BEHIND
THE ROSE

PLAYING RUGBY FOR
ENGLAND

**England
Rugby**

BEHIND
THE ROSE
PLAYING RUGBY FOR
ENGLAND

STEPHEN JONES

NICK CAIN

England
Rugby

First published in 2014 by
ARENA SPORT
An imprint of Birlinn Limited
West Newington House
10 Newington Road
Edinburgh
EH9 1QS

in association with

POLARIS PUBLISHING LTD
c/o Turcan Connell
Princes Exchange
1 Earl Grey Street
Edinburgh
EH3 9EE

www.arenasportbooks.co.uk
www.polarispublishing.com

ISBN: 978-1-909715-19-6
EBOOK ISBN: 978-0-85790-816-2

British Library Cataloguing-in-Publication Data
A catalogue record for this book is available from the British Library

Designed and typeset by Polaris Publishing, Edinburgh

Printed and bound by Kint, Slovenia by arrangement with Associated Agencies, Oxford

CONTENTS

ACKNOWLEDGEMENTS

NICK CAIN AND STEPHEN JONES would like to pay tributes to a number of colleagues for their work in the preparation of this book.

John Griffiths, one of rugby's foremost historians and the sport's most trusted statistical source, played a leading role in creating the outline for this book, researching the memoirs of and articles by some of the great men of England rugby from previous eras, and monitoring all other aspects for accuracy. This book could not have been produced without him.

Brendan Gallagher contributed in monumental fashion to some of the key chapters and also, through his galaxy of contacts, to the earlier chapters. Gallagher is one of the powerhouse sports journalists of his generation across a range of sports and his journalist craft and enthusiasm cannot fail to improve any project. This one is no exception.

We would also like to thank two more outstanding journalists, friends and colleagues in Adam Hathaway, of *The People*, and Rob Wildman, formerly of the *Daily Telegraph* and *Daily Mail*, for their input.

Our most prized interview was that conducted with the Midland legend, Harry Walker, England's oldest-living capped player, in his 100th year. We are grateful to Harry's family, friends and especially his son Richard for arranging the interview, which found Harry on rumbustious form,

Nick Greenstock, assistant secretary of The England Rugby Internationals Club (ERIC), was extremely helpful in putting us in touch with former internationals. ERIC is the honorary association of all England and ex-England players (www.eric-rfu.org.uk).

Thanks must also go to Jane Barron and her team at the RFU and, in particular, to Peter Burns at Arena Sport and Polaris Publishing for his drive and enthusiasm throughout the whole process.

And especially, we would like to thank all the wonderful England players of all eras who so readily shared with us their memories of their times in the England jersey. It is hard to believe that in any sport, the jersey of a national team has been in such good hands for so long.

In June 2014 on the England tour of New Zealand, Kieran Brookes of Newcastle Falcons, came on as replacement to become the 1365th player to win an England cap, and to wear the white jersey with the red rose. Some say that the All Blacks jersey is the most iconic in sport. There would be at least 1365 great men who beg to differ.

Stephen Jones and Nick Cain, 2014

FOREWORD

BY JASON LEONARD, MBE

THERE ARE SOME things you can never imagine happening, even in your wildest dreams. When I was a carpenter in Barking, starting out in rugby with Barking RFC, how could I even begin to imagine the career that lay ahead of me? That in the years ahead there would be a train named after me which operated on the Barking line? Or that I'd become known in rugby circles then world over as the Fun Bus?

Like many young Englishmen I suppose I dreamt of playing rugby for England, but in the early years you never truly expect that you will get there. Fortunately, Saracens saw something in me as a young prop, I kept on working hard, and in 1990 on tour in Argentina, I won my first cap, against the Pumas in Buenos Aires, and the honour of that first appearance for your country is almost impossible to put into words.

The match was fairly indescribable too. It was on the eighth anniversary of the Falklands War, the intensity of the home team and the crowd was frightening – one of the most interesting things that the crowd threw at us was a bathroom tap. Officially, it was billed as a friendly international. I was pleased that I got through it and seemed to make an impression on my team-mates.

When I had the honour of reaching 10 caps for my country, it seemed that it was all over, for Harlequins and for England. I ruptured a vertebra in my neck playing against Wales, and had to have part of my hip bone grafted on to my spine, using the front of my neck as the surgeon's entry point. There were no guarantees, but thanks to brilliant medical people I didn't miss a single England match.

And now? I am the most-capped England player of all time with 114 and five Tests for the Lions – and I have played in four England Grand Slam teams and three Rugby World Cups, finally lifting that glorious prize in 2003.

How did that all happen? Did it happen to me? When I came on as replacement in the England-France World Cup semi-final in 2003, I was then the most-capped player from any country. Others have since overtaken me and, no doubt, I will lose my England status too, and when that happens I will be the first to applaud the new record-holder.

Yet to be England's most-capped player is a very humbling experience when you look back and see all those hundreds of players and all those great men and fantastic characters who have played for England, in all the good and bad times, not only during my career but all the way back to 1871 through to the 2015 Rugby World Cup in England. To have been a part of that brotherhood feels very special.

I often think how fortunate I was to have played in both the amateur and professional eras. We all now know that the game has changed, in many ways for the better, although there was also such an element of fun in those amateur days, sometimes a little outrageous perhaps, which the outstanding professionals of the modern day cannot afford to indulge in. How sad that there must always be stories from the great old days which cannot be re-told in public! I enjoyed picking my all-time drinking XV for my autobiography and perhaps I was trying to keep something of those old days alive because right up until the end of my England career I always sought out my opposite number after a match to have a chat and a beer if possible. No one ever turned me down, which is a good comment on the bond between front row forwards in our own little world but also one on rugby itself – so much of the old camaraderie, team spirit and respect remains even in these ultra-professional days.

Playing for England has been a magnificent adventure, and one which needed sacrifice from my partner Sandra and from our three lovely children, Harry, Jack and Francesca. I am grateful to all my team-mates and England coaches – Geoff Cooke, Jack Rowell, Sir Clive Woodward and all their excellent back-up people – and to everyone who has helped me through my career. It is such a pleasure to relive the experiences of all the decades of England players in this book, and many new chapters will be written on the field in the years to come.

To complete the full cycle of unexpected consequences, I am, as a write, a Vice-President of the Rugby Football Union, a body that had become more sleek and efficient for the modern era. It could even mean that I become President of the RFU for a season. Barking carpenter to RFU President, and all those incredible experiences in between. Unbelievable. What a privilege. What a game.

Jason Leonard, MBE, Vice-President, Rugby Football Union
114 caps for England, 1990-2004; 5 Tests for the Lions

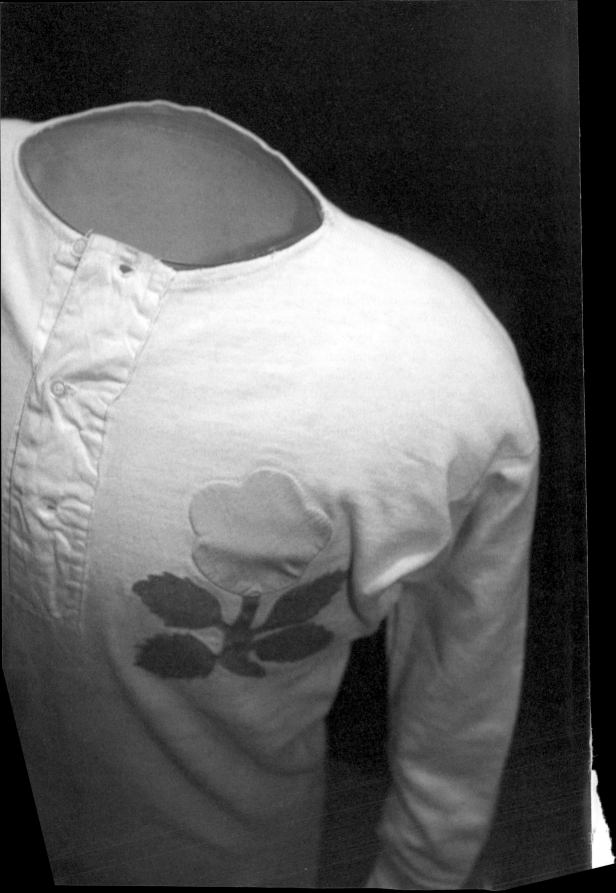

INTRODUCTION

GENERATIONS OF ONE JERSEY

THE FIRST ENGLAND national rugby jersey was a garment of pristine white, save for a motif based on the rose. For those early games at the time of the advent of international rugby, the marvellous men who blazed the path had to bring their own jersey to wear and at a time when selection could be capricious, perhaps it was only ever needed once. The missive informing players of their selection gave details of the tailor from where kit could be bought – the tailor also had the England cap itself for sale.

These days, the jersey retains the Red Rose, but it is a hi-tech garment intended not just to be a uniform for play, but to actually enhance performance. Yet the important aspect is that the pioneers instituted the international rugby game, nurtured it and passed in on for future generations. There is an unbreakable link between the two kinds of jersey, and the men who wore it, now and then and in every match in between. Generations of men almost bursting out of their jersey with pride.

Everything else has changed profoundly, not just the kit. In the leap across the chasm of the years, the players have become paid to play whereas for the first 124 years of England's international rugby history, they could not be, and this was a tenet of the sport pursued avidly by every Rugby Football Union president and committee as a matter of principle. These days, the modern RFU is streamlined and professional and at the forefront of the new sports business era, while retaining the strongest links with the amateur game by proudly reinvesting all its profits back into the sport.

Yet in the following pages we hear the testimony of the player who claimed one penny too much for a train fare, rounding up the amount of his claim, and the RFU, having checked the real fare, docked him the penny. Next time, he added to his claim one penny for the use of the toilet, and was paid.

Nowadays, the elite segment of players wield a commercial appeal to industry that is often lucrative for the game and themselves but significantly, you come across very few rugby followers who begrudge them a penny, for their ferocious dedication, commitment, power and skill, and their bearing in a different and far more severe age.

Opposite: A shirt from the first England Test match, against Scotland at Raeburn Place in Edinburgh in 1871.

Between the extremes of the eras, however the players trained, however much they were paid (or not), how successful they were (or not) and whatever they wore when they took the field, some aspects have been unchanging for those 144 years – the essential goodness, demeanour, vividness, honesty, humour and the pride of the wonderful men who have played rugby for England. A generalisation? All history, and the words of those men inside this book, suggests not.

To wear the jersey for the first time, accordingly to the testimony of the newly-capped, is to cross a narrow but somehow cavernous border. It is as if the difference between having no caps and having one, is far wider than it is between having one cap and 100. It is a step into history.

Stuart Lancaster, the current coach, whose idea of preparation is very different to the steak and beer diet of previous eras, appreciates this link, insisting that every player recognised the ghostly but inspirational presence in the jersey of whatever number, of everyone else who had worn it down the years. Every jersey is on loan to the proud wearer, to be augmented, and then passed on.

Heaven knows, England have not always been successful in international rugby. There have been grim, lingering flat periods, punctuated with some golden eras. The peak of the whole 144-odd years – the gargantuan, world-dominating World Cup triumph of 2003, was the culmination of years of red rose authority over both hemispheres when Sir Clive Woodward and Martin Johnson ruled the roost.

Yet perhaps the glory tasted sweeter when it was a little delayed, and England have produced soaring Grand Slams and Triple Crowns, and courage and bloody-mindedness against the odds.

Social inclusiveness is said not to have been a feature of the years. It is true that RFU and occasionally the England team – especially in the years following the breakaway of the Northern League, later Rugby League, in 1895 but even after – were drawn largely from the middle classes, almost always from the Public Schools, and often from the military services and Oxbridge.

Perhaps some selections were based on non-rugby connections. And on being what was perceived as the right sort of character. Yet the picture is flawed. Sometimes the social historians have been too earnest. Hundreds of England players have come from working-class regions or regions where rugby was deemed as a class-less gathering.

The generalisations have been too easy to make. England's new breed, such as the powerful Manu Tuilagi of Samoan extraction, are no less part of the history than the old greats, such as Lord Wakefield of Kendal, the heroic yeoman figure of Bill Beaumont and the illustrious Will Carling and the others. They are all part, as Jason Leonard says in his foreword to this book, of one brotherhood.

Ronnie Poulton-Palmer, one of the earlier heroes, a wonderful, unpredictable

player and vivid character, once wrote powerfully to the Press demanding that the RFU take no action against some players allegedly accepting payment for broken-time, as it made it too difficult for working-class players to turn out for England if they lost money, and that rugby was for all.

It still is. These days, it is played at the top level by the professional classes – professional rugby players. The president of the RFU in World Cup year of 2015 will be Jason Leonard, the rumbustious prop from the East End of London. Not public school, not from the services or Oxbridge. Just the most capped player in English rugby history, and much beloved.

There is another generalisation that can be made with more confidence. The evidence of history and of our own eyes and ears, suggests that the fraternity of England players has contained some of the finest, most-balanced, least vindictive sportsmen that sport has ever seen; these are behavioural traits not peculiar to rugby but especially prevalent within its ranks. And not least among its top players. In truth, there are enough marvellous characters in the ranks to have worn the jersey to fill a hundred books.

As Jonny Wilkinson, probably the most famous of all the brotherhood, has proved, it is possible, even these days, to touch greatness and retain humanity and humility. It is also relevant to point out that in 144 years, only four England players have been sent off in an international, and it was over 100 years since the first international when the first, the colourful Michael Burton, was despatched – and none have tested positive for performance-enhancing drugs.

You would dearly love to be able to gather together round a table, England rugby players of all the eras. What would they drink? Beer, or isotonic drinks? The former, of course. The old convivialities would be preserved.

The modern players could listen in wonder at the heroics, privations and customs of every era, the old greats could shake their heads in wonder at the advances, on and off the field.

Then they could scratch their heads as the current crew explain to the pioneers the little pocket in the back of their jersey, and the workings of the global positioning system inserted therein.

The pathfinders, in turn, could expand on their roles in establishing international rugby, something sure to remain for as long as sport exists, as one of the finest traditions in sport, and one of the arenas of which England as a country can be most proud. Possibly, representatives of some eras could give vent to their frustration that results were never as good as they should have been.

Of course, many experiences would chime down the ages. The first-ever international saw a major refereeing controversy. Players of all eras would have seen the same. Tomfoolery of various kinds was not restricted to the older days when socialising was so vital a part of the game – it is true that England players were arrested for after-hour activities after a game in Edinburgh in the 19th century.

But also that in the 1980s, a player from each side was seen to be using the Calcutta Cup itself as a plaything on the streets of Edinburgh, long after it had been presented at the end of the match. Damage was so extensive that bystanders called it 'The Calcutta plate'. It was soon restored. Among the pranks of the amateur era, we hear the story of the giant prop that drank after-shave at the post-match banquet, surviving to carry on scrummaging magnificently for his country.

We hear in these pages of the players whose idea of tapering off for the game was to eat 'undercooked meat and beer', and to stop smoking for a day or two as the game approached. One letter advising players of selection referred to the match 'on Monday next' and continued, 'we require you to get yourself as fit as possible by that day'.

Our gathered heroes would be able to talk about shared experiences, but also about so many staggering differences, in their lives and their sporting careers. Yet the jersey they all have in common would give them a profound sense of brotherhood and sense of togetherness infinitely more significant than anything that divided them.

This book is the next best thing to that celestial but impossible gathering. It is the story of what they made of it all themselves, the camaraderie, the victories and defeats, the Grand Slams, the World Cup, the fallow years.

And above all, the passion to play for England, then to play well for England. This is the story of the creation and nurturing and maintaining of a magnificent sporting history, told by the men who wore the jersey.

Stephen Jones and Nick Cain, 2014

ONE

THE FIRST RUGBY NATION

1871-1884

IT ALL BEGAN, *perhaps rather prosaically, with a soccer match. In 1870, the Football Association arranged a London fixture between teams labelled England and Scotland, rather paternalistically selecting both teams for a game which England won 1-0.*
The staging of the game caused a stir north of the Border. The players representing Scotland had but tenuous links with the country, one player's connection being an annual visit to his country estate, while the claims of another were said to be due to liking for Scotch whisky. The Scots claimed that the rugby code was their game and after the soccer defeat they challenged England's rugby fraternity to accept a return match under rugby rules.

Blackheath, the oldest open rugby club in England, acknowledged the challenge and a committee dominated by old boys of Rugby School (Old Rugbeians, or ORs) was formed to select a team. The chosen side comprised ten ORs, including John Clayton, a Liverpool businessman largely responsible for popularising rugby in the North-West, and Frederick Stokes (captain) and Arthur Guillemard, committee members of the Rugby Football Union (RFU) formed in London in January 1871. England's uniform was Rugby School colours: white jersey with brown socks.

The early internationals took place on Mondays, with 20 players on each side. Teams comprised 13 forwards, three halves, a single threequarter and three fullbacks. This was the shoving age. Forwards converged around held players who were ordered by the umpires to 'down' the ball – place it on the ground – whereupon packs formed primitive scrummages, leaning or shoving against one another. Heads were held upright, forwards barging or kicking the ball through. Halves acted as a first line of defence, with the sole threequarter and back-three in support to catch punts ahead, land field goals or claim marks to kick for territory.

Until the late 1880s, matches could only be decided by the kicking of goals. Tries were worthless unless converted. Scotland won the first match by converting a try that was hotly disputed by the English team. Reg Birkett crossed for England's first-ever try in international rugby soon after, but Fred Stokes was unable to convert from wide out. So, long before scoring by points was introduced, Scotland ran out victors by a goal and a try to a try.

England gained revenge at The Oval in 1872 through a magnificent dropped goal kicked by Harold Freeman, but their next visits to Scotland were mired in controversy.

Opposite: The 1871 England team.

England suspected sabotage in 1873 when their boots were mysteriously lost by a local cobbler and, two years later, two Englishmen got so drunk after the match that they were arrested for assaulting an Edinburgh policeman.

Oxford and Cambridge Universities, meanwhile, were in the vanguard of change, experimenting in 1875 by reducing numbers on each side in their games from 20 to 15. International teams followed suit two years later. Reduced numbers made it easier for emerging clubs to field teams. Backs, moreover, had more scope to display skills.

Lennard Stokes, the Blackheath fullback-cum-threequarter, was the outstanding drop-kicker in the land in the second half of the 1870s. Younger brother of England's first captain, he made his Test debut when Ireland entered the international arena in 1875 and the extent to which Stokes relished the transition to 15-a-side can be measured from the fact that he kicked 19 goals in his 12 cap matches.

The first decade of international rugby saw the game evolve from the shoving age. Mauls and 'scrimmages' became less protracted with fewer players in the packs. Blackheath and Oxford University exploited the possibilities. Oxford had a particularly successful side in the early 1880s and the influence of their captain, Henry ('Harry') Vassall proved significant.

Vassall won five caps for England between 1881 and 1883 and became known as the father of the passing game. This began as 'short' passing, an innovation made by Arthur 'Jimmy' Budd [England 1878-1881] at Blackheath in the late 1870s. Vassall, one of the club's forwards, was persuaded by Budd to experiment at Oxford. Short passing evolved to long passing which required more cover among the backs, where typically two threequarters had become the norm, with nine forwards, two halves and two fullbacks.

Vassall moved another fullback into the threequarter line, bringing about the one fullback, three threequarters and two half-backs formation which prevailed until the Welsh adoption of a four threequarter system.

Vassall's ideas permeated England sides in the 1880s. His international call-up was for the first game played against Wales (in 1881), and he was soon cementing his place by scoring three tries in an overwhelming win. So abject were Wales that the fixture was dropped the next season.

Passing benefited back play, releasing the outside men from their hitherto primary duties as defenders, turning them into attackers who focussed on scoring. In 1882-83, England's wings Wilfred Bolton and Australia-born Gregory Wade shared seven of England's 12 tries when, for the first time, all three of the other Home Unions were met and beaten.

England therefore become the first nation to win the Triple Crown. One of rugby's grand oddities is that the Triple Crown was strongly coveted as an honour, but it didn't exist as an actual trophy until 2006.

A H ROBERTSON, F J MONCREIFF, B HALL BLYTH, J W ARTHUR, J H OATTS *(representing the interests of Scotland's rugby fraternity reacting to the inaugural international of 1871.)*

There is a pretty general feeling among Scotch football players that the football power of the old country was not properly represented in the late so-called International Football Match. Not that we think the play of the gentlemen who represented Scotland otherwise than very good – for that it was so is amply proved by the stout resistance they offered to their opponents and by the fact that they were beaten by only one goal – but that we consider the Association rules, in accordance with which the late game was played, not such as to bring together the best team Scotland could turn out.

ARTHUR GUILLEMARD (England 1871-1872, 2 caps; RFU Secretary 1872-1876)

The first International match between England and Scotland was played at the Academy Ground in Raeburn Place, Edinburgh, on 27 March, 1871. An attendance of 4,000 spectators showed that Rugby football had already attained considerable popularity north of the Tweed. The ground measured some 120 yards by 55 [and] it was arranged that the match be played for two periods of fifty minutes each.

The match was evenly contested until half-time, after which the combination of the Scotsmen began to tell a tale, and just outside the English goal-line the umpires ordered the ball to be put down in a scrummage five yards outside the line. The Scottish forwards drove the entire scrummage into goal, and then grounded the ball and claimed a try. This, though illegal according to English laws, was allowed by the umpires, and a goal was kicked.

There is a pretty general feeling among Scotch football players that the football power of the old country was not properly represented in the late so-called International Football Match. Not that we think the play of the gentlemen who represented Scotland otherwise than very good – for that it was so is amply proved by the stout resistance they offered to their opponents and by the fact that they were beaten by only one goal – but that we consider the Association rules, in accordance with which the late game was played, not such as to bring together the best team Scotland could turn out.

Almost all the leading clubs [in Scotland] play by the Rugby code, and have no opportunity of practising the Association game even if willing to do so. We therefore feel that a match played in accordance with any rules other than those in general use in Scotland, as was the case in the last match, is not one that would meet with support generally from her players.

For our satisfaction, therefore, and with a view of really testing what Scotland can do against an English team we, as representing the football interests of Scotland, hereby challenge any team selected from the whole of England, to play us a match, twenty-a-side, Rugby rules either in Edinburgh or Glasgow on any day during the present season that might be found suitable to the English players.

Let this count as the return to the match played in London on 19 November [1870], or, if preferred, let it be a separate match. If it be entered into we can promise England a hearty welcome and a first-rate match. Any communications addressed to any one of us will be attended to.

JOHN CLAYTON (England 1871, 1 cap)
I trained hard for a month before the [first International] match, running four miles or so with a large Newfoundland dog to make the pace, every morning in the dark before breakfast.

I then rode four miles on horseback to my Liverpool office, where I was at my desk from 8am to 8pm, when I rode home again.

As was the custom, I adhered to a strict diet of underdone beef and beer, and lived a frugal and strenuous life otherwise. As a result, I increased my weight and achieved what was regarded as a superb state of fitness for the match.

ARTHUR GUILLEMARD
The first International match between England and Scotland was played at the Academy Ground in Raeburn Place, Edinburgh, on 27 March, 1871. An attendance of 4,000 spectators showed that Rugby football had already attained considerable popularity north of the Tweed. The ground measured some 120 yards by 55 [and] it was arranged that the match be played for two periods of fifty minutes each.

The match was evenly contested until half-time, after which the combination of the Scotsmen began to tell a tale, and just outside the English goal-line the umpires ordered the ball to be put down in a scrummage five yards outside the line. The Scottish forwards drove the entire scrummage into goal, and then grounded the ball and claimed a try. This, though illegal according to English laws, was allowed by the umpires, and a goal was kicked.

HELY HUTCHINSON ALMOND (Scottish Umpire: Scotland v England 1871)
Let me make a personal confession. I was umpire, and I do not know to this day whether the decision which gave Scotland the try from which the winning goal was kicked was correct in fact. The ball had certainly been scrummaged over the line by Scotland, and touched down first by a Scotchman. The try was, however, vociferously disputed by the English team, but upon what ground I was then unable to discover. I

must say, however, that when an umpire is in doubt, I think he is justified in deciding against the side which makes the most noise. They are probably in the wrong.

ARTHUR GUILLEMARD
England then penned their opponents for some time, and ultimately R H Birkett ran in close to touch, but the captain's place-kick, a long and difficult one across the wind, failed.

F Stokes was a most excellent and popular captain, combining a thorough knowledge of the game with admirable tact and good temper, and being gifted with power of infusing spirit and enthusiasm into his team. As a player, he was one of the very best examples of a heavy forward, always on the ball, and first-rate either in the thick of a scrummage or in a loose rally, a good dribbler, very successful in getting the ball when thrown out of touch, a very long drop [kicker] and a particularly safe tackle.

R H Birkett was very useful both forward and behind the scrummage and had plenty of pace.

HARRY VASSALL (England 1881-1883, 5 caps)
We need not pause long to discuss the much-abused shoving matches of the days when twenty-a-side were played. They have gone, never to return, regretted by none.

ARTHUR GUILLEMARD
When the English twenty arrived in Glasgow [for the 1873 match] they found the country under snow, but this quickly thawed under a hot sun, and was followed by a downpour. The turf was consequently spongy and slippery at the top.

The greasy nature of the ground caused the English captain [Frederick Stokes] to direct his men to have bars of leather affixed to the soles of their boots. Freeman and Boyle, who with Finney were considered the most dangerous men on the side, reported, when the cobbler had done his work, that they were each minus a boot. Several of the team proceeded to ransack the cobbler's shop, but without success, and it was not until after the match – in which Boyle played with a dress boot on his left foot – that the canny tradesman produced the missing articles.

ARTHUR BUDD (England 1878-1881, 5 caps)
H Freeman, a great goal-dropper and a powerful runner, was the most celebrated threequarter of his time. The most distinguished halves were S Finney and W H Milton. The most famous forwards were Frederick Stokes, C W Crosse and F H Lee.

The first step towards a faster game was the diminution in the number of players from twenty to fifteen. Lennard Stokes was the greatest threequarter of his day. In the opinion of many [he] has never had an equal before or since, was certainly the greatest drop-kicker the world has ever seen. His kicking combined the great length with the most wonderful accuracy, and an ability to kick in an extraordinarily small compass.

CHARLES MARRIOTT (England 1884-1887, 7 caps)
In 1882, following on a magazine article by Arthur Budd advocating the advantage to be gained by passing, H Vassall, the capable captain of the Oxford team, took up the idea, and developed a system of passing in his team with wonderful results.

ARTHUR GUILLEMARD
[*From the RFU inviting J A Body to play in the 1873 game in Scotland*]
   24 February, 1873
   The Committee desire me to inform you that you have been selected to play against Scotland on Monday next at Glasgow and to request you to get yourself as fit as possible by that day.
      The uniform, (which should be written for by the first mail) consists of white jersey with badge and ribbon, white flannel knickerbockers and dark brown stockings. It is obtainable from J Markham, Tailor, Rugby, as is the cap, which is of rose velvet with silver lace badge. In ordering a jersey, the size of your collar and measurement around the chest should be stated. If you can give Markham a London address where you can conveniently call, it will be the safer plan, as parcels are so frequently delayed in transmission through town to other Railways.
      The 8.40pm express on Saturday from Euston is the train best suited for the XX [the 20 players]. It arrives in Glasgow at 7am. The XX will probably put up at the George Hotel, but further arrangements will be announced and Bell's Life of Saturday morning will contain latest particulars.
      Please inform me by Post whether you propose taking the 8.40 train.
      Yours faithfully,
      Arthur G Guillemard
      Hon Sec

MISCONDUCT OF THE ENGLISH FOOTBALL PLAYERS
[*From* Edinburgh Evening News *Edinburgh: 10 March, 1875*]
On Monday evening a disgraceful scene was witnessed at the Waverley Station, where the English football players, who took part in the international match, assembled preparatory to leaving the city by the 10.40 PM train for the south. It was evident from the shouting and bawling, and generally boisterous conduct of

some of the party, that they had been indulging too freely in strong drink. The railway officials were unwilling to interfere so long as they confined themselves simply to shouting, but they were forced to do so when one of the Englishmen gave an engine-driver a blow on the breast, which sent him reeling against a carriage. The engine-driver, generously enough, did not press any charge against his assailant, and the players were hustled into a carriage and the doors locked upon them. Just before the starting of the train, however, one of them got out and struck a railway policeman. The policeman attempted to detain him, but two of the others, coming to their comrade's assistance, gave the officers some rough treatment. While the party were struggling, the train moved off, leaving the three Englishmen in the custody of the railway officials who came to the policeman's assistance. They struggled violently to free themselves, kicking and using their sticks in a savage manner. The policeman received a severe kick while he was lying on the ground, which nearly broke the bridge of his nose. The prisoners, whose names are Reginald Halsey Birkett and Henry James Graham were taken to the Police Office, but were liberated on finding each £2 bail for their reappearance. When the case was called in the Police Court today, Mr Linton stated that delay for a week had been asked, and as he had no objections Sheriff Hallard agreed to an adjournment. The case will therefore come before the courts again next Wednesday.

ARTHUR BUDD

The elaboration of passing was unquestionably the work of the Blackheath team.

HARRY VASSALL

It was the development of the passing game which was keynote to the success of the [Oxford] team. Short passing amongst the forwards had been adopted by other clubs before this date; but long passing, right across the ground if necessary, was a thing hitherto unknown. The team soon grasped the idea that passing, to be successful, must be to the open, and they learnt very quickly to back up in the open, and only to call for passes when they were in a better position than the man in possession. In this way they used to sweep the ball from end to end of the ground time after time, passing any length with such deadly accuracy that very often the whole team handled the ball in less than two minutes, and their opponents were completely nonplussed.

ARTHUR BUDD

Bolton, a splendidly proportioned man with great pace, ran straight and handed off. Wade had the power of levering opponents off his hips. The English team [of

1883] was largely composed of new men and in every instance laid the foundation of special fame as International players. H B Tristram, as back, demonstrated that he was the best man who had ever officiated in that position. W N Bolton, A M Evanson and G C Wade were the [England] threequarters, and a finer trio never wore the English jersey. Alan Rotherham [became] the half-back of the decade.

'The Calcutta Cup match at Raeburn Place, 1886' by WH Overend and LP Smythe

TWO

SUPER TEN: ENGLAND DOMINANT

1884-1892

A S VASSALL AND *Budd passed from the scene in 1883, another Oxford innovator, Alan Rotherham, put his imprint on the game, developing the idea of passing from the half-backs. Rotherham was credited with being the first to view the half-back role as a 'link' – a feed between forwards and threequarters – and what Rotherham did for half-back play, Bradford's Rawson Robertshaw did for the threequarters.*

English rugby enjoyed a glorious run as the other Home Unions adjusted to their innovations. After losing to Scotland in Manchester in 1882, England lost only once more before the decade ended. The period included a purple patch of ten successive victories – a record that stood until Sir Clive Woodward's reign as England manager in the 21st century.

Household names in a decade that brought refinements to scrummaging were Charles and Temple Gurdon, experts at the ploy of wheeling scrums and breaking off them to lead foot rushes. Charles Gurdon was credited with introducing 'scraping' – heeling or hooking the ball back. Old-timers disapproved of these developments, believing forwards were primarily shovers. Packs, they feared, would become subservient to the backs.

Among the threequarters, the great Andrew 'Drewy' Stoddart and Dicky Lockwood, a Yorkshireman destined to become the first working-class player to captain England, were stars. Lockwood was among the earliest backs to exploit the crosskick while, behind them, Henry Tristram emerged as the outstanding fullback.

For all their success on the field, the RFU encountered immense difficulties off it. A fight to maintain their position as law-makers to the sport saw them shunned by the other Home Unions.

The 1884 England/Scotland game was the showdown of the season with England seeking back-to-back Triple Crowns. Internationals now took place on Saturdays and a record crowd approaching 10,000 gathered at Blackheath to see them win by a conversion. The visitors, however, disputed the try from which Wilfred Bolton kicked England's winning goal.

A Scot had 'knocked back' in the move leading to England's try – an infringement under Scottish rules. England supported the referee, a respected former Irish international, saying his decision was final. Besides, why should Scotland profit from

Opposite: The England team of 1892

their mistake? The Scots wanted settlement by an independent adjudicator and a lengthy correspondence ensued, resulting in cancellation of the 1885 Calcutta Cup match.

The Irish Union intervened suggesting a meeting to consider forming an International Board to resolve disputes. The concept of a Board crystallised in Dublin in February 1886, Scotland later conceding the 1884 match to England on condition that the RFU join a Board comprising an equal number of members from each of the Four Nations. Sensing the Board would become the game's sole law-makers, the RFU rejected Scotland's ultimatum.

And so England were pariahs in 1888 and 1889, before the RFU offered to accept independent arbitration. This gesture of goodwill saw them reinstated to the International Championship in 1890 and when arbitration concluded in April, the RFU lost its law making powers – but held half the seats on the Board.

During the dispute, England played a Test against the first touring side from overseas. The New Zealand Native team, known as the Maoris, undertook a gruelling tour of Britain and Ireland in the winter of 1888-89, often playing three matches a week. It was an epic undertaking, and remains the most heroic sports tour in history.

It was now that the amateur creed of the RFU began to cause serious disagreements, something which was to continue for a century and more. The news that expenses were paid to the Maori tourists vexed the true-blue amateurs of the RFU, while the international itself was a fractious affair. Under Fred Bonsor – the first Yorkshireman to skipper the national side – England fielded 12 new caps but maintained their long unbeaten international record. Disputes marred a match refereed by the RFU secretary, Rowland Hill and some of the visitors withdrew from the field in protest when he awarded England a contentious try.

Then fissures began to appear. The intense club rivalries in Yorkshire and Lancashire Cup competitions brought those counties into sharp focus while England were in the international wilderness. When the RFU launched the County Championship, partly to compensate for the lack of international competition, Yorkshire dominated its early years.

Their packs invariably comprised working men with a reputation for hard, uncompromising scrummaging – the so-called 'northern forward'. They had become integral components of England's recent packs and carried the national side through its next heyday in the early 1890s.

English rugby came of age in 1892 marking the occasion with a Triple Crown without conceding a single score – the perfect season. Significantly, most of the players were from Lancashire and Yorkshire, no fewer than 13 northerners taking the field against Scotland.

All told, in its first 21 years the RFU placed 45 teams in the field, winning 30 losing six, and drawing nine. The game's first rugby nation justifiably dominated. But storm clouds were gathering, destined to tear the northern heart out of the game, sending England's rugby stock into a decline that would take 18 years to overcome, giving birth to what was to become a new code of rugby and creating divisions which lasted way into the future. England were already a great rugby nation, but not every player came from the same culture, or social grouping.

CHARLES MARRIOTT

Alan Rotherham, who, by the excellency of his passing and by the openings that he made for his threequarters, revolutionised half-back play. The threequarters now being recognised as the attacking force, a third was added, the fullbacks being reduced to two.

ARTHUR BUDD

It was not long before the contagion of passing, which had attacked the forwards, spread to the half-backs. Hitherto they had played an individual game, but with three men behind them, who they knew must not be left idle in the cold, and with the means of transmission handy in the mechanism of passing, they were bound to consider their own play as subservient to providing the three-quarters with favourable opportunities. What half first set the example of 'feeding' I am unable to say. Rowland Hill [Secretary RFU 1881-1904] tells me that the first time he ever saw a pass by a half to a threequarter was in 1881, when J H Payne slung the ball out to C E Bartram, who gained a try. There can be no doubt, however, that the man who reduced the art to a science, and thereby revolutionised half-back play, was A Rotherham, of Oxford and Richmond – the equal of whom we have never, in my opinion, since seen.

CHARLES MARRIOTT

Though Rotherham is held to have been the most correct half, credit must also be given in the North to the old Cambridge threequarter, J H Payne, who, having been converted into a half, adopted similar methods. In Yorkshire, Bonsor of Bradford, became a specialist in the new style. Nor must we omit mention of Colonel Manners Smith, V.C., who in the Sandhurst and Blackheath teams, by assiduously serving the herculean W N Bolton, added scoring power to that splendid runner.

ARTHUR BUDD

[Rotherham] was the first to clearly demonstrate that a half-back ought not to run and play for himself, but ought essentially to be the connecting link between the forwards and threequarters, and he showed how this ought to be done, not merely by stationary but by what I may term 'opportune' passing, i.e. running himself and not passing till he had got his threequarters on their legs, and till he had fogged his opponents as to whether they ought to go for him or the threequarters he was intent on feeding. He showed how and when to pass and when not to pass, and how a half ought to run on himself when, by a feint, he had decoyed his tacklers to the threequarter and left an open field for himself.

CHARLES MARRIOTT
Rawson Robertshaw was responsible for a further development in the game, namely, a centre threequarter acting as a supply depot for his wing men. Robertshaw brought this to a high state of perfection.

ARTHUR BUDD
Next development was the passing by the centre threequarter to his wings, and in this the pioneer was Rawson Robertshaw, who, at centre, applied the same principles which Rotherham had demonstrated at half.

[Robertshaw's] game might be described as a reproduction at threequarter of Rotherham's at half, the idea of playing for his wings rather than himself, and feeding them by what I have previously termed 'opportune' passing. Thus he became the last link in the machinery which has brought about the cooperation of forwards, halves and threequarters.

Wheeling is unquestionably the most fashionable method of scrummaging. Having obtained [the ball], the practice is to deposit it behind the first or second-row of forwards, where it lies safe from the interference of your opponents, and to there manipulate it till you screw your adversaries off it and rush on with it yourself. What one now sees in every match is that the moment the ball is put down in the centre of the scrummage both sides try to be the first to pull it back, and you will behold a forest of legs scraping for its possession. Its introduction cannot, in my opinion, be considered an unmixed blessing.

The canker-worm of work is heeling-out. You can bet your bottom dollar that a team who habitually heel-out are no pushers. Their sole anxiety is to get the ball to their halves.

ARTHUR GUILLEMARD
E T Gurdon's record of sixteen matches evidences his sterling worth. In every respect he was one of the best forwards that ever represented England. He was very muscular, and used his weight and strength to the best advantage, and was usually to be found in the very heart of the scrummage. His use of his feet amidst a crowd of forwards was admirable, but better still was his dribbling when he had got the ball before him in the open, and many a time has the ring been wrought up to a pitch of frenzy watching the two Gurdons steering the ball past half-backs

and threequarter backs straight for the enemy's quarters. A grand example was that set by the brothers of resolutely keeping the ball on the ground when they had taken it through a scrummage, knowing how much more difficult it is for a half-back to stop a combined rush of two or three good dribblers than a single man with the ball under his arm. An excellent knowledge of the game and thorough unselfishness helped to make [Temple Gurdon] a popular captain.

C Gurdon, built on a larger scale than his brother, with enormous strength in his thighs and shoulders, was one of the most massive and muscular forwards that ever stripped. In his day a scrummage was worthy of its name. A very zealous worker in the scrummage, [Charles] devoted all his attention to the ball, and was very careful not to overrun it whilst steering it through the ranks of his opponents. When he had got it free he dribbled fast and with unusual skill and success. Halves and threequarters dreaded his rush more than that of any other player.

ARTHUR BUDD

Lockwood, a pocket Hercules, was an exceptionally clever player, and though he was a fine runner, his great forte was his judgment kicking, and he was the first man to start the example of kicking obliquely across the field and running on himself at full speed, so as to put his forwards who were at the spot where the ball pitched onside.

Stoddart was certainly one of the most graceful players who ever donned a jersey. His dodging was simply marvellous. Sometimes he would go right through the thick of a team without a hand being laid upon him, and he was able to field a ball off the ground when running at full speed.

If a ballot [for the world's best fullback] were taken Tristram would probably come top of the poll.

CHARLES MARRIOTT

In 1884 a misunderstanding arose with Scotland over the referee's decision, and this led to no match taking place the following season. In 1886 the matter was adjusted, and the Scottish match again took place, but, unfortunately, differences arose between England and the other Home Unions, and for two seasons England played no International matches with the other Home Unions.

STATEMENT ISSUED BY THE INTERNATIONAL BOARD

[*From Minutes of the International Rugby Football Board – Crewe Meeting: 5 December, 1887*]

All International matches must be played under Rules approved of by the International Board, in terms of which no International match with England can take place until the English Rugby Union agrees to join the International Board.

RFU RESPONSE

[From Minutes of the RFU Committee – London Meeting: 17 December, 1887]

Having regard to the fact that it would be impossible to play International matches if there is great divergence in the Laws of the various Unions, and that in order to continue these matches in future an International Board would practically become the law makers for the game generally, it is impossible for R.U. (recognising as they do the fact that the clubs subscribing to their Union treble in number those belonging to the Scottish, Irish and Welsh unions combined) to accept an International Board on the basis of equality between the four Unions.

LORD KINGSBURGH AND MAJOR F A MARINDIN

[Independent arbitrators defining the Regulations of the Board]

The International Rugby Football Board shall consist of twelve members, six of whom shall be elected to represent England, two to represent Scotland, two to represent Ireland, and two to represent Wales.

Scotland versus England at Raeburn Place, Edinburgh,1892

The Board shall have power to settle all disputes arising at or in connection with International Matches by a majority of their number.

The International Board shall have power by a majority of not less than three-fourths of their number to amend, alter or cancel any Law in, and add new Laws to, the International Code.

HARRY VASSALL

The [England v Maoris 1889] match was hardly a success from any point of view, except that it gave the Committee an opportunity, which they would otherwise have lacked, of putting the England team for that year into the field. The chief interest of the match lies in the proof it affords, coming as it did just after the tour of Shaw and Shrewsbury's team in New Zealand and Australia, of the firm hold which the Rugby game has gained upon the colonies.

ARTHUR BUDD

The only International in which England engaged this season [1887-88] was against the Maoris, who during their visit to this country displayed a remarkable aptitude for disputing the decisions of the officials. The English umpire and referee were anathematised and threatened, and at one period of the game five of the Maori team left the field, but were induced to return by their manager. The English team was an exceedingly strong one, and it was a great pity that they had no opportunity of showing their prowess to the other countries.

CHARLES MARRIOTT

The game had now obtained for some years a high state of perfection in the north, especially in Yorkshire, where it was most enthusiastically followed. Unfortunately the numerous matches made such a demand upon the players' time that in many instances it meant loss of wages, which they could ill afford. To make this up to them all sorts of surreptitious payments were made, which went under the name of 'veiled professionalism'. To still keep in the Rugby Union fold an endeavour was made by various Northern Clubs to legalise the payment for broken time. The Rugby Union, while wishful that their game should not be a class one, and that anyone might take part in it, provided he conformed to their rules, rightly divined that recompense for broken time was only the thin of the wedge of full-blown professionalism.

THREE

SCHISM AND SLUMP

1893-1896

ENGLAND HAD NO *sooner emerged as the pioneer rugby union nation – and the pre-eminent one in international competition – when its triumphal march was stopped in its tracks by a tumultuous dispute which was to cause reverberating problems throughout the sport and which many people deduced was an outbreak of class warfare. The social divisions in Victorian Britain wreaked havoc with the newly established sport, resulting in a near-brutal rift which became known as the Great Schism.*

The traditional view is that working class players and their overwhelmingly Northern-based clubs advocated financial compensation, known as 'broken-time' payment, for any loss of earnings incurred by their participation, their middle class counterparts, especially those in London and the south, were having none of it. Recently, historians have concluded that the class-based battle lines were slightly exaggerated. But to the majority of southern players, earning a living from the professions or business, rugby union was a recreational sport, and their view was that any move to pay players was against the best interests of the game, and its amateur spirit.

A large contingent of northern clubs were diametrically opposed to this outlook, mindful of the need to reimburse the miners and factory workers for any loss of wages, or jeopardise the progress that the sport had made. They knew also that rugby union in the north had rapidly become a popular spectator sport capable of paying broken-time compensation.

The 'pay or not to pay' argument came to a head at the RFU's London AGM in September 1893. Yorkshire, home of the most competitive county cup competition in the land, and also the country's champion county and source of England's most rugged forwards, forced the issue by proposing 'broken time' payment.

By that time some northern clubs were enticing star players with job offers, and transfer stories were rife. This promoted grave suspicions about northern practices in the amateur south, and the stances hardened. Yorkshire's proposal, which they insisted was drawn up to stave off full professionalism, was defeated in a vigorous debate.

Before the landmark meeting, Yorkshire's committee approached their Lancashire counterparts seeking support. Lancashire's president was Albert Hornby, Harrovian, establishment figure, and the first man to captain England at both rugby and cricket. He was notorious for having once declined to play rugby against Scotland because it interfered with his shooting, which was going 'particularly well'. After considering the arguments, Hornby (and his county) declared support, though his former England colleague John Payne, a Manchester solicitor and the county's secretary/treasurer, sternly opposed.

Payne, thinly disguised as 'half-back', wrote to the Manchester press censuring his county. Meanwhile, the bastions of the Rugby Union, President William Cail and Rowland Hill, its 'amateur of amateurs' secretary, mobilised members and arranged proxies for their AGM at London's Westminster Palace Hotel.

Advocating Yorkshire's proposal, the county president recalled that the England team in Dublin seven months earlier had included working men from the northern counties. They had set out Friday morning, played on Saturday and returned on Monday. The working men had their railway fare and hotel bills refunded but lost three days' wages. He asked the assembled members if they called that playing on 'level terms'.

Cail and Rowland Hill responded, tabling an amendment declining to sanction the proposal. Hill, defending amateurism, was backed by the Yorkshire clergyman/ schoolmaster, Rev Frank Marshall, rugby's first historian and upholder of amateurism. Marshall set the cat among the northern pigeons, vigorously opposing his own county. He said one Yorkshire club had seven licensees – it was an open secret that many players were in receipt of 'funds'. Fierce debate followed.

Herbert Fallas, the Wakefield Trinity international, was enraged by Marshall's comments. Harry Garnett, another Yorkshire ex-international and a past president of the RFU, expressed his 'reluctant' support for his county more temperately. Broken time might offer a stay of execution from full-blown professionalism, he argued. Among the Lancashire contingent Roger Walker, the England forward of the 1870s, spoke at length, wondering if broken time payments were practicable.

Despite the northerners turning up at the AGM in numbers on two specially chartered trains they lost the vote by more than two-to-one, 282 votes to 136. The amendment was carried, broken-time rejected. The status quo effectively taxed players from working-class backgrounds and, two years later, in August 1895, the Great Schism began when 20 leading Yorkshire/Lancashire clubs seceded, forming the Northern Union. This was to become the founder body of a new and separate code, rugby league.

Players remained remarkably loyal to their clubs. A case in point was Billy Nicholl from Brighouse Rangers, one of England's 1892 Triple Crown pack. When he started playing as a teenager, Brighouse couldn't afford to pay travel expenses. He became a publican and when the club was among the 1895 breakaways, he felt honour-bound to remain a Brighouse player. The detrimental effect of the schism on the national side was not immediate, even though after 1896 it was profound.

Wales carried off their first Triple Crown in 1893, their success being ascribed to the four threequarter system they had pioneered with mixed results over the previous seven seasons. The upshot was that England embraced the system in 1894, beating them 24-3 at Birkenhead. They won again in 1895 and sent the Welsh packing from Blackheath with a 25-0 drubbing in 1896.

The RFU exercised an even hand about the amateur game in the north. Three of their five home internationals between 1893 and 1896 were staged there. Heckmondwike's Dicky Lockwood, first capped in 1887, was England's skipper in 1894 before falling out with the RFU after they suspended him before a Yorkshire Cup-tie. That precipitated his conversion to the Northern Union, whereupon Billy Taylor, a working man from the impeccably amateur Rockcliff club in Northumberland assumed the England captaincy.

Taylor shared that responsibility for three seasons with the outstanding southern forward of the day, S M J 'Sammy' Woods, a dual Test cricketer for his native Australia and adoptive England. Woods was poles apart on the social scale from Lockwood and Taylor. A strapping Cambridge Blue of private means and bluff character, he was the classic gentleman player right down to the obligatory set of three initials – 'good ole Sarah Mary Jane' they called him in Yorkshire.

Yorkshire talent was still available. Two of their finest forwards, Bramley's bull-necked Harry Bradshaw and Bingley's aptly-named Tom Broadley, were at the heart of the 1894 win against Wales. However, with the upcoming generation of working-class players gravitating to Northern Union clubs, Yorkshire's dominance of amateur rugby waned with fewer selected for England. After extending their County Championship run to seven titles in eight seasons in 1896, another 32 years passed before their next title.

BILLY NICHOLL (England 1892, 2 caps)
We had our own expenses to pay in those days. We couldn't afford railway fares. Many a time we [Brighouse players] trudged to the other side of Huddersfield, played a tough game, and trudged home again. Occasionally we came across a kindly disposed lorryman, or a coal cart, and got a lift on our way in that manner. Despite all these little difficulties, it was the greatest ambition to play. We would have given up anything rather than miss a match.

TOM BROADLEY (England 1893-1896, 6 caps)
On Saturdays I used to work in the mornings and play football in the afternoons. It was hard going. For the England v Scotland International in March 1893 I and three other Yorkshire players selected for the match received the total sum of seven shillings – less than two shillings [ten pence in today's money] each!

LEONARD TOSSWILL (England 1902, 3 caps)
During the nineties the game suffered a shock which shook it to its foundations

and threatened its very existence. This was the great cleavage which split the Union over the question of payments to players for 'broken time.' In Yorkshire and Lancashire, at that time the most powerful strongholds of the game, many of what are called the 'working classes' were playing Rugby, and it was alleged that they could not afford to play unless they were given compensation for loss of working time.

CHARLES MARRIOTT

The game had now obtained for some years a high state of perfection in the north, especially in Yorkshire, where it was most enthusiastically followed. Unfortunately the numerous matches made such a demand upon the players' time that in many instances it meant loss of wages, which they could ill afford. To make this up to them all sorts of surreptitious payments were made, which went under the name of 'veiled professionalism'. To still keep in the Rugby Union fold an endeavour was made by various Northern Clubs to legalise the payment for broken time. The Rugby Union, while wishful that their game should not be a class one, and that anyone might take part in it, provided he conformed to their rules, rightly divined that recompense for broken time was only the thin of the wedge of full-blown professionalism. They therefore refused to recognise any system of payment in whatever shape or form.

JOHN PAYNE (England 1882-1885, 7 caps)

I am clean against the [Yorkshire] proposal [for payment for broken time] as it would in future be a source of infinite misery to the working man footballer.

ALBERT HORNBY (England 1877-1882, 9 caps)

To sum up, there is no danger in the proposal. It is possible to differentiate between the professional pure and simple and the amateur without any difficulty.

LEONARD TOSSWILL

The Rugby Union set its face resolutely against this [broken time] principle, foreseeing that it was merely the prelude to actual professionalism. Thanks to the courage and firmness of the Rev. Frank Marshall, Rowland Hill and other stout-hearted supporters of amateur football, the game was saved for future generations.

HERBERT FALLAS (England 1884, 1 cap)

I am in favour of the resolution for broken time payment. Mr Marshall is a political mountebank. [Fallas was called to order and the latter term was subsequently withdrawn on a ruling of the Chairman, who eventually ordered Fallas to sit down.]

HARRY GARNETT (England 1877, 1 cap)

No one can live long in Yorkshire without being convinced of the necessity for some such payment as proposed. Passing the resolution will not prevent professionalism, but it will delay it for perhaps three years, perhaps more, perhaps less, and it is in this spirit that I have come to support my county.

ROGER WALKER (England 1874-1880, 5 caps)

I do not think either Mr Rowland Hill or Mr Gladstone himself could lay down a scheme for settling this matter. It will be utterly impossible to draw up a feasible scheme, nor does the honest working man want compensation. So long as they are amateurs, they are equal with everyone else, but if they are paid for lost time it will at once do away with that equality.

I have spent a lot of time among that body, and I have always found them a very good lot, but the working man in my day did not enjoy the luxury that the Yorkshire football player of today enjoys. If necessary, let those who want professionalism in Lancashire and Yorkshire separate themselves from the Union. In conclusion, the scheme is neither practicable nor beneficial.

CHARLES MARRIOTT

After a very spirited and, at times, heated debate, the amendment was carried by 282 votes to 136. As a corollary a large number of north country clubs seceded from the Rugby Union, and formed the Northern Union to allow payment for loss of time. As had been anticipated, the Northern Union [subsequently] adopted full professionalism for its players.

LEONARD TOSSWILL

Many of the Yorkshire and Lancashire clubs left the Union in consequence, and it was not long before they had formed the Northern Union on definite professional lines. It is only within comparatively recent times that the game has recovered fully from this blow and the number of clubs affiliated to the Rugby Union has risen above the number which constituted it before the secession of the northern clubs.

JOHN RAPHAEL (England 1902-1906, 9 caps)

The four threequarter formation originated in Wales and was generally adopted in the land of its birth, so far back as the eighties. The additional man made threequarter combination really effective by rendering short, sharp passing practicable. [But] during the nineties we were still imbued with the old ideas and traditions of the game. [England] resisted the new formation as long as they possibly could; they adopted it only when compelled to by force of circumstances.

They considered the additional outside almost solely from the defensive point of view. More time was spent in deploring his loss from the forwards than in bringing him effectively into the attacking line.

DICKY LOCKWOOD (England 1887-1894, 14 caps)
The most amusing incident of my life on the field was when I captained England for the first time, against Wales at Birkenhead in 1894. It was the smartest piece of work I ever saw and the easiest try I ever saw scored. The burly Harry Bradshaw got hold of the ball from a line-out, and scored before anyone knew where he was except [Norman] Biggs, the famous Cardiff man. Someone went up to the Welshman and asked him why he didn't stop Bradshaw. 'Stop him!?' he said. 'Did you see him coming? It took me all my time to get out of his way!'

HARRY BRADSHAW (England 1892-1894, 7 caps)
It wasn't so much they couldn't get round me. [My neck] was such a size they couldn't get round it. It's not so very big. Do you think so? I can wear a twenty-four collar comfortably.

LEONARD TOSSWILL
I only saw the great 'Sammy' Woods at the end of his Rugby career, when he was past his best, but even then he seemed to dominate every game in which he played, and it appeared to be impossible for any of his opponents, however elusive, to escape the clutch of his huge hands. Woods dribbling down the field was an awe-inspiring figure for any hapless back awaiting his approach.

DICKY LOCKWOOD
We had real good fun in the old days. Football isn't what it used to be. It was a real pleasure to play, and we considered the enjoyment of a game sufficient recompense. Some people blame the Northern Union, but I think it was a good move. The Rugby Union is right enough, although they could never hide the spite they had against Yorkshire. Personally, I don't love them much. I cannot see why I was debarred from playing with Heckmondwike in the first round of the Cup tie, when Taylor, of Rockcliff in Northumberland, under exactly the same circumstances, was allowed to do so. Since then I have never played under any but Northern Union rules [for Wakefield].

Opposite: EW 'Billy' Taylor

FOUR
EARLY EVOLUTIONS
1897-1909

THE GREAT SCHISM *cast long shadows. In 1893 there were 481 clubs in membership of the RFU, but three years later there were 383. By 1904 the number had dwindled to just 244. Decline was evident in results too. After the 1892 perfect Triple Crown, 18 years passed before England's next Championship title. Between 1897 and 1910 England beat Wales only once, and half the successful 1892 team were with Northern Union clubs by 1896. It was English rugby's Dark Age.*

Wales, meanwhile, made rapid progress. Forward play there involved physical forwards heeling the ball out for fast, imaginative backs to exploit openings and create overlaps for wings to score tries. Specialisation at half-back began there. Llewellyn Lloyd at Newport and Dai and Evan James, Swansea's famous brothers, were early pioneers of specific stand-off and scrum-half roles.

That practice slowly spread to the West Country through their close ties with leading Welsh clubs. Elsewhere, though, development was stunted. The loss of northern working men hugely weakened English packs. Their game barely moved tactically. The international tide first turned in 1897 at Newport where Billy Taylor, still their captain, put an 11-0 defeat at Rodney Parade down to an awful pitch. But by 1899, Arthur Rotherham, as England skipper, had no excuses when Wales won 26-3, scoring six tries to one.

England hit rock bottom that year, losing all three internationals for the first time, and failing to register a score against Ireland and Scotland. Seven new caps took the field against Wales. Only two – John Daniell among the forwards and the legendary Devonport fullback Herbert Gamlin – would win more than half-a-dozen more caps. Gamlin alone would reach double figures, though Daniell, who became captain in 1900 at the tender age of 21 and went on to lead England six times, would have commanded a place in any international pack.

Daniell was at the helm inspiring England to win two of their three matches in 1902. Only the tricks of Wales' artful scrum-half, Dicky Owen, in luring his opposite number offside with a dummy at a scrum, allowed them to squeak home 9-8 through the ensuing penalty. (Clive Woodward would be similarly hoodwinked in Cardiff 79 years later.)

With Harry Alexander up front, and John Raphael and J T 'Long John' Taylor

Opposite: The England players leave the field, Crystal Palace, London, in 1905 after losing 15-0 to New Zealand. Little Dai Gent, a new cap that day, is the player just above centre, far left.

at centre showing promise, the season brought a rare shaft of light to the gloom that otherwise shrouded the England careers of Gamlin and Daniell. Taylor had begun playing with Castleford before they defected to the Northern Union, whereupon he transferred to amateur West Hartlepool. But he was definitely in the minority by actively dissociating himself from a 'broken-time' outfit.

There was no more acute observer of this period than Dai Gent. Although he grew up in South Wales, Gent moved to Gloucestershire and played for England in the 1900s before swapping ball for pen as rugby correspondent for the Sunday Times. His England debut was against New Zealand in 1905.

The All Blacks had swept through the land. Their focus was on constant backing-up of the player, and they had evolved specialist positions for half-backs and forwards (including the detested wing-forward or 'rover'). England went down 15-0 – five tries to nil – in miserable conditions at the Crystal Palace. The site had been temporarily hired by the homeless RFU to accommodate the vast crowds the tourists attracted. England were overwhelmed. Only the wet conditions and the plucky display of the new Cornish fullback, John Jackett, kept the score down. The press was unanimous – England were lucky to get nil! Wales later halted the New Zealanders' progress, but the visitors left a happy legacy. Change was in the English air.

The catalyst was a Harlequins half-back called Adrian Stoop, first capped in 1905 partnering Walter Butcher for the final game of another Championship whitewash. At the time England still played the naive 'left-and-right' half-back game – halves alternating between fly-half and scrum-half depending on which side of the field the scrum was positioned.

Change took time. Stoop wasn't even an England regular. He returned against the First Springboks in 1906, controversially selected in preference to Devon's James Peters, a black half-back who, it was said, the South Africans objected to playing against. An admin error also saw the wrong forward invited to play that day – Arnold Alcock, an unknown Guy's medic getting called ahead of Liverpool's Lancelot Slocock. Whatever next? England drew 3-3, beat France, who were playing their first away Test, before Stoop was dropped again after losing 22-0 in Wales.

Undeterred, Stoop set about raising his club's profile – in the process making English rugby interesting again. He decided 'stand-off' was the tactical key, and installed himself as the fly-half specialist. Basic skills were paramount. Quick passing, with players running on to the ball at speed, was the mantra.

Harlequins became drivers of English club rugby's revival between 1907 and 1909. Stoop was a magnet to players seeking enjoyment with success, and 'Quins gathered a talented team that played 'total rugby' long before the expression entered rugby's lexicon. A century later, he could have been a coaching blend of John Dawes, Carwyn James and Clive Woodward.

DAI GENT (England 1905-1910, 5 caps)

I watched [Welsh rugby] first between 1897 and 1903, [when] I became a player myself. In the scrummage every man got down into the first position he could find, there were definitely no set positions. Every man got into the pack and was expected to fit himself in as tightly as he could, and *push*. If his side got the ball, he had to help in heeling it out quickly and gently, pushing his hardest all the time, even after the ball had gone! If his side did *not* get the ball, he pushed harder than ever, for he fully expected that the extra attention he could give to his pushing, having no ball to think about, would enable his pack to push the other men off the ball.

The backs were the 'passers', not the forwards [who] were strongly discouraged from interfering with the job of the men behind. What effect had that on the game? Very much, for you did see the seven backs on each side have ample room in which to manoeuvre without the interference of forwards straying about. It made a beautiful game to watch, and I consider it still the most perfect form of Rugby I have ever seen. An intensive close game among the forwards, with the open game almost entirely left to the seven backs on each side. No interference from 'roving' [wing] forwards.

EDWARD BAKER (England 1895-1897, 7 caps)

The English forwards were badly beaten. We backs never had the ball passed out to us at all.

DAI GENT

My very vivid recollection of half-back play in my pre-playing days was of Wales beating England in 1899. It was the play of the Welsh half-backs that really paved the way for a smashing defeat, for the English half-backs were powerless against them. In Wales, then, the separate functions of the two half-backs had become quite stabilised, but in England generally this was not the case.

ARTHUR ROTHERHAM (England 1898-1899, 5 caps plus 3 caps for the Lions)

The Welshmen were most deserving of their victory. There is not the least doubt of it that the best team won. From start to finish the game was played in the most friendly spirit.

ARTHUR BUDD

The brothers James simply waltzed round Livesay and Rotherham.

JOHN RAPHAEL (England 1902-1906, 9 caps)

To play against Wales in Wales with any prospect of success, it is no good settling down to a steady 'dogged as does it'. The team that tries that has usually very decisively settled itself ere the first lap has been completed. It is at a very extended sprint that a game at Cardiff or at Swansea must be played. The grounds are quite different to any one meets elsewhere. Cardiff more particularly can be a real terror. I have played there when not a member of the English team and seemed unable to get a foothold of any sort; and yet the Welshmen were frolicking – well, that's hardly the right word – they were raiding our goal-line with an insatiable and a disgusting greediness that even a hard ground and dry ball would not have justified.

LEONARD TOSSWILL
John Daniell was the greatest forward the game has ever known. I played with and against him in every kind of game. He was not only a magnificent forward but a most inspiring captain. He could get the last ounce out of his men, and was at his best in an emergency. Physically he was the ideal build for a forward, not too tall, with very powerful shoulders, fast and clever in the loose, and a tremendously hard worker in the scrummages. I believe Daniell would hold his own in any company of forwards, from any country and of any time.

DAI GENT
The octopus-like Gamlin. Six feet odd in height, with exceptionally long arms and legs, his face always grimly set, and slightly bow-legged, I can see him now. Here was the greatest tackler I have ever seen. No man passed the ball after Gamlin had laid hands on him: he went headlong, ball and all, with Gamlin's tentacles all round him. Gamlin's genius lay in arranging – yes arranging – when the man in possession should be tackled. It is practically useless to tackle a player just after he has passed the ball. It is the man with the ball you want. Gamlin would watch the movement coming up to him, taking in at a glance its probable development, and then he would, by perfect positioning, force the movement to go in a certain direction, induce a player or two to pass, and then crash into the man on the spot where he [Gamlin] had decided the movement should stop. In his days Welsh football was at its very best, and the greatness of their midfield players used to enable the Welsh backs to burst through the middle of the field quite often, and run up to Gamlin, often three to his single self. Then it was that his deferred tackle came into play.

SAMMY WOODS (England 1890-1895, 13 caps)
I reckon [Gamlin] was the best fullback who ever played.

LEONARD TOSSWILL
The most impressive thing about [Gamlin] was his tackling. This was unique, for although he went for his man fairly high, he never failed to gather both man and

ball in his grasp. A very long and accurate kicker with his left foot, and more than useful with his right foot as well. When playing in front of Gamlin one regarded the most dangerous runs by opposing threequarters with equanimity. Hands alone should never be used for catching the ball, although Gamlin invariably did – but Gamlin was a rule to himself.

JOHN RAPHAEL

Gamlin always seemed to be in a position to prevent you going over the line. I should strongly advise nobody to adopt [his] method of tackling – he was an exception that proves the rule about going low. The way he dealt with his adversaries was uncomfortable and disconcerting to the victims. He dropped on them, as it were, from above. He was a heavy man, too!

I have some idea of what it would have been like, from seeing how [in 1902] he took a large and pacy Irishman, when the latter, coming down at full speed, was about three yards from our line, and perhaps half-a-dozen feet from touch. There was a spring by the Englishman; two bodies rose into the air, and the next thing was a seething mass of humanity lying well outside the touchline. Both men eventually arose, apparently uninjured, and the game proceeded. How precisely it was done I do not know. The most remarkable feature was the distance and the direction they travelled ere reaching terra firma.

DAI GENT

It was gorgeous to watch [Gamlin] control a situation. It was gorgeous, too, to see the duels between Teddy Morgan or Willie Llewellyn and Gamlin, after Gwyn Nicholls or Rhys Gabe had made openings that left their wings with only Gamlin to beat. Yes, not once, but twenty times have I seen Gamlin confronted by this situation, he alone against as many as four opponents, sometimes. Tackling, rush-stopping, and kicking of tremendous length, though not of great accuracy, were Gamlin's superb characteristics, and if ever one man was called upon to hold the fort, it was Gamlin in the games he played against Wales between 1899 and 1904.

JOHN RAPHAEL

The most terrific tackle I ever witnessed was during the [1902] England and Scotland game. The Scottish halves having drawn the defence, put their threes in motion, and [their wing], taking full advantage of the opening, came tearing down the middle of the ground. Unable to pass without some risk of an intercept, he went straight ahead, and, from the way he was moving, no ordinary tackle could have saved [our] line. Fortunately for us, J T Taylor was at hand. They met with a crash that could be heard all over the ground. Instinctively we all paused to see what had happened.

DAI GENT
For my club [Gloucester] I was a 'scrum-half', and, as in Wales, there was never any mixing of the positions. During the 1904-05 season I played for Gloucestershire, and my partner was [Walter] Butcher, who was also one of the England half-backs that season. I remember his asking me in the dressing-room: 'Which half of the field would you like to take?' I wondered what he meant until he told me that it was the custom to take one half of the field (the right or the left) and on that side to 'work' the scrum and throw out of touch, acting as outside-half and standing at the end of the line-out on the other side. This was quite a new idea to me, but I soon tumbled to it. This old tradition of half-backs, ready for either position, continued in parts of England for a little longer, but the visit of the New Zealanders in 1905-06 showed the need of 'specialist' half-backs, and after about 1906 most teams had their scrum-half and stand-off-half, and their different functions became clearly defined.

HARRY ALEXANDER (England 1900-1902, 7 caps)
The total of 15 points to 0 in favour of the New Zealanders by no means flatters the winners. With the exception of about four all too brief intervals, they were in England's half of the grounds, and at half-time the state of the turf at the different ends of the field gave a clear enough proof of where all the play had been. In addition to this, the visitors looked absolutely certain to score on several occasions, and were only stopped from doing so by the barest margin. The way in which the visitors gained possession in the scrum almost every time became very apparent, and no less marked was the vastly superior way in which their half got the ball away to his backs.

Jackett was more than once called upon to stop an otherwise certain try, and collared his man very well each time. He gave a very fine display, and deserves much praise for the way in which he carried out the enormous amount of work that was thrown on him. In every department the New Zealanders were greatly superior to the Englishmen. Their forwards practically always got the ball in the scrums, and about as often out of touch. The English halves were virtually swamped, and could only get the ball out to their backs on two or three occasions, so that the English threequarters had no chance whatever of showing their powers of attack. Their defence was, on the whole, good; and to cope at all with the wonderful passing and extraordinarily skilful variety of tactics displayed by the Colonials, must have been above the average.

DAI GENT
[After] the All Blacks, the game, in England especially, underwent a kind of renaissance. Sides were encouraged to open out the game from all parts of the field, forwards were taught to be a little more mobile, and England was really roused to the potentialities

of the game as a spectacle. It led, too, to the encouragement of the wing forward, the role carried out by the New Zealand captain, Dave Gallaher. I played against him for England. I know how difficult it was to play against this 'wing' forward.

JOHN RAPHAEL

There is no question that the visit of the New Zealanders was largely responsible for breaking the spell of decline that had bound English football. The effect, however, was not very immediate, nor was it startlingly direct. The great lesson, it seems to me, that we learnt from that famous team was that combination is not a mechanical affair.

DAI GENT

Adrian Stoop was the man whose mission it was to infuse, with his own, many of the ideas of the New Zealanders into English football, and the Harlequins club was the instrument he used to bring this about. I have no hesitation in saying that no single individual has done as much to make Rugby an attractive game to watch and to play in as Stoop. He was the best attacking outside half I have ever seen, and I had the great benefit of judging his play on the field, for we played together in international matches. Stoop's policy was: 'Attack, attack all the time, no matter what part of the field you are in.' It was almost a principle of his that the further you were from your opponents' line, the better chance you had of driving your attack home.

The 1909 England team before their 22-0 victory over France at Leicester. Ronnie Poulton (later Poulton-Palmer), on his England debut, far right on the floor and fullback John Jackett seated far left middle row

FIVE

THE FIRST GOLDEN ERA

1910-1914

NOW ENGLAND HAD *a permanent home. Twickenham was to last them down through the generations, and was to eventually provide them with a towering edifice as a tribute to the wisdom of the pioneers and the acumen of their modern-day successors.*

The acquisition of Twickenham, together with the Adrian Stoop-inspired revolution in playing approach, heralded the return of England's former rugby dominance and signalled that the sport was overcoming the effects of the great schism which created rugby league.

In January 1910, the remarkable Stoop captained them in the first international staged at the ground, and they celebrated by beating Wales to open a Golden Era that brought five Grand Slams in ten seasons. It was also in 1910 that the Five Nations Championship truly began, with France playing all four home unions for the first time.

Stoop's defining streak of unorthodoxy immediately showed against the Welsh. Fielding the Welsh kick-off, Stoop initiated a bold attack that led to a try before Wales had handled the ball. It set in train a performance which brought an 11-6 win and fired England to their first Championship title since 1892.

Welsh followers had to wait only one season for revenge after their first defeat by England for 12 years. They beat England in Cardiff and went on to win the Grand Slam, but thereafter England dominated Five Nations rugby until the outbreak of the Great War.

Stoop's side effectively broke up after the draw with Ireland in 1912. In his 30th year, Stoop's last game was a rare defeat against Scotland at Inverleith, where England played with 14 men after Jack King, the 5ft 5in pocket Hercules from Headingley and the smallest forward ever capped by England, left the field early on with injury.

Next to depart the international scene was John Birkett, Stoop's senior centre and lieutenant for club and country, who stepped down after becoming England's most capped player – as his farewell he choose the match against France in front of a hostile French crowd on Easter Monday when another great name in English rugby, J E (Jenny) Greenwood made his debut and the Navy's Norman Wodehouse was the captain.

If Stoop had revolutionised back play in England, Greenwood, a Cambridge Blue and Harlequin, was to contribute in another area. He had already made a close study of scrummaging by the time he made his debut for the national team and his experience garnered as a Test player would soon add authority to his findings. At the time, first up,

Opposite: Adrian Stoop (far right) in 1910.

first down, remained the order of the day (if you arrived first you formed part of the front-row, and so on), though hooking and 'winging' tactics had become established.

Packs often scrummaged in 3-3-2 formation, the asymmetry aiding wheeling, a popular tactic that enabled the 'winger' (wing forward) to break away at the head of a foot-rush. In defence, this specialist's role was hindering the opposition. Other forwards were picked on all-round skills — no specialist props or locks, while the conception of the No 8 forward was decades away.

The wing-forward role evolved with Swansea's Ivor Morgan pioneering the tactic of harassing the opposition fly-half. Charles 'Cherry' Pillman refined the technique to a fine art for England. Fast, with fly-paper hands and a smother tackle that nipped handling movements in the bud, he was the prototype open-side.

Pillman and Greenwood were key components of England's packs in the back-to-back Grand Slams immediately before the Great War. Greenwood preferred the 3-2-3 arrangement, arguing that it enabled a straighter scrum shove.

Behind them in 1913, as they established a strong pack, was a new back division spearheaded from fly-half by a young naval officer, WJA 'Dave' Davies, from Wales. CN 'Kid' Lowe, like Greenwood a Cambridge Blue and former Dulwich College pupil, was a new right-wing, with Bath's Vincent Coates on the left. Ronald Poulton, the famous Harlequin threequarter, was recalled at centre.

Poulton was the poster-boy for English rugby after Stoop's departure. Educated at Rugby School and Oxford, his good looks, natural charm and brilliant rugby skills guaranteed hero status. He became Poulton-Palmer after acknowledging an inheritance from George Palmer, his grandfather who was the co-founder of the Huntley and Palmer biscuit business. Yet despite his privileged background, his empathy with those of a differnt class than himself, and his enduring modesty, were the most striking facets of his charm.

Poulton intervened in 1912 when the RFU conducted a fierce campaign against professionalism, suspending several Devon players over allegations that they had received broken time payments.

Among those allegedly tainted were James Peters and Richard Jago, who had each appeared for England with Stoop. Poulton was outraged and wrote defending 'broken time' to The Sportsman *newspaper. Later, as England's captain, he refused to be photographed with the ball in the official photograph, the captain's traditional privilege, not wishing to be marked out from his team.*

He made his mark on the opening Test of 1913, against South Africa. New-look England opened strongly and Poulton, from a mazy run, scored under the posts. The record Twickenham crowd of 35,000 watched in dismay as Wodehouse missed the conversion. Minutes later Poulton set off on another swerving run only to be hauled down short of the line.

England lost 9-3, but the selectors made only two changes for the visit to Cardiff where Poulton's reputation ensured Wales closely marked him. Davies sent a perfect cut-out pass to Coates when all eyes were on Poulton, enabling the Bath wing to open the scoring early in the second half. Greenwood landed a fine conversion, Poulton dropped a goal and the ubiquitous Pillman completed the victory with a late try.

This launched England's first-ever Grand Slam season, Coates scoring six tries overall. 'Kid' Lowe on the other wing barely received a pass. But he made up for it the next season, scoring eight (still the all-time individual Five/Six Nations try record) when Poulton was skipper.

DAVE DAVIES (England 1913-1923, 22 caps)

Intense backing up was a feature and the main reason for the Harlequin success during the Stoop era. The Harlequins threw the ball about, or, in other words, gave it plenty of air. It was made possible by the plethora of speed outside. Tim and Adrian Stoop, John Birkett, Ronnie Poulton, Douglas Lambert and Henry Brougham [all England internationals] were no slouches. I doubt if a nicer adjustment of speed in a team outside the scrum ever existed. The wings were faster than the centres, centres faster than the stand-off half, who was very quick off the mark, and all above the average – an ideal combination. Nothing approached this standard of excellence in post-war rugby.

DAI GENT

The easiest [half-back] partner I ever had was AD Stoop. I first played with him in 1910, and found it as easy to 'find' him as I did my usual club partner. [In] the historic England v Wales match with which the Twickenham ground was officially opened, we scored in the first minute of the game, and because Stoop played a part in getting that try, the match has often been referred to as 'Stoop's match.'

It was certainly Stoop's fertile brain that made the try possible, for even in those days it was customary for the kick-off to be returned conventionally to touch. That day, instead of kicking, Stoop made off towards the west stand, started a bout of passing, and this movement was so brilliantly executed against a great Welsh side that was hardly awake to what had happened, that we scored through FE Chapman in the right-hand corner of the field, the ball having gone from the centre of the field to the west touch-line (on Stoop's left), and finishing in the right-hand or north-east corner.

My point in mentioning this is that, with all the confusion and excitement of an England v Wales match, it was easy to 'find' one's partner, though thanks mainly, perhaps, to his smooth running and his wonderful sense of position and his excellent handling.

DAVE DAVIES

The wisdom of the Union's policy in buying [Twickenham], although much discussed and bitterly opposed in some quarters, has been abundantly justified since. The only effective criticism that one could make was that, in the light of present-day experience, the ground is not capable of holding the vast crowds who frequent it on international days.

RONALD POULTON-PALMER (England 1909-1914, 17 caps)

I had to come back after a week [at Wengen] to play in a trial match in London [in January 1910]. We were badly beaten, but I succeeded in staying for the Welsh match a week later. After that they had no further use for me!

JOHN 'JENNY' GREENWOOD (England 1912-1920, 13 caps)

[I] was chosen reserve for the English XV against Scotland at Inverleith [1912] in Edinburgh. In order to get back to my Cambridge studies I came down by the night train after the dinner and did not stay the night. In those days we had to travel third-class, and the sole occupant of my carriage was Ernest Ward, the Rugby football correspondent of the *Morning Post*. He was a nice old bloke but unfortunately too fond of the bottle. I was very civil to him and after that he always wrote me up tremendously.

The RFU were very strict about expenses. William Cail was treasurer. On one occasion, when a player had sent in a claim for expenses going to Dublin, when Mr Cail next saw him he asked if he had a good journey. The fellow replied 'Perfectly awful, Mr Cail, it was very rough and I felt terribly sick.' Mr Cail replied that, in that case, he would cancel his claim for lunch on the boat, which he could not have had!

RONALD POULTON-PALMER

Letter to The Sportsman, *December 1912*

THE RUGBY UNION AND PROFESSIONALISM.

It is with much apprehension that I read this morning the finding of the General Committee of the Rugby Union concerning the charges brought against certain players in Devonshire clubs of having received money for 'broken time'.

If it is the desire of the Rugby Union Committee practically to limit the game to players who learn it at the Public Schools, and in the Services and Universities, such a finding is reasonable. But I cannot believe such is their desire.

Was not this, then, the opportunity to put the game on an immovable basis among all classes of the community by making an alteration in the laws of the game relating to professionalism, so as to legislate for a carefully arranged payment for 'broken time' for men who are paid weekly or monthly for the hours they work?

And it is difficult to see how such an offence can be construed as professionalism. A man does not, or under careful regulation would not, receive any addition to this normal weekly wage, but would be paid merely for the hours of work missed through football. Such hours of work would, of course, not include 'overtime'.

He would then be exactly in the position of many business men who, in the enjoyment of a settled income, leave their work an hour or so earlier to catch the necessary train to the match. The most optimistic must feel that such an action as the R.U.Committee have taken will do much to prevent the expansion of the Rugby game, and so reduce the value to England of the most democratic of sports.

I only venture to write this to find out if there are any other present or past players of the game who think as I do.

Yours truly,

RONALD W. POULTON.

16 Portland Place, Reading

JAMES 'BIM' BAXTER (England 1900, 3 caps)

It was in 1913 that [WJA] Davies was first chosen to represent his country, against WA Millar's South African team, and it is worth noting that he was then on the losing side for the first and only time when wearing the glorious white of England.

A fortnight or so later he made amends by helping England to beat Wales at Cardiff, this being the only occasion on which England has been victorious in that city. It was Davies who threw out the long pass which enabled VHM Coates to score the first try England had gained at Cardiff since 1893.

DAVE DAVIES

An urgent wire on the Friday before the match, asking me to play [for London] against the South Africans, put me on the threshold of international football. London beat the South Africans, the only English team to claim this record.

To my great surprise, the next week I was picked in the international trial, and soon afterwards played in that memorable match when England sustained her only defeat at Twickenham by 9-3.

Certain impressions of my first international remain indelibly imprinted in my mind. A great feeling of uneasiness crept over me on entering the dressing-room, as I was a comparative stranger to all the players, and the importance of the occasion rather overawed me.

Of the game itself, I remember certain things very clearly. My disappointment when Wodehouse failed to kick a goal from under the posts, after Poulton had scored a try, was immense.

JENNY GREENWOOD

Unfortunately, I was in the first English side ever to lose a match at Twickenham and this was against the South Africans, largely caused by two enormous penalty goals kicked by Morkel. Both were for minor offences, and I have always thought it quite wrong that a kick in such circumstances should be worth as much as a try. Rugby football is supposed to be a team game, but winning games by penalty goals is often entirely due to one man. Norman Wodehouse was [our] captain, and when we scored a try under the South Africans' post he took the kick and missed. I naturally was disgusted as I had been asked by the selection committee to go to Twickenham the day before and practise place-kicks. We won the Triple Crown that year, beating Wales at Cardiff [for] the first time.

JOHN RAPHAEL

Of brilliant individual bursts, those who saw it will single out one of Poulton-Palmer's in the England and South Africa match of 1913. Receiving the ball well inside his own half-way, Palmer commenced to 'hare' for the touchline. Then he seemed to stop, and his opponents, in doubt whether he was going to kick or to pass to his wing, dashed at various angles to where danger seemed to threaten.

Having drawn off the Springboks on to the wrong trail, a change of foot and one of his own inimitable swerves saw him flying across the face and almost within touch of the nearest foes. Then a feint – and a dodge – and he was through, with only, so it seemed, the [full-]back to pass. Morkel had no chance, and the roar of 35,000 voices urged the runner on to the unmarked goal-line.

The path, however, was not quite clear, for the speedy Stegmann was doing his utmost to cut off England's centre. Another slight change of direction had to be undertaken, and this brought danger from another quarter. The race now was agonising in its excitement, but with Lowe in attendance it looked a certain try. It was not, however, to be.

Three or four yards from his destination Palmer was overtaken, and a splendid tackle spoilt his attempt at passing. It was a sad pity for England that success did not attend him. For thrilling sensationalism this run lives almost by itself in the football of very recent years.

RONALD POULTON-PALMER

The season was made memorable by the visit of the South African team. You feel there must be something extraordinary about the climate of South Africa, when you are easily given twenty yards in a hundred by a McHardy or a Stegmann, when you see the ball propelled infinite distances with perfect accuracy by a Morkel, and when you feel the weight of a Morkel, a Van Vuuren, or a Shum deposited on your chest.

DAVE DAVIES

The following match in 1913 was against Wales in Cardiff. I was greatly impressed with the strong confidence of Wodehouse, our captain, in his belief that we were going to give Wales a good hiding, and his keen disappointment at breakfast on the morning of the match, when it was raining. Of the game itself, I remember little, except Poulton's dropped goal – a marvellous effort, in a quagmire – and a certain satisfaction I had in getting across to tackle their wing on several occasions. It was a very satisfied English team which travelled back to Paddington that evening.

RONALD POULTON-PALMER

'Oh, there you are, my dear fellow. Hurry up, you'll miss the train! You're always late!'

In these words (as usual), I was welcomed by our anxious Secretary, Mr Charles Marriott, on joining a merry party of some two dozen souls bound on January 17 for Penarth, there to obtain the rest necessary for our great encounter with Wales at Cardiff.

On assembling at breakfast the next morning we found that rain was falling steadily, and all hope of a dry ground and ball was given up. The morning was spent in animated discussions of numerous devices for winning the match, none of which by any chance came off during the game itself, except the oft-repeated injunction of our captain, 'Remember your feet and use them, and don't forget the watchword,' – but that, I fear, is unprintable.

However, after a game played on a ground where the blades of grass seemed with difficulty to be holding their heads above the ever-rising flood, England emerged unrecognisable but victorious by 12 points to nil.

LEONARD TOSSWILL

Among the greatest players of a generation was WJA [Dave] Davies [with] his marvellous fielding of the ball, his drop-kicking, and his flashes of inspiration. Davies had as partner FE Oakeley, a victim of the war. He [too] was [among] the most distinguished players the Navy has given to Rugby football.

DAVE DAVIES

Charles Marriott is known to all players in the country. No other official of the RFU will ever occupy quite the same place in the affections of the Rugby football world.

My reputation for carelessness was enhanced in my first away international in

Ireland [in 1913]. I lost my railway ticket. This indeed was a tragedy. How could I break the news to Mr Marriott, who was then in the middle of a heated argument with the dining-car attendant as to whether our party numbered 20 or 21. The news was eventually broken to him, and the result cannot be described in mere pedestrian prose. For the remainder of the journey I was kept under the vigilant eye of the secretary, and was made to travel with him.

RONALD POULTON-PALMER

In all the five games only ten forwards were played. [They] were expected by close, low packing to obtain possession of the ball in the scrum, and to show great speed in the loose dribbling and hand to hand advance.

DAVE DAVIES

The finest exponent of getting away from the lineout in a dribble was Wodehouse. Catching the ball and passing back is one continuous motion. JE Greenwood excelled in this. Numerous attacks were started by him in this way. Possessed of exceptional height, with a rare knack of catching the ball well above his head, it was a comparatively easy matter for him to swing round to pass to his outsides.

RONALD POULTON-PALMER

The English forwards were superior to their opponents in every game, and, time after time, an opportune dribble produced a fifty-yard advance and prevented a probable adverse score. But they were not so successful in obtaining the ball in the scrum, and the heeling was often slow.

The England team before their 20-0 victory over France at Twickenham in 1913.
Back row: William Cheesman, Frank Steinthal, Sid Smart, John Ritson, 'Jenny' Greenwood, Vincent Coates, George Ward, 'Dave' Davies. Seated: "Bruno" Brown, "Cherry" Pillman, Ronnie Poulton, Norman Wodehouse (captain), William Johnston, Jack King, "Kid" Lowe.

LEONARD TOSSWILL
Poulton-Palmer was [a] centre threequarter of the highest type, having a deceptive swerve and sound in defence. [He] was exceedingly popular with a host of friends and admirers.

DAVE DAVIES
Poulton [-Palmer] was my ideal captain [1914]. No one of the present generation stands out more against the background of Rugby football than Ronald Poulton [-Palmer]. One could not help liking him. His easy grace and charm of manner, his versatility on the football field, the characteristic run with the head well back and ball held in outstretched hands, are vivid impressions of probably the greatest figure which ever played Rugby football.

The season of 1914 opened very inauspiciously for me. For the England v Wales match, Oakeley and I were dropped and preference given to the Leicester halves. It was not altogether unexpected, as I was playing very badly at the time, but it was a grievous disappointment to me that I was the cause of Oakeley's departure. However, we were picked again for the Irish and the remaining matches.

DAI GENT
Scrum half-backs are, as a rule, smallish men, plucky, nippy, and made of whipcord. FE Oakeley was like that.

DAVE DAVIES
My first visit to France was at the end of the season, when England won 39-13, although the French team had made a terrific commencement. After the match, one of the selection committee commended Oakeley and myself on our game, and stated that their only mistake during the season was dropping us for the Welsh match.

LEONARD TOSSWILL
Lowe was one of the pluckiest tacklers imaginable and, although a light man, was also one of the most dangerous scoring threequarters produced by any country for many years. He was not exceptionally fast, but had an excellent swerve at full speed and he was a fine kicker.

DAVE DAVIES
I have often been asked my opinion as to the comparative playing strength of the [1921 and 1923 Grand Slam] teams compared with the 1914 team. An answer, which is accurate and without qualification, is hard to find. If the personal element could be eliminated and Rugby football theories treated dogmatically and logically, then perhaps one might conclude the 1914 team was better.

"This is not the time to play Games" (Lord Roberts)

RUGBY·UNION·FOOTBALLERS
are
DOING·THEIR·DUTY
over 90% have enlisted

"Every player who represented England in Rugby international matches last year has joined the colours."—Extract from *The Times*, November 30, 1914.

BRITISH ATHLETES!
Will you follow this
GLORIOUS EXAMPLE?

SIX

THE GREAT WAR

1914-1918

RUGBY PLAYERS FROM *all over England volunteered in huge numbers to serve King and country when War broke out in August 1914. There were even requests from groups of players that they be allowed to serve together in the same regiment, although the government eventually ruled this out.*

Few were quicker off the mark than England's Jack King, who enlisted with the Yorkshire Hussars on 6 August 1914, and left his farm three days later to begin his service career.

He was originally told that he was too short (at 5ft 5in he was one inch below the regulation 5ft 6in). King stood his ground and told the Recruiting Officer in no uncertain terms that he would 'simply stick here until you do take me in.' Military records show that he officially became a trooper on 12 August, undertook his training in Hitchin, Herts and went off to France.

As in most other walks of life, losses to the rugby fraternity in the war were colossal and international players featured prominently among the casualties. Of the 30 players who had taken part in the Triple Crown match between Scotland and England in 1914, 11 were killed in the War and, all told, 27 former England caps were killed in action, lost or died of wounds.

Among them were King (killed in action on the same day and at the same place as Lancelot Slocock), the celebrated Ronald Poulton-Palmer, John Raphael and Robert Pillman, the younger brother of 'Cherry' Pillman whose place he'd taken in the last England side to play before War.

Arthur Harrison, a forward who had played against Ireland and France in the 1914 Grand Slam campaign, headed the list of casualties decorated in battle. He was posthumously awarded the V.C. for his gallantry during the blockade of Zeebrugge.

Opposite: A First World War recruitment poster.

ROLL OF HONOUR 1914-1918

WILSON, Charles Edward (England 1898) KIA River Aisne, September 17, 1914.

WATSON, James Henry Digby Watson (England 1914) Lost at sea when HMS Hawke was torpedoed on October 15, 1914.

OAKELEY, Francis Eckley (England 1913-14) Lost at sea between November 25 & December 1, 1914.

KENDALL, Percy Dale (England 1901-03). KIA Ypres, January 25, 1915.

LAGDEN, Ronald Owen (England 1911) KIA St Eloi, March 3, 1915.

TODD, Alexander Findlater (England 1900) Died of wounds, Ypres, April 21, 1915.

POULTON-PALMER, Ronald William (England 1909-14) KIA Ploegsteert Wood, May 5, 1915.

BERRY, Henry (England 1910) KIA Festubert, France, May 9, 1915.

NANSON, William Moore Bell (England 1907) KIA Gallipoli, June 4, 1915.

TARR, Francis Nathaniel (Frank) (England 1909-13). KIA Ypres, July 18, 1915.

DINGLE, Arthur James (England 1913-14) KIA Gallipoli, August 22, 1915.

LAMBERT, Douglas (England 1907-11) KIA Loos, October 13, 1915. Loos Memorial.

ALEXANDER, Harry (England 1900-02) KIA Hulluch, northern France, October 17, 1915.

PILLMAN, Robert Lawrence (England 1914) Died of wounds Armentières, July 9, 1916.

HAIGH, Leonard (England 1910-11) Died in training at Woolwich August 6, 1916.

SLOCOCK, Lancelot Andrew Noel (England 1907-08) Died of wounds Guillemont, August 9, 1916.

KING, John Abbott (England 1911-13) KIA Guillemont, August 9, 1916.

INGLIS, Rupert Edward (England 1886) Killed rescuing wounded in Ginchy, France, September 18, 1916.

MAYNARD, Alfred Frederick (England 1914) KIA Beaumont Hamel, November 13, 1916.

DOBBS, George Eric Burroughs (England 1906) KIA Poperinghe, June 17, 1917.

WILSON, Arthur James (England 1909) KIA Flanders July 31, 1917.

MOBBS, Edgar Roberts (England 1909 10) KIA, Zillebeke, July 31, 1917.

HODGES, Harold Augustus (England 1906) KIA, near Mons, March 24, 1918.

HANDS, Reginald Harold Myburgh (England 1910) Died of wounds at Boulogne, April 20, 1918.

HARRISON, Arthur Leyland (England 1914) KIA Zeebrugge April 23, 1918.

RAPHAEL, John Edward (England 1902-06) Died of wounds Remy (Messines), June 11, 1917.

SCHWARZ, Reginald Oscar (England 1899-1901) Died of influenza on active service, Etaples, November 18, 1918.

SEVEN

IN THE SHADOW OF THE WAR

1920-1924

LIFE VERY SLOWLY *returned to something approaching normality, and England rugby set about absorbing, in mind and body, the losses they had suffered amongst players throughout the game. International rugby was to resume in 1920.*

The national team were so successful in blending pre-War experience with post-War youth that England enjoyed a wonderful run in the five seasons after the Great War. Twickenham remained a fortress throughout the period and the only defeats were in the levelling conditions of rain and mud at Swansea (1920) and Cardiff (1922).

When internationals resumed in 1920, critics judged the quality of post-war rugby inferior to pre-war days. England, though, possessed experience: WJA 'Dave' Davies and CN 'Kid' Lowe (behind the scrum), and LG 'Bruno' Brown and John Greenwood up front were seasoned players by now.

For their opening match, in the Swansea rain, it was not just the players who were rusty. Bungling selectors also drew criticism. Davies, the pre-War tactical maestro, was omitted and the selectors dropped another player just before kick-off.

Wales won 19-5, but two Englishmen who were to be of great significance in the sport, took their first steps into the pages of international rugby history. They were Wavell Wakefield – 'Wakers' – who was one of the fastest forwards ever to grace a rugby field, and C.A.Kershaw, who was to irrevocably change half-back play.

Wakefield's analytical mind focused on scrum tactics. The 1920 captain John Greenwood insisted on the compact scrum formation that laid the foundations for Wakefield's refinements. Choosing forwards on ability to specialise in the fixed 3-2-3 pack positions, Wakefield eventually consigned to history the 'first up; first down' scrummaging dogma. Specialisation became the norm.

Kershaw was unorthodox, a scrum-half who perfected darting set-piece breaks – predecessors were scrum 'workers', merely feeders and passers, pure and simple. An athlete who excelled at several sports, Kershaw revolutionised half-back play. His solo breaks took pressure off his partner, forcing defences to think about developing wing-forward play: a blind-side to bottle up the scrum-half; an open-side to attack the fly-half.

Kershaw's partnership with fellow Naval officer Davies lasted 14 England matches.

Opposite: England players at half-time after defeating Wales in Swansea in 1924. From left to right: Bevan Chantrill, Alan Robson, Arthur Blakiston, Geoff Conway, Tom Voyce, Wavell Wakefield (captain), Ronald Cove-Smith, Bill Luddington. (Smiling Tom Voyce played most of this game with a fractured rib.)

They never played together on a losing side – Davies and Kershaw were as resonant of twenties' rugby as John and Edwards for Wales in the 1970s

Davies assumed the captaincy with a convincing win over Wales at Twickenham in 1921, compelling the Cardiff Western Mail *to enquire why he didn't play for Wales, where he was born.*

England blooded a dynamic pack nucleus – a 'minder' in the shape of Reg Edwards, an enforcer in Marine Gardner and a skilled lineout operator in Ronald Cove-Smith.

Davies engendered a wonderful team ethic – working men and professional classes mixed freely as a band of brothers, and together they carried off the first post-war Grand Slam.

He then had to withdrew injured before the 1922 Five Nations match in Cardiff where the meteorological gods contrived to provide dreadful conditions. With Bruno Brown in charge, England were beaten 28-6. Against France at Twickenham, only a late flurry of scoring and deadly goal-kicking by Harold Day preserved the Twickenham Five Nations record.

Then, more glory, with the back to back Grand Slams of 1923 and 1924.

England and Scotland met annually on the third Saturday in March, the Calcutta Cup at this time invariably deciding the destiny of the Championship and Triple Crown. They were confrontations to savour, they attracted capacity crowds, including King George V. His Majesty attended Twickenham for pleasure, not from a sense of duty, and the sound of 'three cheers for the King' as he greeted the teams became commonplace.

Wakefield's insistence on fixed pack places in 1923 focused selection procedure. England played two out-and-out scavengers in the back-row, Leo Price and Gloucester's swashbuckling Tom Voyce, against the Welsh and Irish. For the challenge of the unbeaten Scottish, it was felt by the England selectors that a strapping 'stopper', Arthur Blakiston, was more suitable than the pacey Price.

Blakiston's experience proved a decisive element in England's narrow win. So did solid place-kicking. Conversions then were taken with a placer. Timing and coordination between placer and kicker were vital, so the selectors nominated their pair early. Practice paid off for the Naval marines, Luddington and Gardner, the former converting Tom Voyce's equalising try from the touchline for a thrilling 8-6 win.

England's match in Paris was the swansong for three stalwarts. 'Kid' Lowe, the great right-wing, retired as the England record-holder with 25 caps – won successively since 1913 – while Dave Davies and Kershaw signed-off too. Davies, then on his honeymoon, sealed the Grand Slam with a dropped goal from virtually the game's last play. On the following day, a Colonel Clive Wigram wrote on behalf of the King rejoicing at England's achievements and congratulating Davies on his glittering career:

Windsor Castle,
April 3, 1923.

My Dear Davies –

The King wishes me to let you know how delighted he was to hear of the victory of the English team in Paris, and to congratulate you on being captain of the winning team in all your matches.

His Majesty feels sure that you must have created a record by this fitting termination to your brilliant career in international football.

Success percolated down to England's grass-roots. Rugby traditionally relied on the Public Schools as its conveyor belt of talent but from the 1920s, a burgeoning Grammar School system strengthened supply and there were also many converting from soccer. Typical – yet remarkable – was Watford Grammar School in Hertfordshire. There, from 1921 to 1934, the master in charge of P.E & Games was Stanley (later Sir Stanley) Rous. Already an international soccer referee, and later the Secretary of the FA and a FIFA big-wig, he instigated the school's change from the round-ball game.

Newspaper coverage given in the broadsheets to Rugby – always spelt with a capital R – was vast. And riding the crest of rugby's popularity wave, Wisden launched a rugby equivalent to its famous cricketing Almanack *in the autumn of 1923, while the same month saw the launch of the first weekly magazine devoted exclusively to the sport.*

Wakefield was captain of a new-look team in 1924 when newcomer Carston Catcheside became the first player to score tries in every match of a Five Nations campaign. The Percy Park wing even managed to score one over the then-parsimonious RFU. He had put in a rounded expenses claim for £4 following a Twickenham trial match, only to find the claim reduced to the correct rail fare, £3-19-11.

After winning the Grand Slam against Scotland at Twickenham March, he again submitted a claim for £4 – this time boosting the claim by 1 penny for use of the toilets at King's Cross was paid.

England were the rugby rulers of the northern hemisphere when 1924 ended. They had absorbed well the loss of players who had formed the Northern Union, and also those lost in the war. Rugby was growing, so too the importance of international rugby, the list of grand characters the game produced, and the anecdotes which sprouted whenever they gathered.

Yet a different challenge awaited them in the New Year, dressed in black.

LEONARD TOSSWILL

The two greatest players of a generation were WJA Davies and CA Kershaw, who until 1923 played together for England at half-back. I have heard arguments on the question whether Davies made Kershaw, or Kershaw made Davies, but I prefer to think of them – as they would themselves wish – as one pair, the greatest pair of halves probably who ever played for England. Each had his strong points – Kershaw, his lightning passes from the base of the scrum and his dashing bursts of speed as he made for the line; Davies, his marvellous fielding of the ball, his drop-kicking, his flashes of inspiration.

DAVE DAVIES
After the Armistice in 1918, playing in a trial match for HMS Queen Elizabeth against one of the squadrons in the fleet at Forsyth, I met Kershaw. We played together for the Grand Fleet against the Rest of the Navy in March, 1919, and commenced a partnership which lasted until the end of the season 1923. Our esteemed friend, the *Morning Post* correspondent [Ernest Ward], was at the match, and was duly impressed with Kershaw, who first came into prominence from that day. Fortunately for both of us, we were appointed to Portsmouth, where we were stationed for several years, and had ample time and opportunity to develop that understanding necessary for a successful partnership.

CECIL KERSHAW (England 1920-1923, 16 caps)
One of the points of the partnership was that it didn't just happen, it was hard work! We used to meet after work four or five nights a week at the United Services ground so that we worked up a sort of instinctive co-operation. If I got the ball in a game, no matter where I went, I knew if I threw the ball up Dave would be there.

RONALD COVE-SMITH (England 1921-1929, 29 caps plus 4 caps for the Lions)
The English Selection Committee of late years [have chosen] when possible, halves from the same club. WJA [Dave] Davies was first of all chosen to partner Cheesman (Old Merchant Taylors') and then Oakeley (United Services) but made good on his own; then Kershaw was chosen to partner Davies after the war, and he in turn made an individual name for himself.

DAVE DAVIES
Kershaw I can write about with the most unbounded admiration. He, more than any other player, revolutionised scrummage half-back play, and contributed in no small measure, by his great initiative and daring, to the success of the English side during the four seasons following the war.

He was bold enough to initiate attacks from the base of the scrum almost as successfully as the modern stand-off-half. Until Kershaw arrived, a scrum-half fed his partner unremittingly. Kershaw changed all this.

Endowed with all the physical advantages necessary to the attainment of the highest class, and possessed of natural ability for all ball games, his was the premier place in the list of scrummage half-backs.

JOHN GREENWOOD

I had a very easy war, with only a bullet wound through the left arm. I was tired and sore after the [1919] Varsity Match and decided to retire and not play any more football as I was nearly 29 then. However, this was not to be, as a few weeks later I received a telephone call late at night from John Daniell [of the England Selection Committee], saying that they were in a hole regarding a captain and leader of forwards and would I play again. He knew I wasn't keen but when he agreed that it would be for all four matches and that I should not have to play for my place, I accepted.

WILFRED LOWRY (England 1920, 1 cap)

After being photographed with the England team on the pitch at Swansea, five minutes before the match started I was unceremoniously dropped in favour of HLV Day on the score of heavy rain and atrocious mud. This caused quite a furore at the time but perhaps I was well out of it as Wales won 19-5 with Jerry Shea scoring 16 points in a brilliant centre threequarter display.

JOHN GREENWOOD

Our first international was against Wales at Swansea, where we were beaten but not disgraced. The Selection Committee was not very bright, as they played Harry Coverdale instead of Dave – ie WJA [Dave] Davies, at fly-half. Also, after we had been photographed, I was staggered to see when going on to the pitch that they had substituted HLV Day on the wing for Lowrie without telling me! This was the first international for Wavell Wakefield.

WAVELL WAKEFIELD (England 1920-1926, 31 caps)

'Jenny' [Greenwood] was, I always thought, one of the very neatest of forwards in all he did, and [as captain] he had a great faculty of getting to the bed-rock in his remarks before, during or after a game.

CECIL KERSHAW

The moment I'd most prefer to forget was returning to the dressing-room at Swansea after a shower, Wales having beaten us 19-5 in the first international after the 1914-18 war, to find that my first international jersey had been stolen.

DAVE DAVIES

At the beginning of the 1919-20 season, I cracked a small bone in my leg, which prevented me from playing until the England v the South trial match. I was dropped for the match against Wales. I was disappointed, but not surprised as I was very slow. I travelled to Swansea as a reserve and saw the game from the touch-line. It was a very unsatisfactory exhibition.

I was reinstated into the team for the French match. We just managed to beat France and Ireland, and finished up the season in convincing style by beating Scotland, who had previously beaten Wales. The result was that England, Scotland and Wales were bracketed equal at the head of the championships, a fitting result to the aftermath of war.

JOHN GREENWOOD

We only just managed to beat France 8-3 at Twickenham. I landed a penalty goal from half-way, which was the longest goal I ever kicked.

WILFRED LOWRY

Against France I played [wing] outside EDG Hammett – a strange selection this as he had played amateur soccer for Wales and had also played in a Welsh rugger trial. However, he had an English qualification too, though I wonder nowadays if all this would be permitted. Why Harold Locke [my club centre at Birkenhead] was dropped after the one England trial in 1919, I never could understand. He and I were never again given the chance as partners for England. Compared with playing with Locke, Ernie Hammett, a nice chap, was like an old carthorse – steady, sober, adequate but very unlike my normal dynamic centre.

JOHN GREENWOOD

The next match was against Ireland in Dublin in the middle of the troubles, but it passed off without incident; however, we had a very rough crossing both ways and I did not play at my best.

My last match was against Scotland whom we beat, and in consequence my name as captain is engraved on the Calcutta Cup. In this match, four young forwards played who afterwards made great names for themselves, ie Wakefield, Conway, Tom Voyce and Blakiston, the latter becoming Sir Arthur Blakiston, Bart., MFH, in later years. Thus the last game I ever played in was a suitable finish with a win against Scotland.

King George V was a very enthusiastic follower of Rugby football and attended many matches at Twickenham including the last one in which I played. He brought Prince Albert and Prince Henry with him.

WAVELL WAKEFIELD

I remember that we were rather anxious about the [1920] Scotch match, for they had beaten both Ireland and Wales, and it looked very much as if the Twickenham record would be broken. However, Davies and Kershaw played remarkably well together, though I nearly gave the game away myself by missing a pass from Hammett when all I had to do was to run a few yards to score under the posts.

DAVE DAVIES

I was asked by Mr James Baxter, the president of the England Selection Committee, to captain the team [in 1921], a post I was entrusted with for three years. Mine was an easy task, and I should like to place on record now my deep appreciation of the loyalty of every player. I think the success of the English team during these three years was due to the happy feeling which existed among the players – a feeling made possible by the spirit instilled into us and the example set by the Selection Committee.

WAVELL WAKEFIELD

I remember that everyone fully expected that we should be beaten by Wales in the first match [of 1921], but somehow the English team got going from the first whistle, and won easily. We followed it up by beating Ireland, although Davies was crocked in the first ten minutes. His injury was serious enough to send him off the field, and I had to go out on the wing, a change of position which gave me a valuable insight into International threequarter play.

DAVE DAVIES

I don't wish to stir up any controversy about this, but the facts are quite simple. It is quite true that I was born in Pembroke Dock, but I did not learn my Rugby in Wales. All my Rugby was learnt in England, and the first club I played for was an English club at Cardiff, curiously enough. Until I left Wales I knew nothing about Rugby. It was said that I was going to be selected for both the English and Welsh trial. I made it quite clear at once that if I was selected at all I would play for England.

RONALD COVE-SMITH

What joys there are to be found in travelling about the country together and of getting to know one another as a team. I well remember when travelling up to Scotland to play in my first international match [in 1921] how impressed I was by the way the others put their heads out of the windows and cheered Blakiston and Smallwood as we ran into Peterborough and Grantham, at which stations they joined the team. We were more like a happy family than an international team picked from scattered clubs all over the country, and I am sure that a good deal of our success was due to that fact alone.

DAVE DAVIES

Always remember to let the vice-captain know your intentions in cases of emergency. In the Irish match in 1921, at Twickenham, I was crocked with concussion in the first five minutes, and was unable to take any further part in the match. Unfortunately I had omitted to tell LG ('Bruno') Brown my proposed plans. I had discussed them casually with him, so everything was soon in order; but even old Bruno fell into the trap of expediency, so easy in the heat of the fray, of taking Wakefield out of the scrum. No harm was done, but the English team did not settle down until well into the second half, and we won comfortably in the end 15-0.

During my captaincy I was indeed fortunate to have Brown and Wakefield as leaders of my scrum. Both had a most intimate knowledge of forward play, and were ever ready to discuss the smallest point with me, or any other member of the team, concerning the game. Both had the happy knack of getting the extra effort out of their pack when required. Wakefield led by precept and example, always on the ball and leading a forward rush.

WAVELL WAKEFIELD

I thoroughly enjoyed my international football in [1921], for we had a series of victories and the pack was really tough and solid. I was in the second-row then, with Reg Edwards of Newport, and there was always plenty to push against, though we were not too particular about fixed places in the two front-rows [ie the front five]. It is interesting to note that the average age of that pack was over 30, and yet it was as fine a pack as England has had since the war. As a matter of fact, the backs were not much younger, and they were all consistently good.

Before the Scotch match, Scotsmen (my Scotch friends tell me) had always regarded English forwards as soft. This time the English pack was definitely the better of the two. After the game one of the Scotch forwards, ruefully rubbing his shin, complained to me that we had used the boot too much. I told him Scotland had set the example in the past. It was in this match against Scotland that LG Brown scored an outrageously offside try, and looked the most ashamed man in the North Country as he quite pardonably did so.

DAVE DAVIES

I was unable to play against Wales at Cardiff [in 1922]. In my absence the team was captained by LG ('Bruno') Brown. No better person could have led the English team, and it was an irony of fate that, owing to a combination of unfortunate circumstances, the team played very badly. No finer character than Bruno ever stepped on or off a Rugby field. He was the essence of what a Rugby footballer should be – cool, calm and collected.

BRUNO BROWN (England 1911-1922, 18 caps)
London Hospital,
Whitechapel Road,
E.1

January 18, 1922

Dear Dave,
I heard yesterday that through your misfortune and inability to play, I'm to captain the side on Saturday. I'm more than sorry that this should be so, and should gladly have foregone the honour to have had you in your place in the team. We'll not play the same together without you. I wonder whether you'll make the trip to Cardiff. I hope so, for we'd all like to have you amongst us just the same. You must give your old leg a good rest, and no doubt you'll manage to be fit for the rest of the internationals.

Hoping to see you, then, on Saturday, and once more my regrets at your misfortune.

I am
Yours ever,
Bruno

WAVELL WAKEFIELD

There were many changes in the English team after the Welsh fiasco, LG Brown, E Hammett and BS Cumberlege retiring from International football. Personally, I think it was a great mistake that Cumberlege was dropped, for he had much football left in him, and he did better than anyone else would have done in most adverse circumstances. I saw him some ten days after the match and the whole of one side of his body was still black and blue. He was a fine fullback, and it has taken England a long time to find any one who can hope to take his place successfully.

DAVE DAVIES

Our win against Ireland in Dublin the following month did much to restore the prestige of English Rugby. An Irish supporter during a lull near the end of the game, when Ireland were well beaten, said: 'If you can't catch Davies, for heaven's sake ruffle his hair.' In the corresponding match at Leicester [in 1923] I

was brilliantly tackled and my hair purposely dishevelled by GV Stephenson, the
Irish centre.

WAVELL WAKEFIELD

The Irish match was in Dublin, and I led the English pack for the first time.
I thoroughly enjoyed the game, and we won because our opponents kept such
an anxious watch on W.J.A.Davies at stand-off half that they forgot Kershaw at
scrum-half, who continually broke through with great success.

DAVE DAVIES

In pre-war days the attacking powers of a team outside the scrum were reduced
considerably by an excessive concentration on the stand-off-half – until then the
pivot of the attack. Ireland fell into this trap against England at Dublin in 1922.
What was the result? Kershaw cut through brilliantly on four distinct occasions,
from each of which we scored a try. Kershaw's policy made the halves a separate
attacking force outside, and quite independent of, the threequarter line.

WAVELL WAKEFIELD

The French match at Twickenham was an unsatisfactory affair. The French forwards

Paris 1927: Wavell Wakefield's last match and England's first defeat by France. Len Corbett
(right) leads the side out at Stade Colombes with Sam Tucker (centre) and Wakefield (left).

that day were magnificent, and I am afraid the English pack rather lethargic and not going really well together. At the end of the game we felt we had had a very lucky escape from defeat, and I have never known a Twickenham crowd to be so silent as we left the field.

DAVE DAVIES

Ten minutes before the scheduled time to kick off, all the spectators are seated, and the chief actors in the drama are lined up near the entrance to be introduced to His Majesty the King. The King arrives. The band plays the National Anthem, and every one stands and bares his head. The players are introduced. Three cheers are given for His Majesty, and never can cheers have been more heartily given. His Majesty likes to see any form of outdoor exercise; but Rugby football particularly appeals to him.

At the close the players leave the field to the accompaniment of cheers from their fellow-countrymen and to the shouts of 'Well played, England.' They don't get anything more. But what more do they deserve? They have played the game for the game's sake.

HAROLD DAY (England 1920-1926, 4 caps)

France were desperately unlucky not to win in 1922, when they were deprived of their first victory at Twickenham by [my] goal kicking. But as the immortal

Half-time at Cardiff in 1922. Stand-in skipper 'Bruno' Brown (far left), Geoff Conway (centre foreground) and curly-haired Tom Voyce (to Conway's right) deep in thought. England were beaten 28-6 in 'Dave' Davies's enforced absence through injury.

George Gunn used to reply when asked about his famous exploits on the cricket field 'T'aint for the likes of me to say,' I will pass over the details.

I should, however, like to deny flatly the assertion so often made that I had to play in borrowed boots because I forgot my own. In point of fact they were stolen with the rest of my gear while we were at lunch. What a to-do there was to get me fitted out in time, with boots that pinched, shorts like tights, and a jersey that cramped my breathing, and without a rose, there being no time to sew one on before the King arrived.

DAVE DAVIES

England were decidedly fortunate to draw with France at Twickenham, and we owed everything to the wonderful place-kicking of Day. [His] performance was all the more remarkable, as it was done with a pair of boots borrowed from Pitman (reserve), his own having been mislaid during the journey from the hotel to the ground. (Those of us who know Day well, appreciate the fact.) A well-deserved victory over Scotland at Twickenham put England second in the Championship, and again restored the country's confidence in the team, which had been shaken by the ignominiously lucky draw with France.

RONALD COVE-SMITH

A lone French forward, finding himself unmarked in a lineout, shrieked to his compatriot, who was throwing in: 'A moi: je suis tout seul!' Of course, as soon as he had advertised the fact, Gardner and another of our forwards dashed for him, and the poor Frenchie received the ball and both forwards – who weighed well

On the way to the Grand Slam. Captain Dave Davies introduces King George V to Reg Edwards, the England & Newport forward, before the Welsh match at Twickenham in 1923.

over 15 stones – at one and the same moment! Needless to say, for the rest of the game he was somewhat subdued.

HAROLD DAY

Gardner must have been endowed with the toughest of skulls, so hard in fact that in going down head first into a French forward, he picked himself up rather gingerly to see a Frenchman being carried off.

DAVE DAVIES

In 1923, England again won the Championship, defeating in turn each of the other countries. Wales were beaten at Twickenham after one of the most sensational starts ever seen at a Rugby football match. England kicked off against a small gale blowing straight down the ground. The ball was blown into the hands of HL Price, who was following up. He endeavoured to drop a goal. The ball fell short on to the goal-line. Price caught it and fell over the line for a try before the unhappy Welsh team realised the game had commenced. Smallwood dropped a goal in the second half from a lucky pass by Corbett, and England won 7-3.

At Leicester, against Ireland, we played better, and ran out easy winners. It was realised that the English team would be severely tested against Scotland. How would Locke and Holliday [new caps at centre and fullback respectively] acquit themselves on the wind-swept turf of Inverleith? The game itself, played in the presence of the Duke of York and his future wife [later King George VI and Queen Elizabeth] was a series of thrilling changes of fortune. Half-time came with honours even, due to relentless tackling. When Scotland scored their second try, and for ten minutes afterwards, it appeared that England's fate was sealed, but it was not to be.

England's effort in the last quarter of an hour when [3-6] down, and the Scottish team playing strongly, was as brilliant as it was brave, and showed a true appreciation of the spirit of Rugby football. Locke broke away and passed to the ever-ready Voyce, who hurled himself over the line for a try. Luddington's kick at goal was successful and the Calcutta Cup retained. The play of the English team, and the Scottish team as well, bore out the high expectations which had been formed of both of them.

The [final] game played in France was no easy obstacle [but] proved successful. It was unfortunate for England that Lowe and Smallwood were both crocked in the first ten minutes of the game. As on other occasions earlier in the season, England owed her victory mainly to the skill of the forwards.

WAVELL WAKEFIELD

We won that [1923 Calcutta Cup] match through the foresight of Engineer-Commander EW Roberts, who was then on the English Selection Committee, and

Engineer-Commander SF Coopper, who was at that time stationed at Devonport, and helped Luddington and Gardner in practising place-kicking together at Devonport for a week before the match, Luddington kicking and Gardner placing the ball for him. It so happened that just towards the end Tom Voyce scored a wonderful try, and everything depended on the kick from the touchline. As a result of the practice, Luddington made no mistake and the match was won, and the importance of combination between placer and kicker was never more clearly demonstrated.

DAVE DAVIES
To crown a week's hard work by playing football for your country is to gain the greatest satisfaction, and certainly nothing has given me greater joy than to play for England against Scotland. The third Saturday in March comes round each year, with its indisputable superiority over all Saturdays, for it is on that day the destiny of the Calcutta Cup is settled, and more often than not, England v Scotland turns out to be one of the most decisive games in the determination of the Championship.

LEONARD TOSSWILL
CN Lowe has represented England more often than any other player up to now [25 matches]. Lowe, as a wing threequarter, was one of the pluckiest tacklers imaginable and, although a light man, was also one of the most dangerous scoring threequarters produced by any country for years. He was not exceptionally fast, but had an excellent swerve at full speed and he was a fine kicker.

WAVELL WAKEFIELD
Once more [in 1923] we had a tough game in Paris. That game was ended by a beautiful dropped goal by WJA Davies. I still believe he definitely worked for this, knowing it was just on time. I felt he was going to do it when we had a scrum under the posts and a quick heel. He took plenty of time, put in a perfect kick, and thus worthily ended his wonderful International career, for after this he retired from big football. He was a very great player and a most inspiring captain, and he has certainly had a deep and lasting influence on the game.

DAI GENT
Never was there a side – no, not even a club side – that combined so perfectly as did Davies's last England side of 1923, or Wakefield's first of 1924. In both these sides you had an ideal mixture of individualism and combination. A wise Selection Committee, under the almost permanent leadership of Mr James Baxter, and consisting of Messrs. John Daniell and RF Oakes always, were agreed on the sort of team they wanted. They went all out for set places in the

scrummages, and fixed on the precise build of the men who were best able to fill these set places.

WAVELL WAKEFIELD

Considering the famous players who had dropped out of the side, I think 1924 must be regarded as a most satisfactory season, and, save in 1921, I cannot remember ever playing in a better pack. The Welshmen [later] said that we had been like a brick wall to push against, and we ourselves always felt comfortable and solid in the scrum.

The Irish match at Belfast [in 1924] opened the [Ravenhill] ground, and my most vivid impression is that of Catcheside's try in the last minute, when he ran the length of the ground to score. We returned to England that night, but it was very difficult to get everybody aboard the boat. We pushed some players into a cab, only to find that they got out of the other door. When the gangways had been pulled in, Catcheside was still ashore, and he had to be hauled aboard as the boat was moving off.

DAI GENT

There was that most spectacular of all 'jumps' at Twickenham in 1924, when HC Catcheside, a most versatile footballer, playing for England against France, treated the occupants of the Royal Box to a perfect leap over the body of the French fullback, L. Pardo, on his way to score a try. His Majesty the King was present and was immensely struck by it.

CARSTON CATCHESIDE (England 1924-1927, 8 caps)
To third-class railway fare Newcastle to Kings Cross, return - £3-19s-11d
To use of toilet at Kings Cross Station - 1d
TOTAL CLAIM - ....£4 - 0s – 0d
[*From Expenses Claim Catcheside to Treasurer RFU, March 1924*]

WAVELL WAKEFIELD

There was nothing particularly memorable about the French match at Twickenham. It was in that game that there was a sudden upheaval in the scrum and Reg Edwards emerged and let fly at an opposing forward, not without reason, for when the referee went over to find out what it was all about, Edwards simply pointed to his cheek, where the Frenchman's teeth marks were plainly visible, and the game proceeded.

Our backs supported us very well and our forwards at that time fitted in with one another excellently, so that we were able to win by a record margin [of 19-0 against Scotland in 1924], though I must say that everything went right with us and no mistakes were made with our kicks at goal.

EIGHT
STUTTERING FORTUNES
1925-1933

THE ALL BLACKS *have always been a barometer for international teams, and that was why the match between England, who had been unbeaten for three years, and the New Zealand touring side on Saturday January 3, 1925, was seen as a day of reckoning for the men in white. What transpired was a match of huge controversy with New Zealand reduced to 14 men when Cyril Brownlie, one of two brothers playing in their forward pack, became the first player to be sent off in an international following a series of free-for-alls.*

The fluctuating fortunes in the match, eventually won 17-11 by New Zealand, who were subsequently dubbed 'The Invincibles', typified England's rugby pattern in the years up to and including the Great Depression. England met the all-conquering visitors, who were playing the last match of a famous tour, at a refurbished Twickenham. A spanking new North Stand had been built to meet the public's insatiable appetite for international matches, and the anticipation ahead of the showdown against the All Blacks had been heightened by the aura of invincibility surrounding the visitors.

With accusations of sharp-practice being levelled at the New Zealanders there were tremours from the start, with the fault-lines appearing first at the scrum-face. The expectation was that New Zealand's 2-3-2 pack formation would fit neatly into Wakefield's 3-2-3 scrum, the All Black front pair giving Sam Tucker, England's hooker, a loose-head on either side. Not a bit of it. England strived for two loose-heads on their side of the put-in (within the laws of the day) and scuffles erupted as the front-rows ducked and dived for an advantage.

Reg Edwards was England's enforcer. Edwards had history. Three months earlier he had been Newport's trouble-shooter in an abrasive encounter that the All Blacks had won 13-10 — the closest call of their entire tour. Now he was in the thick of several altercations in the first five minutes of the international. The referee, AE Freethy, issued an early ultimatum that any more foul play would warrant a sending-off. And so, in the eighth minute of the game, whistling at the next offence (allegedly, kicking an opponent) he ordered Cyril Brownlie from the field. Jock Richardson, Brownlie's captain, made a measured appeal for reinstatement. Wakefield stayed silent. Freethy upheld his decision and the All Black trudged off before a stunned crowd, the first player to walk the plank in a major Test.

Opposite: Wavell Wakefield and France captain Aime Cassayet-Armagnac before a 19-7 victory for England at Twickenham.

With order restored, England took the lead when Ronald Cove-Smith crossed for a try, but New Zealand summoned inner strength and dictated the game for an hour. It was 9-3 at half-time, then early in the second half Maurice Brownlie collected the ball on the spot where his brother had been dismissed and bullocked his way along the touchline for the match-breaking score, partially restoring family honour. Wakefield roused his men. Len Corbett dropped a goal before Harold Kittermaster, the English stand-off, scored a dazzling try that Geoff Conway converted. But it was too little too late and New Zealand held on to win.

Edwards and new cap Ron Hillard never again played for England. Conway, who always made substantial efforts for the common good, played only once more and big, bluff Arthur Blakiston retired at the end of a season which saw England surrender the Five Nations title to Scotland, who christened their new Murrayfield ground with a late 14-11 win against the champions.

Wakefield began his third season as captain by breaking the England cap record in a 3-3 draw at Cardiff in 1926. He celebrated that occasion with a sprint from near half-way for a wonderful try, but it was a new experience at the end of the campaign to lose to Scotland in his 13th and final game as skipper. Scotland's 17-9 victory marked England's first-ever Twickenham Five Nations defeat – a disappointing swansong for Tom Voyce, the Gloucester wing-forward who had been at the core of so many England triumphs in the twenties.

Wakefield's Test career ended a year later. Injured at the start of the season (when the captaincy passed to Bristol's Len Corbett), he returned for the final away matches of 1927 – losing at Murrayfield and in Paris, where England fell to their first-ever defeat by France. 'Wakers' stepped down with 31 caps to his name, an England record that stood for 42 years, and devoted the rest of his rugby retirement to putting his wealth of experience to good use as an enlightened administrator.

Post-Wakefield there was an unexpected Grand Slam under Ronald Cove-Smith in 1928. Carl Aarvold, a polished Cambridge threequarter, proved the find of the season and Arthur Young, a scrum-half in the Kershaw mould, won kudos for his tactical finesse. In 1930, Sam Tucker was summoned to make an extraordinary last-minute journey from Bristol to Cardiff by plane and lorry to replace a late-hour withdrawal. The first man to fly to an international, he inspired a rare win at the Arms Park and ended the year as captain for a scoreless draw with Scotland that earned England another unexpected title.

These, however, were but fleeting triumphs. Ireland had their maiden Twickenham win in 1929 and England were without a Five Nations win (for the first time) in 1931. The Home Unions, unhappy with the conduct of the club game in France where rumours of professionalism were rife, declared them persona non grata in February that year, leaving the RFU with a delicate fixture to fulfil at

Easter. France won it 14-13 in Paris, captain Carl Aarvold making a diplomatic banquet speech – in French – expressing the players' hopes that matches would soon be resumed.

With more home defeats – to South Africa in 1932 and, for the first time at HQ against Wales in 1933, fortress Twickenham had been well and truly stormed.

WAVELL WAKEFIELD

I had an attack of influenza at Christmas time, just before England played New Zealand, and seriously thought of crying off. Fortunately, I had time to get in three or four days' running about, which put me right.

LEN CORBETT (England 1921-1927, 16 caps)

Our side was in my opinion just about the best that could be fielded from the material available, with its strength where it was most likely to be most needed – in the pack. Most backs of my generation or any other would be well satisfied to play behind the eight which represented England that day – WW Wakefield, AT Voyce, AF Blakiston, R Edwards, R Cove-Smith, GS Conway, JS Tucker and RJ Hillard. At fullback we had young JW Brough from the North, playing in his first international; JC Gibbs, also making his first appearance for England, and myself were partnered on the left of our threequarter line with VG Davies and RH Hamilton-Wickes on the other flank. At half-back AT Young was paired with the sure-handed HJ Kittermaster.

WAVELL WAKEFIELD

It was a remarkable game, and I had determined before it started that the New Zealanders should not assert a moral superiority over us. I think it is not generally understood how many of their matches were won by the assertion of this moral supremacy, and as an instance I may mention an incident in the match between the All Blacks and Hampshire.

One of the Hampshire forwards had the ball when he was tackled hard by [the New Zealand forward] Irvine. Immediately Irvine, who was the aggressor, turned round and said, 'What the devil are you doing? Can't you leave go of me?' The Hampshire forward apologised. 'All right,' said Irvine, 'be more careful next time.' After the game Irvine mentioned the incident and said, 'That forward's no good. Fancy apologising for being tackled!'

LEN CORBETT

Despite rain which had fallen earlier the ground was in good condition and half-an-hour before the kick-off the gates at Twickenham had to be closed. By that time some 60,000 had assembled and the presence of the Prince of Wales and the Prime Minister set the seal on an historic rugby occasion.

I can safely say that all thirty players were glad when the preliminaries were over and the ball was kicked off, for, contrary to popular belief, the 'difficult' period for most of those taking part is not the first few minutes of the game itself but the half-hour or so which precedes it.

LEN CORBETT

There is no doubt that both sides were keyed up to a pretty high pitch and some indications of this were apparent in the first few minutes of the game. I have a pretty clear recollection of the incidents. The referee found it necessary to issue a warning very early to both packs that he did not intend to allow the proceedings to degenerate into a 'free-for-all.' His warning went unheeded, and when a scrummage was formed after seven minutes something occurred which caused Mr Freethy to take the unprecedented action of sending a player off the field in an international match. Unhappily the player concerned was that magnificent All Black forward Cyril Brownlie.

WAVELL WAKEFIELD

I suppose I must say something about that most unfortunate occurrence when one of the New Zealand team was sent off the field by AE Freethy, who refereed the match. First and foremost there is no getting away from the fact that Freethy had warned both sides three times, and it so happened that a New Zealander was the next offender and thus had to pay the inevitable penalty. It might just as well have been an Englishman, though I did not see the actual incident I can say nothing of the rights or wrongs of the case.

JIM BROUGH (England 1925, 2 caps)

The England team did not think Brownlie kicked anybody. England was keyed up to beat the All Blacks and went flat out from the start. Edwards was a tough guy, a bit free with his fists, and others in our forwards were tough, too. We believed that Freethy was so determined to assert control that he decided the only way to do it was by sending Brownlie off the field.

RON HILLARD (England 1925, 1 cap)

If that is international Rugby, I want nothing of it.

WAVELL WAKEFIELD

In New Zealand, I am told that it is sometimes the practice, when a man is sent off, for the captain of the opposing team to ask the referee to allow him to return to the field. I did not do this, for most decidedly such a custom is unheard of in this country, and if a similar situation arose again I would certainly not intervene. Such action clearly undermines the authority of the referee,

JIM BROUGH
Wakefield refused Richardson's appeal because he did not think it possible to ask the referee to change his mind. All of us English players believed that the Prince of Wales tried hard to persuade officials to have Brownlie returned to the field.

LEN CORBETT
To say that the incident had an unsettling effect on either side would be an exaggeration; on the contrary, I would say that, if anything, its effect was to steady the more exuberant and excitable players on both sides.

WAVELL WAKEFIELD
Maurice Brownlie was one of the greatest forwards I have ever played against. The ball had fallen loose between Gibbs and Cove-Smith, when Brownlie came through very fast and snapped it up. I had slightly over-run it, and as I turned I was directly behind him and could see him going straight down the touch-line, though it seemed impossible for him to score. Somehow he went on, giving me the impression of a moving tree-trunk, so solid did he appear to be, and so little effect did various attempted tackles have upon him. He crashed through without swerving ... and went over the line for one of the most surprising tries I have ever seen. It was a great game, and the All Blacks undoubtedly won on their merits.

LEN CORBETT
England went down fighting and the All Blacks had achieved their double ambition – to retain their unbeaten record and to defeat England. They triumphed, as on many previous occasions, more by their superb opportunism than by superior individual or collective skill. It is doubtful whether any side has developed to so great an extent the art of taking advantage of errors by their opponents.

DAI GENT
Corbett's brilliance was almost as effective [as Ronnie Poulton's]. Glorious kicking, drop and punt, thrilling dashes with swerves galore on the way, and a nose for an opening that is only granted to geniuses – these were his main qualities, apart from his very fine tackling.

WAVELL WAKEFIELD

[Geoff] Conway [was] to my mind one of the finest examples of the hard-working, scientific, foot-rushing type of player. His close dribbling and ball control were wonderful, and he went hard from the beginning of a game to the end. His line-out play was also great, and he showed what could be done by determination to jump and catch the ball, though he was shorter and smaller than the majority of International forwards.

He was exceptionally tough, for he was a typical north-country forward and believed in training as hard as he played. He was a truly great player, and it is a pity his career was cut short by the injury he received against New Zealand in 1925.

The Calcutta Cup clash at Twickenham in 1926. Tom Voyce, in his last international, forces his way towards the line for England's first try.

DAVE DAVIES

In any classification of forwards, WW Wakefield must be very near the top. Possessed of all the physical qualities necessary for the highest standard, he obtained very early, by assiduous practice and thorough training, a pre-eminent position in the Rugby football world. Quick intuition on the field, perseverance and physique, combined in his case to make a very formidable player. Skilful in all phases of forward play, his speed was his most striking characteristic, and the momentum of a 14¼ stone forward, six feet high and suitably proportioned, travelling as fast as the modern wing three-quarter, was my strongest impression, yet no one ever worked harder in the scrum or had a more thorough knowledge of the game's details.

DAI GENT

[England had] short bulldog types in the front-row, powerfully shouldered, of boundless energy, and capable with their feet and in open play generally. The names of the best of them will occur to all followers of the game: WGE Luddington and GS Conway.

For your second-row you had slightly bigger men, well able to act as 'binders' of the scrum, and good again at close work generally. R Cove-Smith was a great 'second-row' forward, while Wakefield also frequently took his place in the second-row.

WAVELL WAKEFIELD

When the Welsh match came along in 1926 I was delighted to find telegrams from all my old friends waiting for me at Cardiff, particularly one from CN Lowe, whose record number of English caps I was then breaking. I have always appreciated the telegrams people have sent me. CA Kershaw sent me a telegram at Cardiff, doubtless thinking of our mud-fight there four years before, which said, 'Good luck to you all. Mind you wear your galoshes.'

DAVE DAVIES

[Tom Voyce]'s was not an academic training. The scrum was an unnecessary preliminary to the more open play. He was a distinct type. He was not a winging forward in the way that Charles Pillman was. He possessed the same extraordinary football position or sense, less reluctance to shove in the scrum, but, whereas Pillman revelled in open play, Voyce's speciality was his work in the semi-loose scrums, fighting his way through a host of players.

TOM VOYCE (England 1920-1926, 27 caps plus 2 caps for the Lions)

Many a wing-forward puts defence before attack; his game should be an attacking one. I always worked on the principle of receiving at least six passes during a game and with me the attacking idea came first. This approach not only sets the pattern of play a team is likely to pursue, but also greatly increases a wing-forward's enjoyment.

It is probably true to say that no other forward position so consistently offers a player such scope to show his all-round worth to his team as well as his own ability and prowess.

WAVELL WAKEFIELD

Tom Voyce I always see with the ball in a line-out, struggling to make a few yards with four or five opponents round his neck and knees. I see him also chasing down the field for a cross-kick, with his head well forward and his arms going like flails, moving much faster with that loping stride of his than he would appear to be. We used to hunt in twos and threes, and if we could not get the ball, at least we knew that in our efforts we should put two of our opponents on their backs. Voyce was the happy warrior, the buccaneer of my period.

DAI GENT

Mention ought to be made of the success of R Cove-Smith's side in 1927-28, which won all its five matches, a feat only once performed previously by any country, namely Wales in 1908-09. But it was the poor quality of international football generally, together with Cove-Smith's effective handling of his side, that gave England her victories, rather than the brilliance of her play. It is notable, too, that that was the season of the first appearance for his country of CD Aarvold.

WAVELL WAKEFIELD

Since 1925 England owe a great deal to the power of honest scrummaging which [JSTucker] has displayed. He has been invaluable as hooker, and it is safe to say that without him the English record would not have been so good as it is.

And then there is Arthur Young, a scrum-half who must be included in any story of post-War Rugger, an unorthodox player who has left me with an impression of arms clutching the air, while Young ducks and sways beneath them to break through on his own.

SAM TUCKER (England 1922-1931, 27 caps)

On Saturday morning, January 18, 1930, after having a glass of beer in a Bristol

Action from the Five Nations encounter in Paris in 1931.

hostelry, I returned to my office to clear up a few things when, at 12.25 pm, the telephone rang. It was Engineer-Commander SF Coopper, secretary of the RFU. He said: 'We want you to come over to Cardiff to play against Wales today!' I said it was impossible, as the last train had gone, but then selector John Daniell came on the phone to say: 'You must be there, even if you come by plane.'

The only thing I could do was call Filton Aerodrome, as there was no landing strip in either Bristol or Cardiff in those days. A lady answered the phone [and] said there was a certain 'Captain Somebody' in the air and she would try to get a signal to him to come down.

By a stroke of luck she succeeded and the 'Captain' phoned me at 1pm. He said if I went out at once he would get me to Cardiff between 2pm and 2.15. I was at Filton [by 1.50] and there was the pilot with a small bi-plane two-seater already revved up. He stuck a helmet on my head, strapped me in and, with a roar, we were off.

We arrived over Cardiff at roughly 2pm and after circling around he thought he could land in a field. I thanked him, raced over the field on to the road and waved the driver [of a coal lorry] down [who] did the journey [to the Arms Park] in under ten minutes. We won 11-3, and somehow I became a bit of a hero.

DAI GENT

With the retirement of men like Wakefield, Myers, Young, Luddington and Voyce, this perfect combination of very good players tended to be less and less a feature of English international football, and the game again became rather ragged, which is how I should describe its present state.

CARL AARVOLD (England 1928-1933, 16 caps plus 5 caps for the Lions)

William Wavell – Lord Wakefield of Kendal – was by any standards a very remarkable man, of that special calibre that caused [one] to recognise at once that here indeed was a very rare person: a man with determination, energy [and] superb confidence in himself.

Marked on his features were two irresistible dimples. Try as he might, there always crept into his features the direct look, the lurking smile … [that] proclaimed the sincerity, kindliness, fun and friendliness of his nature.

When you find a man blessed with his physique, his guts, his speed of thought and action, his courage, his adventurous imagination, and his energy and determination you would expect such a man: to play for England – even gain 31 caps and captain the side and every other side he played for; to be an athlete in the class of Harold Abrahams; to swim like a salmon; to excel at squash, and to ski like the proverbial bat escaping from the nether regions.

NINE

BACK IN THE GROOVE

1934-1939

THE GLITCHES OF *the second half of the 1920s/ early 1930s gave way to glory in the seasons leading up to the Second World War. England enjoyed unexpected revenge in another landmark match against the All Blacks in January 1936, winning 13-0 in what was known thereafter as 'Obolensky's match'. This was due to the two spectacular tries scored on his debut by the young Russian prince, Alexander Obolensky. Either side of that, England won two Triple Crowns, and, with France out of the equation, picked up three Four Nations titles –1934, 1937 and in 1939 a three-way share with Wales and Ireland – before War again interrupted official internationals in September 1939.*

The selectors named five new caps, including teenager Peter Cranmer at centre and the South African Test cricketer 'Tuppy' Owen-Smith at fullback, for Cardiff in 1934. England had won there only twice and superstition was rife on the Friday afternoon when the team's motor coach was stopped to allow a black cat slowly to cross the road. Bernard Gadney was captain, but when Lu Booth went down with measles next morning, he must have thought his luck was out. A sixth new man, 'Tim' Warr, came in on the wing.

Gadney needn't have worried. Wales blooded 13 new caps, with their blockbusting tackler Claud Davey, listed to face Cranmer, the only concession to experience behind the scrum. Ron Gerrard, the Bath centre, knew that an early Davey special could knock the stuffing out of his partner so, swapping positions with Cranmer, he gently eased the Oxford University student into international rugby.

England got off to a flyer, winning 9-0, and Gadney, Cranmer and the reliable Owen-Smith behind them became the team's backbone for several seasons. Success in Dublin was the prelude to a tight match at Twickenham where scrum-half Gadney's tactical nous and defensive skills were instrumental in a 6-3 win that wrested the Triple Crown from holders Scotland. It was England's first Crown for six years and, all told, wings had accounted for six of the eight tries scored, but the team stepped backwards in 1935 with a low try count that augured badly for the upcoming All Blacks fixture. Wings, though, would spectacularly reclaim the headlines at Twickenham on the first Saturday of 1936.

If Wavell Wakefield, later the Lord Wakefield of Kendal, had been England's chief protagonist against New Zealand in 1925, Prince Alexander Obolensky was the stand-out in the victory over the 1936 All Blacks. He had fled the revolution with his family to England as an infant to follow an establishment public school/Oxford University

Opposite: Russian Prince Alexander Obolensky. In his first match for England, he scored two tries in the first half against the All Blacks at Twickenham.

education. Obolensky set no records – the wing was only capped four times – but against New Zealand he became a household name, owing to his two first half tries captured for eternity on cine-newsreel that stands as arguably rugby's most iconic film.

Hal Sever, a new cap like Obolensky, scored on the left-wing in the second half and Cranmer's snap dropped goal rounded off New Zealand's defeat. Post-match reaction from the Russian seems rare, only the Mirror *in England eliciting the shy star's hope it might help his application for British naturalisation.*

'Obo' was marked closely in the three Championship matches that followed. The Welsh fullback, Viv Jenkins, remembered sitting through hours of B-movies in a London cinema to catch newsreel glimpses of the Prince's tries. It paid dividends because a fortnight later the two sides who had lowered All Blacks' colours played a scoreless stalemate at Swansea. England then lost in Dublin despite a fine Hal Sever try. John Daniell, their veteran selector, felt wine had turned to water.

'Tuppy' Owen-Smith was captain in 1937 for a season that went down as Hal Sever's year. A Fellow of the Institute of Actuaries, Sever took his profession onto the field of play, underwriting England's Triple Crown season with the winning scores against Wales (dropped goal), Ireland (a length-of-the-field touchline dash) and Scotland (a sidestepping effort in England's first-ever Murrayfield success).

Wings scored tries, forwards won ball. The laws of the day permitted teams to opt for scrums instead of line-outs, and both Bernard Gadney and, later, hooker Bert Toft favoured blind-side put-ins where the choice arose. Toft was the best technician in the business and favoured the South African 3-4-1 scrum formation that shifted the locking of the set-piece to the middle of the second-row. The middle man of the back-row had performed the function in the 3-2-3 arrangement. The heel was much quicker packing 3-4-1. Wing-forwards moved up to flank the middle-row of the scrum, directing their shove inwards through their props to bring pressure on the opposition hooker. The sole occupant of the back-row was left to develop a new game: the Number Eight was born.

England lost at Cardiff in a wind-spoilt game in 1938, but in Dublin enjoyed first use of the gale to rattle up an unassailable half-time lead. The self-effacing Cranmer was dropped in favour of Toft as captain after winning 36-14 – a story he enjoyed telling against himself. England could still win the Championship, but in a match of constant thrills against the Scots at Twickenham – it was the first televised international – there was never more than a converted try between the sides. Then Wilson Shaw scuttled away for a famous late score, regaining the Triple Crown for Scotland.

Toft led England shrewdly to a share of the 1939 Championship, winning unexpected gains against the head in narrow victories over Wales and Scotland. France, it was announced that year, would soon return to the Five Nations, but generally it was a season subdued by the gathering clouds of War. Within a fortnight of the outbreak of the Second World War in September 1939, senior rugby was officially cancelled.

PETER CRANMER (England 1934-1938, 16 caps)

I had been on the Rest side in the final trial and had gone to bed fairly early on the Sunday night, when the telephone rang. My father answered and heard the voice say 'Your son's an International.' I didn't sleep that night.

I was in bed at the hotel in Penarth known to generations of footballers, the Esplanade, sharing a room with my Oxford team mate, Tim Warr, on the morning of the [1934 Welsh] match, when Eng.Cmdr. Coopper came into the room and said: 'Tim, you're playing, Lu Booth's got measles.' We won that match, thanks to some fine tries by Graham Meikle on the left-wing, and I've still got the baby's bottle which the players gave me as the junior member. Henry Rew was given a 3ft long spring, as one Welsh paper said he'd lost some of his. That, of course, was Friday night's paper, for, as always, he played a beauty.

I remember we had to go through the Welsh dressing room and up some stairs to ours. I was amazed at the backchat between individuals of the two sides.

One thing that stood out in that [1934] match was that, when we lined up, I was being marked by Claud Davey. He was probably the hardest hitting tackler in the game at that time and a couple of those tackles could easily put off a young, first cap and indeed lessen his chances of further caps. The other English centre was 'Gerry' Gerrard, who was built on the lines of Claud. He immediately told me to swap places, which we did for the first quarter of an hour and the two granite blocks hit each other. By that time I had found my feet so we swapped back and all was more or less well. That was a typical action of Gerry's.

BERNARD GADNEY (England 1932-1938, 14 caps)

It seemed doubtful how the England side would settle down against [the All Blacks], but I myself felt confident of breaking through and I knew Cranmer could too. If this was exploited, it would give more room for Obolensky and Sever to move in.

The impression of the English selectors, who had seen these All Blacks so often, emphasized the fact that a mistake by England meant a score to New Zealand. Everyone seemed keyed up when we arrived back at the Metropole, and it seemed odd to find the opposition at the same hotel. I myself had a feeling that I did not wish to meet them until the actual day.

PETER CRANMER

We used to meet on the Friday morning, go round the Hon Artillery Company ground in the centre of the city and just do one or two passings up and down. We just met on a Friday – we never got together as such: none of these weekends or that sort of thing – squad training or anything like that.

HAL SEVER (England 1936-1938, 10 caps)

The fortnight leading up to it I kept thinking, don't trip over the pavement or fall down or pull a muscle or something. The day itself I remember going in the bus, Bernard Gadney was captain. I was sitting next to 'Obo' and [the skipper] came and had a chat with us because it was both our first games and he just talked anything but rugby. We had lunch at the Cole Court Hotel, walked to the ground and went and had a look on the pitch. I remember looking all the way round and thinking, this mass of people there, how wonderful it was. I think there was a crowd of 72,000 there that day.

BERNARD GADNEY

A charabanc drive to the Cole Court, lunch, a walk to the ground, and, just before the game, we lined up outside our dressing-rooms under the stand to meet the Prince of Wales. The danger in the excitement of the moment of forgetting any of the players' names was over; the Prince of Wales had gone, and one could see the All Blacks walking slowly on to the field in single file. We all lined up in the middle of the field for 'God Save the King'. I had lost the toss and [Jack] Manchester had taken what wind there was.

JOHN GREENWOOD

During my second year as [RFU] president, the Prince of Wales, later King Edward VIII, came to Twickenham to see the All Blacks play. Instead of going on to the pitch for the players to be presented to him he said he did not want to keep them waiting in the cold and they were presented in the changing rooms. His brother, the Duke of Kent, also came to a match but his staff had let him down badly by not telling him that Rugby football was a very strictly amateur game. The Duke turned to me and said 'Do you pay your players well?'

I was recently reminded by my son that I had taken him and my wife to the [All Blacks'] match. He said that we got a lift to the station in an open police car and that somehow Prince Obolensky had been left behind so that we gave him a lift also!

HAL SEVER

My most thrilling game? I played in many but I must place my first international against the All Blacks in 1936 as the most exciting of all for me.

Not that we had a grandstand finish: we didn't. We won more easily than anyone imagined. But I shall never forget the deafening roar from the capacity crowd at Twickenham when Obolensky scored his two tries. No game could ever quite match that one.

BERNARD GADNEY

From the loose I gave Obolensky the ball, and he was caught and half tackled, a nasty shock, as we had all thought that he would have the legs of everyone. A moment later he set our minds at rest, however, for, receiving the ball, he turned in and ran beautifully for and over the line. A tremendous roar went up from the crowd.

PETER CRANMER

Everything seemed to go right. We played well that day. Everybody played well and of course we had that tremendous man, 'Tuppy' Owen-Smith, behind us, and every time the ball went over the head you never bothered to look behind to see what was happening. Old 'Tuppy' could get himself out of any mess.

BERNARD GADNEY

Things were all going right. Cranmer made a perfect opening: even now I can see his feet half stop and him leaving his man standing, to pass to Candler, who sent Obolensky off once more. I felt this run as discouraging to New Zealand as it was encouraging to us. It was a wonderful scoring effort, and surely the roar which went up from the crowd was worth five extra points to England.

PETER CRANMER

I think people were wrong in saying [Obolensky] was just a sprinter because of the way he saw this sort of avenue when he scored this wonderful try starting on the right and finishing near the corner-flag on the left. He just went absolutely straight through this gap and his feet did the rest for him.

HAL SEVER

Rarely, if ever, has a more spectacular and unorthodox try been scored in such a critical game and on such a big occasion. Obolensky, a right wing threequarter, received the ball near the half-way line on the right-hand side of the field, yet scored his try near the left-hand corner-flag – something rather unique.

As 'Obo' reached the left-wing I thought he was about to pass to me, a few yards short of the line, but anticipating that I would probably drop the ball in the excitement, he confounded friend and foe by nonchalantly running round my opposing wing to score near my corner-flag – to the most tumultuous roar I ever remember hearing.

PETER CRANMER

I must just tell you one thing about this. Just before I went out on to the field, mark you, [the selectors] said: 'Peter we want you to play left-centre not right-centre – so that the ball can get to Obolensky!'

BERNARD GADNEY

Half-time came with a visit from an anxious but obviously happy touch-judge. The forwards were going great guns. We weren't seeing much of the ball, but I did not mind that, as our defence seemed cast iron.

Every second got more valuable now. Cranmer gave Sever the chance for him to run strongly and touch down wide out, and then I felt Cranmer had put paid to everything when he dropped his magnificent goal. When one of their team asked an Englishman for his jersey out of touch, I knew we were safe. Clarke and Webb, the two [second-row] heavyweights, never looked like giving in. Cranmer and Gerrard locked up the midfield, Dunkley was going great guns, and Weston closed up the blind-side.

We work the touch-line as the hands of the clock move on. A quick heel and I kick out for the last time. Faull blows his whistle and a mighty roar goes up, for a grand English side has beaten New Zealand for the first time. Before we had moved, Manchester and his men had congratulated us.

PETER CRANMER

I was credited with making a wonderful opening for the last try by Hal Sever. In fact it wasn't me. It was the wing forward, a fellow called Hamilton-Hill, who came away from the scrum. Anyway, he took on my man, passed to me and there was a gap as wide as Twickenham to go through which I went through and chucked a terrible pass to old Hal Sever, who caught it and ran over.

DAI GENT

England's pressure on the defence first, and then on the attack, was systematic and relentless. The New Zealanders just couldn't make sufficient headway, though, my

Allan Clarke, Alexander Obolensky, and Hal Sever before the All Blacks game, 1936.

Obolensky slides in to score his second try against New Zealand.

word, they tried hard enough. Against this background of English stolidity were flashes of brilliance as spectacular as they were clever – Obolensky's memorable tries, HS Sever's gorgeous finish to a beautiful opening made by Peter Cranmer, and Cranmer's own fine dropped goal – there they are, reminders of an historic match.

PETER CRANMER
I dropped a goal towards the end. We were leading 9-0 and we were fairly near their posts. I was going for the break. 'Pat' Caughey tackled me, or at least he held on to my right leg and so I thought we can drop a goal from here and so I had a go with my left foot and it went between the posts and that more or less was that.

ALEXANDER OBOLENSKY (England 1936, 4 caps)
It is difficult for me to believe that I am anything but an Englishman, and as one I simply did my best at Twickenham.

JOHN DANIELL (England 1899-1904, 7 caps)
The New Zealand victory was followed by a very disappointing drawn game at Swansea – in itself no mean performance – but the game was disappointing because both sides played bad football. What were the selectors to do now? They did very little – changed one forward, and had a second forward change forced on them, through illness. The side was beaten in Dublin, though I feel more inclined to say 'beat themselves' because they had only two scoring chances and took both, while England had possibly twenty and took one!

Now here was a real quandary. A side that was hailed on the 5 January as world beaters had in five weeks become candidates for the wooden spoon! I need not carry on the story, except to say that the reconditioned English XV for twenty minutes out of the eighty minutes played nearly as good football as they did during seventy out of the eighty minutes in the New Zealand match.

'It is devilish hard to get into an England XV, but it is often a damned sight harder to get out' is a truism which, as far as I know, has never been refuted.

BERT TOFT (England 1936-1939, 10 caps)
The phenomenal HS Sever won the game [against Wales in 1937] with an unbelievable drop-goal (then 4 points) left-footed, from 40 yards away and on the touch-line, yet high between the very tops of the posts, after the ball had glanced off the shoulders of an English forward. Sever also won each of England's other games that season, with his long, indomitable heart-bursting gallop against the Irish, and another equally inspired try against the Scots.

PETER CRANMER
At Twickenham in 1937, Hal Sever's year, we won again [against Wales], 4-3, Hal dropping an 'out-of-the-blue' goal from the 25 and touch-line. He went on to score that magnificent try against Ireland from his own 25 all along the touchline – and another against Scotland, which gave us the Championship again as we had in 1934.

BERT TOFT
How does it feel to be 'up against' the spirit of Murrayfield? First there is the transformation from Princes Street in the morning to the ground in the afternoon. Incomparable Princes Street, splendid in the cool, bright sunshine of mid-March, thronged with shoppers and promenaders. Then Murrayfield itself, and no more gentleness and softness, but the stark unbroken vastness of the terraces and the sombre shadow of that giant frowning stand – as far from Princes Street as the boxing ring from the ballroom.

PETER CRANMER
The rub of the green, bounce of the ball or what you will, favoured us [at Murrayfield in 1937] and we came off the field the first English victors on this great ground. A night of festivity I seem to remember. Was it the 'Banana Club' – the Havana to the uninitiated – it was one of those nights which has been magnified with the passing years to Bacchanalian proportions.

PETER CRANMER
Arms Park in 1938, and the greatest moment: leading England on to the field for the first time. It was a year of gales and I lost the toss and we played against it in

the first half. Kicks for touch from the 25, or further up field, were finishing at our own corner posts. By the time we had turned round in the second half, we were too tired to take advantage of the gale, and lost against Wales for the first time since I'd started playing. What a captain!

BERT TOFT

In 1938 the English went to Cardiff sure, we were told, to win. We lost.

PETER CRANMER

Perhaps I may mention Ireland in Dublin of that year. Again a gale, this time I won the toss and we were 23 points up at half-time – we won 36-14, a record for International matches and I was the only player to be dropped for the Calcutta Cup. Such is life!

BERT TOFT

The victory at Twickenham in 1938, which won back for Scotland not only the Calcutta Cup but the Triple Crown as well, was the finest of the four matches [I played in against them]. RW Shaw, outside-half and captain, was the man of the match, and was everywhere described as the best player of the season in any country. The lead changed six times and there were twelve scores in all, two penalty goals and five tries to Scotland and a dropped goal, three penalty goals and a try to England (21-16). Yet the Scottish backs who tore England's defence to ribbons had possession only once to every five against.

HAL SEVER

It was my last game. We lost 21-16 and I always thought we could have won because I made an effort to score a try under the posts only ten minutes from time when we were losing 18-16. If I'd scored we'd probably have converted and won 21-18. I didn't. I got held up and I think it was almost the ensuing scrum the Scots broke away and Wilson Shaw ran pretty well the length of the field. I can see his feet running up the field at great speed and he scored this wonderful try. It's been termed 'Wilson Shaw's match' ever since.

DAI GENT

The very last match before the Second World War was played at Murrayfield and England won it by three penalty goals to two tries! It was very hard lines on Scotland in a way, but I will say I have never seen such a beautiful exhibition of place-kicking. All three goals were from near the halfway line and within a few yards of the touch line. Jack Heaton, the Lancashire centre, was the kicker, and a lovely kicker he was – punt, place, or drop.

TEN

THE SECOND WORLD WAR

1939-1945

WAR AGAINST HITLER *was different from the conflict with the Kaiser. Once again there was no shortage of volunteers from the rugby brotherhood, but the long period of 'Phoney War' enabled rugby, through the organising abilities of the Services, to continue more extensively than during the First World War. By the end of September 1939, an informal season was announced and many fixtures took place between service units, students and even the clubs continued by recruiting from servicemen stationed nearby.*

Red Cross Internationals between England and Wales were staged in 1939-40 before giving way to a long series of Services Internationals in the middle years of the war. Then, when peace was declared, a season of 'Victory Internationals' followed in 1945-46. None of the matches warranted full caps because, it was argued, the best players weren't always available owing to the needs of the services. Even during the post-war 'Victory' series many were still stationed abroad awaiting demob. That was a pity for Ray Longland, the nuggety, barrel-chested Northampton prop who had been a winner against the All Blacks and an England regular since 1932. He played 16 wartime 'internationals' up to 1945 making him the true forerunner in skill, character and endurance of the modern era's Jason Leonard – even though the official record doesn't show it.

This war, too, was remarkable for an armistice between union and league. Animosities were suspended for players in the services and many of the 13-a-side's box-office players – ex-Welsh union star Willie Davies and his famous league compatriot Gus Risman to name two – turned out many times in top-draw union matches. There was even a famous cross-code challenge at Bradford's Odsal Stadium, league's equivalent of Twickenham (which had been requisitioned and suffered damage from a V-bomb blast in July 1944).

There were mercifully fewer killed in action this time, though among the 14 English casualties were two names from the win against the All Blacks: the Bath centre, Ron Gerrard, and Alex Obolensky, who was the first England cap to perish when his aircraft crashed during an RAF training flight in Suffolk in 1940.

Opposite: The England team for the war-time Services International against Scotland at Murrayfield on 17 March, 1945, which England won 16-5. Rugby league players as well as overseas stars serving in England often featured in these war-time internationals.

ROLL OF HONOUR 1914-1918

OBOLENSKY, Alexander (England 1936) Killed flying, Martlesham, Suffolk, March 29, 1940.

COOKE, Paul (England 1939) KIA Calais, May 1, 1940.

BLACK, Brian Henry (England 1930-1933) Killed Chilmark, Wilts, July 29, 1940.

PARSONS, Ernest Ian (England 1939) Killed flying over the Channel, August 13/14, 1940.

TEDEN, Derek Edmund (England 1939) Killed flying over North Sea, October 15, 1940.

REW, Henry (England 1929-1934) Died of wounds, Western Desert, December 11, 1940.

LUDDINGTON, William George Ernest (England 1923-1926) Lost at sea, off Sicily, January 10, 1941.

TANNER, Christopher Champain (England 1930-1932) Died rescuing survivors of a sinking off Crete, May 23, 1941.

WODEHOUSE, Norman Atherton (England 1910-1913) Lost at sea off West Africa, July 4, 1941

DAVIES, Vivian Gordon (England 1922-1925) Killed London, December 23, 1941.

FREAKES, Hubert Dainton (England 1938-1939) Killed Honeybourne, Worcs, March 10, 1942.

BOOTH, Lewis Alfred (England 1933-1935) KIA flying, June 25, 1942.

GERRARD, Ronald Anderson (England 1932-1936) KIA Western Desert, January 22, 1943.

MARSHALL, Robert Mackenzie (England 1938-1939) Lost at sea off Skagerrak, May 12, 1945 at the end of the war.

11 April, 1942: International rugby is staged at Wembley Stadium for the first time. England wing, 2nd Lt A L Evans evades Scottish centre defender, Fl-Lt E C Hunter. Scotland went on to win this Services match, 8-5. Neither Evans or Hunter won full caps.

ELEVEN
POST-WAR RECOVERY
1945-1951

AS THE NATION *gradually recovered after the horrors of the Second World War, sport tried to follow in its wake. Twickenham, eventually, looked a picture – the stadium was quickly refurbished after suffering bomb damage to the West Stand and the effects of wartime use by ARP and fire units, and by the Home Guard for exercises. If the stadium was imposing once more, however, it was not a period of success for the new England team.*

There had been a very popular series of so-called Victory Internationals played in 1945-46, but international rugby officially restarted in January 1947 – England's previous full international had been in March 1939 – with Wales hosting England at the Arms Park, which itself had suffered bomb damage, in the first post-war Five Nations match to be staged in the Home Unions (France had returned to the international fold on New Year's Day, when playing Scotland in Paris).

The team, obviously, was much changed. For that first match in Cardiff, only Dickie Guest spanned the years since international rugby had ceased. Among England's 14 new caps were Norman 'Nim' Hall, Keith Scott and Norman Bennett, who formed a midfield entirely drawn from St Mary's Hospital. Hall, Scott and Bennett were medical students and the brains behind the successful St Mary's side that had dominated other students and servicemen stationed in England in wartime club games. Their club's finest hour was in January 1945 when they ended Coventry's incredible run of 72 successive wins stretching back to December 1941, with an 8-3 win at Teddington. Hall was the architect of that victory, scoring all the medics' points from two four-point dropped goals.

The pack included the new captain, Joe Mycock, and a rumbustious forward from Coventry in Harry Walker in the front-row and the Australian born Basil 'Jika' Travers, a Rhodes scholar, a fine cricketer and who was to win six caps for his adopted country. Walker had emerged from Midlands rugby and went on to serve the game in all kinds of capacities, becoming a senior county administrator in 1985, and in season 2013-14 at 99, was still supporting Coventry matches in person.

In the back-row for the re-start of rugby life, the relatively small but highly-competitive Micky Steele-Bodger, another later to be engaged in a long career in rugby officialdom as president of both the Rugby Football Union and (still, as we write) the Barbarians, made his debut. Outspoken but charming and who remains one of

Opposite: England's Vic Roberts (left), Bruce Neale (in scrum cap) and Eric Evans (right) close around the ball against Scotland at Twickenham in 1951

the most combative and engaging rugby men England has produced, Steele-Bodger is known throughout the world.

The drop-kicking of Hall helped England to win that first post-war international match at Cardiff, and it set the side on course for a share in the 1947 Five Nations. There was to be no Grand Slam, however. In what was the most bitter winter on record, England lost 22-0 against a passionate Ireland in Dublin, but recovered to beat Scotland at Twickenham 24-5 in March – in this match they were inspired by another foreigner, the superb South African-born scrum-half, Ossie Newton-Thompson.

That was the match when Steele-Bodger, then a veterinary student in Scotland, endured a journey of heroic length in order to turn out for his country. He left Edinburgh Waverley on Thursday evening, hit snowdrifts at Carlisle and eventually crawled into London in the early hours of the Saturday of the match, joining the team at Twickenham on the afternoon not long before kick-off. They weren't expecting him to make it and Vic Roberts, the Cornwall customs-officer, was on standby to play. He wasn't needed, but did win his cap a month later.

The game with France, due for February, was postponed until mid-April, but the icy winter eventually relented and gave way to perfect pitch conditions when England, in front of Mr Clement Attlee, scraped home against France 6-3 thanks to a late try by the new cap Vic Roberts. It was the day French rugby, in its first Five Nations for 16 years, showed that very soon it would become a rugby force to be reckoned with.

Steele-Bodger, Roberts, the hefty Northampton forward, Don White (an England coach in later years when coaching as a concept for the Test team was in its infancy) and Travers, were outstanding wing-forwards at a time when the back-row game was developing rapidly in the southern hemisphere.

New Zealand, meanwhile, were developing the ruck as a means of attack, running the ball up to draw in defenders then attacking with second-phase possession. British rugby was a long way behind these forward-thinking rugby powers at the time.

It was no wonder then that Rhodes Scholars, from the advanced nations – particularly if they could play in the back-row – were precious commodities in English scrums of the era. Indeed, the whole question of England fielding overseas players became mired in controversy – then, as now.

Between 1947 and 1951 there were regularly three or four 'foreigners' in the England XVs. One Oxford University team of the period was satirised as 'Springboxford'. The problem of national qualification had never been properly addressed. The view always taken by England's selectors was that if a student was living in England and good enough to win international honours, then there should be no reason why he could not be treated as 'one of us' and selected for the national side.

This meant that many fine English-born forwards missed out on a cap (such as Dudley Wood, the Oxford Blue who would later become secretary of the RFU). The

Four Home Unions Committee finally laid down the law in February 1950: no man should play for two countries. This didn't address the qualification issue, but it certainly made overseas players more reluctant to accept an offer to play for one of the Home Unions if they knew it precluded them from representing their original country when they returned home.

To complete the grand characters of the era who played for England and then went on to become leading administrators, was Bob Weighill, later Air Commodore, and a formidable and respected RFU secretary. He played nine of the 15 Service Internationals before Test rugby officially resumed and also captained the RAF, Combined Services and the Barbarians. During interviews, he rarely mentioned that in terms of casualty rates, his role doing low level reconnaissance flying during the war was one of the most risky operations in the RAF. For his exploits he was awarded the Distinguished Flying Cross.

England had a melancholy season in 1947-48. They lost to the touring Australians, even though a good number of the visitors were suffering from food poisoning – and in the Five Nations of 1948, subsided to a Wooden Spoon, losing three matches and drawing with Wales.

There were extenuating circumstances at Murrayfield where a narrow 6-3 defeat at the hands of Scotland underlined the absurdity of the IRB's reluctance to permit substitutes for injured players. It was a measure which was to continue in operation for 20 more years and which crippled several England performances in the era.

At Murrayfield, England lost Richard Madge, their scrum-half, after 10 minutes because of torn ligaments. Steele-Bodger, who moved from the back-row to deputise, was badly concussed just before half-time. Keith Scott, England's captain and by then a doctor in Cornwall, played the second half with a fractured jaw – and never wore England colours again. The danger of injured players trying to continue never persuaded the authorities of the day that action should be taken and replacements allowed.

The attempt at revival started slowly. Defeats in Cardiff and Dublin were an inauspicious start to 1949. Then, Ivor Preece, the Coventry fly-half, succeeded Nim Hall as captain and fly-half, and the effect was immediate. Preece helped see off an improving France at Twickenham with a sweetly-struck dropped goal (8-3) and on a glorious spring day in March set his backs loose on the way to a boisterous 19-3 Calcutta Cup victory – Preece and his men seemed to run the ball at every opportunity. The foreign element was still significant, as the South African Test cricketer, Clive van Ryneveld, broke through in midfield to score two memorable tries.

If the decade up to 1950 was not a vintage period for the England team, it did see the emergence of players who were later to become prominent in officialdom. John Kendall-Carpenter, a versatile forward later to captain England, made his England debut in 1949. Few men have started their first two Tests for their country playing first in the back-row and then in the front-row. Kendall-Carpenter did exactly that.

Ivor Preece had eight new caps under him for the start of the 1950 season and, again, the foreign controversy raged. Ian Botting, who had toured South Africa with the 1949 All Blacks, played on the wing for England for the opening game of 1950 – against Wales in front of a then-record 75,500 at Twickenham in January.

It was said unofficially that this was the last straw for the Four Home Unions Committee and precipitated their February ruling restricting dual nationality at Test level. Wales, inspired by the 18-year-old Lewis Jones, then a boy wonder, won 11-5 – only the second-ever win for the them in 40 years of visits to Twickenham, and defeats in Paris and Edinburgh brought the curtain down on another English Wooden Spoon. The foreign contingent had hardly galvanised the team and, sadly, another bastion fell in 1951. France won for the first time at Twickenham, a result which was a sensation at the time and which gave rugby across the Channel a remarkable boost.

On-field successes might have been few and far between in those early post-war seasons, but the game in England was booming anyway. In 1947, there were 882 clubs in membership of the RFU. By the early 1950s, the figure had swollen to more than 1400. International matches were so popular that even in the days when crowds could be packed into standing terraces, the RFU finally had to succumb and make their matches all-ticket affairs. International rugby was still rising in importance, and all that was needed was for England to find a way of fully re-joining the party they had begun in 1871.

HARRY WALKER (England 1947-1948, 9 caps)

What did it mean to play rugby for England? Everything. That's all you could say. After years and years of playing tough rugby with Cov [Coventry], you were suddenly in the England jersey. My father was killed in the First World War, I was born 1915 and he was killed 1916, so you thought of him I suppose.

Well, I thought I played well in those days, I was a bit big-headed. I fancied myself against any of these forwards around. I never made it to 6ft but I was 15st 10lb and 5ft 11½in and that was big in those day. I knew my way about.

I thought that the amateur game was wonderful, because it didn't matter if you were a labourer or a factory worker, you'd probably be playing with a solicitor or a doctor and on the park it was wonderful.

Regrets? Yes, that I didn't get in the England team before the war! But so many didn't play for England. I can't grumble.

I loved my rugby for England, though there are some memories before I won my first cap. I was playing for the school against Broad Street and stopped their outside-half, who was a schoolboy international. I tackled him hard by the touch line – then a Broad Street teacher who was also chairman of the Coventry Rugby Football Club came on the pitch and hit me three times across the head with his umbrella. The referee came up and he was another school teacher. He said to me: 'You shouldn't do that, Harold.' To me!

I was only 17 when I played for the second team, when I played for the first team I was probably just 19. Soon after I made the Cov first team we went to Leicester and took them to pieces, pushed them from their 25 line over their line – in the paper they said they wanted to cancel fixtures because we were just a dirty side. Yet we had two 19 year old boys in the pack. We won 11-3. I scored two tries against Leicester from tight-head prop and had another one disallowed, I came off the park full of it. When we got into the cricket pavilion, which was where we changed, our second-row Arthur Wheatley sat me down and he said, 'Your job isn't to score tries, your job is to put your head down and get that ball back for far better players than you.'

What did we wear for England? Well not those running pumps they have today. How long are the studs on those? How do they expect to stand up in any sort of weather? We had two types of studs, one lot for wet weather and one for dry weather. We hammered the studs in with nails.

Our training was different too. I worked in a factory, so I used to run every

The first post-war Twickenham cap match. Pre-war cap Jack Heaton lines up for the anthems as captain with his England team to face Scotland, 1947.

night, even in the snow. Round the streets, more or less in the dark. With England, in my time in the team after the war, the only training session we had was on the Friday before the game. We used to go to Rosslyn Park for about an hour. We just had a few scrums and the backs mucked about a bit.

You got a cap – just one. We had to buy our own shorts, and as Coventry's shorts were blue I had to go and buy two pairs of white shorts. All they gave us were the socks and shirts, and after the games they'd even go through your kit to get the shirt back. They never gave us anything, which you could understand a bit, clothes were on coupon. I do know that in the two years I played every game and they'd come in afterwards and make sure they got jerseys 1 to 15 safely back.

Expenses were tight too. There was a clamp-down on those as well. We used to go down on Fridays for home games. One day the train was very, very late. When I got off the train, Micky Steele-Bodger was on it and we were running behind. Micky suggested a taxi and we got in.

Anyway, before the end of the weekend, Doug Prentice of the RFU had us in, one after the other. He said we don't pay expenses for taxis, and in future you take a earlier train. We were invited to the Anglo-Scottish ball after a Scotland match once and they invited girlfriends and wives but we had to pay for them. There wasn't a penny extra at all.

MICKY STEELE-BODGER (England 1947-1948, 9 caps)
Playing for England meant such a huge amount to us all. We were very passionate, although perhaps not in the extrovert manner the Celts sometimes have. We were desperate not to let anybody down.

HARRY WALKER
My first cap was in the first game after the war in Cardiff. Eric Coley was the England head selector. He played for England and Northampton. He came round after the war when rugby started and I got picked for the first trial – that was in '47, the first season after the war. I was in the Rest, not in the England team, but I was picked for Cardiff. We won that one 9-6 too.

We more than held our own up front. We scored a great try by Don White, although I didn't see much of it, and though we went behind we won when Joe Mycock, the captain from Sale, caught the ball, got it back to the scrum-half, straight back to his outside-half Nim Hall, and Nim dropped a great goal. Wonderful.

BASIL 'JIKA' TRAVERS (England 1947-1949, 6 caps)
In the game today the penalty has come into prominence for two reasons: first, the defence has been so organised and planned that it is now difficult to score tries,

thus when penalties are scored they often win matches. Second, the penalty kick is no longer charged by the opposition. This will explain a number of successful penalty kicks that are given in the game today. But there is a third reason why the penalty is so frequent, and that is because the number of possible infringements has been increased in recent years.

HARRY WALKER

The next game was away again for some reason, in Dublin against Ireland. The previous time I had crossed the Irish Sea for a festival game in the war we had been zig-zagging to avoid U-boats.

On the train coming back from Cardiff, Doug Prentice of the RFU and all the selectors were on the same train as me. They sat in another carriage but half way through the journey, they invited me to sit with them. They told me they'd picked the team and made two changes. I said: 'You can't make two changes, you'll knock all the confidence out of us.'

They told me that I was in but I just wanted to win the game. They made two changes and we got stuffed 22-0. Jack Heaton came in at centre but I don't know who the other centre was, he only played the one game. He was awful. To me their pack was about half a yard quicker than us and I wasn't too happy about midfield, but when you're up front you don't realise that. Jackie Kyle was at fly-half for them, wonderful player.

After the game the selectors came to the dressing room and they walked the length of the room to where I was sitting, and expected me to tell them what had happened. I told them to ask Bod [Micky Steele-Bodger]. I was too full up to say anything. After the match there was a big dinner. The Irish Union president got up and his speech was, basically, 22-0, 22-0, 22-0. He murdered us!

MICKY STEELE-BODGER

That awful winter of '47 seemed to go on forever and I was still up at Edinburgh University doing my studies to become a vet. I had just broken into the England side, we beat Wales 9-6 down in Cardiff then none of us played for two months – except in the middle of February we went across to Dublin where the conditions were better, and got hammered 22-0; no match practice, you see, plus a good Ireland side beginning to hit their straps.

England made four or five changes but I survived the cut for the Scotland game and come the Thursday afternoon, with mainland Britain still under a thick blanket of snow, I had to make the decision whether to try the East coast line or the West coast line. It was the toss of a coin. The Scotland team were gathering at the station at the same time and went down the East coast and somehow got through unscathed, I went down the West coast and immediately ran into fresh blizzards.

We got as far as Carstairs and ground to a halt with ten foot snow drifts across the line at one point. It was Scott of the Antarctic territory. There was nothing for it – all able-bodied men had to climb out and dig the train out with the snow shovels that somebody had thoughtfully loaded onto the guard's carriage. It was hard work, I can tell you.

Eventually we crawled into Carlisle Station and I managed to send a telegraph saying I was on my way, but it was still pretty grim. The buffet had a couple of buns and some hot tea without milk because, obviously, the milkman had not made it through that day.

Onwards we went, very slowly, and occasionally we had to jump out and go to work again with our shovels. The Flying Scotsman it wasn't. We eventually got into Euston about 3am on the Saturday morning and I jumped into a taxi and got down to the England hotel at god-knows-what-hour. I had been put in a room with a very young Eric Evans who had been called in as a reserve for the first time. I was exhausted and slumped on my bed and wrote a note asking him to wake me up in the morning.

When I woke up, the hotel was absolutely deserted. It was late morning, England had already departed for a pre-match lunch and Eric had failed to wake me up because he was so excited.

Damn. So I took a taxi out to a hotel we used to go to for lunch. That was closed. I was getting a bit anxious by now so I just pointed the taxi in the direction of Twickenham, marched into the dressing room and put on my jersey, number seven.

Eventually the England party arrived and Vic Roberts had already been told he was playing in my place, which didn't go down well. I told the selectors that I hadn't gone through those two days for damn all, and after a bit of discussion I was reinstalled in the team. Luckily I knew Vic very well and he was capped soon afterwards.

I seem to remember that the pitch was frozen solid and both side finished with 13 men, with some nasty injuries. I had one of my better games. Well, having caused such a fuss I thought I had better perform! Afterwards, I ate my first meal since Thursday lunchtime.

HARRY WALKER

That was my first home game and they made changes. One of the great things as far as I was concerned was the new scrum-half Ossie Newton-Thompson. I thought he was the best scrum-half that played for us, Thompson, he was a smasher and we won comfortably. To play at home before 70,000 was wonderful. Well, you're top of the pops, you've got to play well.

BOB WEIGHILL (England 1947-1948, 4 caps)
I was very lucky because although I was flying operationally doing a low-level photographic reconnaissance job [for the RAF during the war] most of it was done either in the early morning or late at night. So, I had most of the days free, and I was able to do a lot of training and was very fit.

I had a lot of fun – and there were a lot of very good players around. In the good old days we had all the 'professors' from rugby league playing with us [in the wartime Services Internationals]. When you think of an RAF pack containing Ray Longland, Bert Toft, 'Beef' Dancer, Joe Mycock, Eddie Watkins, and Ike Owens from rugby league – one of the best flankers ever – and myself at No.8, it was great stuff.

Injuries kept me out of the games against both Wales and Ireland for two years in a row, in 1947 and 1948. The second year it was a broken ankle, and the first a freak accident. I was training after the big freeze-up in 1947. I was stationed at White Waltham near Maidenhead, and I went to Littlewick Green to kick a ball about – hoofing the ball, running after it and scooping it up as handling practice. It was teeming with rain and there were these two little boys sitting under a hedge sheltering under one of those old wartime gas capes watching me. Anyway, I had just kicked the ball and as I bent down to pick it up one of them ran out from under the hedge – he had big farm boots on – and gave the ball an almighty welt. It caught my middle finger on the end and shattered it… there was bone everywhere. That put me out for six weeks.

The boys hadn't seen me reaching for the ball, and thought they were helping. They ran off laughing, thought it was a huge joke. They didn't realise they'd done that much damage of course. I had to run two miles to find a doctor.

In 1948 I came back for the last two games against Scotland and France, both away losses, and was made captain in my final Test against France.

HARRY WALKER
We had a wonderful day against France at Twickenham in 1947, Ossie Newton-Thompson made a lovely break and Vic Roberts scored. The next game was after Christmas against Australia. Eric Evans was brought in and said that he wanted to play tight-head. I told him I couldn't care less, I could play both sides, so he started practising at tight-head.

Then on to the park came the selectors and they asked me what I thought I was doing. I told them that Eric wanted to play tight-head. They looked at Eric and told him that if he wouldn't come round to the loose-head side he could bugger off. Eric was a good hooker, he was never a prop, his propping was not very good.

MICKY STEELE-BODGER

The war was a very recent memory and there was an understated toughness about players. Everybody has seen so much worse [in the war] and we were reluctant to make a fuss over 'minor' injuries. In the 1948 match at Murrayfield we were captained by a very phlegmatic Cornishman at centre, Keith Scott of Redruth and Oxford University – he then became an outstanding medic. Talk about leading by example.

Early in the match our scrum-half, Richard Madge, badly tore ligaments in his knee and couldn't walk, let alone run. He had to be carried off. I had the dubious honour of deputising at scrum-half.

Remember that no replacements were allowed in those days – although God knows why, because every team always travelled with reserves in case anybody fell down ill or injured the day before. They were sitting up in the stands at Murrayfield but still we were not allowed to call on their services.

A couple of minutes after the unfortunate Madge departed, I took a terrific blow to the head and didn't know what day of the week it was. I should probably have come off but stayed on, we were short-handed enough. Then Keith sustained a broken jaw in another collision. You could see instantly what had happened. He had a crack right down the symphysis where the two jawbones meet, upper and lower – but for the time being there was no displacement.

I remember to this day one of our chaps running on with lemons at half-time and Keith calmly asking him to order a taxi to be waiting outside the England changing room on the final whistle to take him directly to Edinburgh Infirmary, where he would need his jaw wired. And with that he turned back to his team and gave a stirring half-time talk before leading us back into battle. I was rather impressed although, alas, there was no fairytale ending.

HARRY WALKER

I stayed in the team for 1948. We drew 3-3 with Wales at Twickenham and we lost Syd Newton, our fullback, in the first half. Jika Travers, our biggest forward, had to go back to fullback. Then we lost at home to Ireland and Jackie Kyle play so well again. Really, he was one of the best players I've ever seen, he was magic. We could have won that game but it was touch and go.

Against Scotland we had two bad injuries and lost 6-3, then in Paris we got stuffed 15-0. We had a new team and France were too good.

After 1948 I got dropped. I carried on with Cov for four years and I played for the Baa-baas [the Barbarians] against Australia at Cardiff Arms Park where the tourists lost 6-9. They had beaten Scotland, Ireland, England and France. Doug Elliott of Scotland was a great back-row forward for us.

JOHN KENDALL-CARPENTER (England 1949-1954, 23 caps)

I played my first international in Dublin in 1949 in the back-row. In my initial Twickenham international, against France, I was nearly carried off the field before the first scrum was over. In one of those strange twists of fortune, Jika Travers, the vast Australian who had been my reserve in Dublin, took over as No 8 and I was moved up to the front-row.

It was when the three French juggernauts Soro, Moga and Basquet were in their prime, and as the scrum went down for the first time their front-row opened up and an enormous fist whistled past my ear. More out of fright than anything else, I grabbed a hairy arm and was still holding it when the scrum collapsed and broke up. Clearly this was the moment to be firm, so I said in my best schoolboy French, 'Taissez-vous!' I'll never know whether it was out of suspicion or compassion, but it worked, and Moga – for it was he – did as he was bid.

IVOR PREECE (England 1948-1951, 12 caps plus 1 cap for the Lions)

At the first mention of 'great moment' one would readily think it an opportune time to revive a famous victory or to recall a personal triumph.

But, after reflecting more deeply, I feel that there are few moments, no matter whether in victory or defeat, to equal that which comes to a player immediately after 'no-side'. After having given his all on the field of play he is completely exhausted, yet blissfully happy, when he sinks into the bath 'comparing notes' with his opposite number, with whom no quarter was given or taken.

Very few other games offer this experience – a truly great rugby moment!

BASIL 'JIKA' TRAVERS

Against Scotland in 1949 [Brian] Vaughan broke away from a lineout on the Scottish 25, passed to [Geoff] Hosking who scored about ten yards to the right of the post. England had been winning the ball regularly from the lineout, and towards the end when the try occurred Scotland were looking for the ball to be passed back to the English backs. Thus, when the ball was taken from the lineout instead of being passed back, the Scottish defence was taken by surprise.

JOHN KENDALL-CARPENTER

[In 1951] I was busy winning my greatest distinction in the game – that of captaining the first England XV ever to lose to France at Twickenham.

TWELVE

A FORMIDABLE FORCE

1952-1960

T HE AUSTERITY OF *1950s post-war Britain was offset by an upswing in England's fortunes during which they developed into a formidable force, including the advent of two of their most inspirational captains, Eric Evans and Dickie Jeeps. They either won or shared the Five Nations Championship five times from 1952-60, with the crowning point the 1957 Grand Slam won by the side led by the Shakespeare-quoting hooker Evans. The uplift was sustained when the indomitable scrum-half, Jeeps, led a much-changed team to secure a Triple Crown in 1960.*

The England players during this period had almost all been through the National Service mill, and the sense of national unity and purpose seems to have carried across, at least in part, to the team. There is very little evidence, for instance, of the tensions that arose in the seventies and eighties between administrators and players of different generations.

Post-match functions had a 'demob-happy' air about them, including an attempt to deposit a donkey in the hotel room of an England selector on one trip to Paris. The light-hearted moments included Carston Catcheside, the chairman of selectors, declaring before the game against New Zealand in 1954 that, 'If we didn't get the ball to the wings it was about as much use as my a*** is for shooting partridges.'

However, while there were off-field japes and pranks, England meant business on the pitch. They were runners-up to Wales in 1952, with the English producing one of their most effective packs for years, and Evans reaching the height of his playing powers as the most technically proficient hooker in the British Isles. England had more or less universally adopted the 3-4-1 formation, with John Kendall-Carpenter as eighthman, giving a model demonstration of how the modern back-rower should operate. This allowed them to break the Five Nations hegemony of Wales and Ireland, who had ruled the roost from 1948-52.

The versatile 'Nim' Hall was back at fly-half and captain. Safety-first was the order of the day and Hall drew criticism for his strict adherence to the prevailing customs. His kicking was brilliant, but as a creator of openings he was lacking. This was a pity because the new wings, the powerful Ted Woodward and Chris Winn – both swift operators – had few chances to excel against defences that marked man-for-man and tackled hard. Even so, after Wooden Spoons in 1950 and 1951, England finished the 1952 Five Nations with three successive wins and second place in the table.

Opposite: England versus Australia at Twickenham, 1958. England players left to right: Peter Robbins, Ned Ashcroft and Peter Jackson.

The promise of '52 turned to Five Nations honours in 1953 when, with Hall still captain but now at fullback, England landed their first outright Championship title for fifteen years. They were unbeaten, with a draw in Ireland the only blot on the copybook. Hall's soccer-style round-the-corner place-kicking was a novelty in 1953, but it paid off when he landed eight kicks at goal. The nucleus of the 1952 pack was still available, but the selectors chanced their arms behind the scrum, blooding an adventurous midfield in Martin Regan (Liverpool fly-half against Wales), Jeff Butterfield (Northampton centre against France) and the forceful young Cambridge centre Phil Davies against Scotland.

The following season, with the captaincy passing to Wasps prop Bob (RV) Stirling, England won the Triple Crown before losing to France at the Stade Colombes in the last match of the Five Nations, and being forced to share the title with the French and the Welsh. As was customary at the time, the 1954 Championship was interrupted by a game against the New Zealand tourists, which, because it came after England had beaten Wales, and Wales had beaten New Zealand, had seen Stirling's side installed as favourites. They lost a fiercely contested game 5-0 in front of 72,000 fans at Twickenham.

The 1954 side showed a growing will to attack. Regan was the key player among the backs, challenging defences with his running and bringing out the best in Jeff Butterfield in the centre (with Davies, for part of this season operating as a wing.) These were times of tight marking, however, and strong back-row defence by New Zealand and France bottled up Regan.

Injuries, illness and retirements brought the selectors fresh problems in 1955. Stirling, Kendall-Carpenter, Alec Lewis and second-row Peter Yarranton had all played their last international rugby in 1954. England scrabbled for a settled side and their only victory came at the end of the season in a grim 9-6 struggle with Scotland.

After that dip England's selectors settled on Evans as captain in 1956, and, after a mid-table finish, they kicked off the 1957 season with an away win in Wales (3-0) and followed it by beating Ireland at Lansdowne Road (6-0), thanks to an opportunist try by Peter Jackson, the brilliant Coventry wing. Jackson followed that with a brace of tries against France at Twickenham, and with another from skipper Evans, the French were outscored three tries to one (9-5).

The Grand Slam – England's first since 1928 – was clinched at Twickenham with the home side, who were constantly on the attack, outscoring Scotland by three tries to none (16-3) in a match attended by the Queen and the Duke of Edinburgh. That 1957 Calcutta Cup game also brought England the Triple Crown and Championship, and was notable for the first use in the press of the term 'Grand Slam' to denote a clean sweep.

Evans' 1957 Grand Slam side was fashioned from the ten new caps that lost to Wales in 1956. England also remained unbeaten in 1958, a season that featured a famous victory over Australia, including a mazy, ghosting run by Jackson which left a trail of bamboozled Wallaby defenders and finished in a winning try that became part of English rugby folklore.

The composition of the team barely changed during those years. It later emerged that match programmes had shown Evans' age to be four years younger than it was: Listed as born Droylsden, near Manchester, 1 February, 1925, the Sale man's date of birth should have read 1921.

Line-out law changes had come into effect in 1954, effectively doing away with all manner of support for jumpers. In David Marques, England found the perfect player to exploit the new line-out. Athletic, supple with good hands, he was the tallest man to play international rugby (at 6ft 5ins) when he entered the side in 1956. His two-handed catching was to provide the English backs with a stream of good possession which, from 1957, Dickie Jeeps put to good effect by launching a superb backline spearheaded by Richard Bartlett at fly-half, oiled by Butterfield and Davies (or occasionally Lou Cannell) in the centres, and completed by Jackson and Peter Thompson, on the wings.

Evans was the perfect captain, an effective, hard-grafting hooker, and there was a dynamic back-row of Peter Robbins, Reg Higgins (flankers) with 'Neddy' Ashcroft at No 8. John 'Muscles' Currie was Marques's minder in the second-row, a useful occasional place-kicker and a prodigious mauler.

All played their parts in England's return to glory days, but, in the view of his team-mates, none more than Evans. The captain was famous for his fitness, and trained regularly with Manchester United, joining the football pros in their lung-busting runs up and down the Old Trafford stands. Seven days after that famous win over Australia he had to do it all again against Ireland, back at Twickenham. In the middle of that week, many of those Man United players with whom he trained perished in the Munich air crash. Evans picked himself up and kept England's unbeaten record intact, leading them to a 6-0 victory. Finally, at 37 – the oldest man to captain his country – he stood down after a draw at Murrayfield left England (who had also drawn their opening game against Wales) as champions for the second year running.

Jeff Butterfield led England in 1959. He had six new caps in a mud-bath encounter at Cardiff where Wales triumphed 5-0, but hamstrung by safety-first edicts handed down by the selectors his side failed to score a try in the Five Nations. This was France's year, the Tricolores winning the Five Nations outright for the first time but failing to beat England. A dull game at Twickenham ended in a 3-all draw – one penalty goal apiece – and stalemate struggles between the two sides were the key to the 1960 and 1961 Championships.

Dickie Jeeps became captain in 1960 and, for the first time in Championship history, a team went through the Five Nations unchanged. On the field that is. Before the Welsh match Bev Risman and Larry Webb had to withdraw at a late hour and Oxford student Richard Sharp and the veteran Northampton prop Ron Jacobs stepped *in to take their places. Sharp, one of seven new caps on the day, played a blinder to put paid to Wales. After the try-drought of the previous season, the Twickenham crowd were sated by two brilliant first half tries scored by left-wing Jim Roberts. Sharp tore the Welsh apart – it was 14-0 at half-time and a new attacking England team was born.*

Ireland were beaten thanks to a late David Marques try at Twickenham. Mike Weston scored a try at the posts in the Championship showdown of the season against France in Paris, but Don Rutherford missed the easy conversion and the sides that went on to share the Championship finished drawn at 3-3 for the second season running. Another glorious display of open rugby masterminded by Jeeps and Sharp brought England the Triple Crown at Murrayfield in a 21-12 win.

Increasing live television coverage of international rugby brought the game to a growing audience in the fifties, with many of England's finest matches extending rugby union's appeal to armchair viewers unable to make the journeys to big international matches. Clubs, however, still objected to the practice – TV undermined their gates, and the RFU, together with their fellow Home Unions, were careful to ration live broadcasting.

It seems hard to believe in this day and age, for example, that as recently as 1959 only the second half of the Wales-England game from Cardiff was shown live. Different times, but for England a sea-change in terms of international success.

ERIC EVANS (England 1948-58, 30 caps)
It may sound trite, but to develop a perfect team spirit, the foundation of this is laid off the field. I made a point of finding out as much as possible of a fellow's background, problems, likes and dislikes. It is amazing how a thoughtless word or action can destroy confidence.

PHIL DAVIES (England 1953-1958, 11 caps plus 3 caps for the Lions)
England was everything. I was born in Worcestershire 10 miles from Edward Elgar's cottage with all the Pomp and Circumstance of Victorian/Edwardian/George V attitudes, and the threatening age of the 1930s, with its recession and rearmament. My parents were a Chaplain POW and Nurse in the First World War and equally involved in the Second World War with Home Guard and Mobile Midwifery.

Armistice Day was so poignant and prominent, with Gustav Holst and 'I vow to thee my Country' staying in the memory. His Jupiter theme later became the first World Cup anthem with Kiri-te-Kanawa singing. A land of service, a Land of Hope and Glory. A strange haunting feeling. Jingoistic, no. Just upbringing and respect for the past.

We would go to watch Gloucester wonder centre Chris Tanner, later commemorated as a Naval Chaplain on Cheltenham College Chapel walls for his

Albert Medal in rescuing two shipmates from his bombed destroyer off Crete, but losing his life as he swam to a third. A hero.

There was a prickly family moment when in 1934, at age six, I was deemed too young to be among the crowd to watch the All Blacks at Villa Park. It took another grumpy twenty years and a frozen Twickenham on the wing for England before I came across the All Blacks again.

My time in RAF rugby and with my first club Evesham, and later Cheltenham, showed what was possible. There was an honours-even clash with 'Billy the Wiz' Boston playing for Pontypridd, later a world star at Wigan.

Early Harlequin games against Service sides reinforced my interest in the rugby league players who were allowed to play union, and the strength of the north and midland clubs generally. The south was softer. Gordon Rimmer had been a PE Sergeant at my Basic Training Camp, RAF Yatesbury, only for us to meet up five years later, in 1953, for my first England cap. He was scrum-half whilst Nim Hall from Worksop was fly-half.

So, a tremendous feeling of pride and massive nervousness not to let the side down. Total commitment. That's how I felt about playing rugby.

JOHN COLLINS (England 1952, 3 caps)

I was one of the few players in living memory to win an England cap out of Cornwall. When I first got picked against Ireland, it was all very controversial and the old King himself – George VI, God rest his soul – died the very next day. Must have been the shock of a Cornishman being selected, well that's what we all said.

The game was re-arranged for later in the season and I was left sweating to see if I was still in favour for the next match, up at Murrayfield. I survived the cut and we beat the Scots before the re-arranged Ireland match. That was a strange one, dreadful Arctic weather and snowstorms on the last Saturday in March. It was so cold that our captain, Nim Hall, ordered us back into the changing rooms at half-time, the first occasion that had happened in an international, I believe. Until then we used to stay out on the field. A hot cup of tea and a nip of something strong saw us scrape home 3-0.

We beat the French in Paris the very next week, but that was it for me, three matches and three wins. My knee went bad the following season and, though Cornwall arranged for me to see Denis Compton's surgeon in London, it never really came right again. Not for rugby anyway. Of course I should never have played for England really, I was professional. I used to charge 3s 6d for my journey from Camborne up to the 'Midlands' – Truro – to catch the Paddington train. Any fool knew it was only 3s. Disgraceful behaviour.

GEORGE HASTINGS (England 1955-1958, 13 caps)
It was the be-all and end-all for me when I was selected for my first cap against Wales in Cardiff. I felt great excitement. However, there was no cap ceremony, and I'm pretty sure that mine came through the post. Does it mean as much to a professional as it meant to an amateur? I don't know. You thought, who are you marking, what are you up against, and what opportunities will come your way? I was familiar with the Arms Park because my first game for Gloucester had been against Cardiff at the ground. Before the Wales game I'd had a letter from Tom Voyce, the great Gloucester and England wing-forward. In it he wrote, 'You are playing for the team, of course, but don't forget to do a bit for yourself.'

BEV RISMAN (England 1959-1961, 8 caps plus 4 caps for the Lions)
Playing for England meant absolutely everything. I'd come through school and university level in England. The only hiccup was Wales also came in for me – my dad was from Wales – but I regarded myself as an Englishman with Welsh connections, because I was born in Salford and my mum was English. My father understood, and agreed with my decision.

JOHN YOUNG (England 1958-1961, 9 caps plus 1 cap for the Lions)
I was very proud of wearing the England shirt, and remain a patriot. At the time it bolstered my confidence in running and organising my life at Oxford. It gave me influence also in developing my City career, and led to my involvement at Harlequins as a player, and Dorking RFC, where my grandsons play and who I've supported for over 40 years.

MALCOLM PHILLIPS (England 1958-1964, 25 caps)
I was playing for Oxford [University] at the time and went to the *Oxford Mail* offices because I'd had a tip-off about England selection and had been invited to go down there by their rugby correspondent, Ron Grimshaw. He let us into the wire room – I think John Currie was there too – and we saw the team coming over on the wire. A letter from Doug Prentice, the RFU secretary, followed in the post a few days later!

TED WOODWARD (England 1952-1956, 15 caps)
We were very patriotic. It meant a lot to us. The comradeship, even today, is unbelievable. You learn an awful lot from playing, because you understand people more. It is a wonderful feeling to play for your country, to reach the top. It gives you confidence, and was a wonderful part of my life.

The most exciting thing is to run out at Twickenham in your first international.

The biggest thrill is to be picked for England, and to hear 70,000 people cheering at the home of rugby.

NED ASHCROFT (England 1956-1959, 16 caps plus 2 caps for the Lions)
It was the supreme achievement – something everyone wanted, and never thought they'd get.

RICHARD SHARP (England 1960-1967, 14 caps plus 2 caps for the Lions)
My first game was over half a century ago, 16 January, 1960, against Wales at Twickenham. I played in the final England trial that season for the Rest, and I didn't have a bad game. However, my heroes, Jeeps and Risman, who had been on the 1959 Lions tour, were playing opposite, and I didn't expect to be picked.

I went back to Oxford University and on the Thursday before the Wales match I got a telegram from my dad at our home in Redruth. It said that Mr. Prentice from the RFU had been in contact and told me to be at the Star & Garter in Richmond on Friday. Bev Risman, who I had huge regard for, had torn a hamstring and I was in the team at fly-half.

I wasn't the only replacement. The prop Larry Webb was also injured, and Ron Jacobs was called up. I shared a room with Ron and, because he had to attend to his farm, he didn't join us until Friday night. The headline in *The Daily Telegraph* on the morning of the match was, 'Jacobs, 31, Sharp, 21, Come in as Replacements'. Ron was most indignant.

ERIC EVANS
One of the great highlights of my time with England was, undoubtedly, when Jackson went over for the winning try against Australia at Twickenham in 1958. There was a minute to go and I couldn't have had a better birthday present.

DICKIE JEEPS (England 1956-1962, 24 caps plus 13 caps for the Lions)
The skipper: such enthusiasm! Eric Evans never stops talking, except for five minutes before the kick-off, when we all have to preserve complete silence and concentrate on the job ahead. Beating Scotland before the Queen [at Twickenham in 1957], when Eric led us to victory, is one of my greatest rugby memories.

GEORGE HASTINGS
I did a bit of goal-kicking – a straight toe-end kicker – and I usually took over when everyone else failed. My most memorable kick came in the game against Scotland at Murrayfield in 1958 when we had missed a few and were down 3-0

with 15 minutes remaining. Eric Evans said to me, 'You have a go George.' It was the equaliser, and it won the Championship.

TED WOODWARD

It all started when I was 17 and played in the Middlesex Sevens final for Wasps at Twickenham. I scored three tries when we beat Harlequins in the final, and after that the press said that I would play for England.

I was picked in an England trial while I was in the RAF, but couldn't make it. However, another invitation came when I was 20. There were three trials culminating in England versus the Rest, who I played for, and scored three tries. I was then selected for my first cap against South Africa in 1952, and won the last of them in 1956 against Scotland.

I never played against a wing as big as me in international rugby. I was 6ft 2ins and 15 stone, whereas Wally Holmes, one of the England props, was 14st 7lbs. I'd won the All England Schools 100 yards championship in 10 seconds at 17, so was fairly quick, and had also been in the RAF as a PE instructor, so I was pretty fit.

I don't mean to be big-headed, but when selected for my first cap I was totally, utterly confident. It was a wonderful feeling. I was never concerned by who I was playing against, and never thought anyone could beat me.

PHIL DAVIES

The highest point was to return to the side in 1957 against France after a good deal of criticism to be part of a Grand Slam. I was able to give the wonder runner Peter Jackson two perfect passes from which he scored. The press were dumbfounded! Fingers had been pointed, and, with no TV, were raised back (regrettably).

BEV RISMAN

I was in for the 1959 season, overlooked in 1960, and back again in 1961, before crossing codes to rugby league. Over those three years we didn't achieve anything, so it's difficult to have a highlight. I suppose kicking the winning goal against Ireland to win 3-0 at Lansdowne Road in 1959 is one – but it was totally different to any other rugby I had played. At that time England had a no-risk policy, and we never scored more than eight points.

JOHN YOUNG

Getting picked and going on the 1959 Lions tour to New Zealand after winning only one cap for England was obviously a great highlight. I got that cap against Ireland at Twickenham in 1958 as a temporary fill-in for Peter Jackson, the king of the wing. One of the selectors, Micky Steele-Bodger, was very keen on me following my win in the AAA, becoming the 100 yards champion in the summer of 1956, after recording a best time of 9.6 seconds.

MALCOLM PHILLIPS

Scoring a try on my debut against Australia in 1958 was the highest point of my England career. It was an outside break, and I went round my opposite number and then the fullback from about 40 yards out. They had a great big picture of it on the wall in the clubhouse at Fylde, my home club, for many years.

RICHARD SHARP

Dick Jeeps' first game as England captain was also my first cap, and we had only half-an-hour training together. Afterwards in the team meeting Dick said, 'We've got two changes but it hasn't weakened our side at all. I've complete confidence in them.' I've never forgotten that. [England beat Wales 14-6.]

TED WOODWARD

Beating Wales at Twickenham in 1954 and scoring two tries was a highlight. For the first one I really had to run for it, and left Gerwyn Williams their fullback with a busted shoulder before scoring in the corner. There was also a penalty I kicked against Wales when we won in Cardiff the previous year.

GEORGE HASTINGS

In the game against Ireland there was a ruck and Nick Labuschagne, England's South African hooker, broke free and when I got the ball I had to go about 10 yards. You don't think about anything until you've got the ball down over the line, but I was very proud, and pleased.

NED ASHCROFT

They tended to get rid of you after about two or three years – after that they thought you were past your best. In fact, you were probably improving. I was at my best after I finished playing for England, because I was still fit and had more experience. I carried on playing until I was in my fifties, playing in all six teams at Waterloo handing on what I could to the youngsters.

PHIL DAVIES

The lowest point was being injured and having to cry off before a first cap in 1953. The week before I couldn't travel away on a Saturday from Christ's Hospital (where I was teaching), and so I played for the Harlequins Wanderers against Coventry at Teddington, taking a boot in the stomach and bruising some muscles. I went to the most effective sports injury physiotherapist of the day, Mr. Bill Tucker [who had been capped three times by England between 1926 and 1930], in Harley Street, and recall a lady assistant who marvellously, and with decorum, draped my genitals with a pre-warmed towel. Half a month's salary for one visit spent joyfully, with electrotherapy, but to no account!

DICKIE JEEPS
We were being introduced to the Duke of Edinburgh [before the 1957 Grand Slam game against Scotland] and as the Duke walked down the line of Scottish players Eric Evans noticed the great big smile on the face of the Scottish fly-half, Gordon Waddell, who was winning his first cap. Evans whispered to Robbins, 'If you haven't knocked that smile off his face in the first ten minutes I shall want to know why.'

ERIC EVANS
Within reason one should go on the field temporarily hating the opposition. Many of our opponents were, and are, great friends of mine, but during the 80 minutes of the match victory was the only aim.

JOHN CURRIE (England 1956-1962, 25 caps)
Peter Robbins was the best open-side I ever saw. He was a great constructive player, he never stopped running and, of course, he was a tremendous character. No one was safe from his practical jokes, except me. I always shared a room with him.

RON JACOBS (1956-1964, 29 caps)
Eric Evans was so enthusiastic and good-hearted. He was thoughtful to all his players and we were all very fond of him. He used to train at Manchester United with the 'Busby Babes' and he even took some training sessions because he had some qualifications as a PE teacher. Of course he was devastated when the Manchester United plane crashed in Munich in 1958, but he had to rouse to beat Ireland when we assembled the morning after that crash.

ERIC EVANS
Everybody said I was a good captain and if I was a good captain, it was because I had Peter Robbins beside me. He was terribly intelligent: he worked me out straight away, realised I was a chippy Northerner and he was incredibly kind to me. I had a special relationship with Peter and for my part it was based on his sincerity. He was a great asset to me as a captain as he was always there to lean on. He understood people and he understood me. He built me up, his image did not

signify what a genuine guy he was. He would obviously have made a very good England captain [but] I had one advantage over him: I was much more noisy. He was the greatest wing-forward I ever played with and one of the greatest characters I ever knew. He was totally reliable, had tremendous skill and if you think of wing-forwards as rip-roaring rugby players, Robbins was more than that. Robbins was sheer class.

PHIL DAVIES
Ricky Bartlett was a wonderful quietly-spoken England fly-half and Harlequins captain, and giver of the softest of passes – each with a hint of a break. I played with him first at Cambridge, for the LX Club against Oxford. The programme listed 6 future internationals. He died so young.

For his understanding of the top game and need for fitness and preparation, as well as the most fluent of passers and deceptive running, Jeff Butterfield was the best I played with. He was from Yorkshire, with direct speech and viewpoints, and also from Loughborough, with its then enormous influence on the game. I am proud to be godfather of his racing driver son, Giles.

For his Lancastrian brand of Agincourt language and leadership, Eric Evans, as captain always sticks in my mind. His rhetoric was spiced by practical plans such as, 'Belting his man at the first line-out' and taking it from there!

GEORGE HASTINGS
We had a very good captain in Eric Evans. He was not the greatest player, but he had fanatical enthusiasm. Whenever we were going to the ground I can remember Eric urging the police to get a move on from the door of the bus.

JEFF BUTTERFIELD (England 1953-1959, 28 caps plus 4 caps for the Lions)
Jeeps was the toughest, hardest player around. He was relentless in pursuing a win. He didn't play rugby for fun. Part of his essential gear contained a catapult: he was a grown-up 'Just William'.

DICKIE JEEPS
Butterfield was the classic centre. Peter Jackson didn't have blinding pace, but he made space for himself. Peter Robbins was a tremendous asset at flanker [and] the great pair of locks, David Marques and John Currie, gave us so much ball.

TED WOODWARD
Nim Hall was an incredible guy. He was extremely versatile, playing fly-half and fullback for England, and scrum-half in sevens.

BEV RISMAN

I played my first match at fly-half with Steve (SR) Smith at scrum-half. Dickie Jeeps had been dropped because Steve was the first of the long passers – although each of his first few passes missed me by a mile in pretty atrocious conditions at the Arms Park.

One of my greatest friends at Lancashire was Alan Ashcroft, so I had a mate already in the side. Jeff Butterfield was such a classy player. He had the old-fashioned swinging hips passing style, but he delivered the ball perfectly. He was a good captain and a strong character.

My main inspiration was Dickie Jeeps. He carried me through my first season, and only gave me the ball when it was to advantage. He would take on the opposition forwards.

Jeeps was an imp. He was up to mischief all the time, a very cheeky and abrasive character. He was absolutely dedicated to winning whatever the cost, and also winning for the team.

JOHN YOUNG

Peter Jackson was an amazing wing with a wonderful sidestep. We both played on the same 1959 Lions tour, and I was privileged to replace him for two seasons. It wasn't a low point to lose my place to him after that.

Eric Evans. I cannot forget his pre-match short talks, standing on a chair in his jockstrap with his England shirt tied under his armpits before the match. My father had died in 1956 before my first cap and I remember Eric said to me very kindly, 'I'm sure he will be looking down and wishing you well.'

MALCOLM PHILLIPS

Peter Jackson was the outstanding guy. He was incredibly elusive, able to ghost and feint past people. Tony O'Reilly was the star wing of those days, and he was faster, but he didn't have Jackson's ghosting ability. When I look back on the try he scored against Australia I'm still not sure how he did it – and I'm not sure he was either.

DICKIE JEEPS

We scored more tries with Ricky Bartlett at fly-half than at any other time. He stood rather close to you and liked taking the ball very near to the advantage line. He played to his centres Jeff Butterfield and Phil Davies, and also had two good feet.

DON WHITE (England 1947-1953, 14 caps)

Jeff Butterfield was a superb passer of the ball, a joy to play with. He had a wonderful ability to sum up a situation and decide what to do, and wings loved playing outside him.

NED ASHCROFT

It was the captain who got you together. Eric Evans was the inspiration, and I remember his talks winding us up before the big matches. Apart from that he just played. He got stuck in. My mate Reg Higgins in the England back-row was good. He was just tough. We got together and didn't let anyone get past us. There were no missed tackles and anyone who came our way got 'bunged'. Marques and Currie weren't hard – they were a bit posh, you see – but they were good at their jobs.

TED WOODWARD

There was a fair social mix. I was just a butcher's boy from near High Wycombe, whereas people like Marques and Currie had been to Oxford and were highly educated. I remember sharing a room with Chris Winn, who'd also been to Oxford, and was worried he might be a bit posh for me – but we got on like a house on fire. There's a fantastic camaraderie when you are in a changing room and you know that you will all play for each other.

DICKIE JEEPS

Bob Challis, our fullback, overslept before the Irish match [of 1957] in Dublin. For me, that would be impossible. I'm nervous – fortunately: I wouldn't be the least bit of good if I wasn't.

MALCOLM PHILLIPS

Jeff Butterfield and I had a spell together. I liked playing with Jeff, he never put you in trouble. Eric Evans lived near me. He was an enormous character – not much bigger than me, but very wiry and tough. If you want a patriot, he was it. Dickie Jeeps was another hard nut. He was a farmer, and when you tackled him he was all muscle. It's always said that the best scrum-halves can play well behind a losing pack, and he was one. As tough as nails. Those characters help to drive it, but at that time England teams were self-propelled and self-reliant. It was a team game, but played by individuals with a lot of self-sufficiency.

ERIC EVANS

Undoubtedly among the greatest I have played with and against are Dickie Jeeps and Peter Jackson, for my money the greatest opportunist of them all.

JEFF BUTTERFIELD

We took things in such a modest manner [after beating Scotland to win the 1957 Grand Slam]. It was just a game that we'd won. We weren't going hysterical because we'd won the whole Championship. The memories of the game are not quite so much with playing, apart from playing a very technically sound game, it's rather of shaking hands with the Queen. That's when I was at Twickenham. And that's when we took it all. I don't think in that particular game any one player was particularly outstanding. We just took it in our stride and we knew we could beat the other four countries at that time.

GEORGE HASTINGS

There was not a weak link in the 1957 team. Ron Jacobs was a very strong prop, I was a fairly loose front-row forward, and we had big second-rows for the time in John Currie and David Marques – about 6ft 4in or 6ft 5in. The loose forwards included Peter Robbins, who was a very good footballer, and Reg Higgins, and with players like Jeff Butterfield and Peter Thompson, a good quick-thinking wing, we had speed and penetration in the backs. Winning the Grand Slam was a landmark, but we didn't hug each other. It had happened, and that was it.

DICKIE JEEPS

We had captaincy by committee [in 1960] because there were some old campaigners in the pack and we decided that I would break more often and the wings would get a run. Left wing Jim Roberts scored twice in the first half against Wales and we rattled up seven tries and 46 points that year, very high for the game played then, and we shared the Championship. We would have won the Grand Slam but for Don Rutherford hitting the post with a conversion in Paris when we drew 3-3.

RICHARD SHARP

We won the Triple Crown and shared the Championship with France in 1960, after drawing with them in Paris. I made a break and Mike Weston scored under the posts. Then Don Rutherford, who had kicked impeccably all season, hit the post and France -- who kicked a penalty, which was worth 3 points, the same as an unconverted try – got a draw. We fielded an unchanged side throughout, which at that time was incredible.

PETER JACKSON (1956-1963, 20 caps plus 5 caps for the Lions)

All I remember [of the 1958 match-winning try against Australia] is being exhausted by it. Peter Robbins had to haul me to my feet.

JEFF BUTTERFIELD

That's got to be for any English guy [against Australia in 1958], probably the greatest game they played in.

At half-time we were down to 14 men – Phil Horrocks-Taylor had to go off. I went up to outside-half and Peter Robbins came out of the pack into the centre, and Peter just played like a centre.

I was knocked-out four times in that game. Vivian Jenkins [in *The Sunday Times*] wrote something to the effect 'First time-ever booing at Twickenham' when Peter Thompson was trodden on by an Aussie. The Australians really did want to put us off the pitch. They tried very hard.

Why it was such a sensational game for me was I'd moved into outside-half, a position I always enjoyed, but they didn't play me there because I couldn't kick – I hardly ever kicked the ball.

However, before the last line-out of the game I was knocked-out for the fourth time, and on that occasion I didn't recover. They put me on a stretcher and they carried me to the touchline. Suddenly the feeling of numbness in my right arm disappeared and I ran back on.

MALCOLM PHILLIPS

At Oxford Peter Robbins kept telling me that he was a centre and I kept telling him that he wasn't quick enough. But he was just about the best open-side of his day. He gave me my scoring pass [to tie the score against Australia]. I had a bit to do, mind. I had to run round the centre and the fullback, but Robbins never let me forget that try. It was typical that he should make such a good fist of playing centre at international level.

PETER JACKSON

Butterfield was hammered to the ground and as he lay writhing, Eric Evans, the captain, began exhorting us to try harder, harder, and while all this was going on, Robbins turned to me and said, 'I don't know about you, Jackson, but I'm knackered and if I get the ball, you'll get it straight away.' He did get the ball and I did get it straight away. But it wasn't because he was knackered; it was because he had this marvellous vision, because he knew the value of a quick pass.

JEFF BUTTERFIELD

Jackson's winning try [against Australia at Twickenham in 1958] was unforgettable. It not only produced a fantastic climax, but it was magnificently executed. John Currie started the move, winning a line-out 25 yards from the Australian line. Like a flash, Jeeps passed to me. A rapid exchange between Malcolm Phillips and

Peter Robbins, a flanker playing centre, gave Jackson the ball 15 yards from the touch-line and room to operate. He weaved and dodged to beat four defenders before touching down. That try illustrated the importance of being able to catch and pass quickly.

ERIC EVANS

You can't make yourself 10 feet tall, but you can make yourself fit. It needs guts and discipline to go to bed early, particularly over Christmas. [Training with Manchester] United I had to go far beyond [where it hurts]. I had to go far, far beyond that. I didn't think I could do it. What kept me going? Pride. The bloke in charge said: 'Now we'll do some steps.' I didn't know what he meant, but I soon found out. It was to the top of the terraces, down again, up again, down, up, down.

ALAN ASHCROFT

We thought about the [1957] game [against Wales] a lot, worked out our individual roles, tightened everything up as a unit and the trick was to get Peter Robbins to fly out, harass the opposition half-backs and drive them inside to Reg Higgins and myself. That game at Cardiff was perhaps the best we had, for Wales had Cliff Morgan and Onllwyn Brace at half-back and to bottle that pair, as we did, was a fair achievement. We didn't let Cliff get across the advantage line in the entire match.

DICKIE JEEPS

[In 1960, Wales's] Haydn Morgan was marking Sharp and when we senior pros had our little team talk just before kick-off, [Peter] Robbins suggested that as it was important to take the pressure off young Sharp, I ought to go for the break from scrum-half from the first scrum. This I did, it confused the Welsh defence and from then on Sharp had a field day. That was typical of Robbins for he was a superb tactician.

BEV RISMAN

It was not until I played for the Lions in 1959 that I was able to unleash. With England it was very much safety first. I loved the honour of playing for my country, but the matches were fairly non-descript. The intention was always to play an open game, but if the forwards weren't winning the battle the backs had problems – and our forwards were not dominating at that time.

We had some very good backs including Jeff Butterfield, Malcolm Phillips and Peter Jackson. But a perfect example of the mentality came in my first year when I thought if I could move the ball quickly to Jeff Butterfield in our own half the

Irish backline would be a bit jagged. 'What the effing hell are you doing?' he said soon after I'd passed it. He didn't want the ball in the England half.

PETER ROBBINS (England 1956-1962, 19 caps)
I recall one occasion at a [France-England] post-match banquet when our second-row John Currie saw off Robert Baulon in a little drinkies competition. In those days we preferred to drink wine rather than aftershave lotion. Poor Baulon thought he was Division One, and he may well have been, but our man was World Cup standard.

I believe it was the same night one of the selectors, who has to remain nameless, joined the orchestra, indeed led it, scraping a violin to produce the most awful sound. That in itself was extremely amusing, but the fact that he was scantily dressed added to the moment.

It was definitely the night that a 2am decision to get a donkey into the hotel at St Lazare was taken. It was destined for one of the selectors with a hyphenated name [Micky Steele-Bodger?], and several pulled the beast and one or two pushed. We got it up the steps as far as the doors where it refused, thus incurring three penalty points.

PHIL DAVIES
One of my clearest memories was as a reserve at Murrayfield. The heather-purple face of a piper unblinking and with cheeks puffed escorting the ceremonial haggis at the post-match dinner. He then downed a tumbler of neat whisky unmoved and impassive.

We had trained at North Berwick using the fields of a Prep School and having finally got the ball to the wings without dropping it we took tea... supervised by Matron. I had grown up under such a regime and knew the form, so was aghast when Carston Catcheside, the Chairman of Selectors, in thanking her said: 'Thank you, however the cheese and onion sandwiches didn't half make one fart.' I think she too roared with laughter.

DONALD 'SANDY' SANDERS (England 1954-1956, 9 caps)
Jeeps was a water-pistol man. He was dedicated, exuberant, analytical and a great team man.

DICKIE JEEPS
Yes, I like a lark. Give me a bucket of water, a firework or a nearby swimming-pool and somebody is going to get a surprise. I got fed up with a long-winded president in Paris and the equally long-winded interpreter, so I crept under the top table and exploded a banger. When Carston Catcheside performed a full strip at an after-

match banquet in Paris, the lady violinist skipped out just before the last garment came down.

MALCOLM PHILLIPS
The post-match functions were usually hilarious, and there was no restriction on drink. Characters like Alan Ashcroft would make the most of it. We would usually stay at the Mayfair Hotel in London, where there were plenty of drinks cabinets, and on one occasion Alan filled his overnight bag with bottles of spirits. As he was on his way out through the hotel lobby his bag broke and there were smashed booze bottles all over the floor.

ALAN ASHCROFT
Way back in his youth [Peter Robbins] went through a water-pistol era. He turned up at the Chiswick Empire one night before an international, sat in the front-row and let fly at Lonnie Donegan on stage. But before the next international, Donegan had been forewarned and he came to the front of the stage and retaliated with a siphon of soda. But it was all very amiable and we had a drink with Lonnie in the bar afterwards.

At the Folies Bergere one night there was a ramp leading down from the stage and as all the showgirls came down it, bosoms bristling, they were hit with ice-cold water from both sides.

ERIC EVANS
It's amazing how much notice people take of the year one is born. A front-row forward does not come into his own until he is at least 28. Let us say the press and the public got the year of my birth wrong.

PHIL DAVIES
We had no coaching, but were given match direction. Before the All Blacks match in 1954 (we went down 5-0) we were issued with free woollen vests and pants because of the frozen pitch. Soon afterwards Carston Catcheside announced that, 'If we didn't get the ball to the wings it was about as much use as my a*** is for shooting partridges.'

TED WOODWARD
The selectors were God. They didn't talk to you. They picked you because of what you were – and told you to get on with it. The only advice I ever got from an England selector came from Carston Catcheside. He said, 'Woodward, I want you to head to the corner flag as fast as you can.'

We came back by boat in 1955 after drawing with Ireland in Dublin, and on the coach journey back Steele-Bodger came and sat next to me. It was unheard of, and he was very charming. As nice as pie. I thought it was a bit strange. The next game I was dropped.

I played one more game for England. I was rung-up at short notice the following year by Doug Prentice soon after I'd cut my hand working in the butcher's shop. He told me I had been selected to play against Scotland at Murrayfield, and I told him I couldn't because of the cut. He said you must – and so I did.

MALCOLM PHILLIPS

Prentice was a former England international himself, and while a bit of a martinet he was a great man who had our respect. On one occasion he had a run-in with Lou Cannell, who played for St Mary's Hospital, a club that happened to have the same colour socks as England. As a consequence Lou never seemed to have any England socks when it came to international days, and this tested Prentice's patience to the limit. So much so that shortly before kick off in one match Cannell was in the changing room with his boots on but no socks – before Prentice burst in and chucked a pair at him.

PHIL DAVIES

As reserve in Ireland and thus non-playing I well remember in immediate English post-rationing days Lobster Thermidor and a steak as pre-match fare. Others, the forwards, led by [John] Kendall-Carpenter especially, liked a stiff sherry with a raw egg in it.

Kit and expenses? Very limited. A set of stockings per season which shrank in the wash, and a shirt for each game – all given away. A splendid cap, tie and badge but we provided the blazer.

Boots were the key equipment as Cotton Oxford sold a heavy strong protective-of-ankle model which I found heavy and not nimble-feeling for acceleration. Again the lads from the north spoke of Foster's of Wigan, boot-makers. My very light hand-made £27 pair of Kangaroo hide were my pride and joy.

NED ASHCROFT

We had good social occasions, dinners where you were treated like lords. Other than that there were very few perks – you even had to wash your own England shirt.

ERIC EVANS

I have never found it meant a thing [public schools, class and the old school tie].

Basic ability was far more important. I went to a grammar school at Audenshaw and never found it a drawback. The public school influence in rugby is grossly exaggerated.

PHIL DAVIES

Selectors, officials and most of us had been in the Services, so we understood 'good order and discipline' and its value. There were new ideas about from the PE teachers and each team had a handful, Jeff Butterfield, Frank Sykes, Alan Ashcroft and Pat Quinn among them. To some extent we were told what to do, but left to sort out how. Colonel Prentice as RFU Secretary was a stickler for punctuality

Bev Risman in full flight.

and arrangement, and was much appreciated. You knew where you were. Others had been through the Second World War with distinction. We were much in awe of Brigadier Hugh Llewellyn Glyn-Hughes, who was the first high ranking Army medical officer into Belsen on its recapture. Then there was Colonel Alfie Aslett – a real stickler and easy to offend!

They were a group we respected, but had little conversation with. We kept strong views to ourselves having seen colleagues blot their copybooks with unasked for comment.

TED WOODWARD

My dad had a butcher's shop, and when he died I had to leave the RAF and take it over. When I was with Wasps I worked in the shop on Saturday mornings before playing in the afternoon. I did that for 10 years, and playing rugby helped me tremendously in business. After that I had a sports shop, and because I was known and had contacts, I'd supply jerseys to Llanelli, the Barbarians and Middlesex. It helped me to build the business so that I was eventually able to open four shops.

Dickie Jeeps gets his backline moving during the 14-0 victory over France at Colomes, 1958.

I was offered big-money, and a butcher's shop, to go to rugby league by Salford, but I asked for advice from my old headmaster at RGS High Wycombe and a few others, and they advised me not to. I'm glad I didn't.

BEV RISMAN

The RFU was very hidebound, but I did get a very nice letter from John Tallent, the RFU President, wishing me well after I went to rugby league. So, I left on good personal terms, but at that time the national bodies went and hid behind the regulations.

At Brunel and West London Institute (Borough Road), I could coach both the rugby union and rugby league teams because it was part of my teaching career. But outside that I could not do any rugby union coaching.

For instance, I was helping John Robins with the England Students and it was suggested I represent them on an RFU committee in the 1970s. I got a personal letter from the then Secretary of the RFU, Robin Prescott, who said it would be a step too far.

PHIL DAVIES

Once we were staying in a hotel at Keswick for a trial and missionary visit to Workington. We were sharing with a rugby league side and there was a wonderful picture taken in the bar with the union selectors in duffel coats at one end, and at the other end the league directors with horn-rimmed glasses and Yorkshire woollen suits, with the mixed players in the middle.

BEV RISMAN

What drove me is selfish reasons. You do it for yourself to get into the England team and show what a good player you are – but then it becomes a team thing when you play for your mates.

There is no doubt that the 1959 Lions team spirit was very strong – probably stronger than England. But we did not get the bonding that Stuart Lancaster manages now. You met your team-mates the day before the match and often you hadn't trained together for much more than an hour.

I had 10 years of rugby league. Looking back, at international level the Lions tour was brilliant, but in my day rugby league was more physically demanding, and more skilful. There were many stoppages in union, but not so many in league.

Now rugby union is fantastic – with all the ball handling props – and I would love to play it these days.

PHIL DAVIES

I look back with pride. England were winning again, and playing less and less in 1958 I was happy to declare myself not fit enough and hand over to the very polished Malcolm Phillips.

MALCOLM PHILLIPS

The publicity was mainly newspapers, and based on the rugby itself. There was very little personality stuff. The game was very low profile in those days. I used to go to the cinema to catch up on footage of the internationals on the Pathé News, including seeing my own try against Australia for the first time.

THIRTEEN
NOT SO SWINGING SIXTIES
1961-1969

FOLLOWING THE FALSE *dawn of their Championship winning 1960 season which, in all truth, should have garnered England a Grand Slam, the 1960s slowly descended into a frustrating decade of under-performance, missed opportunities and poor selection, punctuated with seemingly random moments of brilliance, either individual or collective.*

Predominantly the rugby was grey, tentative and seemingly always played in clawing mud or six inch high savannah grass, but occasional memorable and illuminating shafts of sunlight lit up the drab landscape. Richard Sharp and Andy Hancock scored two of the greatest Test tries in history for England during this period while, by the end of the decade, David Duckham was beginning to weave his magic out wide, his hair going one way and his side step the other. Sharp was a figure so dashing and 'English' that author Bernard Cornwell named the military hero of his famous Sharpe novels after blonde fly-half from Redruth.

It was during the early 1960s that England became the first home union to organise an Antipodean tour, starting with a bang in New Zealand and Australia, much more of which anon, while England also recorded a first ever win over the Springboks during this time. The talent was there – it always is with England – but getting the strongest and most appropriate team on the field for any particular match proved a major challenge and England often seemed to lack a killer instinct. England and the RFU were still unambiguously glorying in amateurism while, even at this stage, big overseas opponents were beginning to flout IRB regulations and teams like Wales had started to hold squad sessions.

After the Championship winning success of 1960, England, although always hard to beat, endured two middling Five Nations campaigns, claiming fourth and third – although that record might have looked much healthier if they could have converted any of their three drawn games into victories. Indeed, England were remarkably prone to drawn games for much of the decade, recording seven in the Championship alone between 1961-66, which statistically is way above the average for international rugby. England sometimes seemed unable or unwilling to go for the jugular in a number of games which led to the impression that they simply lacked the confidence and self-belief to finish games off.

Opposite: Philip Judd readies himself to pounce on a loose ball against France at Twickenham in 1967.

The 1963 season, despite an atrocious winter that matched even Steele-Bodger's epic of 1947, was a last spike of excellence before a general malaise seemed to set in. A Sharp inspired England took the Championship and but for a 0-0 draw in Dublin they would have completed a Grand Slam. There was, however, a bittersweet feel to the season.

Call up the footage of England's game against Scotland in March of that year and just gasp in awe, again, at the majesty of Sharp's sensational try against the Scots in which he sold three dummies on route to the line. It is a try that routinely tops the podium when punters are invited to vote for their favourite England try and is possibly the most aesthetically 'beautiful' try of all time and yet consider this. Sharp was 24 at the time and theoretically approaching his pomp yet that try for the ages was effectively his farewell to England rugby. He knew and was leaving us something to remember him by.

In those strictly amateur days earning a living was a harsh reality that often derailed our sporting gods, and after National Service, and four years at Oxford University, Sharp considered it time to marry, settle down and pursue a career as a schoolteacher at Sherborne. He turned out occasionally for Wasps and then Bristol but retired from international rugby save for one bizarre recall in 1967 when England, at a very low ebb, persuaded Sharp out of retirement to captain the side against Australia,

There were still sporadic moments when England rugby threatened to flex its muscles and one came in the summer of 1963 when they embarked on their first ever overseas tour, a strenuous trip to New Zealand with an add on Test against Australia. It was a bold, progressive initiative, even if six full-on games in 17 days, including three Tests, was bordering on suicidal for a streamlined squad of 23 that was already lacking Sharp (who was taking his finals at Oxford before venturing into the wider world).

The tour to Australasia was considered a success despite losing all three Tests and England might have been expected to kick-on after such a seminal rugby experience and the bonding that automatically comes from such trips. Alas that wasn't the case, and a steady decline set in over the next three seasons, all dominated by Wales in the Championship, which saw England go from third, to fourth, to Wooden Spoon 'winners' under the captaincy of Budge Rogers in 1966 when they could manage just a draw against Ireland.

Selection just seemed so random. Players of known quality were wantonly discarded while others joined them in purdah after just one appearance. Talking to all concerned, a sense of paranoia clearly set in, the retention of your place in the team often becoming the priority rather than the success of the team itself.

Random moments of mesmerising brilliance, notably from the glorious David Duckham towards the end of the decade, began to taunt, as well as delight, England supporters. Sometimes it's the hope that kills you. Subconsciously England fans were always trying to whistle up another Sharp moment and, in 1965, with England staring at a miserable 3-0 defeat against Scotland on another cabbage patch of a pitch at Twickenham, it duly arrived. Two 'once in a lifetime tries' in the space of 24 months. With the game slipping away from England, the previously unheralded Andy Hancock scored one of the most exhilarating length-of-the-field tries the game has ever seen, a score that would have won the match under modern scoring values and a stunning effort that has been replayed for ever and a day. For years Hancock's wondrous effort featured on the starting reel for BBC Grandstand every Saturday afternoon and at times, during lean periods, seemed to mock England's latest efforts.

The visit of Brian Lochore's New Zealand side in 1967 further emphasised England's deficiencies, while the Lions tour to South Africa was an eye opener for the likes of England players such as John Pullin, Bob Taylor, Bob Hiller, Keith Savage and Peter Larter, who all made the tour party. The South Africans would gather for a week before the game, contrary to IRB regulations, and displayed a level of fitness way above that found in the English game.

England carried this mind-set into 1969. Something had to change and with South Africa visiting in the late autumn of '69 a mighty challenge loomed large. England seized the nettle spectacularly by deciding to name an England captain – Bob Hiller – in advance of the game and a thirty man training squad that would meet on three or four Sundays at a venue in the Midlands, either at Coventry or Leicester. It required a considerable commitment from players who had hitherto spent Sundays sleeping off a hangover or licking their wounds from the day before, but this was the level of commitment that was now required to be competitive at the top level.

The result was a stunning success, an England victory that never received the accolades it deserved mainly because history has tended to rubbish that South African team and the tour itself as the frequent anti-apartheid demonstrations dominated the news.

RICHARD SHARP

I always get rather embarrassed talking about that so-called 'try of the decade' against Scotland in 1963. Mike Weston made it with his perfect dummy run.

I had shouted a pre-arranged call with Mike that we would try a scissors – that was the actual call – but of course that always gave me the option of pulling off a dummy scissors. He cut behind me and that caused the defence to hesitate so I carried on my way. Then came another dummy which got me through the two Scotland centres – David White and Brian Henderson – and finally I was just about to pass to Jim Roberts when I could sense their fullback Colin Blaikie had already committed to covering Jim so I decided not to pass and score myself. It was definitely the right decision.

There was a thunderous noise from the crowd, the old Twickenham was a wonderfully noisy stadium when full, but the reaction on the pitch was very understated and English. In those days everybody would always look to congratulate other people rather than accept any plaudits themselves which was still considered rather poor form. I notice from the video footage – my grandchildren like to look at it on YouTube – that Malcom Phillips, who was my first captain at Oxford, did pat me on the back in a very unostentatious way.

BUDGE ROGERS (England 1961-69, 34 caps plus 2 caps for the Lions)
Richard's try was a great moment and I was lucky to probably have the best view in the house, tracking behind him doing the old openside flanker's banana run. Do they still do that?

Moves like that were Richard's great strength and genius. Richard wasn't a stepper, he had great speed and could beat almost anybody on the outside and that was the line he liked to take. He was without any doubt the greatest natural talent, along with David Duckham, I was ever privileged to play with in an England shirt. A glorious player, such speed.

RICHARD SHARP
I really worked on my speed in those days in quite a determined way, especially my speed off the mark which is so crucial. I was fitter than ever before with the possible exception of the early part of the 1962 Lions tour before I got injured. I used to go running all the time during the holidays in the fields around Redruth

Richard Sharp touches down against Scotland at Twickenham in 1963.

and I also took my togs with me whenever I played cricket, which was almost all the time every summer when I was young.

MIKE DAVIS (England 1963-70, 16 caps. England coach 1979-82)
I would like to say I was on Richard's shoulder waiting for his final pass but TV evidence suggests otherwise. In truth, after we had broken up from the scrum and got our bearing, I only caught glimpse of that final dummy and touchdown, although of course in subsequent years I have seen it many times on TV. A very special try by a special bloke. England rugby saw nowhere near enough of him in his prime.

RICHARD SHARP
The simple truth is that my career as a serious rugby player ended there that day with my try in the Scotland game, despite a rather curious recall out of retirement four years later against Australia. I had already made myself unavailable, a long time in advance, for the New Zealand tour in 1963 because my College at Oxford had been extremely good the previous year and delayed my finals exams for a year so that I could accept an invitation to tour South Africa with the 1962 Lions.

But by that summer of 1963 my life was entering a new phase. When I came down from Oxford I got married to my dear wife and obviously I needed to find a job and earn some money. To a certain extent the party was over.

While teaching at Sherborne I helped coach the Sherborne XVs which I very much enjoyed and could only play sporadically for Wasps, and it was proving almost impossible to make the matches some days. I would also have to rush off afterwards and miss the enjoyment of relaxing with friends. I switched to Bristol but again that was difficult as I would be teaching until Saturday lunchtimes and I'm afraid I had also reached that stage of life that when we were at an away match and the team had a vote whether to stay on for a dance or a few drinks all I wanted to really do was get home to my family.

MICKY STEELE-BODGER
I was the assistant manager and touch judge, would you believe, for the England tour of New Zealand and Australia in 1963, and looking back it was an extraordinary affair. Six matches in 17 days after taking nearly three days to get down there. The itinerary was put together by the Kiwis who were rather keen to show us off, and bury us at the same time.

Mike Weston was captain and we only took 23 players which was nowhere near enough – and John Owen, the Coventry lock, got injured very early on. We were quite clever in one way in that went out westaways – London, Amsterdam, Vancouver and then we stopped off in Hawaii for the best part of a day en route

down to Auckland. Economy all the way, naturally. Hawaii proved pretty popular, the surf was up and they served some interesting cocktails down in the beach bars. As you can imagine, the boys were pretty relaxed by the time they climbed back into the plane and slept all the way to New Zealand.

Once we got to Auckland, we headed straight for Wellington a game three days later against the locals which we only went and won 14-9, which rather shocked the New Zealand media. Then it was down to Dunedin four days later and another 14-9 defeat, this time against Otago before the first Test in Auckland, where we played very well indeed for an hour and led 11-3 before running out of steam and losing 21-11. We were outplayed in the end at Eden Park and then had to play Hawke's Bay at Napier a couple of days later – we ran out of steam there – but England definitely deserved to win the following week when we went down 9-6 at Lancaster Park in Christchurch. That was one of the best displays I ever saw from England.

Our front-row of Phil Judd, Bert Godwin and Ron Jacobs absolutely murdered their opponents and our scrum was a great source of strength. They twice shoved the All Blacks back over their own line, but we got nothing from the ref.

On the way back home we popped into the Sydney Sports Ground three days after that second Test and went down 18-9 to Australia in a very wet game when we didn't adapt to conditions. We still scored three tries, mind. It was a mission impossible if you like, but England dug very deep.

MIKE DAVIS

Jetlag hadn't been invented, so we didn't know we were expected to feel rubbish for a week after we arrived. Whether by accident or design we took the scenic route out and that stopover in Hawaii proved an inspired call. Poor old 'Bomber' Thorne, the Bristol hooker who was on tour with us, took too much sun in Hawaii on one of the canoe riggers we all went out on. He was bare-chested and got terribly burnt and tried to hide it from the management, which worked up until the dreaded moment came for the first training session in Wellington and half an hour's scrummaging practice was ordered. Ouch.

I injured my left shoulder pretty badly in the second Test, in fact I dislocated it, but in those days you couldn't bring on replacements. There was a strong spirit in the side and we really fancied out chances of winning so I was very reluctant to go off. I stayed on and packed down on the right hand side of the scrum and sort of threw my left arm over my second-row partner David Perry for every scrum. It was pretty painful but just about doable.

Opposite: Richard Sharp heads to the dressing room having steered his side to victory over Scotland at Twickenham in 1963

At the first line-out after my injury, I leapt and caught the ball one handed basketball-style, which so surprised Colin Meads that I charged 15 yards upfield and set up a promising attack. We seemed to take heart after that and played very well indeed. It was our game really, we should have had a pushover try decision and in the end we were denied the draw in an odd fashion. Don Clarke kicked a 60-yard goal from a mark at the second attempt. Phil Judd and Ron Jacobs, I think it was, had charged his first attempt early so the ref awarded a re-take with no charge allowed. We were a bit pissed off with that.

BUDGE ROGERS

It was a completely ludicrous schedule but great fun, an extraordinary mix of old style touring and some high quality rugby from us in the two New Zealand Tests. Anybody who witnessed that second Test in Christchurch will tell you it was daylight robbery, a real miscarriage of justice. It was the closest I ever came to beating them in nine meetings.

I was one of the five lucky buggers who got to play in all six games on tour and I was ready to drop by the time we headed home via some ridiculous route, the cheapest possible no doubt. I'm pretty sure we ended up in Rome for an afternoon at one stage. The tour was very ad hoc, a pioneering effort and none the worse for it. Of course we had no physio or anything like that.

Micky Steele-Bodger ran the touch line and I have this ever-lasting image of him jumping up and down and screaming blue murder in one of the New Zealand Tests when I dropped on a ball and got a boot in my back from Colin Meads for my trouble. Meads was a hell of a player, I had a lot of admiration for him and indeed New Zealand rugby generally, but he could be a bit naughty. We always had some very tough, durable guys in England teams but we never really bred players like Colin. It wasn't in our DNA. England, as supposedly the originators of the game, were rather expected to be above all that.

MIKE WESTON (England 1960-68, 29 caps plus 6 caps for the Lions)

Ah, Andy Hancock's try against Scotland in 1965… What a beauty! When the ball came out I realised there was no winger on the left side but someone was approaching me fast from that direction. I managed to draw him and get the ball away to Andy.

ANDY HANCOCK (England 1965-66, 3 caps)

My wife Heather, then my fiancée, is a very proud Scot so I'm not sure I wasn't in the doghouse afterwards. It was the strangest thing, but my memory is of complete silence through the entire run, although I am told the crowd was going mad. I was in my own world. I never scored a try from that distance either before or since, it was a complete one-off and I must admit a source of much pride although, I've got no reminders in the house except for a team picture of the day, not that I need any reminders. You never forget a moment like that.

I was reasonably quick and I was one of those rugby players who was a yard quicker again in rugby boots and with a ball tucked under my arm, but I still think it was my overall fitness that got me through at Twickenham that day, my endurance as much as my speed. I could not have been in better shape.

The previous month I had been called into the team late on the Friday night to make my debut against France at Twickenham the next day. I was at work and my mother phoned to say I was needed at home straightaway because some chap from England had been on the phone. I went straight back, mother handed me a packed bag with all my kit and a dinner jacket, or at least the poshest jacket I possessed. I didn't ever have time to be nervous about the forthcoming match.

A month later against Scotland I was the first choice at Twickenham and in many ways I looked on it as my debut proper. It was a well-taken try but a little bit lucky as well. We, and by that I really mean Micky Weston, caught the Scots out by deciding to run it from so deep. It was such a dreadful day and pitch, it just wasn't a day for running rugby. And then Ian Laughland was a little unlucky when he slipped as he tried to tackle me for the first time. Budge Rogers was running hard in support and I think he then distracted Stewart Wilson who thought I might be thinking of the inside pass.

The try line seemed miles away but I kept going and Ian Laughland only got back to me right at the end and tackled me around the ankles but I was over the line. I was absolutely exhausted but suddenly, as I lay there for a second, I could hear the crowd.

My abiding memory, or thought, after the game is that I must, at some stage in my senior career, score another try like that to prove it wasn't a fluke, but alas it wasn't to be. I suffered a lot of injury problems during the first half of the following season and then when I finally got back in against France in Paris I suffered a very nasty hamstring tear early in the game. I should have come off but we weren't allowed replacements in those days and I stayed on the pitch doing untold damage. Madness.

Playing for England was a wonderful experience and my only regret is that it was such a fleeting part of my career. It was a bit difficult to come to terms with for a while but in the amateur days you just got on with your life and job. Happily, when the hamstring finally healed, I enjoyed some of the best rugby days of my entire life as I stepped down a few levels and played with Stafford, and, would you believe, the Chelmsford Undertakers, who were a great veteran over-35s team dedicated to playing good rugby and having fun.

BUDGE ROGERS

For the second time in two years I had a ringside seat for one of the great England tries. Andy Hancock was a very interesting player indeed. He didn't have a long England career and through sheer hard work and dedication he elevated himself to a level of all round fitness and strength that was almost unsustainable as an amateur. He trained so hard, he was like a prototype of what might be achieved in terms of conditioning in the professional era. As he ran I tried to track him all the way, in fact there was the hint of a dummy to me at one stage. It was a tremendous, heroic run that late in a gruelling old muddy game.

BOB HILLER (England 1968-1972, 19 caps)

I was lucky enough to be one of the England guys who toured South Africa with the Lions in 1968, and it was pretty obvious to all of us that if ever England wanted to be competitive on a consistent basis at the top level we just had to be better organised generally. There had to be a better system. We didn't have any leagues, no competitions, you couldn't win a prize or a cup, England had no coach, we coached ourselves along with the captain and the selectors. We would meet on the Friday and decide how we were going to play there and then. Even as amateurs it was pretty unsustainable going forward.

For the 1969-70 season, for the first time, the RFU decided to appoint a coach and turned to Don White. They also selected a squad of 30, I was made captain and a number of Sunday training sessions were organised at Coventry and Leicester in the two or three months leading into the game. We had to pay our own expenses, of course, and in fairness that wasn't just the RFU being tight. The point was if they had paid us expenses we would be deemed to have 'met' in an organised training session as a team, which was still very much against the IRB regulations

The famous Don White story comes from our first session that autumn. He gave us a bit of a pep talk about how things were going to change from this point onwards and England were going to be a lean, mean machine etc and finished off by saying, 'Right lads, let's get this session underway. Take up your usual positions.' At which point we all went and stood under the posts waiting for a conversion.

MIKE DAVIS

I took over as captain when Bob Hiller went off with about ten minutes to go in the mtach against South Africa and we spent the entire time camped in our 25 under the old North Stand. We won the game but we were hanging on at the end. I only had one decision to make during my entire 'reign' as England captain and that came at a scrum right on our line when somebody else had gone off injured and we were temporarily down to seven men in the pack. As we went down to try and resist a pushover try I got a tap on my shoulder; it was Chris Wardlow, the big centre from Cumbria, and he asked, 'Can I help?'

I said, 'We will make our own arrangements thanks very much.' A bit ungracious perhaps, but we were in the zone, just concentrating on keeping the Boks at bay. Sorry Chris, you didn't deserve that, it was a nice thought!

BOB HILLER

It was my first match as England captain and the importance of the win caught me by surprise. I'm not sure many of us realised at the time that it was England's first win over the Boks but it was definitely a big boost. When I look back on my England career that was the highlight right there, certainly from a team point of view. It was a pretty good team we fielded that day. Alas it wasn't long before the selectors started to split the team up again.

DAVID DUCKHAM (England 1969-1976, 36 caps plus 3 caps for the Lions)

Some of the boys insist they didn't know it was England's first win over the Boks but that must be the crew who never read the newspapers! I was very well aware of our poor record against them and felt very nervous – in a good way – but also a bit daunted before the fixture. What was it about these southern hemisphere teams that made them into supermen and apparently unbeatable? I survived the axe after the big defeat in Wales and come early autumn England surprised everybody by naming a 30-man training squad and pre-selecting Bob Hiller as captain with Don White as coach. It was pretty radical stuff for England, although New Zealand and Wales, with Ray Williams at the helm, had been doing it for a few years.

It was a hell of game, incredibly physical and intense, and a bit of an overlooked classic in my opinion.

BOB TAYLOR (England 1966-1971, 16 caps plus 4 caps for the Lions)

It was Dick Greenwood, Will Greenwood's dad, who looked up the IRB regulations which stipulated that a 'team could not gather for organised practice until 48 hours before kick-off'. Dick considered this for a moment and came up with the suggestion that as a team obviously consisted of 15 players there is no reason why 16 or 20 or 30 of us shouldn't meet at any time which suited us for a spot of practice.

I found those sessions great, I loved them. Yes, it was a big commitment in those amateur days and we were paying our way, but the players welcomed it. We knew it would give us a better chance of beating the Boks, and England, generally, were fed up losing to these big teams.

BUDGE ROGERS

The squad system came too late for me, agonisingly so. When I was made captain for the '66 Championship I rang around the team and suggested we start trying to gather on Wednesday nights at Richmond, under the lights, and have the occasional ad hoc training session. The very next day I had a phone call and stern talking to from the RFU secretary Bob Weighilll: 'I want to be able to assure the RFU President that you are not going to have this run around.' I had to back down, the game was up.

I felt very frustrated not being involved in '69, but I was part of the cull following our big 30-9 defeat against the Welsh in our previous game at the end of the 1969 Championship. We got hammered – it was the day Maurice Richards scored four tries – and there was always going to be a fall out. As captain I knew I was well and truly in the firing line.

I wasn't quite 30 and felt I had a good deal still to offer, but that was it as far as Test rugby was concerned. I did, curiously, get recalled for a warm-up match before the RFU Centenary game between England and a President's XV. I'm never sure if that was a capped match or not but the warm-up was hard going against essentially a World XV. I remember early on I got a kick in the back from Colin Meads – another one – who as we got up informed me 'That's for Waka.'

Long memories those Kiwis. Back in 1967 I had been playing for the East Midlands against the All Blacks and was having my usual ding-dong battle with Waka Nathan at the back of the line-out. He was a great player but used to get away with absolute murder and finally I let him have a short arm jab and connected so sweetly that I broke his cheekbone. That was his tour over and there was a bit of a fuss about it, although I have never met an All Black who wouldn't have done exactly what I did! Anyway, four years later, in a celebration Centenary game in front of a packed house, it was payback time!

BOB HILLER

The modern day rugby players and fan will find probably it curious but the trial system – three matches of increasing importance – was a big thing, and of course it was the system that existed if you wanted to play for your country, so you just had to get on with it. It started with Whites versus Blues then I think we went to Probables v Possibles, which of course we all renamed as 'Improbables v Impossibles', and the final game was always England against the Rest.

Wales had a built-in advantage in that although they had 17 or 18 first class clubs, although in reality the vast majority of quality players gravitated to four clubs – Llanelli, Swansea, Cardiff and Newport – and they played each other four times a season in front of big crowds. Those games were a big step above any domestic rugby we played in England and provided that sort of halfway house to Test rugby. I fancy they also made selection a bit easier by concentrating the talent. There were many more club combinations used to playing with each other.

International rugby seemed five or ten yards faster than most England clubs games. Of course there were English players who could make that step up, but identifying them was not an easy business. I spoke to Jeff Butterfield, who had been a selector, and he admitted it was virtually impossible, logistically, to do the job to their satisfaction. The selectors then didn't have a motorway system, travel was pretty difficult and they just couldn't get around to slightly lesser clubs. There was no TV coverage worthy of the name, no internet, video clips, YouTube or anything. Having said that, some selections were just incomprehensible. Mike Davis was a world class lock throughout the sixties, it was madness that he was ever dropped. He should have finished with 35-40 caps like Budge.

RAY FRENCH (England 1961, 4 caps)
Those trial matches were strange old games. There were three at various outposts around the country and except for Alan Ashcroft I didn't know a soul and socially felt very out of my league. It was difficult. Before one trial, in Coventry, the RFU put both teams up in a hotel and we all dined out together the night before the match, a full six course banquet. Lobster Thermador was one of the courses and I sat there in a blind panic not knowing what to do. Alan told me I could pick it up and eat with my hands but I thought it was a wind-up and waited until I saw some of the big names and Varsity players do just that before I dived in.

I was primarily a No 8 as a union player, but to my surprise I was selected at lock next to David Marques for the opener again Wales at the Arms Park, which was an absolute quagmire in those days. They outscored us two tries to one and the reports suggest it was a decent game, but I remember hardly any rugby being played. Quite why 60,000 people would pay good money to watch that I have no idea.

JOHN PULLIN (England 1966-1976, 42 caps plus 7 caps for the Lions)
I might be out on a limb here but I used to find the old trial matches incredibly testing and among the hardest games I ever played. In that respect they were good. It might just have been my position, hooker, which puts you right up against your direct opponent all the time. One of the most depressing moments in sport was at half-time of a trial match when the selectors switched you from the Probables to the Possibles.

My two best rugby experiences with England, later in my career, were the 1972 tour to South Africa and then New Zealand the following year when there was just a manger, myself as captain and maybe one selector travelling with us. I had a much bigger input, which meant the senior group of players indirectly had an input because obviously I spoke to them all the time. I didn't win every call but the team that took the park was pretty much the team I wanted and trusted.

BUDGE ROGERS

Obviously we had no coach so the only time we discussed our tactics was at the Friday night meal. In fact in my entire playing career – and at one time I was the most capped England player ever – only one person ever talked to me about playing flanker, my approach and tactics, and that was Don White who used to go through the game with me over a post-match pint when I first broke into the Midlands side and played alongside him. And that was the sum total of my 'coaching and analysis' in my entire senior career.

The England practices on Fridays were nothing more than walk throughs – a few lineout calls for the forwards and a couple of set-piece plays in the backs. There was no opportunity to do any live scrummaging with just a couple of reserves and arthritic selectors in suits knocking about the place. There was no such thing as an England tracksuit, you just wore your often unwashed club kit from the week before. We had to provide our own white shorts for every match and make a pair of England socks last the season. We were given new England shirts for every match.

MIKE DAVIS

When I made my debut against Wales in 1963 I couldn't afford proper rugby boots so I bought a pair of much cheaper football boots and dyed them black. In those days your England cap – the very reason you played the game as an amateur and made all those sacrifices – was simply posted to you a few days after your debut. There was no fuss at all and none of those initiation ceremonies, the compulsory singing of songs and much worse. My cap arrived safely enough but a couple of seasons later – 1965 – when I was in the Navy doing National Service at HMS Raleigh, I got a message from the sentry gate to come down and collect a parcel addressed to me. It was an international cap intended for Dave Rosser who had made his debut against Wales earlier that season. I sent it back to the RFU by return of post, I hope Dave got the cap OK.

There was no TLC those days with phone calls and quiet chats ahead of the selection. If you were dropped, it was pretty brutal. And pretty random as well. In my debut season, 1963, we started with a win in Wales – our last for 28 years – and then a 0-0 draw in the mud at Lansdowne Road, which actually cost us a Grand Slam at the time. I was then dropped for the France game and had also been dropped for the next game against Scotland but played in circumstances that you would never countenance these days. I heard, on the radio news as usual, that I was a travelling reserve for the game at Twickenham which was no big deal really because of course there were no replacements allowed on the pitch. What it meant was that I had to travel up with the team on the Friday just in case one of the second-rows turned an ankle at the gentle Friday afternoon run-out.

I was at St Luke's College at the time and you scarcely get to draw breath down there. On the Tuesday night of the Scotland game, as well as the normal activities during the day, I played in a big basketball match in the evening – I loved my basketball – and then on the Wednesday night I played a pretty hectic St Luke's College rugby match at Torquay, my home club. The Devon sides used to love having a pop at the students, so there was no holding back, but I was among friends and afterwards had a fair few beers, as you do. And then on the Thursday night I played another important basketball match for the team – it was the crunch part of our season – before finally getting on the train for London on Friday morning. I arrived for a late lunch and really tucked in – starving impoverished student and all that – and then I got a tap on the shoulder from Dick Manley who said, 'Mike, listen to this,' at which point Tom Pargetter appeared. 'Mike I've got tonsillitis and thought I would shake if off but it's no good I can't play tomorrow,' whispered poor old Tom. Would that happen these days? I do not think so.

BUDGE ROGERS

I don't agree with people who think the old Twickenham was noisier, by the way. The crowd was hugely well behaved in those days, very polite. No booing ever, silence for all kicks, which was good, but some didn't know the game well enough to cheer in the right places, which wasn't so good. We had anthems but no presentations.

And of course we had the anthem at the end as well. I was sprawled on the ground at the end of the 1962 game against Wales when the band struck up again with the anthem. I had broken free and had chipped over Kevin Coslett who took me out with a body check and I did an AC shoulder joint. I would have scored for certain but the referee Mr Taylor from Scotland was unmoved. It would have won the game, as it was it finished 0-0. Another draw.

NIGEL HORTON (England 1969-1980, 20 caps)

I was 19 when I was selected as an England travelling reserve in 1968, so I was lucky enough to achieve that at a very early age. However, things weren't quite what I expected. When we got to Paris on the Friday before the France game the first thing the reserves did was assemble in the hotel lobby and it was then decided that we would have a drink in every bar on the side of the road our hotel was on. It was a long boulevard and none of us got back in a fit state.

I had a bit of a chip on my shoulder because I was working class, whereas the majority of people playing rugby were middle-class, or teachers. I wanted to get there, and to wear the jersey, and to have the Queen shake your hand at Twickenham was a tremendous honour.

I also had issues with the selectors. One of them cost me two years of my England career. I won my first cap against Ireland in 1969 at Lansdowne Road, and although I kept my place throughout that Championship I was young and not worldly when England played their last game against Wales at Cardiff Arms Park. At the post-match dinner, Wales were one of the few countries that went for suits rather than black-tie, mainly because many of the players were working-class and black-tie was something that they would rarely use. I only had one suit, but it was heavy, and it had been a beautiful day so it was quite warm. The Welsh and English players sat on mixed tables that evening, and because it was hot I took my jacket off.

A selector came up to me and said, 'Nigel, I think you should put your jacket on, it's upsetting a few people, and they are talking about it.' I turned to the other players on the table and asked if it was upsetting them, and they said it was no problem. That wasn't good enough, so I said, 'Are you telling me as a selector to put my jacket on?' He said, 'Yes', and so I did it.

Then, at two o'clock in the morning when I wandered into the players' room, the selector in question was in there having a drink and wanted to discuss it further – and I didn't. He was insistent, and I told him where to go. I didn't play for England again until 1971, which was the same season that selector left the panel.

JOHN PULLIN

I never for a moment started my rugby career with the dream of playing for England let alone captaining them in front of 70,000 people. I started playing with Bristol Saracens to get a day off working at the family farm – with England, it was partly pride in representing your country and partly self-pride in not being considered second best to anybody else in your position.

And that emotion stays with you. I was dropped for good by England in 1976 when Peter Wheeler took over – and it was the right decision, I can see that now – but I kept playing for Bristol, for another couple of seasons, and all the time you are physically 'able' you think deep down you should still be playing for England. Working on the farm kept me very fit and, ridiculous as it sounds, right up to my late 40s even when I was long retired I thought deep down I could still be doing it for England.

Mentally I've never retired. If England phoned up tomorrow and asked could I get up to Pennyhill Park to help out I would be there like a shot! Seriously I would.

I have never understood any player who 'retires' from international duty. It's not your decision, mate. If you are fit and playing you must always be available for your country. What 'retiring from international rugby' normally means is that the player concerned isn't big enough to handle being dropped and senses the axe is coming.

MIKE DAVIS

I'm an English patriot, passionate about rugby and wanting to play for England was such a part of my make up that I took it for granted, it wasn't even worthy of comment. I was never the emotional type on the pitch and I found it very easy to detach myself totally from that side of it. I became ultra-practical and clinical, perhaps abnormally so.

When I was a trainee teacher at Luke's, one of my major thoughts all the time when playing for England was how much I was learning and how all this experience must surely make me a better coach and teacher. There was so much to be learned by playing for England. Not the most romantic approach, I know!

All those selectorial changes didn't help. When you get selected you meet up with the team and you look around and you couldn't help yourself. You think, 'Yes he's a good player I'm glad he's aboard,' and I'm afraid in a few cases I would look at somebody and think, 'What is he doing here?'

RICHARD SHARP

I felt very simple emotions when I played for England – pride, and what a privilege it all was. For a number of matches I was in a state of virtual disbelief that I was partnering the great Dickie Jeeps at half-back and that he used to come and pick me up at my College in Oxford and drive me down to Richmond on a Thursday night before a game. But I got a little surge of confidence whenever I pulled on the white jersey. I used to think, 'Well, I can't be that bad because here I am again, they have picked me again.' I felt very fulfilled with my England career, no regrets. My only regret in rugby was getting injured in South Africa in 1962 when I was in my very best form.

One of my fondest rugby memories was driving from Twickenham to the post match banquet at the Hilton in London with my girlfriend, soon to become my dear wife. I rather fancy it was after a good win against Ireland in 1962. Anyway a bus drew up alongside and it was rammed to the gills with Cornwall supporters in the county colours. Trelawny's Army, or at least a detachment thereof, up in town for the match.

They had recognised the two of us, in fact a number of them were friends, and proceeded to provide an escort to the Hilton singing all of our wonderful Cornish rugby songs at full volume – Trelawny's song which is the 'Song of the Western Men', 'Lil Lize', 'Lamorna' and all the others. I was there to play for England and they shouted themselves horse for England but at that moment it felt a very Cornish occasion as well. A marvellous moment combining all the great loves of my life, really.

I've only got one England shirt, which is of course for the family. I gave Redruth a complete set of shirts from the Five Nations I had collected through swaps. They hang in the saloon bar which is the best place for them. I still follow all the England games closely on the TV; I was quite ill in 2007 and don't get about much these days. I love these evening games when I can have a cup of tea before the start and a glass of whisky at half time, although I'm not so sure I would have enjoyed those evening kick offs if I was working as a rugby correspondent any more.

BOB TAYLOR

I look back on my England career with total pleasure. There is a temptation to feel disappointed at not winning more matches but I was, and remain, immensely proud of my 16 caps. Playing for England meant absolutely everything to me and encompassed everything I had learned at school and then Northampton. Many people – parents, friends, club colleagues, work colleagues – had a hand in my rugby career and those caps were their reward as much as mine.

A lot of people underestimate English passion at their peril. English people generally are extremely tolerant, generous and mild mannered – it is one of our most admirable traits as a nation – and there is sometimes this expectation that our rugby team will play in that image. Well that impression is not wholly correct. As a nation we might queue politely and let traffic out with a friendly nod of the head but as a rugby team we liked to roll our sleeves up and get stuck in. If you make it up the ladder and get picked for England you will be a passionate rugby player, believe me.

BOB HILLER

It sounds trite but I did literally dream of playing for England, running out at Twickenham, as a sports-mad youngster. And although 40 years on our preparations might seem a bit casual and Heath Robinson to the modern generation, we were always very passionate about trying to win for England, it meant everything to us. I was never one to wear my emotions on my sleeve, there were no tears or great emotion at the anthems. I was very competitive. To use the modern expression 'I was in the zone', and I was operating in my own space for much of the time. During the match I would occasionally let the crowd in but most of the time I was deep in concentration which was a product of my pretty manic desire to win.

I have a feeling that ultra-competitive nature might have made me a bit of a bully as a captain, although we had a reasonable record when I was in charge. I took the same full-on approach at whatever level I played, even for the Quins 5th XV – I often got accused of playing those games like I was 'still an international Hiller'.

DAVID DUCKHAM

I was always pretty emotional about playing for England and although, in all honesty, our national anthem is not the most inspiring piece of music, every time I hear it I immediately find myself back at Lansdowne Road in 1969 when I made my debut against Ireland. A big part of it for me was living the dream and connecting with my hopes and inspirations as a youngster.

My sidestep was totally down to the great Peter 'Jacko' Jackson, the brilliant Coventry wing, watching his as a schoolboy and trying to mimic him, as you do. I didn't really have exceptional pace at Test level so I had to develop another weapons. You knew it was coming with Jacko but it was still unstoppable. And on top of the side-step he used to sell a dummy as well and that was real skill which I spent years trying to replicate. Put a sidestep and a dummy together properly and you really are in business. I can feel my heart racing now remembering watching him and whispering to myself: 'Give it to Jacko, give it to Jacko.' He was my hero and inspiration without any question.

I was lucky enough to get to know Jacko very well and very early in my career, just before my England debut, I enjoyed a pint or two with him one night after a game and, well frankly, asked him how I could make a success of things if the England call came. I was desperate to do well for England. Peter had a think and boiled it down like this: 'Whatever your pre-match routine for Coventry, David, make it exactly the same as your England routine, but always be aware that your early matches in an England shirt will pass in the blink of an eye. The way you first survive and then flourish playing international rugby is that you do exactly the things you do for your club and county, but twice as quick. You speed the film up, if you like.'

FOURTEEN
WE MIGHT NOT BE ANY GOOD...
1970-1975

IN TERMS OF *wasted talent entwined with occasional wondrous results, there are few eras in the annals of international rugby that eclipse the extraordinary tale of the England team during the 1970s. It was a decade graced by some of the greatest players and biggest characters to have worn the red rose – among them John Pullin, David Duckham, Roger Uttley, Fran Cotton, Tony Neary, Bill Beaumont, Peter Wheeler, Andy Ripley and Mike Burton – but it was also one of stark underachievement and heartache for players and supporters alike.*

There was no period of bust and boom quite like it. It was a decade in which England failed to win a single Championship title outright and in 1972 they had their worst finish in the tournament, losing every match. The high point was a share of the title in a five way split the following season.

What is notable in an era in which they were overshadowed by exceptional Welsh and French sides in Europe, is that although England lost frequently they were not easy-beats, and the margins of defeat were rarely emphatic. However, the most riveting aspect of a topsy-turvy decade was that it was marked by two resounding against-all-odds away victories over the big southern hemisphere superpowers, beating South Africa in Johannesburg in 1972, and New Zealand in Auckland in 1973.

To this day that makes England the only home union side to have won Tests in South Africa and New Zealand. On both occasions England were captained by the phlegmatic 1971 Lions Test hooker Pullin, a Gloucestershire farmer who was not only a fine player and a calm, steadying influence on the pitch, but also had a gift for droll understatement off it.

In between those two landmark overseas victories there was a highlight closer to home of even greater magnitude which took rugby into the political arena around the Irish 'Troubles'.

Despite the Welsh and the Scots refusing to travel to away matches against the Irish the previous season (1972) for fear of terrorist reprisals, the RFU was determined to honour the fixture. After a cursory debate, the majority of the England squad agreed with their union, and the team that took the field at Lansdowne Road in February of 1973 was met with a standing ovation that lasted, according to some accounts, for the best part of five minutes. After defeat in Dublin, Pullin's remark that, 'We may not be

Opposite: The two forward packs compete at a lineout during Ireland's 18-9 win in Dublin in February 1973.

any good, but at least we turn up,' delivered at the post-match dinner went down as one of sport's great one-liners.

Pullin's predecessor as captain was Bob Hiller, another Englishman with a dry sense of humour. In 1970, England lost to Wales, Scotland and France, and in 1971 the RFU's Centenary season fizzled out as they succumbed to Wales, were beaten by Scotland twice, and were outclassed by the RFU President's XV. Hiller, one of the best goal-kickers of the era, scored 49 out of England's 55 points in his five appearances in 1971.

When Hiller was axed midway through the 1972 Five Nations, a whitewash followed before Pullin took over as captain – with prospects for their forthcoming tour of South Africa looking bleak. Instead, they went through South Africa unbeaten before recording one of the all-time upsets, sending the Springboks to an 18-9 defeat in front of 77,000 spectators at Ellis Park. Even at altitude the Springboks had no answer to an inspired England outfit in which two new caps scored all their points – fullback Sam Doble kicked 14 of them, and wing Alan Morley added the remainder with a try – and a third, Gloucester flanker John Watkins, was outstanding.

There is no doubt that the England team of the seventies was sprinkled with stardust, with players such as Duckham, Pullin, Peter Dixon, Cotton, Uttley, Neary and Wheeler in the world class category. Nor, despite the constant setbacks, was there a suggestion of anything other than great pride in wearing the red rose jersey, with players such as Burton describing it as a life-altering experience. The downside, however, was that the team suffered from a dysfunctional national structure and inconsistent selection policies. Clubs were strongest in the Midlands (Coventry and Moseley) and the South West (Bristol and Gloucester), and to an extent in London and the South East, but with a county and regional overlay. This contrasted with the North, where the clubs were smaller, and, underpinned by Lancashire and Yorkshire, county and regional rugby was king. This resulted in the best often not playing the best and, with national selectors invariably pushing players from their own regions, there was a great deal of player movement in and out of the England team, which had the effect of often undermining both team morale and confidence. A case in point is that of Jan Webster, the buzzing Moseley scrum-half who was the man-of-the-match in the 16-10 victory over New Zealand in front of 72,000 at Eden Park, but who was dropped two months later for the first match of the following season against Australia. Webster, who was the linchpin in the three tries to two triumph over the All Blacks, was stunned – as were most of his team-mates.

With this perplexing selection process in place, players became afraid to express themselves, and often there was a safety-first mentality which undercut the team's self-belief. With the exception of Cotton there was barely anyone, even a 1971 Lions Test flanker like Dixon, who did not get the chop.

Occasionally the selectors stumbled on the right formula, such as in 1974 when

England held the monstrous French pack to earn a 12-12 draw at the Parc des Princes and followed it up by recording their sole victory of the decade over Wales, 16-12 at Twickenham.

Apart from that the only time when things came together was on tour, where, away from the vagaries of selectorial meddling the Englishmen bonded, forging a team spirit and unity of purpose against the foreign foe which carried them to victory in South Africa and New Zealand.

BOB HILLER

I used to try about ten drop-goals a match for Harlequins and drive them all quietly mad. We had a winger, John Cox, who was my best man, who must have scored 30 tries chasing my missed drop-goals over the seasons.

I tried a drop-goal in just about every match I ever played. I had landed a few drop-goals from that same position (45 yards out) over the years for Quins – but never two in the same game from the same spot as I did against the Irish in 1970. The first wasn't hit very well, it was a bit scruffy, and it crept over. But the second was probably the best I ever hit. It came straight out of the middle and went for miles. You hit two or three of those in your life.

MIKE DAVIS

We lost 14-5 at Murrayfield (in 1970) and as usual I got the first hint of my fate on the one o'clock news the next week when I wasn't in the team. Mike Leadbetter came in for me to partner Peter Larter. Because I wasn't picked I played for Harlequins against London Welsh at Old Deer Park the day England were playing France, and the result of the England v France game was read out over the PA. We were just gathering for a line-out when the announcement was made and five of the London Welsh pack shook me by the hand for missing the game [England lost 35-13].

ROGER UTTLEY (England 1973-1980, 23 caps plus 4 caps for the Lions)

The whole of the 1970s was chequered. I'll never forget that when I was England coach and we went down for one of the first warm weather training sessions in Portugal in the late 1980s Geoff Cooke introduced me to the squad. He said I was part of the worst decade in English rugby. Ever. I gave him a sideways look.

PETER DIXON (England 1971-1978, 22 caps plus 3 caps for the Lions)

It was an honour playing for England and I look back on it with great pride. I made my England debut against the President's XV in 1971, but that was legitimised by the 1971 Lions selection that came before it.

PETER ROSSBOROUGH (England 1971-1975, 7 caps)

After I'd won my first England cap in 1971 and been dropped immediately after losing to Wales I felt absolutely desperate. Despair. Obviously, also reading it in a newspaper didn't help. Being picked was a source of tremendous pride – for my family also, because it came a couple of years after my dad had died. We lost 22-6 to the Welsh, and I was travelling back up by train to Durham University, where I was student, after playing for Coventry against Richmond at Coundon Road. When I had to change trains at York I picked up a paper and read about it. I guess you couldn't contact players as easily then as you can now with mobiles. I was not thrilled with the way I played – after spilling a high ball by Barry John I was hit hard by Arthur Lewis, and Gerald Davies scored. The only two players dropped were me and my Coventry teammate Barry Ninnes, but there were plenty of others who didn't play as well as they could. After that Bob Hiller came back, and Tony Jorden also came on the scene, and it took me two years to get back into the side.

CHRIS RALSTON (England 1971-1975, 22 caps plus 1 cap for the Lions)

I played my best rugby at the age of 23, but I didn't get to play for England until I was 28. I was long-haired, and slightly anti-establishment. On one occasion Albert

Nigel Starmer-Smith spins the ball to his backline against Wales in 1970.

Agar, who was one of the England selectors, came up to me after a game when I had just moved from No.8 to second-row, and said to me that I should be playing No.8. I didn't know who he was and was irritated, so I told him to get lost. I guess that might not have helped.

TONY NEARY (England 1971-1980, 43 caps plus 1 cap for the Lions)
You usually heard about England selection through the local press guys, like the *Manchester Evening News*.

NIGEL HORTON
I was dropped again at the end of the 1971 season, along with Jacko Page, after the first of two consecutive games against Scotland, the first in the Championship at Twickenham, and the second the Centenary celebration match at Murrayfield. I was at the post-match dinner in London and we had such a good time that I didn't hear one of the speeches. However, Jacko and I must have offended certain alickadoos who were at the dinner because we were both dropped for the match at Murrayfield, whereas the Scottish players on our table both played.

Gordon Brown, the Scotland and Lions lock, later made a fortune from telling the story on the after-dinner circuit how delighted he was that I was dropped because after we trooped off the pitch at Twickenham I'd said to him, 'Gordon, I'm going to sort you out next week.'

BOB HILLER
We lost to Scotland twice in a week in 1971 – we went up to Murrayfield seven days later for the SRU Centenary game – which was pretty typical of us in those days. Somebody decided that we were going to run everything that day, and that included if Scotland kicked long from the kick-off. Anyway they did kick-off long. I caught it and passed it inside to Jeremy Janion and on to Cowman. Cowman passed to Spencer, who promptly dropped it, and John Frame picked it up and scored under the posts. The recording afterwards showed us that the score came in the 13th second of the match, but I can tell you we looked at the clock and it hadn't even reached 3pm. We had kicked off a minute early so we were five down before the game had even started! A lot of good players in that Scotland team, mind.

MARTIN COOPER (England 1973-1977, 11 caps)
After being picked for an England trial from Wolverhampton in 1971 I was invited to join Moseley. The following season I scored a try on the wing when the Midlands Counties (West) beat the All Blacks 16-8 at Moseley. A few weeks later I had a call from Air Commodore Weighill, the RFU secretary, whose first words to

me were, 'Cooper, have you got a dinner jacket?' I didn't have one, but I told him I had a club blazer. He then told me to get down to Porthcawl because I was needed as a replacement for the England match against Wales in Cardiff.

MIKE BURTON (England 1972-1978, 17 caps)

Eventually I got picked to start a match – in the 1972 Five Nations, against Wales at Twickenham. When we were in the tunnel ready to go out, Gerald Davies was there with his top button done up, looking immaculate. I was trying to work out how I was ever going to get my hands on Gerald. Then there was Gareth Edwards, JPR Williams and all the others. When you go out at Twickenham you are the bravest man in the world … but then the sound hits you, and you wonder what you are doing there, and you realise what a massive thing it is. But I didn't have any fear at that time. I had played in Wales, I knew them all, and I had done okay. I remember on that day at Twickenham, thinking about all the notes and wishes that people had sent me, from my school, from my little club, from the Gloucester Council, and from all those people and coaches who had helped me along the way. We lost 12-3, but I will never forget that day.

My England career was wonderful, it was a major thing that triggered change in my whole life. I used to hear about Tom Voyce, the great Gloucester flanker. And Lord Wakefield, and all those other greats. Then there was Obolensky, and his famous tries. I couldn't match any of that. But I think that Mike Burton stood up when he had to.

DAVID DUCKHAM

To say England's performance were inconsistent during my time in the side would

The England and Scotland teams come together for a Centenary celebration photo, 1971.

be a grotesque understatement. Part of the reason was certainly selection, there were way too many people discarded after just a couple of games, but I can't blame the selectors entirely. We still had a lot of absolutely cracking players in our teams, and we still occasionally beat the world's best. What we really lacked was self-belief.

I remember playing for England – well I say playing, but I tore a hamstring in the first game against France – in the World Sevens in 1973 and I looked around and man for man we could match anybody. We had Rippers [Tony Ripley], John Gray, who was amazing, Fran Cotton, Steve Smith, Peter Preece, Geoff Evans, Peter Rossborough and Keith Fielding, who was the fastest player I ever saw, a yard quicker than JJ Williams in my opinion. We beat everybody including the Welsh, who had JJ, Gerald [Davies] and Gareth [Edwards] playing. My fondest memory of all was dear Rippers sprinting away from Mike Gibson, who couldn't lay a hand on him. The point is we had the raw material, we had a fantastic array of rugby talent at our disposal. Thinking back that is the only thing I ever won in an England shirt – and even then I was sitting in the stands with my torn hamstring!

JAN WEBSTER (1972-1975, 11 caps)

Playing for England was the pinnacle of my sporting ideal. Rugby wasn't my first game – football was – and Joe Mercer, then manager of Aston Villa, asked me to go to the club as an apprentice. My headmaster at St Mary's Walsall said no, because I was playing rugby for the school. It was hard work for me to get an England cap because of my lack of size and lack of a long pass at a time when Gareth Edwards and Chris Laidlaw had made it in vogue. I worked at it, but I couldn't do it as well as them, or as well as Steve Smith, who was my main England rival – a big lad with a long spin pass. My aim was always to get the ball from A to B as fast as possible, and if that meant a dive pass, then so be it.

I'd been in the England squad in 1967 and 1968 as a reserve, so it was almost as much a feeling of relief as joy when I was picked to start against Wales in 1972.

STEVE SMITH (England 1973-1983, 28 caps)

We were organised on tour whereas at home we weren't. That's why we did so well on tour. Players such as Fran Cotton and myself had a head start because Jim Greenwood at Loughborough was light years ahead of any other coach in the game. We'd get to England training and think, 'This is the dark ages.' Don White was a lovely fellow, but he just didn't know what to do with us. The good England coaches you could count on one half of one hand. I don't think the RFU were particularly clear about how they saw coaches and coaching. On one occasion I was firing out 30 yard spin-passes in training and I remember Dickie Jeeps telling me to get on my belly and dive pass.

PETER ROSSBOROUGH

Coaching at that time was very much in its infancy. Don White was the first England coach, and while he was a fine back-row forward, there was no theory involved – you just leaned on your playing experience. There was also a tendency for coaches to be teachers, like Carwyn James, John Elders and, later, Ian McGeechan, because they were good at standing in front of people and communicating. Elders (in New Zealand) and John Burgess (in Japan) were tracksuit coaches, and good coaches. However, the RFU were not in the vanguard of employing coaches until Don Rutherford got it formalised.

BOB HILLER

Carwyn James was on a different level. He was miles ahead of any coach or rugby thinker I had ever worked with, and when I came back from the 1971 Lions tour we certainly tried to introduce some of his thinking at Quins – but it didn't seem to change England's approach at all. I only played a couple more times in 1972 before I was dropped and quickly off the international scene, but I don't recall any great determination by England to try and mimic the Lions way.

Alan Old clears for touch against France at Colombes, 1972.

PETER DIXON

To me, coming from Oxford University, where we had Roy Bish as coach and Chris Laidlaw (the All Black scrum-half) as captain, and were well organised in training, England seemed amateur – in all senses. It was ludicrous that you knew your line-out drills at your club inside out but when it came to England there would always be some sort of debate, such as whether we were going to use numbers, with someone saying they should be long and someone else saying short. Meanwhile the backs were huddled in another corner trying to get their moves together. Then, before it was sorted out, the chairman of selectors would run on and say, 'That will have to do because we've got a sherry party to attend'.

CHRIS RALSTON

We had several different coaches with different ideas. John Burgess was an extrovert, loud and demanding, whereas John Elders was the opposite, quiet and unassuming. Whichever coach, we were pretty organised up front.

BILL BEAUMONT (England 1975-1982, 34 caps, plus 7 caps for the Lions)

John Burgess was very passionate. Very organised. Very structured. In actual fact, very honest with you. You couldn't hide from him. If you hadn't played well, then you knew it. He wasn't the type of bloke to say, 'Tough luck today mate.' He gave it as he saw it.

STEVE SMITH

The first good England coach we had was Mike Davis, who made sure there was consistency in selection. If you're not a good selector that means trouble because it is two thirds of your job. When the Northern lads got together and were travelling down for internationals we'd look down the team list and think, 'Why have they picked him?'

JOHN PULLIN

Back in 1972 after a disastrous whitewash in the Five Nations they offered me the captaincy for England's South Africa tour, because they couldn't find anybody else in truth. I accepted quickly, mainly because if I didn't I suspected I might not make the tour at all. Right from the off the tour party seemed to click. To be honest I never suffered one bit from altitude, but others did, and whether by accident or design our schedule was perfect.

We had four matches at sea level including two really good games against Natal and Western Province, who were strong in those days, and then we flew up to Pretoria just two days before the Northern Transvaal game – which was like a Test really – and that's how the sports scientists like you to do it these days. We drew 13-13.

Then we had a final week to get ready for the Springbok Test with a midweek match just for good measure. I wouldn't say the Test win was comfortable, but 18-9 was a fair enough scoreline. We dominated the line-outs through Larter, Ralston and Ripley, Jan Webster was very good and Sam Doble kicked his goals. It sent a few shockwaves around the rugby world. The Boks had only lost one of their previous nine Tests and were huge favourites.

MIKE BURTON

I was 26 by then, but I didn't have a passport. I had to rush round to get one when they told me I might be going. The RFU at that time was like the Foreign Office, there was always someone in there directing you what to do.

ALAN MORLEY (England 1972-1975, 7 caps)

The apartheid situation never crossed my mind because I wanted to play rugby at the highest level. We had issues with anti-apartheid demonstrators before leaving, and when you were selected you were also asked if you had any concerns about going to South Africa.

I was 21 at the time, and when we got there the situation struck all of us as odd. We spoke to people in a decent manner, and because they hadn't been spoken to like that they were taken aback. When we asked for something we said 'please', which the Afrikaner wouldn't do.

We went into Soweto and played a game. They were overjoyed that we had turned up, and although we won by 60 points they scored one try and celebrated as if they'd won. Afterwards some of the spectators said, 'We'll take your blazers and dry-clean them for you,' but we decided to hang onto them!

JAN WEBSTER

You had your own thoughts about apartheid. Peter Hain and his mates ran out and lay in front of the coach when we were leaving for the airport, but when you get out there you are just a bunch of blokes on tour who get on well.

STEVE SMITH

South Africa was my first England call-up, as a replacement after Lionel Weston was injured. I was called out for the last week, and sat on the bench for the Test. For me it was fantastic. I'd never been on a plane before, and I'd never been to a place like South Africa. I was star-struck – I had no idea how big rugby was out there and the crowd of 80,000 people at Ellis Park just blew me away. Apartheid? I didn't really know what it was, and just spent my time walking around a beautiful country.

JAN WEBSTER

South Africa were the unofficial world champions, but we went into it thinking if we brought out our best game we could win. In our own minds we were not underdogs because it had been such a good tour that each one of us was confident. South Africa did not play well that sunny afternoon, but we didn't allow them to play well.

I remember putting Alan Morley through for his try – I wouldn't have wanted to play anywhere else but scrum-half because you are everywhere. I used to take quick taps a lot, and I liked to play at pace and set people up by getting them quick ball.

MIKE BURTON

The Western Province game in Cape Town was massive. Stack Stevens was another little prop, and he and I were running out when we spotted the two Western Province props, Walter Hugo and Des van Jaarsveldt. Players then were not as big as they are now but those two were well over 19 stone. Stack watched them go by and said to me: 'I don't like the look of yours much.' But I understood things. I learned that if you give some of those weightlifters something to lift, they will lift it. What you do not do is pack down on their shoulders. I'm giving Robert Cockrell, their hooker, the back of my head in every scrum. They are so used to the loose-head holding the scrum high that they didn't know what to do, and we nicked a couple. I knew what was going to happen. Van Jaarsveldt shifted his feet as he went to hit me, so I hit him first. He said: 'Classy.' Then his mate Cockrell was standing there with his mouth open, so I hit him too. The Kray twins used to offer you a cigarette and, as you opened your mouth to get it, the other one would hit you.

FRAN COTTON (England 1971-1981, 31 caps plus 7 caps for the Lions)

Before the Test side was announced I thought I was the front runner for the tight-head spot having played four of the first five games, but I was able to swallow my pride because I respected Mike Burton as a player and for once the selectors gave me a logical reason for my non-selection.

MIKE BURTON

I found that Fran and I had the same philosophies, and playing up front against those giant men we had the same problems. I went on the next few tours with Fran and we became firm friends. When you're grafting together like that, you have a care for each other because you need each other.

We played in the same team only rarely, probably because Derek Morgan, who was in charge then, and others, always said that props couldn't switch over. History has proved them wrong and especially in the case of Fran, who went over to the loose-head side on the 1974 Lions tour. He didn't manage that switch badly, did he?

Normally Fran and I were competing for the tight-head spot, and after we played the provincial games they announced the team for the first Test. I was in, and in training we were not friends. When we went down for the first scrum in practice he was up against me and I could feel the passion and the emotion and frustration coming out of him.

FRAN COTTON
It brought myself and Mike together as friends because he appreciated I had played well and that he was somewhat fortunate to be selected. More importantly, he had seen that I was big enough to accept the decision.

JOHN WATKINS (England 1972-1975, 7 caps)
I will never forget training at Ellis Park when John Elders got us in a circle and read the England team out. I'd played well, but I never remember thinking 'I'm in' – I never assumed that. At that time, when he read my name out, it was the most important thing that had ever happened to me.

TONY NEARY
That win over South Africa in Johannesburg was a typical English backs-against-the-wall reaction. There was a realisation that they were a better organised side, so we had to restrict their possession – and we did that.

South Africa's lethal weapon was Joggie Jansen, a huge centre, but Jeremy Janion was also a big lad. He was asked to stand up to Jansen, and he did. Our guys cut them down. Sam Doble at fullback was a brilliant kicker, and at altitude he kicked everything, while Jan Webster was a very lively scrum-half – he didn't have the pass, but he was very jinky and linked well with the back-row. He also had a very good box-kick.

STACK STEVENS (England 1969-1975, 25 caps)
It was a relatively short tour, and we went into the Test full of confidence. We had a very strong set of forwards who adapted well to the fast hard playing surfaces and took the game to the South Africans.

ALAN MORLEY
Pre-Test we were told by the media in South Africa, 'You try to tackle Joggie

Jansen and you will break your arm.' They didn't seem to register that we were five games unbeaten, or that we had trained together for three weeks.

The remarkable thing about my try was that there is a photo in which you can see the touch judge and the referee at the moment I grounded the ball and was hit into the corner flag by their fullback, Carlson. All the officials in the Test were South Africans, and it was a close enough call that they could have ruled I was in touch. Thinking back I should probably have scored three that day – if I'd been a little more experienced I could have turned one or two more chances into tries. However, the game went so quickly that it is the only incident I can remember.

After the match I ran off the pitch to get my tour shirt with my opposite number, Jan Muller, and when I went back into the changing room the others were all sat there with their heads in their hands. There was just sheer relief and disbelief, and tears in their eyes at that result after such a horror season.

At that time South Africa didn't lose at home. Years later I remember going to Belfast for a 1974 Lions reunion with the then captain of the Springboks, Hannes Marais, who said he is only remembered in South Africa for losing to the Lions despite also being captain of the side who won a series 3-1 against New Zealand in 1970.

However, when they say that the 1974 Lions were the first team of the century to tour South Africa unbeaten, that was not true. We were!

MIKE BURTON

Their prop up against Stack was Sakkie Sauermann from Northern Transvaal and mine was Niek Bezuidenhout, who was a real killer. I gave Sauermann the best sidewinder in the world but in the second half someone kicked Stack in the head and sliced his head open. I could virtually see his brains. Don't forget there were no blood replacements in those days so we had to carry on with 14 men.

John Pullin is a fantastic player, and he wanted me to switch over to loose-head. Pullin is saying, 'All we need to do is win our own ball and keep calm.' But I've got to switch to prop against Sauermann, and now he's going to kill *me*. He's actually grinning. On the tight-head side is little John Watkins, who is 14 stone sopping wet, who has had to move up from the flank to prop. I saw his feet soaring up through the scrum. They almost squashed him. I gave Sauermann a thump on the head to try to dissuade him, but we managed to somehow protect our own ball. Alan Morley scored a try and Alan Old kicked some goals and we won 18-9, it was one of those great games. It was one of those great things, and I still see all those blokes.

JOHN WATKINS

I was playing in the Gloucester 1972 cup run, and there were a number who couldn't go on the England tour, but I was on standby before being called up. The next four weeks were like a dream. I played in the opening win against Natal, against Northern Transvaal, Griqualand West, Proteas and Bantu.

After the Natal game Tommy Bedford said to me, 'Wait till you go up top' (to Johannesburg and the altitude on the high veld). And it was a bit of a shock. You were gasping for air in training, and there was nothing coming in. Eventually you get a little accustomed, but at first everyone was on their haunches trying to get some breath.

All I can remember about coming off the field at Ellis Park is that I cried my eyes out. I picked up the ball as the final whistle went. When someone ran up I thought he was going to fight me for it, but he patted me on the back instead. Jan Ellis and Pieter Greyling came in and I asked if I could swap my tour shirt, which had a No.25 on it, and they agreed. That Springbok jersey is now on the wall at Kingsholm. After that, Joggie Jansen came up to my hotel room and gave me his tracksuit.

The South Africans turned up at the dinner very late – it had obviously been a bit of a shock to them. We played seven games with 25 people, and finished the tour unbeaten. The South Africans were big, bullish, with not a lot of skill, and they tried to thug us. Stack Stevens went off with a cut eye, and I had to go up to the front-row. Tony Neary was too good an openside to go up… and everyone looked at me. Micky Burton moved across to loose-head and I went to tight-head. The bloke opposite was built like a brick wall. Micky says I was there for 20 scrums, but I'd say it was for three or four.

We outplayed them. We scored a try where they didn't, and Sam Doble was amazing. In club rugby when I played against Sam I thought he was arrogant, but then I roomed with him and he was a lovely man with a lot of humility. That's also when I became so friendly with Andy Ripley. We just got on from the start, and it was a lifelong friendship. He stopped at my place, and me at his – he was a smashing bloke.

FRAN COTTON

I remember Jeremy Paul Aubrey George Janion being fined at the Players Court by the Judge, Chris Ralston, for having too many names.

JAN WEBSTER

Rugby is a game full of characters and big personalities. Micky Burton was one of those in South Africa, and so were guys like Andy Ripley and Chris Ralston. They all had something to offer off the park. Then there was Jeremy Paul George Aubrey Janion, a big strong boy who played a great game in defence in the Test. Can you imagine going on tour with a name like that? He was fined every morning! There were no cliques, and we got down to playing winning, successful and enjoyable rugby.

MIKE BURTON

The Test was one of the greatest ever England wins, but in the middle of a Test match you thought that life could not get any worse. You were playing this game against the monsters, we were thousands of feet above sea-level on the baked hard pitches, and there wasn't a single supporter on the trip, so there was no one shouting for England. There was kikuyu grass and the referee was a South African, no neutral refs in those days. And your mouth was as dry as dust because in those days they never even ran on with a drink of water.

JOHN PULLIN

Those two wins – against South Africa in 1972 and New Zealand in 1973 – were the highpoint of the time I played with England. When you travelled down those parts you started every Test match nine points down straight away because of the home refs. I'm not saying they were cheats as such, but such was the pressure on them that you knew that when push came to shove on three or four crucial penalty decisions, that could go either way, it would go against you. They just did. It made winning down there even more of an achievement.

STEVE SMITH

My first cap was 1973 in Dublin, and it was after Scotland and Wales had not gone to Ireland in 1972. The feeling was that if we didn't, Irish rugby would have been dead for 10 years. At the time I said that I'd play for England in a minefield – which may not have been the right thing to say.

It meant so much to me. I didn't just want to play for England, I wanted to win for England. I never put my shirt on in front of my teammates. I always put it on in a cubicle in the toilet, and kissed the rose. It was a private ritual.

I was a working-class council house kid and I'd never seen a rugby ball until I was 11 and went to King's Macclesfield. On the first two Saturdays I was picked to play rugby I didn't turn up because I didn't want to play it. I played Stockport Schools soccer, but I soon discovered that rugby was far away the better social sport, and more organised.

NIGEL HORTON

In 1973, after Wales and Scotland had decided not to play in Ireland the previous season because of the Troubles, the RFU said England would go to Dublin. That decision did not offend me, but the way it was done definitely did. We had lost to Wales in Cardiff, where I was a reserve, but were told that there would be an England team meeting at 9 a.m. on Sunday, the morning after the post-match dinner.

We all turned up, and were told by the chairman of selectors that the RFU's position was that an England team would go, whether it was the first team, second team, or third team. We were also told that if we decided not to go they would respect individual decisions and it would not affect your future selection chances.

We would probably have decided to go as a group, but what offended me was that we were not being asked our views at all, we were being told – even though we were out there representing our country.

In the end there were five players who for various reasons didn't go to Dublin. I was one of them because, as a policeman, I was asked to attend a meeting with my chief constable, and he suggested I should not go (for security reasons). I believe that none of those five, me included, played for England the following season.

MARTIN COOPER

I went to the Ireland game in Dublin as a sub, and although the RFU told us it wouldn't be held against anyone if they didn't go, I'd have gone to the North Pole if it meant a cap. As it transpired, David Duckham broke his cheekbone, but he wouldn't come off, so I had to wait a little longer.

JOHN PULLIN

I was and am a Gloucestershire farmer and knew little or nothing of Irish politics, so, if I am honest, none of that swayed my decision to play at Lansdowne Road. I was always going to travel for the simple selfish reason that I was the England captain and hooker, and I valued both positions. I would have hated it if somebody had come in and done such a good job that I was dropped.

Looking back and knowing just a little bit more about the politics I appreciate now that it was a big deal. The situation was very bad in the early seventies, there had been a spate of bombs on mainland Britain, there had been that Bloody Sunday incident the previous year, and you could see that the appearance of the England rugby team in particular might pose a few security problems.

DAVID DUCKHAM

Two or three of the boys dropped out – Jan Webster, Sam Doble and Peter Larter – and I could see at a squad session we had in Coventry that quite a few were very nervous about the whole thing so I said I would phone Willie-John who I had got to know pretty well on the '71 Lions.

So I did and I remember his words to this day: 'You must come, don't let the terrorists win.' That's all he said, and it sent a shiver up my spine. He didn't dress it up with any false promises about guaranteeing our safety – how could he? – and stuff like, 'If they get you they will have to get us as well,' which I have seen reported from time to time. At training the following week, six days before the match, I reported back and we decided to go for it.

We got off the plane, walked down the steps and straight onto a bus which looked more like an armoured personnel carrier than anything. Police outriders everywhere, high security. But the Irish Rugby Union, bless them, in case the IRA weren't quite sure who we were, had put a big cardboard poster thing saying England rugby team!

The bus headed for the Shelbourne and I was sitting next to Rippers who was next to the window. He started rocking to and fro in a rather alarming and bizarre manner and after five minutes – on behalf of all the lads – I asked him what he was doing. He looked at me and said, in a loud voice that everybody could hear, that he was trying to make it as difficult for the snipers to get him as possible. There was a brief pause and then we all cracked up and the mood relaxed. Rippers was

Andy Ripley, centre, leads the charge against Australia during England's 20-3 victory in 1973.

such an intelligent man, and that was what he meant to happen all along. It was his way of making us chill. It was a wonderful moment.

It was a crazy, ridiculous weekend and actually running out at Lansdowne Road was the proudest I have ever felt in an England shirt.

ALAN MORLEY

After the 1972 South Africa tour my next game was playing against New Zealand at Twickenham, with Grant Batty opposite, and losing. Then it was Wales, and John Bevan, and we lost that too. The next game, against Ireland, was all pretty traumatic. We were told on the Sunday morning after the Wales game that England were going to Dublin, but that the likes of Nigel Horton couldn't go because he was a policeman. David Duckham said that he'd go but that he wanted to take his wife – he said, 'If we're going to die, were both going to die together.' That was the pre-match talk. We trained in England on the Wednesday and Thursday and then flew to Ireland on Friday. The Garda were on the tarmac to meet us, and we had four outriders with guns, and when we got to the hotel there were armed guards on the doors. Yet, it was a bit surreal, because on the Saturday morning we were out on the streets of Dublin having a walk around.

My dad went across to watch the match and play a bit of golf the day before. Not many England supporters had travelled over so when he was asked what he was doing, and he told them he was watching his son, for the rest of the trip he didn't buy a drink.

Terry Moore charges off the back of the Irish scrum, supported by Johnny Moloney (left) and Fergus Slattery (right), against England at Lansdowne Road in February 1973.

JOHN PULLIN

A school teacher friend of mine brought around some documents and press cuttings a few years back about the other Bloody Sunday in 1920 with British troops shooting civilian fans dead at a GA game at Croke Park, and again I realised looking back that this was potentially an explosive situation given what was going on.

Anyway my ignorance was bliss, plus I had also got it in my mind somewhere that the IRA were on the record somewhere as having said they would never target a sports event in Ireland. Most of us decided to go, and you were very aware of heightened security to start with. We had armed security guards on the bus and on our floor at the Shelbourne Hotel, but strangely they seemed to clock off on the Friday night and we never saw them again. I fancy they had a big night and that was it. The authorities were very clever and put the two teams in the same hotel which would be pretty unusual these days. If the bombers wanted to get us they would take half of the Ireland rugby team as well.

Other players and commentators talk of the noise when we ran on but I never noticed it – but I'm not a good judge of these things. As ever I was just concentrating on the match, and getting on with it. I hated all the formalities.

DAVID DUCKHAM

When we ran on we were greeted by a wall of sound so huge that you didn't hear it, you felt it, it was noise that could have split your eardrums. A few of us broke down, including me. I was very tearful for a few moments. I do remember thinking it just can't be better than this. It was an unbelievable moment and I have to concede that the RFU were absolutely right committing us to fulfilling the fixture, even if they didn't ask our views first!

JOHN PULLIN

You can joke about it, but I felt pretty exposed throwing in at the line-outs in the match. I was a sitting duck, as were the wings. I remember Alan Morley admitting he really didn't enjoy the experience one bit and I thought it very unfair that his performance that day seemed to count against him selectorially. He didn't play much for England after that.

ALAN MORLEY

I'd had a new gumshield made, but I left it behind at the hotel, which wasn't the best start. Then we walked out onto the pitch for a standing ovation which went on for at least five minutes. You didn't know where to put yourself.

At that stage I was very nervous before matches, whereas at the end of my career in 1975 I was much more comfortable. I picked that moment to play the worst game of my career. I couldn't catch anything, and it went from bad to worse.

At the dinner that evening I sat next to Moss Keane – who was not the easiest man to understand – and they came in with lighted candles shaped like mini rugby balls. Moss gave me one of them as a keepsake and told me to put it in my pocket. I've still got it.

After the match I had to travel back from Heathrow in a car with two fellow Bristolians, the chairman of the selectors, Alec Lewis, and captain John Pullin, knowing that I would be dropped. The three of us were together again the following evening at a South West sportsman's boxing evening at the Grand Hotel in Bristol where they made a presentation to me of a small trophy for my debut try in the win over South Africa. In accepting it I motioned towards Alec and John, and said, 'I'm glad they're here to see it' – but it didn't stop me being dropped.

DAVID DUCKHAM

We lost the game, the result didn't really matter in a deep way, and then JP crowned it all with his famous comment that 'we may not be any good, but at least we turn up'. Hospitality was wonderful that weekend, we were given then freedom of the city.

JOHN PULLIN

My little speech? Well, I'm not sure it deserved the acclaim it got, but, yes, it was a pre-planned line. When I was England captain I always used to scribble a few thoughts on a piece of paper, usually on the coach to the hotel before the dinner, and that was definitely one of the lines I wrote down. I've got no idea what I would have said if England had won, but there was little chance of that. Irish hospitality didn't extend to gifting us anything on the pitch. They were well worth their 18-9 win.

PETER DIXON

My England highlight came at the end of the 1973 Championship. We were going well as a team and I scored two tries in the 20-13 victory over Scotland – I actually scored a third but was pulled back across the line. However, my career highlight was playing for the 1971 Lions in New Zealand.

PETER SQUIRES (England 1973-1979, 29 caps plus 1 cap for the Lions)

When I opened that first invitation card on the doorstep at home it was everything you had dreamed of and hoped for. Then you were hoping you didn't get injured until you played. I made my debut against France in 1973, and all I can recall is I was just pleased to have caught the ball after hearing the hooves of the big French forwards coming towards me.

I was pleased to have got through the game okay because at the time I had only been on the wing for 18 months – and that was playing for Yorkshire, not my club, Harrogate. For the club I'd be the scrum-half initially and then a fly-half, and I'd only played on the wing once before I was 21. At Yorkshire it was me on one wing and Ian McGeechan on the other.

MARTIN COOPER

It was the stuff of boyhood dreams when I won my first cap in a 14-6 win over France at Twickenham in 1973. The irony was that I was at fly-half despite playing on the wing for Moseley, whereas Peter Squires, who also won his first cap that day on the wing, was usually a fly-half at Harrogate. I had come to the selectors' attention after scoring a try against New Zealand when the West Midlands beat them at Moseley. I was on the wing and went round their fullback, and that made me useful to put on the bench because there were a few other positions I could cover, including fly-half, centre and fullback.

DAVID DUCKHAM

It was the strangest dynamic. For Coventry, Warwickshire, Barbarians and the Lions I was having an absolute ball and winning a lot of rugby matches in fine style, but when it came to England it was very frustrating. And they, of course, were the team I wanted to win with most! I felt sheer frustration at the lack of success, and I don't mind admitting it got to me a few times. I had a distinct wobble in form in 1974-75 when I was struggling for motivation and asked myself if I wanted to keep on making the sacrifices you have to make as amateur to play for your country.

ROGER UTTLEY

With wins over France and Scotland in the 1973 Five Nations, and then over New Zealand, I was on the winning side on three of my first four internationals. When Australia came in the autumn we dominated in the tight, and won again.

JOHN PULLIN

The win on the 1973 tour to New Zealand was quite a bit different from the success in 1972 in South Africa, which I must confess came a bit out of the blue. We hadn't been too bad in the 1973 Championship. It was the year of the five-way tie at the top with all the teams winning their home games and losing away. New Zealand didn't quite have that invincible feeling around that time. The Lions had beaten them in 1971, the North West Counties and Midlands had beaten them on the 1972-73 tour and then of course the Barbarians had beaten them. That doesn't mean to say they weren't going to be formidable on their own turf, but we had picked a decent squad, there weren't too many selectors on tour to mess things up, and we certainly thought we had a sniff.

DAVID DUCKHAM

It was so typical of England in that era to suddenly find these performances from somewhere. From the moment the first whistle went I felt New Zealand weren't quite as sharp mentally as they normally are.

I would single out five players who made that win happen. Jan Webster enjoyed an extraordinary match and completely outplayed Sid Going, and the back-row of Rippers, Tony Neary and John Watkins were superb. Fran Cotton had a fine match. He did one dummying 60 yard run that nearly resulted in one of the great tries by a front-row man. Fran was so much more than just a prop.

FRAN COTTON

Even though we were beaten by Wellington in a poorish display and then by Canterbury in an excellent performance from them, we never allowed ourselves to become despondent or believe that we were on a hiding to nothing in the Test. We had a full week to prepare and spent it up at Waitangi in the north of the North Island, the historic point where Maori chiefs ceded the country to Queen Victoria in 1840.

ROGER UTTLEY

We had a little break in the Bay of Islands before the Test. The rain stopped, the weather brightened, and because it was sub-tropical it was like being somewhere different, and it gave us a lift. I remember walking through an orange grove on the way to training. We were talking, and saying, 'Let's do something.' We got stuck into them, and as our confidence rose they were presented with problems they hadn't expected, and they had a fly-half in John Dougan who was a weak link.

TONY NEARY

Playing the All Blacks was a great experience, and a formidable prospect. We were up against some of the great names that I'd watched on TV, like Ian Kirkpatrick and Sid Going, and then to be actually playing against them was quite something. I scored a try after Jan Webster broke and Alan Old put me through… I think I fell over the line. The other thing was that throughout the 1970s the England pack could front up to any opposition in the scrum and line-out.

JOHN PULLIN

We started with a very tough win in Fiji who were a strong bunch around that time and that really helped knock us into shape. We didn't win any of our provincial games – Taranaki, Wellington and Canterbury – but I thought we were playing okay. The match that really mattered, against Canterbury a week before the Test, we could have won on another day. We were in that nice situation of being quite confident within the camp while the Kiwi press was writing us off. To them, it was a matter of how many points the All Blacks would score.

ROGER UTTLEY

Alan Old, who suffered a lot at the hands of the selectors, was at fly-half at Eden Park. He was always outspoken, and I'm not sure it did him any favours with them. On one occasion when the pack had been praised he offered an alternative viewpoint. He said, 'Yes, of course you're very good – but very dull. You stick it up your jumpers, and when you can't think of anything else to do, you give it to us.' He was always accused of kicking too much, but he claimed he was always given static ball – which was quite valid. For the North, and for the 1974 Lions, he was outstanding and showed what he could do.

FRAN COTTON

The Test selection between myself and Micky Burton that had occurred in South Africa was reversed and he took the decision with good grace. Little did I realise that the 1972 Test would be the last time I was to be left out of an England team for nine years.

JAN WEBSTER

Alan Old was at fly-half against New Zealand and the ball didn't go past him more than three or four times. If I didn't kick then he kicked – but this was the day you devised a tactic, and it came off. When you plan something and it works there is no better feeling.

ROGER UTTLEY

The quality of that England backline was comparable with the North side that beat New Zealand in 1979. It had David Duckham, Peter Preece, Geoff Evans and Peter Rossborough, who all played for Coventry. Preece was very quick – we called him 'Beep-Beep' after the Roadrunner cartoon character – while Evans was muscular.

PETER SQUIRES

We made history with the win against New Zealand, in New Zealand. No-one gave us much of a chance, but we became the first nation from the British Isles to win there. Jan Webster had a cracking game, very gutsy, and he put me in after he broke on the 22, although I beat a man to get over the line.

JOHN PULLIN

We were very good value for the 16-10 win – three tries to two – and the pack went very well that day. We pretty much controlled it, and our back-row of Andy Ripley, Tony Neary and John Watkins played a very good All Blacks back-row off the park. John Watkins was probably the most underrated England player I can recall but, as ever, the selectors messed him around soon after and discarded him. They started getting him to stand marking the five yard area at line-outs, and that made it really difficult for him to get involved like he usually did. He should have had 30-40 caps John, he was magnificent down in Auckland as he had been the previous summer in South Africa.

Ripley too. People always talk about him being a character and all that, but they forget what a great rugby player he was – a great athlete, very difficult to tackle with those high knees, very good in the line-out, and very competitive. He wasn't that tight big-tackling No. 8 that some prefer, but he was tough enough in his own way. Very competitive on the pitch, relaxed off it. He was short-changed in terms of England caps and he was unlucky to come up against Merve 'The Swerve'

New Zealand scrum-half Sid Going kicks ahead as Jan Webster presses him from a scrum at Eden Park, Auckland, 1973.

(Mervyn Davies) for the Lions spot in '74. He would have been brilliant in the Tests as well. The other star that day was Jan Webster, again, who got the better of Sid Going. Not many did that. Full of guts and heart Jan, and another poorly treated by the selectors. I don't know what the selectors were looking for most of the time.

JAN WEBSTER

I got my first cap with Andy Ripley, and we got friendly. At that time Adidas and Puma were asking people to wear their boots, and being the sort of figure he was with his long hair, he was in demand. I think he ended up with both Adidas and Puma and so he decided to wear one boot from each manufacturer! To do what he did coming to rugby late was remarkable, and the sort of person he was – he was great fun. Characters like that are priceless. We'd meet every year in Langan's in London, myself, Andy, Roger Uttley, Tony Neary, John Watkins, Chris Ralston, and we did it until Andy passed away... and it's still done now.

I tried to get on with everyone, and I cannot remember anyone I played with on those tours that I wouldn't go and meet. Rugby gave me what football wouldn't have done socially, and over the length of my career I've had far more friends because of it.

Chris Ralston out-jumps Samuel Strachan in the line out at Eden Park during England's their first victory over the All Blacks since 1936.

CHRIS RALSTON

I played my socks off against New Zealand in Auckland. I had flu in the week before the game but it all came together in the match and we dominated the line-out.

FRAN COTTON

We were confident but what we hadn't reckoned on was our domination of the set-pieces and with Chris Ralston also out-jumping Sam Strahan in the line-outs it allowed our half-backs to keep us going forward and released our back-row of Neary, Ripley and Watkins to pressurise the All Blacks into mistakes. Just the sort of game in fact that the All Blacks had used for years – but for once it was an English side in the driving seat.

PETER ROSSBOROUGH

That game was the high point of my career, becoming the first England team to beat New Zealand in New Zealand. I remember Sandy Sanders, the tour manager, saying, 'England have plucked the crown jewel of rugby.'

FRAN COTTON

The most important part of the game for me was in the last minute when I broke around the front of a line-out and sold Going a perfect dummy. He was in the third row of the stands before he realised I still had the ball. This was followed by a dainty little sidestep past John Dougan their fly-half followed by an almighty welly downfield which was chased all the way by Andy Ripley, who almost scored.

STEVE SMITH

Fran Cotton was the only player I know that was never dropped by England in that era. The only one. What characterised Fran is that he is very smart. His degree is in maths, and he knew how to work out the angles as a prop. He went on to become a world-class prop on both sides of the scrum – although, when I first played against him for Cheshire against Lancashire he was a second-row. He was also a great handler of the ball, a fly-half in a fat man's body. He almost signed for St Helens in the mid-seventies. When England won the World Sevens at Murrayfield in 1973 he was the only prop in the whole tournament. He would take out three tacklers and lay the ball off. I was on the bench against New Zealand in Auckland in 1973, after being dropped. In the last minute of the match England were denied a further try when Fran dummied, made a break, and chipped through for Andy Ripley to score – only for the referee to blow for full-time.

ROGER UTTLEY

Back in the 1970s New Zealand was still extremely colonial and provincial, and in the winter the weather was like being back in Britain. We were flying around in Fokker Friendships, and people were very friendly but it was all rugby, rugby, rugby.

We had some fun too. Nick Martin was a lock from Bedford whose booming post-match clarion call was always, 'Let's hit the piss!' On one occasion he got hold of a big red snapper which found its way into someone's bed.

FRAN COTTON

'We play better on this side of the equator,' was John Pullin's comment afterwards. The following November at Twickenham we played Australia and we won by the handsome margin of 17 points. I am sure the ease of victory was one of the reasons the selectors completely misjudged what would be needed to beat Australia on our Tour out there in 1975.

JOHN WATKINS

On the New Zealand tour we lost the three provincial games, but there was not much in it. I suppose New Zealand thought, 'We'll turn them over,' and took their eye off the ball.

Jan Webster was the man of the match. How he got some of the ball away I just don't know. Jan was like a rubber ball, you could never put him down on the floor, and he'd take off on these little darting runs. Neary was the speed man, and played No.6. I killed the ball and took a shoeing, although I had to fill in on the wing at one stage in Auckland.

After every game we played we'd go and have a couple of beers. Before that Test I was rooming with Peter Rossborough, and they brought some glasses of sherry around just to warm us up a bit. I had a couple of them just before we left the hotel for the ground. I guess it was a pretty intimidating prospect, because we knew New Zealand's history, and I was a bit nervous, as we all were.

After the final whistle I ran past a ball boy and took the match ball off him, and it is now in the clubhouse at Longlevens. A lot of people think that the New Zealand side we played was weak, but it wasn't. They were a really good side. Ian Kirkpatrick, Alex Wyllie and Ken Stewart were in the back-row, Tane Norton was at hooker, Sid Going at scrum-half, and Grant Batty and Bryan Williams in the backs. But they picked a first cap fullback (Bob Lendrum), and it was windy conditions. He struggled a bit.

Jan Webster was the inspirational figure by far in both those wins – he was the linchpin – and Tony Neary was outstanding too. John Pullin was a quiet man, but a good captain who led from the front. I'm always asked why we didn't win the Championship, and I don't know why we couldn't do it.

I was always very shy, and after club matches I'd stick in the corner and have a couple of beers, but going on tour with an England team you had to gel. I was a good tourist, and I'd muck in and do anything. That gave me confidence, and I came out of my shell.

I used to say I was 6ft, and I played at 14 stone. I started on the wing as a youngster but then I moved to the back-row. Once Gloucester tried to get me

Stack Stevens watches as Roger Uttley vies for the ball with Tony Shaw of Australia in 1973.

propping, and I had two or three games there – one of them against Stack Stevens, who picked me up and marched me around the field.

I was single at the time, and didn't have a house, and I never got a penny from work, but they allowed me to go. I was a machinist in an aluminium plant, so it was four weeks in South Africa and then back to standing in front of a Bridgeport milling machine for eight hours a day. It was fantastic – and then back to reality.

After the New Zealand win I played in the next game, which was a 20-3 win over Australia at Twickenham. After that I was on the bench seven or eight times, but at the time replacements were only for injury, and I was never able to find that tour form back home. They brought me back for a couple of games in 1975, against France and Wales, but I'd have liked to play against Scotland and Ireland.

I wanted to produce that form on English soil – but I'll take those three wins.

STACK STEVENS
The away wins over South Africa in 1972 and the All Blacks in 1973 were the highlights of my career. They were two of the best all-round team performances by a side that I have ever played in. It was a bonus to score a try in the New Zealand game and great to beat both sides in their own back yards.

A key factor in the victories over South Africa and New Zealand was the consistency in selection. Even though we were white-washed in the Five Nations we kept the core of the team for both tours.

STEVE SMITH
Chris Ralston was the best second-row jumper in the world. In those wins over South Africa and New Zealand he won so much line-out ball. He was an unsung hero. Unbelievable.

CHRIS RALSTON
The great moments were winning in South Africa and in New Zealand because no Home Nations country had gone there and beaten either of them. We were not successful in the Championship, but we were on tour. There was team spirit, we got it together, and the side was more settled. At home changes were made all the time – in my time there were about 15 different scrum-halves. Jan Webster was nippy and read the game well, and although his service was not perhaps the best, he was a good scrum-half and effective on the hard grounds. We had a good pack of forwards, but we were always experimenting at half-back.

JAN WEBSTER
The sad thing was that after that New Zealand win in Auckland in 1973 I was

the only England player dropped for the next game just two months later against Australia at Twickenham. Sandy Sanders, who was the chairman of selectors, wrote me a letter saying it was the hardest decision they had to make. I'm a sensitive person, and if things go wrong I tend to brood on it until I can put it right. I was 27 or 28, and it's still in my head now. I should have said I'm going back to play for my club, and that's it, but I agreed to be a sub. I'd no problems with Steve (Smith), he was a different player to me and a likeable lad – we had a good rivalry.

I wasn't a great player and many in our team weren't great players, but they were very good players – and they showed it. When you beat South Africa and New Zealand on their own turf for the first time, you ask how did that happen from a supposedly average team?

As a team we just had good days – great days – and I was lucky to be part of those two wins. And for all the disappointments after it, time is a healer. And if people remember those two games, that's fine for me. I never played more than a few games consecutively for England, so it was a rocky road. But on that road there were some highlights that will stay with me forever.

STEVE SMITH
England selection was so terrible. We could have had a team a lot earlier than 1980 but we didn't because of the amateur side of it, the lack of organisation and training. Alan Old was a fantastic player, as were Les Cusworth and Johnny Horton, but they weren't picked to do what they did best.

MARTIN COOPER
At the next training session after the 1973 New Zealand tour I gave Jan Webster and Steve Smith a lift back up to Birmingham. They were scrum-half rivals but there would always be plenty of chatter, however this time things were very quiet in the car and after we dropped Smithy off to catch a train on to Manchester I said to Jan, 'You're quiet, Sprat'. He said, 'Yes, they've dropped me'. How much would you hate being king dog on tour, and then they drop you? There was no logic to that, and that's how you felt a lot of the time.

PETER DIXON
Captaincy was a funny thing back in those days. For instance, in 1972 Bob Hiller was given the England job for the season and then dropped after two games – and that was when I was made captain.

There was a history of the skipper bearing the brunt, so when I told the other members of the team the overall response was, 'Glad it's you and not me.'

When I was asked to captain the side I said, 'Are you sure?' What terrified me most was giving the post-match dinner speech – I am not keen on public speaking, and it was always a burden. I felt more comfortable as a 2nd Lieutenant suggesting to a captain like Roger Uttley that he should tell the coach this or that.

TONY NEARY

I was appointed captain for the last game of the 1975 Championship when we beat Scotland at Twickenham, and then led the squad on the Australia tour that summer. It was obviously an honour, and I'd captained Lancashire with some success. However, you do question how you get the chance, and whether it was your turn because you'd been around a long time?

STEVE SMITH

John Pullin was a good lad, but not inspirational. However we had massive respect for him, and would follow him over the top. Billy Beaumont and I had a perfect relationship – I'd say get us the ball, and we (the backs) will work it out. Later on he was a great leader by example.

JAN WEBSTER

John Pullin was behind the New Zealand success. He had acquired the ability to be the best person in the job he was doing, and he communicated to people what he wanted and expected. And having been a Lions Test forward in 1971 he knew what it took. He had a dry sense of humour, but he didn't say a great deal – he didn't have to. He got the best out of the lads. Those wins can't happen without a happy group, and he was central to both of them.

CHRIS RALSTON

We didn't have a Willie-John McBride as a leader – John Pullin was a great player and a nice guy, but wasn't a terribly inspirational person.

MIKE BURTON

I missed most of 1973 because I broke my leg training at Twickenham. In those days there was very little medical back-up. They put me in one of those RFU minivans and took me to West Middlesex Hospital.

Before the international season in 1974 I broke my jaw. I had the wiring out of my jaw three days before I sat on the bench for the Ireland game, but decided not to tell anyone about it so no one noticed when I played the home game against Wales. Bobby Windsor was hooking and their props were Glyn Shaw and Phil Llewellyn, so they didn't have a scrum. We punished them, and we scraped home

16-12. Then I went to Paris to play against Jean Iracabal, the French prop who was one of the best I ever played against. He wasn't as big a beast as Gerard Cholley, but Iracabal was a great technical operator.

Syd Millar had been appointed manager of the Lions to go to South Africa that year and he came over to watch that France game. We did well against them in the scrums, I had a few runs and we drew 12-12. They announced the 1974 Lions team on Monday, and I was in it. To go on that tour with Willie-John, Cotton, Gareth, Phil Bennett, Gordon Brown, Mighty Mouse [Ian McLauchlan] and all those guys was beyond your wildest dreams.

STACK STEVENS

I had to turn down selection for the Lions in 1974. I had been away the three previous years on tours and could not be away again because of commitments at home on the farm. I had to decline the invitation to go. I remember with great clarity Don Rutherford phoning me and trying to persuade me to change my mind. It is obviously something I regret.

PETER ROSSBOROUGH

It's hard to put your finger on why the best wins were away from home, and not at home. Perhaps it had something to do with the level of expectation at Twickenham. Recently, coaches and managers have quite deliberately harnessed the power of Twickenham, whereas maybe in the past there was a sense of apprehension. England are just starting to remind people of their heritage.

PETER WHEELER (England 1975-1984, 41 caps, plus 7 caps for the Lions)

There was a big distinction back then between being a club player and an England player. It was a big step, and a big honour. Also, at Leicester, we had very few internationals. These days you trip over them every day.

JOHN PULLIN

Throughout 1974 I had a really bad ankle problem and I used to have it 'washed' every Wednesday night before an international at the local hospital down here in Bristol – bathed in cortisone – to get me through the game at the weekend. I could hardly walk around the farm let alone run and train in between times, but I wanted to keep that England shirt. That's what always drove me on. I'm not sure if that is what people mean by passion and pride, or just being obstinate and bloody-minded. Still, it paid off. I got to play against Wales in 1974 at Twickenham, the only win I needed to complete a set of victories against all the other seven major rugby nations as they were then. I wasn't great, but we won.

I always got on with the Welsh boys brilliantly. I spent most of my club career playing against them, and went on two Lions tours with many of them, and I took plenty of good natured stick over the years. I walked tall that night even though my ankle was killing me.

ROGER UTTLEY

In the 1974 Five Nations we lost to Ireland, and then drew with France in Paris. In the next game, at Twickenham, we beat Wales for the only time in the 1970s. Andy Ripley had a great game that day and overshadowed Mervyn Davies. It was one of the reasons Andy got picked for the Lions. Against me at the front of the line-out was a Cardiff policeman named Ian Robinson, and line-outs at that time were a fight. I was held back and swung my arm. There was a clunk – and I'm expecting retaliation to rain down – but when the game stops there is a prostrate figure on the 10 yard line. Robinson had to go off with a dislocated jaw after my forearm hit him. It was not deliberate, but in those days you were just scrapping for survival. There was some thuggery, and the forward contest could be a scary

Ireland's scrum-half John Moloney is tackled by Steve Smith as Andy Ripley looks on during their Five Nations match at Twickenham in 1974.

place because you didn't know where it was coming from. And if the ref didn't see it, that was it. There was no retrospective citing stuff.

It was mystifying that England could not replicate that 1974 win. But when Gareth Edwards got a game in his grip, and JPR Williams – one of the most competitive men you will ever meet – was on song, it was not easy. Also, as I discovered with the 1974 Lions, Phil Bennett and JJ Williams had a great rapport, which was fantastic when you are playing with them, but less good when you were against them.

JAN WEBSTER

What's the point of picking Duckham and Spencer if you are not going to use them? I played against Wales four times in what was a great era for them, and only won once. They were a brilliant side, and we tried everything – but what's the point in kicking the ball to them so they can run it back? I'd love to be playing now and being given the licence to go out and play your game in the way Stuart Lancaster has with Danny Care. At Moseley we were playing a high tempo game. If I have a downer in my rugby life it was not playing the same way for England as in club rugby. They told you to put the ball up in the air all the time, but when you are playing for your country you want to go out and show your ability – not be told to go out there and not make a mistake.

PETER SQUIRES

To beat Wales in 1974 was pretty special. Overall I played against world-class wings including Gerald Davies and JJ Williams for Wales, and Grant Batty and Bryan Williams for New Zealand. There were also other big athletic wings like France's Jean Gourdon and Ireland's Tom Grace.

PETER WHEELER

I played in non-cap games against Japan on the 1971 Far East tour, so from then until 1975 you had played for England… but not played for England. I'd been on the bench a number of times for John Pullin but to actually win a cap you had to play against one of the foundation unions. The coach John Burgess had called a training session at Coventry on a Sunday morning a week after England had lost in Ireland, I was sitting in the dressing room listening to the team announcement. I heard him say that they had decided to leave Pullin out of the team. Then he read out the team against France with my name in it at hooker. It was a very big moment, and quite stark, because it is what I had been trying to achieve for a number of years.

That is why I feel badly that John Raphael was on the bench 19 times for me. But it never even entered your mind that you would come off the pitch, although I wish for him that I had in the last few minutes of a match or two.

I remember virtually nothing about that debut game. I got an opportunity off a loose French line-out tap at the front, but I knocked it on. If I'd caught it, I would probably have scored. However, I do recall the arrival at the stadium. We had been shut up at the Petersham Hotel, then you got on the coach to the ground and saw the crowds building, and arrived in the west car park where people were picnicking and cheered you in. It got you emotionally keyed-in. You virtually never played against French teams, so your only experience of them was internationals. They had Alain Paco, who was a very quick hooker, and they always had ferocious props and second-rows like Cholley, Paparemborde, Palmie and Imbernon. A little later they had Philippe Dintrans, who was physically very strong – more like a professional – and a very good hooker. One quirky statistic is that it was Jean-Pierre Rives' first game for France too. It was a shared experience that gave us a special bond.

ROGER UTTLEY

I was selected for the Calcutta Cup at Murrayfield but when we were training at North Berwick I did one of those steps into nothing on a bit of uneven turf and put my back out. Don Rutherford drove me back down to Newcastle in his Vauxhall where we met my physio who treated me in the back of the car – but to no avail. It was the start of a train of back injuries which dogged me during the seventies. I have an extra sacrum vertebrae which makes my back a little long, and wear and tear put it out. It affected me from time to time, and I went from being a consistent presence for England to being a bit of a risk.

I was knackered after the 1974 Lions tour, where I played 16 out of 17 matches. Soon afterwards I was due to play at an England trial held in Bristol. We drove down and went to a petrol station to get some fuel, and I reached in my back pocket for my wallet and my back went again.

BILL BEAUMONT

If John Burgess hadn't been the coach, I wouldn't have been picked for that game in Dublin in 1975. They would have picked Nigel Horton. There were lots of good second-rows around, but Burgess knew me and because I was on the bench it was easy to put me in. So, I had gone from not being in the England U23s in October to playing for England in the January against Willie-John McBride. Willie-John was, apart from Gareth Edwards, the great name in world rugby. I remember Fran [Cotton] was captain. He said: 'You'll beat him. Don't worry about him.' Willie-John was like God, because the Lions were the pinnacle. He was on 'This Is Your Life' with Eamonn Andrews.

PETER ROSSBOROUGH

My last cap came against France in 1975. Although we lost 27-20 at Twickenham, I scored a try and kicked four penalties. I was dropped again, and had no expectation of it at all. Let's leave it at that.

ALAN MORLEY

I was fortunate to go out as a replacement for the 1974 Lions, but my next game for England after losing my place came two seasons later against Scotland in 1975, when they dropped David Duckham for the last game of the Championship. I was flabbergasted at the decision, but we beat the Scots and I scored when Peter Warfield kicked it into the in-goal area and Andy Irvine and I both dived after it bounced and I was given it.

MARTIN COOPER

I always looked up to David Duckham. He had pace, strength, skill – and he was great in the card school.

DAVID DUCKHAM

I absolutely craved to be part of an England team that could win Championships and Grand Slams. My taste of rugby heaven with the Lions in 1971 made it quite difficult to get my head around our lack of success. In the seven, nearly eight seasons, I was involved with England we never won more than two games in a season and we shared just one Championship title, that year when everybody won their two home games and lost their two away matches. I think somebody, probably a Welshman, worked out the points differences and calculated if that system was being used we would still have 'won' the Wooden Spoon!

JAN WEBSTER

My father collected scrapbooks of me. There are 35 of them and occasionally I have a look and they give me a lift. My mum and dad used to drive to matches when Moseley were away. They had this little Morris Minor and the coach would pass them on the motorway, and I'd see them, but when I got home he always asked me, 'How'd you get on son?', and I'd say, 'You know'. But he never liked to let on that they'd been at the game.

David Duckam in action against Scotland in 1975.

FIFTEEN

GATHERING MOMENTUM

1975-1979

ENGLAND'S TOURING MAGIC *did not last, because no sooner was the team back on home soil than the issue of inconsistent selection raised its head again. If Webster's axing was the most obvious instance, selectorial indecision was also reflected in a relay of captains, with the selectors moving on from the veteran Pullin and passing the baton to Dixon, Cotton, Neary, Uttley, Beaumont and Wheeler in quick succession.*

The inability to develop continuity between the players (and amid specific units in the team) was a self-inflicted disadvantage that England could ill-afford because, as Steve Smith and others comment, the Five Nations competition was fierce with British and Irish rugby enjoying a halcyon era which reached a peak with the resounding Lions tour victories in 1971 (New Zealand) and 1974 (South Africa).

Wales had the superb Gareth Edwards spear-heading one of the most talented teams in its history, while Willie-John McBride's Ireland and a Scotland side boasting the mercurial talents of Andy Irvine and Jim Renwick were difficult opponents. To make life tougher, by 1975 France had developed a monster pack around giant tight-head prop Gérard Cholley, an ex-Army heavyweight boxing champion. Add two great footballing flankers to the mix in Jean-Claude Skrela and Jean-Pierre Rives, and the direction offered from scrum-half by 'le petit general', Jacques Fouroux, and the French were a formidable proposition.

In 1974, despite the draw with France and victory over Wales, England still finished bottom of the table. In 1975 they finished last again, and only a 7-6 home win over the Scots prevented a whitewash. Matters then went from bad to worse when a selection experiment aimed at injecting young blood into the England squad came adrift in an acrimonious tour of Australia.

The Australians, who needed little prompting when it came to taking offence at any sleight from Mother England, real or imagined, decided that they were not being taken seriously enough – and opted for boot and 'biff' as their means of retribution. With seasoned campaigners like tour captain Tony Neary and pack cornerstone Cotton ruled out by injuries early in the script, the Wallabies opted for orchestrated thuggery as their primary tactic in the two Test series.

After winning the first Test in Sydney (16-9) hostilities were renewed a week later in Brisbane where in the opening minutes the Australian forwards started swinging punches in a premeditated mass assault. The upshot was that Mike Burton sought retribution, and the Gloucester tight-head prop became the first England international player to be sent off when he used an elbow to floor the Wallaby wing Doug Osborne.

With England reduced to 14 men after just three minutes, and Bill Beaumont moving up to tight-head, the Australians clinched the series. Yet, at no stage in the 30-21 loss did the tourists capitulate, and afterwards RFU officials were so incensed that they considered cancelling Australia's return fixture at Twickenham. They relented, and, after both sides were read the riot act to prevent any further feuding, England made their point on the pitch early in 1976 with a 23-6 victory, with Neary captaining a side that scored three tries to nil.

It was not an end to inconsistency. In 1976 England suffered their second Five Nations whitewash, with the sadly under-utilised David Duckham giving way to Mike Slemen mid-Championship. Slemen was informed of his England selection in his Merchant Taylors' (Crosby) school staffroom in a telephone call from the Press Association's Terry Cooper.

Having plumbed the depths again, gradually, from 1977 to 1979, England began to consolidate and build a team based around a core of gnarled, experienced northern forwards like Cotton, Beaumont, Uttley and Neary, and an increasingly influential scrum-half in Smith.

In 1977 and 1978 England finished mid-table in the Five Nations, and in 1979 the North achieved a landmark victory by overwhelming the bulk of the New Zealand Test side 21-9 at Otley, scoring four tries to one. It remains one of the most resounding defeats ever inflicted on the All Blacks. Yet, despite the North selectors seeming to have done the job for them, the England selectors made different choices in key positions a week later, ignoring the claims of Dixon and Uttley in the back-row and Old at fly-half, before suffering a 10-9 reverse at Twickenham.

By that stage new coach Mike Davis had detected that he had the makings of a dominant team. At its core was a pack of hard-bitten forwards who could command possession and territory – and believed their time had come – and a backline which could translate those advantages into points. As the seventies drew to a close the stage was set for England to stand and deliver.

BILL BEAUMONT

The drive was always to play for England, especially at Twickenham. Playing for England became a way of life. It's not obsessional. But you loved that build-up as it once was, the Thursday get-together with all the lads, training on Thursday night. Training on Friday. The match build-up. The bus going to the ground. All the people in the west car park. All of them wishing you well.

Then the changing rooms, some fantastic changing rooms in those days. Well, nothing compared to what they are now. But they were still fantastic. I can still remember the highly-polished parquet floor that they had there. You could eat off that floor.

Your jersey was hanging up waiting for you. Number 4 for me. As you went into the dressing room, you would start at Number 1 and work your way round. I always had the same peg. Always remember peg 4 – always had the same.

One thing that Stuart Lancaster has done in the current era is to benchmark the standards he expects of his players. Everybody else in the game looks at the England team as role models. It is about getting back to what we were.

There is the strong identity that means that you connect with all the people that have worn that jersey all the way back. You just hand the jersey over to somebody else. You have been lucky enough to wear it. In the England dressing room you see the name of every single player who ever played for England on the wall. You look and you think: 'It's not that many. Not that many. As a nation, we are not cocky, we are just solid. I always think we are solid, reliable, dependable and we get out and we do a job.

TONY NEARY

We treated that 1975 trip to Australia as an experimental tour, and the Wallabies decided that they should be treated better than that. You could see what would happen – it was planned intimidation. It's the way Australia approaches any game, and it's what you expect if you go on their patch. We had a young fly-half, Alan Wordsworth, and a lock, Bob Wilkinson, both from Cambridge University, on their first tours. It was not the place to blood them.

CHRIS RALSTON

I was dropped by England for the Australia tour in 1975, and didn't win another cap. They said it was due to a bad knee, but it upset me because in my view I was okay to tour.

FRAN COTTON

The England tour to Australia in 1975 had such far-reaching effects that it took English rugby at senior level four seasons to recover. The 1974-75 season had been a poor one with just a win in the last game against Scotland, and the results were a warning bell. But for the Australian tour the selectors obviously saw it as more than just a pruning job and decided to uproot the whole team and replace it with a new-look team full of youth and enthusiasm, but with little or no experience of senior rugby, let alone international level.

In fact, they sent a bunch of schoolboys, and not very good ones at that, to do what turned out to be a man's job. From the players selected only seven of the

25 went on to make any significant contribution to the England cause over the next five years, and of those seven only two were newcomers – Bill Beaumont and Alastair Hignell. It was a disaster before we even boarded the plane.

ROGER UTTLEY

The most annoying thing was the selection of young guys like Alan Wordsworth and Steve Callum when guys like Alan Old and Peter Dixon were left behind and both had to be flown out mid-tour. I was concussed during the first Test. I got smacked and I can remember bawling my eyes out in the toilets afterwards.

The Australians viewed it as payback time for their defeats at Twickenham. It is a great country to tour, but their coach, Dave Brockhoff, was a nutcase, and they wanted to make a name – I suppose a former colony wanting to make a point. They had punchers like Steve Finnane and Ray Price, but also some very good players, and that along with home referees and injuries to key players like Tony Neary and Fran Cotton meant it was all uphill.

ALASTAIR HIGNELL (England 1975-1979, 14 caps)

England had a disastrous 1975 Championship, and then I got this card saying that I'd been picked to go on tour to Australia that summer. By that time I had gone from scrum-half, where I had played for Bristol the previous season, to fullback for Cambridge, and then as soon as the Varsity match was over, back to scrum-half. That's why I asked, 'Who's the other scrum-half?' Only to be told that I had been selected as one of two uncapped fullbacks, along with Peter Butler. England took a whole load of youngsters: at fly-half Wordsworth and Neil Bennett had one cap between them, and at scrum-half Richard Harding and Brian Ashton also had no caps.

I remember the first Test in Sydney mostly for cricketing reasons, because at the time my main focus was cricket, as I was on Gloucestershire's books. It was at the SCG and the rugby pitch was right across the cricket square, which I thought was sacrilege.

From the kick-off at Ballymore in the second Test there was kicking, punching and stamping from the Australian pack, Our blokes had had enough of being pushed around by that Test. Dave Brockhoff and John Burgess were both tub-thumping coaches of the 'no step backwards' approach, and they whipped their players into a frenzy.

After the punch-up farce the referee blew and gave us a penalty. However Mike Burton had unfinished business with their prop MacDougall and dropped the nut on him. The referee reversed the decision and when Australia missed the penalty we cleared to them. Their winger Osborne caught it and ran the ball back when Burto intercepted him with his elbow. For anyone to be sent off in an international back then was extraordinary. You thought it was the forwards sorting it out, as often happened, but you didn't expect him to be sent off. I think Burto had also been sent off in my first game for Gloucestershire!

From there it was 14 men, and we knew it would be uphill. We learned later that at half-time Brockhoff got a message from the president of the Australian Rugby Union which said, 'Brock, call them off.'

We lost 30-21, and when we played Australia at Twickenham the following season there was a strong appeal by the RFU president to both sets of players not to indulge in anything like that ever again. We beat them 23-6 by turning good old English tactics on them on a better surface for us, and scoring three tries to nil. I kicked a few penalties as well, although you didn't worry too much about percentages in those days.

FRAN COTTON

I injured my back in the second match of the tour and took no further part. Tony Neary, the captain, ended the tour with a rib injury in the first Test, Brian Ashton had to fly home on a personal matter, and half a dozen players were on the injured list before the last game. It was most revealing that the tour party seemed to be strengthened every time a replacement arrived from home, which served to emphasise the weakness of the initial selection. A scapegoat had to be found afterwards and John Burgess, the coach, resigned.

BILL BEAUMONT

The turning point for me was Australia in 1975 where I replaced Tony Neary in the first Test after he broke his ribs. I played quite well. And then I propped every scrum in the Battle of Ballymore when Burton got sent off. When I came back with three caps I thought, 'Well, I may never play again, now that I have three caps under my belt.' But then the drive was to play at Twickenham.

ROGER UTTLEY

The Battle of Ballymore. They kicked off to us, and it was premeditated. They just ran through and smacked anything in white. When Mike Burton was sent off I thought the world had gone crazy – just Pommy bashing, hitting anyone. In the England side there were not many who would have a go apart from Nigel Horton and Fran Cotton, although Mike (Burton) would dive in and out if there was trouble.

MIKE BURTON

The first thing to say about the Battle of Ballymore when I became the first Englishman to be sent off – and this was after 103 years of international rugby –

is that I never, ever had any regrets about what I did. It was the second Test of a brutal series in which Australia set out to treat us like dogs; the opening stages of the second Test were like a war, they were kicking and punching everything as if it was a war – as if on a pre-arranged signal. The scenes were astonishing.

Thirteen years later, I took Andrew, my son, to Australia and I took him to Ballymore and showed him the place on the field. They had cleaned up all the blood. At some point, someone sent me a DVD of it and my grandchildren gathered round to watch. They saw all the fighting, a head-butt by me, and all that sort of thing, and it was quite a sobering moment. They were all there eating sweets and fruit and watching the film. 'Cor,' they said.

Right at the kick-off they started pummelling us, and kicking us, and in charge was a local Queensland referee, Bob Burnett, refereeing an international in Queensland – he didn't find anyone to send off in the Australia team, even though Ray Price of Australia must have thrown 14 punches. This is why I would not have done it any other way. Before the sending-off I got in a head-butt on MacDougall in the earlier shamozzle, and Burnett saw it. He said, 'Burton, I saw that Gloucester kiss.' Someone had to step up and react to what they were doing. Just after that incident I was warning Australian players. 'Burton's got the biff on,' someone shouted. After only three minutes played, I followed up a kick a long way down the field and late-tackled Doug Osborne, the Australian wing. I was sent off. It was unfortunate because that left 14 men, and Bill Beaumont never forgave me because he had to spend 77 minutes as a tight-head prop.

Now we have a bit of a laugh about it. The other chap wasn't actually mortally injured. And as for the late tackle, there were only three minutes of play gone so it couldn't have been that late! Bill got that joke and he used to use it on a Question of Sport. He filched the story. I am not concerned if the incident gave me any notoriety, which it did. It was a reflection of the way I played the game. At Pontypool, or Gloucester, no-one would have said anything about the tackle.

ALAN MORLEY

My last two Tests came on the 1975 tour to Australia. They were just out to beat us up, and in the second Test when Mickey Burton retaliated and was sent off after slotting their wing Osborne – he arrived as quickly as he could – we were up against it. You cannot play an international with 14 men.

FRAN COTTON

Australia will never know just how close they came to having the English part of their British tour cancelled for the following season. When Mike was sent off I immediately rushed down to the changing rooms to console him. Already in there was Billy Beaumont having stitches put in his eye which had been cut during the brawl at the kick- off. As I put an arm around my tearful colleague the door burst open and Ken Chapman [RFU President], Alec Lewis [tour manager] and John Burgess stormed in, their anger being directed at the Australian Rugby Union, and not towards the disconsolate England player who was the first to be sent off while wearing the white jersey. Chapman was fuming, threatening to cancel the following season's tour and was about to leave the ground in disgust. The emotional Burgess was having none of it. 'No-one is leaving this ground while there are Englishmen out there.'

STEVE SMITH

Andy Ripley played 24 times on the trot for England – which was unheard of at that time – and then he was never selected again. When he was dropped in 1976 they picked Gary Adey, who was a lovely guy but not big enough against the French who had huge forwards, like No.8 Jean-Pierre Bastiat. Rippers was a very big, impressive athlete, and we had France coming up. I said to Don Rutherford, 'You've got to play Ripley against Bastiat,' but it didn't happen.

Before going to Paris we all went to the Stoop to train. Our No.10 Martin Cooper was carrying an injury and he had a fitness test in which he had to tackle Fran Cotton, Bill Beaumont and Micky Burton. If he wasn't injured beforehand he was certain to be afterwards!

Before we went out there was this bloke in the corner of the changing room, who turned out to be Chris Williams, the Gloucester and RAF fly-half. I had never met him before in my life, but when Martin failed the fitness test it was Williams who replaced him, despite England having Alan Old available.

Old had been on the bench all year, had loads of England caps, and had been impressive on the 1974 Lions tour. When he heard about Williams, Old went up to Alec Lewis, the chairman of selectors, and had a massive row with him in the middle of the pitch – with us training around them while it was going on. Lewis was a lovely man, but clueless. We lost to France 30-9 at the Parc des Princes, and I never saw Chris Williams again. That was the low point for me. I had never been stuffed like that.

ALASTAIR HIGNELL

In my first Five Nations Test against Wales at Twickenham in 1976 I came into the line at a good angle and got through. I just had to get past JPR Williams and either score or set up someone else. Whereas most tacklers at the time were more passive, JPR advanced into the tackle and hit hard, and he messed up my timing. The atmosphere before that game was incredible – so different to the Australia game. The Welsh fans with their red scarves and leeks brought passion with them. The Twickenham crowd didn't ever wake up in the same way the Welsh did.

Gareth Edwards is the best rugby player I've ever seen, and at that time he was at the peak of his powers. The Welsh had some fantastic players – Ray Gravell and Steve Fenwick were very powerful – 'Grav' was a monster. They were fitter, faster, and spent more time on the game.

MARTIN COOPER

Scoring the winning try in Ireland when we won 4-0 in 1977 was my highlight, although my foot was three feet in touch. I'm so pleased it was in that era because today, with the TMO, it would have been no try. Years later I got a call from a business colleague inviting me to play a round of golf at Wentworth. He said we could play our round and that he had fixed up for us to watch the Ireland-England game at a nearby pub afterwards. I jumped at it, and was waiting to be picked up early on Saturday morning when the doorbell rang and there was Jan Webster. When I asked him what he was doing coming round at that hour he admitted to arranging the Wentworth wind-up and said, 'You're coming to Dublin, because we've got two tickets – and it's the 30th anniversary of your try.'

STEVE SMITH

The seventies was the most successful period ever in British and Irish rugby, with the Lions win in New Zealand in 1971 its greatest achievement, and victory in South Africa in 1974 not far behind. It was the period of the best Welsh team that ever existed, France were also a great side with the likes of Jean-Pierre Rives and Jaques Fouroux. Ireland and Scotland were good too, so there was fierce competition compared to today when there are two weak teams. It meant the Five Nations was horrendously competitive, and the number of good players was borne out by the success of the Lions – and they should have won again in New Zealand in 1977. I was a reserve for the 1974 and 1977 Lions tours, and I reckon I had more reserve cards than anyone. There was huge competition at scrum-half with Gareth Edwards, Dougie Morgan, Roy Laidlaw, Chris Patterson, John Moloney and John Robbie, and only two went.

TONY NEARY

It was quite an uncertain time, with the England team in transition. Wales were the yardstick by which every team was measured, whether in coaching, club system, or world-class players. By comparison, the whole of English rugby was in a very amateur state in terms of organisation. We had a great bunch of guys, and some great individual players, but in terms of an organised squad it was not quite there.

NIGEL HORTON

There is no doubt that in the last 10 to 15 minutes of matches my level of play dropped off. That's because in the 1960s and 1970s it was considered sissy to drink water at half-time. All we had was a slice of orange. One of the main reasons it all opened up towards the end of games was because we were all dehydrated – there were no water bottles. The average game ball-in-play time in those days was about 24 minutes, whereas now it's more like 35 minutes. Even so, we were probably covering more ground in the forwards. Today they play in pods and take their place in the defensive line whereas we had to go to every single maul and ruck.

PETER SQUIRES

It was a great Welsh side in the 1970s, there's no two ways about it. England versus Wales was a massive game. We had a couple of peaks, the New Zealand Test win was historic, but we underachieved in many respects. The other nations, aside from the Welsh, we should have beaten more. The selection, coaching and rugby structure was so fragmented.

ALASTAIR HIGNELL

Politically there was a strong anti-English feeling in Wales at that time, with cottage burning going on, and having played for Bristol on the other side of the bridge there was some tough, unpleasant stuff. There was also a lot of 'rugby in our blood' talk, so we were being patronised, beaten, and often beaten up.

MIKE BURTON

Gloucester wasn't the most fashionable. It all seemed a different world to Harlequins and all those. Northampton players always seemed to be in with a great chance of getting a cap, but when I saw some of the blokes England used to pick, and the Gloucester players left out for some soft Varsity type, I wondered how they would cope with playing against Brian Thomas. Brian was the legendary hard man at Neath. He used to say: 'All right, Burto? You want a nice smack in the mouth now?' I thought that this was the way I had to play if I wanted to be somebody. I hit Thomas early in one game and Micky Booth, our scrum-half, panicked. 'What have you done Burto, he's going to kill us all now!'

CHRIS RALSTON

In the England trials everyone was out for themselves, and the game in the second-row was very much dog-eat-dog. There was no lifting, no TMO, and the referees were pretty lax. There was all sorts going on in the line-outs, and when you were hit, it depended on how you reacted. I was never really a violent player, but you had to look after yourself.

MIKE BURTON

I was in and out of the England team for years, and they'd always find someone to bring in instead of me for the easier games. They never really let me feel a regular in the England team. Some of the props they picked couldn't push their mother off a piss-pot. When it came to the away game in Paris, they always seemed to find a reason to pick me again to meet Cholley and his mates. They might have ignored me for a season but they never ignored me for the Paris match. It was all rather condescending when I eventually got the call to put on the kit.

We used to go to the stadium with police outriders who kept kicking at the cars to get you to the venue. That French team, there were three balls they were interested in – your testicles, your eyeballs and the football. Jean-Pierre Rives, the captain, used to be an interested spectator from the flank when all this was going on up front. I saw him again in much later life when we were all together having a meeting about the Barbarians. He remembered a clash of heads between Cholley and myself. 'Today, Mike, rugby is a game for babies,' he said.

Back to Cholley and France – Robert Paparemborde, who was on the tight-head for them, used to bore his way right across so that his head was on your chest across the other side of the scrum. Cholley was huge and very mean. One day I went over there for a kind of celebration match thinking it would be much easier than usual. I saw Cholley before the game and he was even smiling and waving at me. Then in the first scrum, smash, he threw one.

MARTIN COOPER

It was difficult for England to gel with all the various factions. England were very much coach-driven. John Burgess loved anyone north of Stoke-on-Trent, but he couldn't get to grips with southerners like Ralston and Ripley. In the North it was all county, not clubs, in the Midlands it was more club based, and in the South West and London it was a mix of both. To be fair to the selectors, it was difficult to knit it together.

PETER DIXON

I retired because I just got too old for it all – it was too much like hard work. I remember after my last England game in 1978, which was against New Zealand at Twickenham, that I found it such hard work that it took me half an hour to get out of the bath.

STACK STEVENS

With the introduction of the squad system and monthly training sessions it was a huge commitment. Squad sessions were always either in Coventry, Leicester or Moseley. It was quite a hike from Cornwall in those days. I used to hitch lifts with the cauliflower lorries when I could. I trained an enormous amount on my own. The nature of my farm work was manual, no fork lift trucks in those days. After a day's work I would go that bit extra and run the beach and sand dunes on my local beach at Praa Sands. I enjoyed all my rugby, it was great to have the rugby/farming work balance, unlike today where the players just do the rugby. Looking back over my career I would not change anything. I think I had the best of it.

ROGER UTTLEY

When I look back and think of the players we had like Andy Ripley, Fran Cotton, Tony Neary, Peter Preece, Steve Smith and Alan Old, that whole era was a missed opportunity. Alan was the form player in the early part of the 1974 Lions tour and but for a knee injury was favourite to be picked for the first Test ahead of

Barry Nelmes (holding the ball), Maurice Colclough, Fran Cotton, and John Scott shield the ball at a lineout for scrum-half Malcolm Young against Ireland at Twickenham in 1978. England won 15-9.

Phil Bennett. There was a whole heap of players the England selectors went through but never allowed to develop. The selectors were very regionally based, and there was not much interaction. Selection was done on an anecdotal and horse-trading basis.

TONY NEARY

What made Roger Uttley, Peter Dixon and myself work so well as a unit was that we all played together for the North, and we understood each other's play. Peter had gone to New Zealand with the 1971 Lions and had learned how to carry and protect the ball very effectively. As far as back-row play was concerned I learned a lot from John Robins. He had coached Loughborough and the UAU, and was fantastic at passing on skills that weren't really taught at that time.

MARTIN COOPER

I played fly-half 10 times for England, and I came on at centre when Geoff Evans was injured in the win over New Zealand in Auckland. I never played fullback or wing, although fullback was probably my best position. However, at Moseley they said initially that I couldn't play fly-half because they already had John Finlan, and therefore that I would be a centre or wing. Moseley played fast tempo rugby, but for England I was picked as a kicking fly-half.

At that time the selectors would put their tracksuits on and come out onto the training pitch with us. On one occasion Derek Morgan said he had seen me pass it on my own 10-yard line and advised me it would be much better to kick the ball into the opposition half before passing it. In some ways you can see why, because we'd made some really bad errors inside our own 25 yard line – but you always felt you were living on a knife edge, and that you couldn't make mistakes.

NIGEL HORTON

Over my career I was in and out of the England team on five different occasions, and not one of them I believe was due to my playing ability. One was for injury, and the others were all about off the park incidents. I'm not sour about it, and I had great satisfaction fighting my way back in, because I was the best second-row of that decade.

PETER SQUIRES

Maybe one of the reasons I bucked the trend when it came to being dropped was because I didn't see more ball! I was frustrated at times; but it was an honour. Even if you didn't get many passes, you still had that honour, so I don't whinge or squawk about it.

ALASTAIR HIGNELL

Here's how amateur we were. The biggest thing on a Friday before an international was not training but getting your car from Richmond, where we stayed pre-match, to the Hilton (Hyde Park), and then getting the train back. The Hilton was where we had the post-match dinner and stayed on Saturday night, and you wanted your car there to make an easy getaway on Sunday.

PETER DIXON

We could have been better. Once or twice we did try to influence the selectors, asking what sort of game we were trying to play. It was never quite clear – it was also never clear whether the coach had the final say in selection, or the six selectors. The whole way through the 1970s you had people who coached, but who were not particularly strategic.

ALAN MORLEY

With the likes of Cotton, Uttley, Dixon and Neary I can never understand why we didn't do better. England had such depth. You have to look at the way the selectors played their part in never letting the team settle. Often we were sent out with mixed signals, and in the backs were left to pick our own moves. The selectors

were not known for their staying power. One mistake, and you were out. They also did things that made no sense, like picking Les Cusworth for the way he played for Leicester and then telling him to kick the leather off the ball.

PETER ROSSBOROUGH

Looking back, I didn't make as good a fist of it as I might have. Sometimes I felt badly treated, and I wish we'd won more, but I still have many friends and great camaraderie from my England experience. Sometimes I feel honoured and proud, and other times a little upset I did not achieve more – which is probably why I went into coaching.

Tony Neary.

CHRIS RALSTON

We were never settled beyond the pack, but I played 22 consecutive games, so I can't complain. We had a good pack, but I don't think we really played to our strengths by playing a tight game.

MARTIN COOPER

It was a real mix of people from around the country, and when I first went into the England dressing room and pulled on the shirt surrounded by the likes of Duckham and Neary, I thought, 'I've no right to be here.' But the good thing was there was very little 'us and them', and it was always a good dressing room despite more downs than ups.

PETER WHEELER

There was very little consistency in coaches or selection in the 1970s. We had some good captains, like Fran Cotton and Tony Neary, but usually only for a season. Fran had the capability to be a great captain, even a Lions captain, but there was no long-term planning. In 1978 the Midlands & North side that played Argentina featured about 12 of the 1980 Grand Slam team – but otherwise they were never picked together. By 1980 we had a very good, experienced international team, but unfortunately it broke up very quickly. It took us too long to get it together.

STEVE SMITH

There was a decent pyramid in the North from club rugby, to County rugby with Lancashire, and regional rugby for the North of England. I don't think I lost a game playing for the North. On one occasion we beat the Midlands by 60 points – we just hammered them. The problem was that going from the North to England was a step down. In terms of coaching, organisation and unity it was not as good.

BILL BEAUMONT

In those days county rugby in the North was strong. We were playing the Gloucestershires and all these sort of teams. Then you went into those divisional games, which the North were good at. We quite liked those. Then you had the old final trial. I was lucky because I came into a Lancashire team that had a very good coach, John Burgess, and Lancashire suddenly started producing international players: Fran, Smithy, Tony Neary, myself, John Carleton, Mike Slemen, Jim Syddall, Wade Dooley. But a lot of other good rugby players too, a guy like Richard Trickey, who played for Sale for years. A good, good player. You would have Irish internationals. Barry O'Driscoll, the fullback from Manchester. Kevin O'Brien. Colin Fisher, the Scottish hooker. The North has produced a lot of good rugby players. So club rugby was quite a decent standard. My problem would have been – and Wade's problem, too – if we had been dropped. Whether playing for Fylde would have been good enough to get me back in the England team, I doubt it.

ALASTAIR HIGNELL
Unfortunately, I got another ankle injury in 1979 – my sixth in seven years – and a specialist told me that there was so much scar tissue that I had to give up rugby if I wanted to continue to play cricket. Where most people have cartilage in their ankles which acts as a shock absorber, they discovered that I've got an extra bit of bone instead. That's why I wore high sided boots and always taped-up my ankles. So, I retired at 23. The attitude to sport then was that it was something you did on the way to something else.

ALAN MORLEY
I would love to have played more games for England, but I took the breaks when they came. I was dropped when I should have been dropped, and I didn't get back in because the others were playing well. I have no regrets. Much as I'd like to have been paid to play the sport, I loved it and wouldn't have missed it.

STACK STEVENS
The social side was all memorable for me, be it club, county or internationally. My rugby career was a great and colourful journey. I made some great friends, met some wonderful characters and got to see places in the world that without rugby would never have happened for me.

NIGEL HORTON
When you play with someone in the second-row it's a marriage. Chris Ralston and Peter Larter were good players, but also nicer blokes than me. John Pullin, Peter Dixon and Roger Uttley were quality players – the problem was not the forwards, it was the backs.

STEVE SMITH
Tony Neary had played basketball for England Schools, and he had fantastic hands. He was not quite as quick as Fergus Slattery, but he was a better handler. He was also a brilliant reader of the game, hard as nails, and highly competitive. They picked him ahead of Dave Rollitt, who should have had the openside shirt for a number of years – he was a big man, and very effective. Then, when 'Nearo' became world-class, they dropped him.

Alan Old was very confident, and would play it his way. I like fly-halves who are a bit gobby, and he could kick miles off either foot. When I last saw him he said to me that he wished he'd stood further away (to make more of my pass). Me and Jonny Horton just fitted together, and he had a great sidestep on him.

ROGER UTTLEY

I was offered the captaincy in 1977 and I very much enjoyed it out on the field, talking to refs like Norman Sanson and Clive Norling and establishing a rapport.

BILL BEAUMONT

I was made England captain the week after returning from the 1977 Lions tour, but my first game as captain was against France in 1978, and we lost 15-6. Old dropped two goals. It was a great day, but I was nervous. Originally, I probably only looked upon myself as short-term because Roger [Uttley], the captain, was injured and I thought: 'Well, are they only going to keep me until he is back?'

My first challenge was on the Thursday training at Richmond. We were on the scrummaging machines. Fran was injured. There was Burton at tight-head, Peter Wheeler, and Robin Cowling on the loose-head. Burton was going, 'Cholley, Paco, Paparemborde, we can't afford to take them on, you know.' Burto was a little bit wary about it because two years before Cholley had put him about six foot up in the air in the scrum. He had never forgotten it, and I said: 'Look, it doesn't matter if it's the first minute, the first scrum, the last scrum – you have got to take him on. Head on.' That was the moment when I said that is what we will do.

We lost 15-6 in Paris. We just lost to Wales, 9-6, at home. Then we finished off by beating Scotland away 15-0, and we also beat Ireland 15-9 at home. By England's standards, it was alright. We hadn't had a bad season.

PAUL DODGE (England 1978-1985, 32 caps, plus 2 caps for the Lions)

To be there at that age [19] against that great Welsh side in 1978 was unbelievable. I'd only recently been watching them on TV. I was not really expecting it, although I was in the final trial and knew I was in the pecking order. It was a typical rainy February afternoon, and I spent the whole game chasing kicks – I think I touched the ball twice.

That season I also kicked a penalty against Scotland. We had a gale force wind behind us, and it was just inside our own half in front of the posts. I hit it well, but I didn't need much help with that wind.

The break against Ireland? You tend to remember things like that vividly – I could see Peter Squires in a lot of space, and he put Mike Slemen over.

ALASTAIR HIGNELL

When Peter Colston, the former Bristol coach, became England coach [in 1979], I was suddenly picked at scrum-half in an England senior trial – without having played there for eight months. I was finding it difficult to get any match time at scrum-half having played for Cambridge in the Varsity match at fullback, until the Old Perseans stepped in and asked me to play against a correctional institution in Bedford. So the media turned up in force at a prison on the outskirts of Bedford to see how I got on at scrum-half on a rock-hard frozen pitch – that's how crazy England selection was at that time.

I even played an England trial at scrum-half, and then the following day, Sunday morning, the selectors decided they would have another full-on contact session. I got a rib injury, and so could not get any more scrum-half time and

Bill Beaumont on the charge against Twickenham at Murrayfield in 1979.

polish up. At heart I was always a scrum-half – I loved it – but I never had a proper crack at it.

PAUL DODGE

In the big defeat by Wales in 1979 in Cardiff I had a really poor game, and was very disappointed with how I played. I had Steve Fenwick opposite. He was underrated – whatever he did was the right thing at the right time, and he was a goal-kicker too.

BILL BEAUMONT

We weren't very good. That was the disappointing thing. In '76, we didn't win a game. In '77, there was a change of captain. Rog came in as captain. We beat Scotland at home. We beat Ireland away 4-0. Martin Cooper scored a try. Then we just lost 4-3 to the French Grand Slam team when we should have won. Higgy didn't have one of his better days.

ALASTAIR HIGNELL

I tell the story that I'm the only England fullback ever to win three Grand Slams. Against France when we lost 4-3 in 1977 at Twickenham I missed a few kicks and France won a Slam. In 1978, again at Twickenham, I missed four kicks against Wales when we lost 9-6 and they went on to win a Slam. And in 1980, when I'd retired, England won a Slam.

I was a sporadic kicker, but it did not have the same emphasis or importance that it has in the professional game. There was not the same focus. I remember that Peter Jackson came down to do a piece on me for the *Daily Mail* when I was coming back from injury, and reporting on my intensive goal-kicking preparations. I was school-teaching at the time, an amateur practising in my lunch break on the school pitches. He calculated that I had taken 290 shots at goal that week, and because I did it alone I fetched every single one of those balls. Jonny Wilkinson did 1,000 place kicks a week, 200 every day.

PETER WHEELER

The first time I captained England was against Tonga on the 1979 summer tour when Billy Beaumont went down with a bug. The Tonga stadium had one stand and we had been advised to arrive already changed. We were shown to a room at the back of the stadium but the groundsman didn't have a key. When he eventually opened the door our changing room was also where he kept his bicycle. The King of Tonga's nephew was on the wing for them, and the pitch had patches of sand with small shells and was fringed with palm trees.

STEVE SMITH

The build-up to the Grand Slam was the 1979 North of England game against New Zealand. We didn't just beat their Test team at Otley, we killed them four tries to one. The selection for that team was superb. The back-row was Uttley, Dixon and Neary. Dicko was a great ball-playing No.8, and Roger was a world-class blindside, but England usually picked them the other way round. I told Des Seabrook that I wanted him to pick Dixon at 8 because of his hands.

TONY NEARY

John Burgess was the most effective coach in England at that time, preparing the North side that beat New Zealand 16-14 at Workington in 1972, and the North side that beat them at Otley in 1979. He was national coach for a short period, but

Maurice Colclough rises to win a lineout against New Zealand at Twickenham in 1979.

he found the transition from the North to England difficult.

He was able to select people in the right positions, which was something England found more difficult. When England played New Zealand in 1979 a week after the North's victory those who came into the team were all good guys – but why would you change a winning combination for a scratch combination? Where was the logic?

BILL BEAUMONT

Judging by the number of people who have come up to me and said they were at Otley that day the crowd must have been 35,000. And it was the only time as a Lancastrian I ever ran out on the field in Yorkshire and they didn't tell me to piss off. But it was a great day. And if someone ever said to me in all seriousness 'What's the greatest 80 minutes you had?' – on the rugby field I hasten to add – then that would be it.

STEVE SMITH

For a few months before the game the North trained once a week at Roundhay, which was not the easiest place to find. It was the days of the Yorkshire Ripper and people would run for cover when anyone like Fran Cotton or Jim Sydall stuck their heads out of the window to ask for directions.

FRAN COTTON

Des Seabrook [Burgess's first lieutenant as Lancashire captain] was the perfect choice to follow John – and they were the two people who should really take the credit for what happened in 1979. And it wasn't by chance. It was down to quality coaching and total commitment to the cause over many years.

I'd played in many games against the All Blacks for England and the Lions, but the significant thing that day was that, when we stood there and the Haka was going on, I looked at our team, then at theirs, and said to myself, 'We've got better players – and that's why we're going to win.' It was a belief we all had.

ROGER UTTLEY

I didn't play again for England in that 1979 season, although in the autumn I played in the North's victory over New Zealand at Otley. After that game we drove down to Leicester for an England training session where they announced the team to play the All Blacks. We'd smashed them but they put me on the bench, and Peter Dixon didn't get selected at all. That's when he said, 'That's it, I'm finished.' When he heard about it Des Seabrook said, 'Those bastards had already made up their minds what the team would be.'

BILL BEAUMONT

One of the biggest problems in English rugby before 1980 was consistency of selection. We very rarely had a settled team. When you look back basically the players were inhibited on the field. They didn't want to make a mistake. Nobody wanted to make a mistake. If you were a back you'd just pass it on to the next guy.

SIXTEEN
OASIS IN THE DESERT
1980-1981

IT WAS A *desert out there. No Grand Slam in 23 years and just three Five Nations Championships, two of them shared, during that entire period. While England struggled badly to consistently produce their A game, Wales had been playing rugby from the gods, and France – all muscle, magic, menace and mystery – weren't far behind. Individually England appeared to have the talent but collectively they were still underperforming, their confidence often shot to pieces, and in the Five Nations the decade ended with one of the worst results in memory, a five tries to nil 27-3 drubbing in Cardiff, their heaviest defeat against Wales since 1905.*

Things had to change, and they did. An exceptional generation of players – Tony Neary, Roger Uttley, Fran Cotton, Peter Wheeler, Mike Slemen, Bill Beaumont and Steve Smith – had enjoyed only sporadic success with England against the game's giants. Playing for the North or the Midlands Counties, the Barbarians or the Lions seemed to be a much more successful and enjoyable rugby experience. How could that be? How was it that England often appeared to be less than the sum of all the parts? It's difficult to quantify but after that humiliating defeat down in Cardiff the main impetus for the 1980 Grand Slam and the brief oasis during the years 1980-81 was the sheer bloody-mindedness of the players.

The appointment of Mike Davis, after a highly successful spell with his all-conquering England Schools XV, was also important. Davis, a world class lock who had been messed around by England for much of the sixties, shared the England players' frustration and became a catalyst for change. Greeted initially with suspicion by the England squad – he had, after all, no experience of coaching at senior level – Davis quickly won the squad over and the impact of his organisational skills, honesty and plain common sense should never be underestimated. Davis made no guarantees to the senior hands in terms of selection but respected their rugby nous and wisdom. If they performed and dedicated themselves to the task at hand he would involve them and value their input like never before, a radical change from the 'them' and 'us' policies that had been the norm in previous England camps.

One or two encouraging signs began to emerge. The timely and well organised Northern Counties tour of South Africa in 1979 – designed to help produce a North team capable of defeating New Zealand at Otley in the November – was a huge success while a less demanding England XV tour of the Far East that summer also enabled

Opposite: Bill Beaumont is carried from the pitch at Murrayfield in 1980.

Davis to impart his rugby thoughts on prospective players – and in turn listen to their thoughts. Bill Beaumont, going above and beyond the call, played on both tours and was beginning to really emerge as a forceful captain after an uncertain start which had included that calamitous defeat in Cardiff. Beaumont's solid yeoman qualities typified an understated passion, connecting with both the fans and his players, and his flowering as a captain was to prove vital to the cause, although little did we expect that the unassuming northerner was going to become one of the most important, and best-loved, figures in English rugby history.

So too, was a young and clever centre who had emerged from Loughborough Colleges and who was to have a reasonably short career as a player, but an epoch-making stint as coach. Although that, in 1980, was all in Clive Woodward's future.

England's narrow 10-9 defeat against New Zealand in November 1979 was Mike Davis's first game as coach but when the dust settled there was, happily, no loss of momentum following the boost the North's famous win over the All Blacks at Otley had provided. There was still a rare optimism about the 1980 Five Nations campaign and that was picked up by the England fans before a shot had been fired in anger. There was a now-or-never feel to the campaign which added an unusual intensity to proceedings.

The England players, recognising that now was the moment, demanded more squad sessions, before and during the tournament, and these were generally held under the lights at Stourbridge on Monday. These sessions were intense no-nonsense affairs and Davis was happy for the public to attend – to make England comfortable with the feeling of being under the microscope, but also to foster an appreciation that there were many passionate England fans out there rooting for them at all times.

The opening match was against Ireland at Twickenham and there were no less than nine changes from the side that had lost their last Five Nations game, away to Wales. Among those was a selectorial coup, a player that neither the rugby media (nor indeed the senior England players who Davis consulted) had ever really mentioned in despatches. Gloucester's pocket battleship prop Phil Blakeway was catapulted into the limelight and went on to play a huge part in England's success. Just sometimes selectors get it very right indeed.

Initially, though, it didn't go smoothly for England who, despite dominating affairs from the off up front, slipped 9-3 behind as Ireland's fly-half Ollie Campbell kicked his goals. It was crunch time. Despite all the brave talk, what was this England team really made of? The answer was emphatic with quick tries from Smith and Slemen and a dominating second half performance despite the disruption of Sale centre Tony Bond breaking his leg. Smith had another try disallowed in the second half but John Scott completed a 24-9 win with a pick up try from No 8 and England were on their way.

Next up was France in Paris and in many ways the signature match of England's campaign. England hadn't won on French soil since 1964 and nothing of major significance could be achieved until that state of affairs was altered. Game on. Again it started unpromisingly with France in full cry and an early try for Jean-Pierre Rives and French backs leaving vapour trails everywhere. Up front however, with Fran Cotton to the fore and leading the resistance, England were beginning to get the better of the French pack and were soon rewarded with a well taken try by centre Nick Preston and a nicely worked try down the blindside by John Carleton. Two dropped goals by John Horton increased that lead to 17-7 before England had to defend for their lives in the final quarter to claim an historic 17-13 victory at the Parc des Princes.

Which brings us to Wales and one of the most discussed games in rugby history. Where did all that intensity and hate come from? Who knows for sure, but the build-up in the media was like nothing we had witnessed before. Wales had convincingly defeated France in Cardiff 18-9 in an extremely physical opening game and then faced a long month to get excited – over-excited? – about the prospect of slaying England at Twickenham and a swift return to the glory years of the seventies. England, meanwhile, were finally flexing their mighty muscles and had shown in Paris that this team would not be messed around. Although still relatively early in the Championship, certainly for Wales, it was undoubtedly a titanic clash in the making, but as the media coverage intensified, the fixture seemed to take on a life and momentum of its own. You rather suspect that February 1980 was an otherwise quiet time in the sporting calendar because the build-up seemed out of proportion and somehow became associated with one or two hot political potatoes – the imminent closure of mines and steel works in South Wales. The game predictably boiled over into an ugly battlefield with Wales, reduced to 14 men after the dismissal of Paul Ringer, digging deep to outscore England two tries to nil before falling to a dramatic last minute penalty by Dusty Hare.

England needed every day of the month gap that followed before their final game against Scotland to recover, but they clinched the long awaited title in style in the best game of the entire tournament against a classy Scotland side who recovered from an England blitzkrieg in the first half to really test England after the break. England were in no mood for succumbing though and closed out the Grand Slam with a 30-18 win with Bill Beaumont being chaired off by two of the greats of English rugby, Fran Cotton and Tony Neary.

But was this a beginning or an end? For a season England rugby supporters held their breath. England played some very decent rugby in 1981 to finish second in the Championship (two wins, two defeats) but a last minute reverse in Cardiff when Clive Woodward strayed a foot offside and Steve Fenwick kicked the winning penalty seemed to slow the momentum. A hard earned series win in Argentina followed, but the storm clouds were gathering. Cotton, Neary and Uttley had retired while Phil Blakeway was experiencing serious injury problems, and then came the hammer blow of Beaumont's premature enforced retirement after another serious concussion. England gradually slipped into bad habits again and as they entered a necessary transitional period

selection became more difficult and erratic again. The 1980 Grand Slam and the
1981 series in Argentina alas proved to be false dawns. Hard times were just around
the corner. Again.

MIKE DAVIS

By 1980 the England rugby players, and the England rugby community, were sick
to death of this underperforming label that had been placed around our necks and
particularly always coming second best to Wales throughout the seventies. The
truth is it haunted us. So this quite exceptional group of players, who had achieved
so much when playing for other teams, consciously made it their mission to right
the situation. They were brilliantly captained by Bill Beaumont who had known
the tough times but was passionate about England and still believed the years of
failure and under-performing could be transformed into something much better.

BILL BEAUMONT

We went on a summer tour to the Far East in 1979 and that's when Mike Davis
came on board as coach. Now, Mike was sharp. He started off as the very successful
coach of the England Schools XV but he quickly realised he couldn't use the same
language talking to a load of seasoned players, some of whom had been on Lions
tours. He was clever though, he would say things like, 'Have you thought of doing
this?' or 'Could it work better doing it this way?'

Consistency of selection, as everybody comments, had been a huge problem
but Budge Rogers had been made chairman of selectors, and Mike invited me
down to London early in November after a game and appointed me as captain for
the season and said, 'Look these are our thoughts, this is what we are thinking of
doing.' It was a rare thing to be included like that in those days.

MIKE DAVIS

As a coach I was very lucky with the tremendous pack I inherited in 1980, still
possibly England's best ever pack although it didn't actually play together as a unit
for very long. One way or another we had six England captains in that pack, past
and present. They were so experienced and streetwise savvy although, as many
commentators rightly point out, that with the exception of Phil Blakeway they had
all been around for years so why hadn't that pack been assembled before? Fair point.
Alas Peter Dixon retired after the North's win over the All Blacks and it remains
extraordinary to think he, Tony Neary and Roger Uttley only played together once
for England.

There were great combinations everywhere in the 1980 team augmented by one
or two others stepping up at exactly the right time. John Horton was a lovely Welsh

style fly-half – he loved to dance and step around – and I told him he could dance and step around as much as he wanted, but I was going to give him boundaries, a corridor he could work in. When he worked in that corridor he was fine, when he started stepping out of that corridor he would over-crowd the centres and I didn't want that. Steve Smith may have been the slowest scrum-half in the world but he was very quick mentally and he made great decisions. I remember saying to Steve once that I thought he was winding up his pass a bit and as quick as you like he came back, 'Mike how can you rush perfection?' He won that little exchange game set and match.

We arrived at the Five Nations in good shape. You can argue about the omission of Roger Uttley and Alan Old against New Zealand after their contribution to the North's win a week earlier – many have – but my abiding memory after that 10-9 defeat against the All Blacks was how upbeat Billy Beaumont was immediately after the game. He pulled me aside for a minute and said, 'Mike, we are going to have a really good season here, I can feel it.' We had a quick debrief. OK we had lost narrowly to New Zealand but let's not lose momentum here, we were going in the right direction.

That 1980 group was very hungry. They wanted more squad sessions and the rugby was getting so physical by then that we decided there was no point in gathering anywhere on Sunday mornings, the lads were too sore from playing the day before, so we decided to move the sessions to Monday night and chose a central destination, Stourbridge, which had a really good playing surface. We worked really hard, with tremendous purpose for an hour and a half or more, the guys couldn't get enough, and those sessions became occasions in their own right. I remember nearly missing one because I got caught in a traffic jam of local fans who we encouraged to come along and watch. Afterwards the Stourbridge club laid on a tremendous spread for the guys which was much appreciated. Our time at Stourbridge was one of my happiest rugby experiences.

The other thing that worked massively in our favour in 1980 was that our weekend off – i.e. the period of the tournament when each team got a month rather two week's between matches – came right after that highly draining match against Wales. I wouldn't have particularly enjoyed going to Scotland straight away for that visit to Murrayfield. We were able to recover properly, mentally and physically, and put in a couple of intensive sessions at Stourbridge. That was the luck of the draw if you like, and every team needs a little of that.

STEVE SMITH

After the All Blacks defeat Mike Davis realised, as the senior players did, that all the selectors had to do was pick the right side and we could pull off the Grand

Slam. The defeat against New Zealand was a blow to our hopes and disappointing to those of us who had beaten them so comprehensively with the North just seven days earlier. It was frustrating because we all knew England should have beaten them but the selectors hadn't got the line up quite right and Mike Davis, at coach, hadn't got the thing together.

It was an unhappy start for Mike but his strength was that he was a good learner. His other qualities were that he was a good bloke anyway and a good selector (and there weren't too many of those around). He also had the ability to get on with people. Budge Rogers wasn't the easiest man to get along with but Mike seemed to be one of the few able to persuade him to change his rather set attitudes. Mike was well liked and that was nearly nine-tenths of the battle.

FRAN COTTON

Mike's appointment did not meet with everybody's approval, particularly that of the Leicester players who felt that 'Chalkie' White should have been given the job after more than ten years of service and latterly great success with the Tigers. A number of players, including myself, were not available for the tour of the Far East, but word got back that Mike was approaching the job in much the same way he had done with the schools team using new terminology. Instead of ruck, maul etc 'whoosh' replaced ruck, while 'wide shoulders' and 'narrow shoulders' described different ways of driving into tight and loose situations.

At the first squad session it was all I could do to keep my face straight and I could almost hear the senior players thinking: 'Where have we got this joker from?' By the middle of the international season Mike had gained the confidence and respect of all the players which is a measure of the sensible overall approach he adopted by bringing in the views of senior players and allowing them to develop a style of play which they had decided best suited their strengths. It was a shrewd assessment and was exactly what was needed to overcome an initial resentment and cynicism and replace it with acceptance and confidence.

This confidence in each other's ability was extended to the chairman of the sectors, Budge Rogers, and the captain Billy Beaumont establishing a level of communication between players and selectors which had never previously been achieved. I must say the selectors played their ace by selecting Phil Blakeway at tight head after just his fourth game of the season.

PETER WHEELER

It was not a question of players taking over sessions as such, but a sensible discussion of the overall tactical approach as opposed to a blind faith in the coach's ideas. It was not a teacher-pupil relationship between coach and players at international level, more a matter of co-ordination to ensure that the players are all operating towards the same end.

BUDGE ROGERS

There were definitely mistakes. We got it wrong as selectors with the 10-9 defeat against New Zealand in the November by not selecting Roger Uttley and Steve Smith for the game just a week after their magnificent win over the All Blacks at Otley. My line of thinking was just wrong. I went back to 1967 when I was in a Midlands team that performed well against New Zealand the week before the Test and got selected pretty much en bloc against the All Blacks... come the Test match we hit the wall and couldn't repeat the intensity or performance. That was my worry in 1979 but I got it wrong and I must take the blame. I like to think, however, that the mistake was quickly rectified and, realising that something special was happening for England, we got the team right in just about every respect in 1980.

Mike built up a very good relationship with that senior group of players and in turn I like to think that they felt that their views were being heard. But ultimately as a selector you have make the call and you have to stand by it. We got the Uttley-Smith non-section wrong against New Zealand but I wonder how many of the senior players, hand on heart, would have come up with Phil Blakeway at prop – and yet that has been acknowledged as a very good selection indeed. You try your best.

There were some tough decisions made for the best of reasons. Maurice Colclough was our first choice to partner Bill Beaumont in the second-row, he had played very well against New Zealand, but missed the first game of the campaign against Ireland through illness, so Nigel Horton came in and did well. I liked Nigel a lot as a player, he was a very tough guy, but Maurice was our first choice and again I remembered back to my playing days how it could be soul destroying to win your place in the England team over a number of years and then to find yourself simply discarded if you fell ill or were injured. So I introduced a policy that if a player dropped out through an illness, he would return for at least one match the moment he was match fit again. He had to be given a chance to defend that hard earned position if you like. Harsh but fair, and I believe above all else players value a fair and honest approach.

When I became Chairman of Selectors, at the end of 1979 ahead of the summer tour and the 1980 Grand Slam, I also decided I wouldn't allow a vote around the table over a particular player or position. Votes can be divisive. I insisted we sat and argued out a selection until we had a consensus, a unanimous decision. When I took over I made changes and brought in John Young and John Finlan and, of course, our coach Mike was made part of the selection panel.

I had become a selector at Dickie Jeeps' invitation in 1976 which, looking back, was possibly too close to the end of my playing career, but I was very keen to get involved and try and put something back. It was a bit more organised than some give us credit for, although I accept it was a difficult job and far from ideal. Throughout the season we would go off and watch as many games as possible, write a report on them all and then meet up at least once a month, sometimes more, normally at a motorway service station, and debate everything we had seen and written.

We used to pick and update five theoretical England XVs starting with the first XV and work downwards. Often we would spend more time debating who was the second and third XV hooker, or whatever position, than the actual team because we wanted an agreed pecking order which gave us something solid to base our comparisons and ratings on. Remember this is all before video footage, internet and widespread TV coverage.

Physically getting to view all the players you needed to see, in games that counted for something, was very challenging. Logistically it could be very hard work. I was working up at Manchester for much of the time and can remember on many occasions slipping away from work at about 4pm to dive down to a match in Gloucester or Bristol and then driving back late at night to be in place at work again early the next morning. Later on there would be flying visits to check on Nigel Horton and Maurice Colclough playing in France.

Very quickly after I became involved we veered away from doing a general report on the game, which had been the method, and concentrated on specific players and positions. If I was looking intently at the back-rows I could be pretty oblivious to the fact that the fullback had just kicked seven penalties or the left wing has romped home for a hat-trick. I exaggerate slightly, but I was there for one reason and that was to watch the back-rows and make my assessment.

STEVE SMITH

So we had Ireland first up and it was a tough start. We went 9-3 down but then our pack produced a splendid spell of pressure and after winning a series of rucks I was able to dart over for a try. We were just a yard out when Fran ripped the ball out and I went to drive really hard for the line and almost fell over and dislocated my shoulder because the anticipated cover wasn't there. We had succeeded in sucking in so many players that my mother could have scored.

BILL BEAUMONT

Ireland was a big win. They had just beaten Australia 2-0 in a series down under the previous summer and unearthed a guy called Ollie Campbell. We wondered who he was, who was this player they had dropped Tony Ward for, who? Well we knew soon enough as we went 9-3 down to three beautifully struck Campbell penalties. But we played well that day, in fact we ended up giving them a really good hammering.

CLIVE WOODWARD (England 1980-84, 21 caps and 2 caps for the Lions. England coach 1997-2004)

I think I had been spoiled a bit in my playing career before my first cap, because I had been playing at Loughborough Colleges under the coaching of the great Jim Greenwood, playing real attacking and positive rugby, and I enjoyed it more than any other rugby I was to play.

But of course the England cap was the target. I was a replacement for my first and I was sitting high up in the stands, there were no tactical substitutions in those days so the only chance you had of getting on was when a player was injured. When Tony Bond broke his leg in the second half I remember having a problem getting down to the tunnel, trying to find my way down the backstairs of the old West Stand. I was still taking my tracksuit off as I got to the tunnel and it was only as he was being carted off on the stretcher to hospital that some official said, 'You are on.' There was half an hour to go and it was great getting on but I was conscious of not doing anything wrong. I don't actually remember touching the ball.

NIGEL HORTON

I played against Ireland because Maurice Colclough was unavailable through illness. We won 24-9 and I had a reasonably good game, but Colclough was the man in possession and I didn't mind being dropped under those circumstances. However, the manner in which I was dropped was unbelievable. I was enjoying myself at the post-match banquet at the Hilton when one of the selectors came up to me and said, 'Nige, you've been dropped.' I couldn't believe he was saying that to me on the Saturday night, rather than waiting until the Sunday morning, so that at least I could enjoy the evening. So, the end of my career wasn't pleasant. I said to my wife, 'We're leaving,' and walked out.

STEVE SMITH

Next it was France at the Parc des Princes in Paris. A scrum broke up early in the first half with Fran Cotton flattening Robert Paparemborde, the French prop. Referee Clive Norling called Fran over while the crowd bayed for him to be sent off and delivered a stiff lecture. That was the only comment made on the incident. Normally Billy would have gone over to the player concerned and given him a rollicking, but you never spoke to Fran when he was in that mood. Half an hour passed before I could pluck up the courage to ask my old pal if he was all right.

Fran just turned around and snarled: 'If he does that again he will get another one.'
He was psyched up to the eyeballs.

Afterwards we celebrated long and hard and at one stage ended up in nightclub
where nobody knew who we were. Suddenly Fran and Nero appeared on the stage
doing their version of the can-can which had the lads falling about. Eventually our
heroes were dragged into the wings, Fran fluttering his eyelashes and falling back in
mock horror every time one of the waiters tried to put a hand on him. The bewildered
audience were trying to decide whether to laugh or cry when our undaunted pair
suddenly reappeared doing a wheelbarrow across the stage. It was a wild night which
continued into day and it was an extremely well-watered Steve Smith who arrived
back home in time to pop into the local for a pint clad in Rives' shirt.

FRAN COTTON
Yes, the first ten minutes were played at such a pace that we were in danger of
being run off our feet, but two things happened to bring it under control. Maurice
Colclough took a two handed catch in the middle of the line-out and the second
was an altercation between Paparemborde and myself. Even though the incident
cost us three points and I apologised to Budge Rogers immediately after the game,
it gave us a psychological ascendency over the French pack as they stood and
watched their anchor man being shown no respect. It was quite an emotional
moment coming off the pitch particularly when my great mate Steve Smith, who
had played four years previously with me in Paris when France had taken us apart
limb by limb, sidled over with his Burt Lancaster smile and said, 'We can drink
with the men tonight, Fran.' My hangover on the Sunday morning was, by some
way, the worst of my life.

DUSTY HARE (England 1974-84, 25 caps)
It was an incredibly tough, physical game and I had total respect and awe for the
way Fran Cotton took them on. Fran was a hard man on the pitch, he had a hell
of a game and the pack followed him. The French at home in those days were just
out-and-out dirty and Paris was a hard place to play. If your forwards didn't turn
up you got a pasting, it was as simple as that, but our forwards turned up that day.

PAUL DODGE
You want to play in every game, but in 1979 Nick Preston was playing well, and
Lancashire had also gone well with Tony Bond. It was a bit of a shock because
we toured Fiji, Tonga and Japan, and everything seemed all right, but maybe my
form was not quite there. Then during the 1980 tournament Clive Woodward
came in for Tony Bond – who had broken his leg – and then Nick got injured.

That meant the Leicester pairing of Clive and myself were selected for the third match, against Wales.

CLIVE WOODWARD

We were always seen as a pair and I loved playing with Paul Dodge. No bones about it. I felt really comfortable with him. He had a great passing game, a great kicking game. And he was also a great defender. A lot of stuff came off him and I could do a lot more running off his passes. He was very quiet off-the-field but on-the-field he was a really good talker. A really good organiser. Just a really talented player. And it was an honour to link up with him on the field.

DUSTY HARE

For the first time ever in our careers that week before the Wales game we seemed to be on the back page and even on the front page of every newspaper in the build-up, and I've never really understood why. It seemed to come from nowhere. Wales had only played the one match – a good win over France – and we had only played the two games. It's not as if this was a Grand Slam decided between the old enemies. I suppose it shows just how desperate for success English rugby was.

I have never seen a game like it before or since. The verbals started right from the start along with the late shots. It all got pretty heated. Out at fullback I wasn't too bothered by it all and I never let any occasion get to me so my big concern was the absolutely atrocious pitch. It was a muddy wasteland as Twickenham often was in those days. Wales had seven shots at goal and didn't land one, I had seven shots at goal and landed just three although happily one of those was the winner right at the death. It was horrendous trying to kick off the floor, it was so soft and spongy. There didn't seem to be any grass management at Twickenham in those days whereas now it's the best playing surface in the world. Twickenham was a disgrace throughout most of my career. It was either a muddy mess or the grass was a foot tall and it was like playing in a meadow.

My last-minute kick to win the game was the most important kick of my career. It was quite wide out on the right but I didn't mind that at all because that was the only area where the pitch condition was half decent. I fancied it. I was oblivious to the crowd throughout my kicking routine but for one of the few times in my career I allowed the crowd into my consciousness when I trotted back into my position. It was absolutely deafening, I can hear it still. It felt like a very big moment for English rugby. I knew instantly I made contact that it was going right down the middle, just like when you cream a drive through the covers. It was nigh on perfect that little beauty and I was running back long before it went through the sticks.

I never had a kicking coach in my life but I was methodical and repetitive and relied on a routine I had worked out myself. Gradually I became a 'shunter' whereby I was pushing it and giving the kick what it needed rather than going with a full blooded follow through. For me goal-kicking is much like the golf, hitting shots off the fairway. I used to form a mental picture of exactly where I wanted the ball to go – not just through the sticks but exactly where it would go through the sticks, which sector. The ball doesn't need to go high and handsome it just needed to go through. I would take the wind and elements into account, the conditions underfoot for my non-kicking foot and I would shape the shot in my mind like a golfer at a tee off. I practised on my own a huge amount on the family farm – we had a grass paddock with a telegraph pole in the middle of it and I used to practice by aiming at it. I didn't hit it very often, it was a bit like getting a hole in one, but it was a target and I got to the point where I was never far away.

PAUL DODGE

It was revved up by the media, and worked out badly for Paul Ringer, who I knew. He had been playing for the first team at Leicester when I was in the youth team. I don't think the incident was as bad as was made out, and would probably just have been a yellow card these days. The Welsh gave penalties away and Dusty kicked well. When it came to the final penalty, I had seen him put them over week in week out at Leicester. It was huge pressure, but knowing Dusty was confident made me confident.

Clive Woodward makes a break against Wales at Twickenham.

STEVE SMITH

Unfortunately the game was built up to such an extent that we almost expected Clint Eastwood to walk out of the sunrise with his guns slung low. The press went a bit over the top and a war of hatred that didn't exist was stirred up. At Twickenham that day there was an atmosphere as we ran out that was electrifying. It was very different from the normal high spirited crowd and there was a feeling of hatred coming from what seemed to be a seething mass of people. There was no real cheering as you would normally expect and the whole experience chilled the blood.

The England dressing room afterwards was like a battleground. There was a queue of about eight England players waiting to have stiches in an assortment of cuts. I was last in line because I only needed three in a cut beneath my left eye. Typically of rugby though, the lads mixed together after the game and nobody mentioned what had happened. We sank a few beers and I remember joining the Welsh lads in a singsong at one stage. The players on both sides had been the innocent victims of the build up to the game. The whole affair had become political and, at the end of the day, had nothing to do with rugby. I toured with Jeff Squire some time later and he told me Wales had never recovered from it that season. They were mentally and physical finished.

TONY NEARY

Wales was always going to be hard. I cannot remember any Test match being built up bigger than that anywhere, in either hemisphere. The whole build-up was charged with emotion, and it was a very strange atmosphere because of the level of animosity. The Welsh had been successful for so long, often at England's expense, and the emotions among spectators spilled over into the changing rooms and onto the pitch. It became a cauldron even though most of us had toured together, and knew each other well. It was just 80 minutes of mayhem.

In terms of Paul Ringer being sent off, the incident was not that damning. John Horton would have got that, and worse, most weekends at club level. That distorted the game because they only had 14 men, which was very unusual. It was a massive forward battle on a pretty heavy Twickenham pitch – and for Dusty Hare to make that winning kick was some achievement.

PETER WHEELER

I don't think Paul Ringer would have been sent off today, but although we were playing against 14 men we had all suffered at the hands of the Welsh, and it was an opportunity we didn't want to lose. If anything the sending-off steeled the Welsh resolve – it can sometimes swing emotionally to the side with 14 men – and only

Dusty Hare's kicking kept us in the game. When that final penalty was awarded it was on the angle, on the wrong side of the pitch, with a Gilbert leather ball. It was a huge pressure kick. In a really important match, when there was a really important kick, you could always bet your money on Dusty kicking it.

It was a brave action on Burnett's part to send Ringer off, but most of the players were aware that having made his gesture it was unlikely that he would do it again and so the dismissal had little effect on an already aggressive game. It may sound extraordinary in view of all the subsequent publicity, but I was not aware of the extent of the foul play in the game. It was hard and committed but then so are most internationals and it came as a surprise to read the fiery criticism in the papers the next day and to see afterwards the film of various incidents in the game.

The one incident I do recall was lying trapped at the bottom of a ruck and seeing one Welsh forward coming towards me. He was a man with whom I had toured with several times and although I did not expect him to walk around me I was surprised when he looked down at me, stamped on my head and was off. Looked at another way, and without intending to make light of what was not a funny situation, I suppose you could say that if we had not been friends on tour together who knows what he might have done.

Ringer did no damage to Horton in the late tackle which caused his dismissal though that may have been more by luck than judgement. Paul played for Leicester between 1973-75. He had been a good friend of mine and was popular among the players, though not perhaps with the committee. He was a skilful, aggressive, sometimes ruthless footballer and there were occasions when he went over the top. Yet in many respects he could be described as a good influence. Away from the field he was a delight to be with. After the game I sought him out and found him at one of the hotel bars with Derek Quinnell. Both of us wanted to console him but his only thought was that he had let his team and country down.

ROGER UTTLEY

I remember a big thing being made of Terry Holmes and John Scott, who were teammates at Cardiff, being painted as arch rivals. I was injured when I fell on the ball, and missed it. So did Geoff Wheel, who swung his foot at the ball but kicked my head instead. The next thing I could feel was where my nose had split, and there was blood everywhere. Tony Neary came over and said, 'Christ!' My face felt like a football. Mike Davis asked me when I was on the touchline whether I was fit to go back on. I said, 'I don't think so.'

There was very little rugby played, everybody was at each other's throats and growling instead of watching the ball. People were giving 'verbal', being niggly, posing and generally taking the fun out of rugby. The ball seemed the last concern.

I was interested to see on television what had necessitated my withdrawal from the cauldron. Very revealing it was too. No wonder I was a shaken. As I gathered the ball Geoff Wheel, with a swing of the boot, had belted my head in a clumsy attempt to hit the ball. If I had faced him instead of turning my back there is no knowing what damage he could have done. How much of a face can they sew back on? Whether it was a deliberate action or not I didn't know but it certainly was in keeping with what had gone on before. Looking in the mirror I was worried about the kids. What would they say when they saw their father coming in the next day looking like this? How could I explain that I played rugby because I enjoyed it? As it was, typically, they took no notice at all.

BILL BEAUMONT

It was the only time I ever beat Wales in my career. It was probably the worst atmosphere of any game I have ever played at Twickenham. It wasn't an enjoyable sort of game, in fact it was an awful game really. But it was a game that you just wanted to win. When Steve Smith had his kick charged down and Elgan Rees scored, the only thing going through my mind was: 'What is John Reason going to write tomorrow about us?!' We didn't play well. That was the annoying thing about it. Paul Ringer probably didn't deserve to get sent off, it was just an accumulation of bits and pieces. I remember going into the Welsh dressing room at the end of the game and going up to the lads that I had known. We had all been together on Lions tours, we were hoping to go on the next Lions tour, and we all just shook hands and had a beer. That is what we did.

TONY NEARY

The last game, against Scotland, was played on a dry pitch on a fine day. Murrayfield was the best of the pitches at that time, and the Scots who had Andy Irvine, Keith Robertson and Jim Renwick in their backline, liked an open game. Given those conditions it was natural it would be more open, and England had an accomplished backline. We had a virtual club pairing at half-back with Smith and Horton, and our centres Paul Dodge and Clive Woodward complemented each other perfectly. The wings Mike Slemen and John Carleton had speed and skill in attack and were good defensively, and with Dusty Hare at 15 it was a good back three.

The feeling afterwards was one of great joy, a certain amount of relief, and great satisfaction. Many of us had played for 8 to 10 years without winning anything. Contrary to what is sometimes thought I did not retire immediately and in fact intended to play the following season. I was selected, but the old rib cartilage injury flared up so it wasn't to be.

ROGER UTTLEY

If Twickenham was the agony then Murrayfield was the ecstasy as rugby, and England rugby, found itself again. Rugby only had to wait a few weeks before the memory of Twickenahm was exorcised by our thrilling attack display at Murrayfield.

PETER WHEELER

There was one scrum at Murrayfield which I regard as the best I have ever been part of. It took place near Scotland's line, our own ball, and Billy called for a double shove. The ball was heeled, the scrum locked and pushed and I can still recall the feeling as we surged forward like a supercharged car going into overdrive. The sensation from that scrum was an uncommon experience at international level.

BILL BEAUMONT

The plan was to play territory, scrummage, win the lineouts, drive hard in the mauls and work for pushover tries. Then Clive Woodward scored a try. It wasn't planned; he just picked up a ball, beat three or four defenders down the left hand side and scored. Then he did the same and made a try for Slem, and John Carleton ended up scoring a hat-trick. We did play good rugby that game. All of a sudden, the English rugby supporters who had been starved of success for years had a Grand Slam to celebrate. When you looked at the dressing room there were many of the same guys who had hidden from the fans in airports with me on a Sunday morning coming back from a walloping in Paris. Some would come up and say, 'Unlucky lads.' And you are thinking, 'Punch him!' Just the disappointment of it all. But now we had our own Grand Slam.

CLIVE WOODWARD

I just felt totally at home up in Scotland. I kept looking at our team and thinking: 'Wow, the preparation – there is no way we can lose this game.' Not that the game we played was the one we prepared for. The whole plan revolved around our forward pack and we were just going to kick for possession. I was new to the team. I was not going to question the tactics of the game. But deep down, I was thinking, after looking at their back division, then looking at our back division, that we should attack.

And then what happened in the first half? We played this all-singing all-dancing game, scored three tries and were 19-3 up at the break. Billy Beaumont got us into a huddle – you didn't go off for half-time in those days – and was about to say something when Fran Cotton teed off. 'Billy! Before you say anything, what happened about keeping it tight?' Of course, all the players just burst out laughing.

MIKE DAVIS

I've always had a theory that every world class Test side will have a spine of five absolutely world class players – individuals who would command a place in a World XV for that era. With Wales in their pomp it was clear to see: Gareth Edwards, Mervyn Davies, JPR, Gerald Davies and then whoever they picked at fly-half – Barry John before he retired, or Phil Bennett.

For the 1980 Grand Slam, for the first time in decades, it seemed to me that England had five world class players on the park – Fran Cotton, Peter Wheeler, Roger Uttley, Tony Neary and Mike Slemen. I didn't include Bill Beaumont initially in that group but he grew as a player throughout the season and from the Lions tour that summer through to the premature end of his career in 1982 Bill was a world class lock.

The name of Slemen might surprise some but I was a huge fan. I always remember one afternoon at Twickenham, and we had TV monitors installed by then for the coaches. I looked out at the field and Mike was standing hands on

hips in that rather trademark pose of his watching the play develop. I looked down and there he was on the monitor as well. My attention was distracted for a fraction and I looked down at the monitor again and Slem was no longer there. With that incredible rugby brain he had ghosted away from the left wing and was heading for some reason to the right and sure enough seconds later he was on hand to give a try scoring pass. Slem was priceless for a coach, he was so adaptable and I would have had no hesitation starting him at fullback had either Dusty or Marcus Rose been injured.

Coaching that team was easy on match day, it was full of leaders and players on a mission. I might have a few relaxed words in the changing room in the build-up but then I would deliberately vanish. There

Clive Woodward attacks in Edinburgh.

were so many great players in the house that the last thing they needed was me bashing on the tables and doors and kicking up a noise. I never really asked what was said and by whom but it always seemed pretty calm when I made my exit. The art surely is to do all the preparation beforehand; a good winning team shouldn't need much extra revving up. Despite all the big names around him, Bill was the perfect captain really, a bloke they all respected. Players like honesty and sincerity from their leaders and Bill ticked both of the boxes perfectly. The way some of the great names of English rugby chaired him off the field in Scotland said it all really.

CLIVE WOODWARD

Billy was actually very similar to Martin Johnson. Billy's big strength was that he led by example. It was not luck. He was a great player and was very good at understanding that he had a really experienced team. Steve Smith was massive for the team as well. Just like Matt Dawson was massive. John Scott was a great leader at No 8, as Lawrence Dallaglio was to be later. The key spine of the 1980 – you look at Wheeler, Scott, Smith, those are some seriously good leaders and communicators. Billy's great gift was to see that and set an incredible example.

STEVE SMITH

I was having a quiet pint with Fran soon after and I pointed out that the 1980 Grand Slam team had been around for five seasons. Apart from Clive Woodward, we had all been around and I thought back to a combined North and Midlands side that had defeated Argentina at Welford Road. The back division that day? Hare, Carleton, Dodge, Bond, Slemen, Horton, Smith. Up front we had Wheeler, Cotton, Beaumont and Neary, while Peter Dixon and Roger Uttley were seasoned internationals by that time. The 1980 Grand Slam was so tough. We sat there after we won it, and thought about the likes of Mike Burton, Andy Ripley, Chris Ralston, Peter Dixon. It was very pleasing to finish in such style and although we knew some of the lads were approaching the end, the selectors should have tried to get another couple of seasons out of a few to help the transition. Instead, it was all change again.

CLIVE WOODWARD

I looked around a very emotional dressing room and thought, 'Why has winning a Grand Slam been so difficult?' We had an amazing team, a mighty forward pack and many of them had been around for years. Why had winning a Grand Slam taken so long? It really wasn't that difficult. Why has this only happened now? That still puzzles me. England had been massive underachievers.

I was just thinking: 'You can't take this away from us, we have won the Grand Slam, we have all played well.' That was the biggest thing to me. Yet I think that is what playing for England is about. That is why you have just got to win. It's not about playing for England, it's about winning. I kept seeing so many people who were grumpy or depressed about their England careers and I didn't want that to be me.

BUDGE ROGERS

That 1980 team was so committed, so hungry. They couldn't get enough of those extra sessions at Stourbridge on Monday nights. It was John Jeavons-Fellows' club and he organised it all splendidly. The facilities were good; it was a good pitch, the squad worked like dogs and the club used to lay on a tremendous spread for the lads afterwards. John's father-in-law was a butcher and would arrive with a supply of all the best cuts for the boys: roast beef, chops, and steaks. Great fun, tremendous bonding nights; they were a very happy group on a mission.

MIKE DAVIS

We started again in 1981 with high hopes and we were competitive enough for the next two years but it was a difficult transition period, no question, with so many of the big names disappearing off the scene. Tony Neary was a super player, possibly the most difficult of all to replace. He read the game so well he was actually one of our best line out players. He had great hands and was the master of running backwards at the tail of a line-out to take the ball. There was nobody round who could take his place like-for-like. Mike Rafter was a very fine player in a different way – he had a great tour of Argentina where he completely bottled up Hugo Porta, and David Cooke was promising for a couple of years. Peter Winterbottom eventually made the place his own, a wonderful player but very different to Nearo.

I started to lose out on a few important selection calls. As the coach, I was only one voice in six in the selection process and gradually I found it very frustrating indeed – and if I am honest, it spoiled things at the end. It had been so good during 1980 but then we regressed again. I still wanted Dusty Hare and Mike Slemen in the team. The critics said Dusty was a carthorse – he wasn't – and there was still nobody better to kick your goals. He was a badly underrated player in my opinion.

Slem was class and when you drop a player like that not only do you deprive yourself of a world class player, but everybody in the team is suddenly on edge. 'If they can drop Slem they can drop anybody.' And then you are back to that situation I outlined before when people start playing for their places rather than doing what is absolutely right for the team. I had decided quite early on that 1982 would be my last Five Nations, I still had a demanding job at Sherborne to fulfil and it was time to step back. It was a memorable spell full of incredible memories of working with great and committed individuals. As a player with England I played 16 Tests and only appeared in five winning teams. As a coach I was in charge 16 times and we won ten. It redressed the balance a little.

CLIVE WOODWARD

We were never the same side the year after, the Slam team had a lot of players coming to the end of their careers, they stated to drift away and Fran, who was immense, had heart problems on the 1980 Lions tour to South Africa. I am a massive supporter of the Lions but still believe that the individual nations who provide a big contingent suffer for it in the season afterwards.

We did manage to beat Scotland in 1981 where I scored a try that they still replay now and again. I was an instinctive player, probably didn't think too much about what I was doing when I had the ball, it was all instinctive. I can remember Huw Davies called the old-fashioned 'Rangi' move named after Ron Rangi, the All Black, where the 10 comes across and scissors the outside-centre. It's one of the oldest plays in the book. So, I came on the scissors with Huw Davies, took the ball and then I looked up to see what was ahead and instinct just took over. I can remember beating a couple and putting the ball down.

It's so funny. No one is congratulating you. Even I looked a bit embarrassed. I put the ball down, sort of walked back. The odd person came up and said, 'Well done.' These days you get half the team rushing up to celebrate with the try scorer.

BILL BEAUMONT

1982 brought the close of play for me. It all began when I played for Lancashire in a short tour to the south of France to celebrate their centenary. I didn't really want to go. I had been away with England in Argentina and hadn't been on a family holiday and I had some work to do. I didn't play in the Agen game but they said I had to play against Beziers, they had sold out the game saying that I was coming.

So I travelled down there. 9pm kick off in August and midges everywhere under the floodlights. We made the mistake of taking the lead in injury time. I remember waiting for a kick-off, watched this ball come out of the floodlights and then somebody put me out. I don't know who it was. And that was when I started feeling cramp. I went and saw a doctor and they said, 'You are okay.' But I never felt 100%. Nowadays of course you would have scans and stuff.

Then came a county game for Lancashire against the East Midlands at Moseley. At the Reddings. Suddenly I couldn't really see the hooker. I couldn't pick the hooker out throwing the ball in from the crowd that were behind him. 'This is strange,' I thought. I went off and I thought I would be alright for next week. But then I had all the tests done. The bloke said: 'You could do yourself some serious injury.' So, really it was an easy decision in one way although at the time I thought my whole world had come to an end because playing for England was my life. My ambition had been to be the first player to captain two Lions tours, to earn selection for the 1983 party to New Zealand, but I soon got things in perspective. I looked back at 34 caps, 33 consecutive appearances for England, a Grand Slam, two Lions tours etc etc. It had been a good run.

There have been some fantastic moments and some fantastic people. People ask about my best win. They bring up the 1980 Grand Slam, of course. But the best win that I had, outside of the Grand Slam, was beating Argentina 12-6 in Buenos Aires in the summer of 1981. The first England team ever to win over there. And not many have done it since against the full Pumas team. It was a tough old game. They had some great players. Hugo Porta. Tomas Landajo, the scrum-half. Alejandro Iachetti, he played. They had Topo Rodriguez, the scrum master who went to Australia. Pete Wheeler didn't go, Maurice Colcough didn't go. Quite a few of the normal team didn't go. We had a young team and we absolutely knuckled down. Woody [Clive Woodward] scored a try in injury time of the first Test, we drew 19-all. Then we beat them 12-6 in the second. Happy days. Happy days.

Winning in the England jersey in games like that was special. Great memories.

The Grand Slam team before the Scotland game at Murrayfield.

SEVENTEEN
THE SLEEPING GIANT
1982-1986

ANY OPTIMISTS WHO *believed that the 1980 Grand Slam, followed by the series win in Argentina, was the start of a brave new dawn for England were soon disabused of the notion. The dozy giant, having briefly awoken and flexed its muscles, stumbled back into the stygian gloom and promptly fell asleep for another seven year spell.*

The 1982 season started promisingly, with Bill Beaumont leading England to a hard-fought 15-11 win over Australia at Twickenham in January. It was a match remembered for a topless streak by Erika Roe, a buxom interloper whose presence on the pitch soon commanded the attention of all the (male) spectators in the stadium – however, disruption of a more serious sort was just around the corner.

The heart was ripped out of the team rebuild when, after a 9-9 stalemate against Scotland in Edinburgh at the start of the Five Nations, Beaumont was forced to withdraw before the Ireland match due to a head knock. It ended in a 16-15 home defeat, and for the captain brought to an end a run of 33 consecutive Tests.

Worse was to follow when Beaumont announced his retirement before the France match following medical advice after a series of concussions, leaving only Phil Blakeway, Peter Wheeler, Maurice Colclough and John Scott from the Slam pack. By contrast, although most of the backline was serviceable – with Steve Smith, John Carleton, Paul Dodge, Clive Woodward, Mike Slemen and Dusty Hare all still available – the selection vagaries that dogged England throughout the 1970s soon resurfaced.

Initially, however, England rallied from the setback, and new captain Smith led the side to a mid-table finish. The highlight was a 27-15 victory in Paris, and after such an emphatic win over the French the English players were in high spirits by the time the post-match dinner started, with the larger-than-life Colclough in the mood for practical jokes. The England second-row decided to start the drinking games with an act of subterfuge designed to snare one of his team-mates. This involved emptying a small bottle of after-shave, given to the players as a gift by their French hosts, and re-filling it with white wine.

Colclough's plan became part of rugby folklore because when he toasted his team-mates and swigged his 'after-shave' back in one, Colin Smart, England's formidable loose-head followed his lead. Soon afterwards the prop began to feel unwell and was rushed to hospital while his team-mates caroused on into the night. Fortunately, Smart

Opposite: Stand-off Rob Andrew celebrates his match-winning drop goal in injury time against Wales at Twickenham, 1986.

made a full recovery – and the following morning may even have felt better than his badly hung-over colleagues.

The feelgood factor continued when Wales were dispatched 17-7 in front of a full house at Twickenham, with an enterprising England side finishing the season on a high note. It started with Smith putting Slemen over on the narrow side, and Carleton scoring the second try with a 30 metre dash from the back of a ruck.

Yet the core stability, which had been established in 1980-81 with Beaumont and coach Mike Davis as the main pillars, started to crumble almost as soon as the 1982 Five Nations was over. No sooner had Beaumont been forced to bow out than Davis, who had gained widespread respect, resigned as coach at the end of the season to concentrate on his teaching career.

Davis was succeeded by Dick Greenwood, but the high point of the new coach's tenure did not come in the 1983 Five Nations – in which England finished last – but the following autumn in a rare England victory over New Zealand.

By that time Wheeler had replaced Smith as captain, and New Zealand had opted to tour with an experimental side. The 15-9 win was fuelled by a sense of injustice among the English players who had been overlooked for the 1983 Lions tour of New Zealand – like Wheeler and his Leicester club-mate Paul Dodge – and by those, like Dusty Hare, who did go but felt hard done by in selection.

A Colclough try gave England the edge and Hare's goal-kicking saw them home, but it was a false dawn. England were mired in mediocrity throughout the middle to late 1980s with the lack of competitive leagues holding back the development of the national team. This was reflected in promising players like Peter Winterbottom and Jamie Salmon going overseas to develop their skills, with Salmon becoming the first dual New Zealand and England international.

There was not so much as a Triple Crown in sight, let alone a Five Nations title, and England finished in the bottom two from 1983 to 1987. There was an occasional raising of the red rose standard, accompanied by the blooding of three players who were to become English rugby icons. The debut of ace finisher Rory Underwood coincided with a narrow home win over the Irish in 1984, while in 1986 Wales were beaten 21-18 thanks to six penalties and a drop-goal from fly-half Rob Andrew, and Ireland edged out 25-20 thanks to two tries from new No.8 Dean Richards.

Overall, however, club and country organisation was poor and national coaches came and went, with Greenwood giving way to Martin Green after the 1985 Five Nations. Neither were able to break the also-ran mould, either at home or on tour.

With John Scott replacing Wheeler as captain for an ill-fated short tour of South Africa in 1984, a makeshift England squad had no answer to the power and pace of the supercharged Springbok centre, Danie Gerber, and were well beaten in both Tests.

It was a similar pattern a year later in New Zealand, this time with Dodge as captain and Salmon swapping New Zealand black for England white. A new-look England outscored the full-strength All Blacks two tries to nil in the first Test in Christchurch – with touchdowns from Mike Harrison and Mike Teague – but were overhauled 18-13 through six penalties from Kieran Crowley. In the second Test in Wellington, the hosts were on a mission to intimidate, and although the English stood up to be counted in a mass punch-up, they came a distant second on the scoreboard, losing 42-15.

PETER WINTERBOTTOM (1982-1993, 58 caps plus 7 caps for the Lions)

It was always going to be a challenge after that great side of 1980-81 started to disintegrate, but it didn't have to become the shambles it became. England rugby's big curse is that we are always boom or bust. We are not good at transition periods.

Old players are kept on one season too long, young players are left kicking their heels when they should have been introduced. This is where the Kiwis have always been ahead of us and others. No matter how big the name, they are kicked out once they are over the hump and somebody is playing better.

CLIVE WOODWARD

Looking back now, I was incredibly spoilt. Probably my one regret is that it went downhill from the Slam and became very, very chequered. Then you are looking back and thinking, 'How can this be?' That is what I think set me up to coach England. When I got the job, for whatever reason, I looked in the mirror and thought, 'You've either got to put up or shut up now because you are in charge. All this stuff you have been thinking about for years, you have got to do it.'

MAURICE COLCLOUGH (1978-1986, 25 caps plus 8 caps for the Lions)

Keeping a nucleus is one of the most important factors in making a successful team. The 1980 side was formed around experienced players like Cotton, Beaumont, Uttley, Neary and Steve Smith. That experience was very important to the younger players coming in – they had a base to work from.

I didn't realise what a good captain Billy was until he went. And it was certainly no fluke that Mike Davis was there in '80 and again in '82 when we should have won the Championship again – it was a pity to see Mike go so early. Although we were lucky to replace flankers like Uttley and Neary with youngsters of the calibre of Winterbottom and Jeavons so quickly, we failed to build on the success we'd had. The English structure didn't help the players – but then we didn't help ourselves either.

PETER WHEELER

When we were more dominant in 1980 we should have maintained it over a longer period, stretching through 1978, 1979, 1980 and 1981. There was a tendency in the Five Nations, and even now, for no-one to have a successful team for much longer than that.

CLIVE WOODWARD

That Lions tour of 1980, a lot of the Slam team were on that, led by Billy Beaumont. It wasn't the most successful tour. The Lions are interesting. Deep down I love the Lions. But with my England hat on, you wonder if they hamper England perhaps. Does it do your national team any good? No. I just don't think it does. For the good of rugby, I think it's the right thing to do. But if it is all about England, I'd say that the Lions is something you could do without. Again we didn't recover from that tour. Fran didn't play for long after that, for one.

MIKE DAVIS

It was my decision to quit. I said I was going to retire at the end of the 1982 season – I still had a proper job at Sherborne that needed my attention. We started losing the mafia, Steve Smith, Uttley, Neary, Fran. They were the people who if they said do it, young players in the squad did it.

STEVE SMITH

When I was made captain in 1982 after Bill Beaumont was forced to retire I tried to make a difference and bridge the gap between the players and the selectors. Then, the following season after we'd drawn in Cardiff they dropped me again.

PETER WINTERBOTTOM

Pretty soon we were on the slippery slope and we went from being very competitive – we had a great win over France in Paris during my first season and we beat the Welsh as well – to being average and then going downhill. From the end of the 1983 season until the first game of the 1987 World Cup I played in 22 England games and was on the winning side just six times.

STEVE SMITH

I found out I was captain when I heard it through the press. It beggars belief – it's basic man-management. We were treated like serfs. All in all I did my bit. Regarding the Cotton Traders success in life after rugby, after 10 years of watching the England selectors, we'd learnt how not to do it.

If I said I loved every minute of playing for England I'd be lying. But I enjoyed the vast majority of it, even though there were some huge frustrations. I'm delighted I came back in 1979, and to win a Grand Slam in 1980 after all the frustrations in the decade before, in the end it was all worthwhile.

MIKE DAVIS

I first saw Winters [Peter Winterbottom] in a Steele-Bodger's game against Cambridge University – it was his ticket to get into the England set up and he gave the students a hell of a tough time.

PETER WINTERBOTTOM

I had a couple of decent Divisional games and next thing I knew I had been picked to play against Australia in January 1982, a game remembered mainly for the appearance of Erika Roe and her friend – who never seems to get a mention! We had a good 15-11 win and outwardly it seemed pretty promising. But it was all about to fall apart. The first six years or so of my England career were pretty difficult and at times, if I am honest, we were close to being a shambles.

It was always in my mind to play rugby. There was a little incident when I was aged seven and we were in Spain on a family holiday. Dad spotted a couple of players from Coventry in the bar and got chatting with them – Brits abroad and all that – and I was introduced to them. 'What are you going to do when you grow up son?' was the friendly question. 'Play rugby for England,' was my instant reply. I remember the moment very well. I earned a guffaw and a friendly pat on the head but I was for real. I really meant it.

In my first season things were already beginning to look problematical for England. There had been a raft of big name retirements – Neary, Roger Uttley, Fran Cotton – and Phil Blakeway had picked up a serious injury. Then Bill Beaumont got another knock on the head, one concussion too many, and was told to stop playing. Bang, that's five members of possibly the strongest England pack in history gone, with one of them – Beaumont – the team's much respected captain. On top of that the coach, Mike Davis, who had done so much to pull that group together, decided to retire at the end of the season. Suddenly, we were lacking leadership and direction – and the truth is that it wasn't until the Geoff Cooke and Will Carling era that we got that.

PAUL DODGE

From 1980 onwards I really began to enjoy it at international level, because I was on top of my game and knew I could cope with the pace and physicality. The win over France in 1982 was the only game I played in Paris. It was played in early spring sunshine which was meant to be French conditions, but we outdid them. There was a breakaway try by Clive Woodward, and then John Carleton scored the clincher.

MIKE DAVIS

The Friday night before we played in Paris in 1982, John Scott and Maurice

Colclough came to me and said, 'Mike, you've got it all wrong'. I got them a beer, which we were allowed to do in those days, and said, 'Where have I got it wrong, guys?' They said we were trying to play too open a game and we want to stick it up our jumpers a bit more. I had to point out to them they were now the mafia.

That weekend I went up to Maurice in the changing room in Paris and I said, 'I am fed up having to justify picking you for every game, can you pull your finger out?' I did it in calculated way and then just walked away. He played a blinder.

PETER WHEELER

After we beat France in Paris we had the usual journey from the Parc des Princes into the centre of Paris for the post-match banquet and the England players were seated at two separate tables. As is the custom after French games there were little gifts at each man's place; sometimes it takes the form of a record, or a cigarette lighter, or aftershave. On this occasion there was a bottle of aftershave for each player and, sitting with Maurice Colclough, I saw him empty the perfume from the bottle and refill it with white wine.

Strange, I thought, until Maurice stood up and shouted: 'Aftershave!' There had been contests between the two tables all evening of course... And this was just one more challenge. Maurice whipped the top off his after-shave bottle and drank the contents. When Colin Smart, at the other table, rose in response and repeated the feat I thought: 'He's in on the joke too.' But an hour later Colin complained of feeling unwell. He must been taken in by Maurice's drinking 'feat', and he was taken to hospital, post-haste, leaving chaotic scenes behind him.

The English committeemen were shooting black looks at the players, who by now had napkins knotted round their heads and trousers rolled up to the knee, aping the traditional Englishman abroad. One of the problems was that in Paris the visiting teams tend to drink wine in the same way as they normally drink beer, by the potful. The bread rolls were flying around and things gradually deteriorated.

DUSTY HARE

It was one of those occasions you will remember to your dying day. Not many beat France in France, so everything about it was memorable. We were on two tables of 10, the French hadn't arrived, and we'd had a few beers – drinking games such as boat races, one against one, and the like. When Colin answered Maurice's 'toast' and swilled it back we were all shouting, 'Don't do it!' When he started feeling unwell Dr Leon Walkden took him to the gents, and then he puked in the ambulance. That's probably why he felt better the next day than the rest of us. However, I can't say anyone noticed he'd gone. We were too drunk to care. It was only the following day that we asked, 'How's Colin?'

STEVE SMITH

Colin was in a bad way – but his breath smelt lovely.

DUSTY HARE

When Smarty got back to Newport he was in the clubhouse having a bite to eat and chuckling as he was telling the tale on himself when one wag walked by and said, 'Glad to see you're back on solids, Colin...'

Dusty Hare, who kicked 11 points in England's 15-9 victory over the All Blacks at Twickenham in 1983, their first victory over New Zealand at home in 47 years.

PETER WINTERBOTTOM

There were a variety of reasons why England struggled in those days, but one thing I did know for sure was that the clubs system that existed then wasn't challenging enough week-on-week for us to compete with the world's best. There were no leagues, every match was a friendly unless you were involved in a cup run. I deliberately took myself off down to Hawke's Bay in New Zealand after the 1982 season to learn my trade as an openside flanker playing every weekend against some of the best in the world. But not everybody has the freedom to up-sticks and do that.

PETER WHEELER

New Zealand came to play us at short notice in 1983 after Argentina withdrew because of the Falklands War. It was only three or four months after the Lions tour, which I had not been selected for, so it was a chance to make amends. I had broken my thumb playing for the Midlands when we beat New Zealand at Welford Road on the Wednesday the week before the international. I had thrown a bad punch at their tight-head and caught his chin after he had grabbed me at the front of a line-out so Murray Mexted could come round the front. There was no way I was going to miss the chance to play the All Blacks at Twickenham, and fortunately it was my left hand rather than my throwing hand. You weren't meant to have painkillers in those days, but the Doc took me into one of the cubicles and gave me an injection before the game. I didn't feel the thumb at all.

PAUL DODGE

Prior to the 1983 Lions tour England had not had the best Championship, and although all the pundits said I'd be in the squad going to New Zealand, I was so disappointed when I wasn't selected. It wasn't the end of the world, because I'd gone out to South Africa as a replacement in 1980 and played in two Tests for the Lions, but I was looking forward to New Zealand coming to the UK in the autumn of 1983. When the Midlands beat them we knew England could win the Test, and although it was a very close game, we did so.

PETER WHEELER

It was a tight game, and although they were not the best New Zealand team, they still had Hika Reid, Cowboy Shaw, Jock Hobbs and Mexted in the pack. It was a great opportunity to beat the All Blacks twice in 10 days – and there are not many people who do that. It was a new coach and new set up with Dick Greenwood as coach and for once England picked the right team. When he was asked about the basis for selection he said, 'We believe the evidence of our eyes,' referring to the Midlands victory.

The All Blacks kept themselves to themselves more in those days. They always had great captains and were very good at getting the refs onside.

MAURICE COLCLOUGH

Let's face it, rugby is a physical game and a certain amount of contact is acceptable. I think you make a choice: if you're cheating and lying on the ball in a ruck you're taking a risk, and if you get trampled on, then fine. I condone people being rucked off the ball if they're deliberately stopping it coming out – I think the New Zealanders had got that right.

I remember the horrified reaction in England when they saw (Peter) Whiting going up somebody's back because he was on the wrong side of a ruck, but in fact that's not too dangerous. It may take the skin off your back so you have to sleep on your stomach for a week, but it's not dangerous in the same way as a kick to the head – and it doesn't compare to the sort of attitudes that existed in French rugby.

PAUL RENDALL (England 1984-1991, 28 caps)

There weren't many to beat Maurice Colclough in size or in sheer character. He must have been the biggest, strongest man to have played rugby in our era, and he was a great player for England and the Lions. Everyone enjoyed his company at Wasps, where he could always be found propping up the bar, drinking copious amounts of Guinness. I remember once, during a court session, fining Melly (Nigel Melville) for too much whingeing and whining on the pitch. His punishment was to drink for the night with Maurice.

BILL BEAUMONT

Maurice was a powerful and very athletic rugby player who made a massive contribution to the clubs he played for, to his country and to the Lions. He had a huge heart.

FRAN COTTON

Maurice Colclough was the strongest scrummager I ever came across. His calf muscles were like footballs. They were so big he had to cut the sides of his socks to get them on.

RORY UNDERWOOD (1984-1996, 85 caps plus 6 caps for the Lions)

It was a great moment for me when I made my debut against Ireland in 1984. The match went very quickly, and I slightly twisted my ankle in the first 20 minutes. We had one opportunity and I passed it to Clive Woodward when I probably should have gone myself.

I wasn't expecting it, I was just a 20-year-old, and the call came out of the blue although I played in the trials for the Possibles. However, you had John Carleton and Mike Slemen, and David Trick and Tony Swift were coming up, so you could never be sure if you were going to make the cut.

My first try came against France in Paris that same Championship. It was a massive relief that I wasn't a one-cap wonder, and also to get a try in your second game. I fly-hacked the ball down the wing and it bounced nicely for me, but Peter Wheeler has always claimed a share of it because he did a bit of manoeuvring to stop a French tackler from getting to me – or so he says.

CLIVE WOODWARD

I stopped with England after the '84 Five Nations, aged 29. Is that young? Did I ever miss the 15-20 extra caps that maybe I could have won? No. I got 21 caps for England. I never got dropped. That was over four or five years. I decided to go to Australia with Rank Xerox – it wasn't a career move, it was a business move. I also wanted to go when I was still young enough to play rugby.

PETER WHEELER

In 1984 the Scots won a Grand Slam and were much more difficult in that period, while our best result was a draw in Cardiff. By the end of the 1984 Championship I was getting to the point where, at 34, I thought England needed to move on and lay new foundations, and I made myself unavailable for the South Africa tour.

PETER WINTERBOTTOM

We were so off the pace against South Africa in 1984 it wasn't funny. I suppose that we were also aware that players in other parts of the rugby world were being treated better than us, but I just don't have the answer other than we got caught in a vicious cycle of diminishing confidence. And that is difficult to extract yourself from.

MIKE TEAGUE (England 1985-1993, 27 caps plus 3 caps for the Lions)

I was bitterly disappointed in South Africa in 1984 when I didn't get a Test place. England were always looking for a tall No.8, and on that tour they put John Scott, who was not really a lock, in the second-row. I'd always played No.8 at Gloucester, and it was between me and John Hall at six and me and Chris Butcher at eight. It was a controversial tour because of apartheid, and they were pleased to see us because they had been starved of international rugby. We had good players but we couldn't cope with the likes of Danie Gerber in the backs – whereas our midfield of John Palmer and Huw Davies was a bit lightweight, and once Dusty Hare jumped out of Gerber's way. It wasn't a serious tour.

RORY UNDERWOOD
The 1984 tour to South Africa was a real problem because of the apartheid sanctions issue. Although the RFU decided that England were going, being a member of the Armed Forces was always delicate, and I had a word in my ear from the powers that be that the RAF felt that it would be better if I didn't go. As a result I got stuck into my flying training, and I had no regrets because I needed those five weeks to do that.

STUART BARNES (1984-1993, 10 caps)
I didn't want to go to South Africa in 1984. I was invited, and I was first choice fly-half, but I was also clear in my political view. On that occasion being unavailable was a question of personal conscience rather than being a miserable git.

DUSTY HARE
There were a lot of guys from Bath drafted into the squad to go to South Africa, and they were not quite experienced enough. We went to South Africa that summer with a poor team. They picked John Scott in the second-row, and he was not quite big enough against those Afrikaners they had. It was a funny old selection, and when I came back I decided I'd had my time after ten years of being in and out of the side. I called it a day with England and continued with Leicester. I thought it would be for two years, but it ended up being four, and I thoroughly enjoyed it.

NIGEL MELVILLE (1984-1988, 13 caps)
I was on the bench for the North when they beat the All Blacks at Otley in 1979, and my first England training session was at Leicester the following day. I went to Argentina with England in 1981, North America in 1982, and I'd played for the Lions in 1983 in New Zealand before I was eventually capped by England in 1984 – although a knee operation ruled me out of the tour of South Africa that summer.

I had been around during the Grand Slam in 1980, and then I saw the transition between the team I had been brought up watching – and then trained with, and got to know with both the North and England – and the new generation. With players like Billy Beaumont, Roger Uttley, Tony Neary and Mike Slemen starting to retire, and Des Seabrook and Mike Weston falling out with the England selectors, that crew was disappearing and players like Steve Bainbridge, Wade Dooley, Nicky Youngs and Huw Davies – who were really my generation – were coming through.

Winning that first cap as captain against Australia in 1984 was the culmination of so much. I had been wanting to play for England since I was a little kid. I'd played at representative level all the way through for England, but then it occurred to me that I could end up like guys like Andy Simpson and John Raphael, two hookers who never got off the bench.

I'd had 16 games on the bench over three to four years, but Smithy (Steve Smith) never came off – and if they didn't come off injured you could not go on in those days. He never even went down, and I never saw him get treatment, whereas Bob Hesford, who was covering the back-row positions at the same time, got about 15 caps. Bob used to strip off in the stands and say, 'I'll be on soon,' and usually he was right.

STUART BARNES

I'm not a patriot. For me international rugby was more about achieving personal objectives. However, I chose not to be available for Wales despite having been selected in their squad as a teenager. I had gone to school in Wales but I am English, and therefore felt I should represent England. Fans support their country and pay money to do so, and the granny and great-granny stuff has never felt right to me.

NIGEL MELVILLE

We were well beaten by that magnificent Wallaby side of 1984, but we did reasonably well compared to some of the other home unions. My opposing scrum-half, Nick Farr-Jones, also made his Australian debut in the same game.

However, the senior England team was one in transition. I remember a training session was called at Worcester on the Monday night before the Australia Test, but it was a waste of time because half the team were injured from the previous Saturday. By comparison, the Wallabies were on tour, and had been training together for at least 10 days. For England you got together very rarely and it was almost like playing for a Barbarians side. The coaches couldn't do anything much other than basic organisation.

STUART BARNES

I expected to play in that game against Australia in 1984, and I'd had whispers that I would – I'd been on the bench the previous season. I remember Mark Ella standing incredibly flat and thinking, 'Jeez, this is how fly-half should be played.' It was a privilege to have played against such an important Wallaby team, because they put Australia on the road to being a frontline rugby nation. I got on well with Michael Lynagh, who I'd met already when Oxford University had played Queensland University, and they were a friendly bunch so I had a good night out with them in Chelsea after the match. I was fascinated by the way they used their brains.

NIGEL MELVILLE

My first ever pass in an England jersey was from a line-out. It was a really wet, windy day – the wind was swirling – and it was at a time when the grass at Twickenham was allowed to grow long, which slowed you down. Then, instead of playing with the Mitre balls we used in club rugby, which had pimples on them for better grip, we had to play with the leather Gilbert ball. These were quite pointed, and they put dubbin on to stop them soaking up all the rain, all of which meant that it was like handling a bar of soap. Then, when I looked at Stuart Barnes, my fly-half, he seemed to be standing miles away. He was like a speck in the distance, and he's not the tallest so the grass seemed to reach his shorts. I thought, 'My God, where's this pass going to go?' Fortunately, because it was a spin-pass, it sort of arced round before going straight into his hands.

STUART BARNES

My form was outstanding at club level at the time, so to be dropped from the starting line-up for the next game against Romania was very disappointing. I was surprised, but they wanted to have a look at Rob Andrew, who had had a great Varsity match.

Rob was quintessentially an English fly-half, and I was quintessentially a Welsh fly-half. Rob would not have been as treasured as a fly-half in Wales as he was in England. Of his type he was very good. He was tough physically, and mentally strong. He liked to play in a pre-ordained pattern, but although typecast as a kicker he could also run.

MIKE TEAGUE

I'd never played against a French side when I made my debut in 1985 at Twickenham as a replacement. We drew that one, and I was never on a losing side against France. When I eventually got the cap I remember how pleased the boys were for me – Les Cusworth went and got me a French shirt so I could keep my first England one, and Albert Agar, who was the manager, gave me a signed programme wishing me luck in my career.

I was training very hard, and I'd gone through the England U23 progression. I was delighted: every rugby player wants to play for their country. When I look at Andy Simpson, who sat on the bench 20 times and never got a cap at hooker, I count my blessings.

JAMIE SALMON (New Zealand 1981, 3 caps. England 1985-1987, 12 caps)

The biggest difference in the early to mid-1980s between rugby in England and New Zealand was that in New Zealand you didn't go to training to get fit. I remember a Kiwi coach telling me, 'It's not my job to get you fit, it's to make you a better rugby player.' You went running at lunchtime in New Zealand to get fit, whether at club or provincial level.

It was different in that respect, and in terms of the expectation levels. The All Blacks were expected to win, full stop. In England the attitude was do your best, but don't worry too much if it's not good enough. I came through the English system, but I didn't get an England U19 trial. In fact, my main memory of English rugby at the time was a Kent U19 selector saying to me after a trial game for Kent, not the most successful rugby county, 'You're not good enough.' I was 18, I wanted to get to the top, and thought I'd played quite well. It was the final thing that turned me – I thought, 'I'm not going to make it here, so I may as well go.' I wasn't alone. John Gallagher will tell you the same story. There was a reluctance to promote youth, and I hate to think how many players England might have missed out on.

Anyway, I was playing for Blackheath seconds with a couple of Kiwis and they said, 'We'll take you,' meaning their club in Wellington (Wests). I arrived in New Zealand in 1978 and within six weeks I was playing for Wellington against Counties and came off the bench with half an hour to go to mark Bruce Robertson. He was an All Black legend with nearly 40 caps, which would be worth double that now. In the same Wellington side there was Allan Hewson, Bernie Fraser and Stu Wilson, all of them All Blacks. It was surreal.

I soon qualified for an NZ passport, and after three years I was eligible to play for New Zealand. In those amateur days my view was, 'Do I turn down being a New Zealand All Black?' I didn't know what was round the corner, and so I didn't hesitate. I made my New Zealand debut against Romania in Bucharest in the first Test of the 1981 All Blacks tour of Europe, scoring a try.

After that tour I came back to the UK for a while but went back to New Zealand and in 1983 played for Wellington against the Lions. I came close to All Black selection again, but just missed out – and then I did my hamstring and decided it was time to think about a career. Rugby-wise I thought that I had made my bed, and that my international career was over when I returned to England again. That was when David Cooke, who was a friend of my brother's, suggested that I come and play at Harlequins. I had to wait a three-year eligibility period to be able to play for another country, in my case my homeland, England.

STUART BARNES

I was back at fly-half for the tour to New Zealand in 1985, and that was my most enjoyable time with England. Brian Ashton was the backs coach, and I liked the pressure of running the team. We almost beat the All Blacks in the first Test, scoring two tries to their six Kieran Crowley penalties, and it was very memorable because we were a patched together team which played decent rugby. The best game I played in an England shirt came on that tour in the provincial game against Otago – a 25-16 victory.

JAMIE SALMON

When I was picked for the first Test in Christchurch I was lying on my bed when there was a phone call, and a familiar voice said, 'Well done mate on becoming a double international.' The voice added, 'But normal rules apply, and if you come on the switch I'll knock your head off.' It was Murray Mexted.

MIKE TEAGUE

Scoring a try on my debut proper in the first Test against New Zealand in 1985 was the crowning glory of my career to that point. What it would have been if we'd won! Nigel Melville put in a deft kick into the left corner and I touched down, but the New Zealanders never give up, and they fought bitterly to the end and nicked it. The punch-up in the second Test was always coming, and what I realised quickly about New Zealand rugby is that if you lay on the ball you got shoed. Destroyed.

It's not the easy games but the hard games on tours when you find out about the players around you, and what it is to be an Englishman. Everyone wants to beat the men in white. But for me, the rose, the white shirt, and singing the national anthem… It was everything.

PAUL DODGE

I had reservations about the captaincy – it was not the easiest job – but I felt I couldn't turn it down as an experienced player. I'm not a natural captain, but I took it on. We didn't do too badly after bringing in a lot of younger players, many of whom pushed on to become part of the 1991 World Cup team. It was a

Stuart Barnes.

hard tour, and we certainly could have won the first Test. In the second Test we were in the lead after the first hour – but in the last 20 minutes we just ran out of steam. It was a heavy scoreline at the end, but we were not overwhelmed at all.

NIGEL MELVILLE

We had a coach who didn't know what was going to happen, in terms of how New Zealand would come at us. Because I'd been there in '79 with England Schools, and in 1983 with the Lions, I knew. It was a very tough game. In the first Test in Christchurch I kicked the ball through from a scrum and got smashed by Cowboy Shaw, so I didn't see a thing as Mike Teague scored – I just heard the roar. I also had seven bells kicked out of me at the first line-out when John Orwin tapped a loose ball back and I went down on the floor to tidy it up. It felt like I was being shot by a machine gun as the All Blacks rucked over me, and as I came out the other end I almost gave the ball to their scrum-half, David Kirk.

STUART BARNES

The second Test was one of the most violent matches I played in – it was epic in its violence. There was a 28-man punch-up at one stage in which I jumped in and rabbit-punched Cowboy Shaw. As he turned round the New Zealand centre Steve Pokere pulled me down and punched the ground next to my head. He said, 'The Cowboy's looking for you – keep your head down!' He saved me, but I couldn't even buy him a drink afterwards because he was very religious and a teetotaller. I'll remember it till the day I die. We had a go, and we were closer to the All Blacks in the fight than we were in the rugby. The only England players who didn't get involved were Huw Davies and Simon Smith, the two pacifist Wasps backs, and the two most intelligent men on the pitch!

NIGEL MELVILLE

We were there when there was a lot of controversy and anti-apartheid protests over the proposed NZ Cavaliers tour of South Africa [which took place in 1986]. On one occasion we were trying to take off from Auckland airport and when we got to the end of the runway there were all these demonstrators with placards protesting against the tour. Then someone called in a bomb alert and we had to evacuate the plane by jumping out of the cargo hold. I remember it was pissing with rain with us all standing on the tarmac. Then, when we were given the all clear, we had to get back in through the cargo hold and while Andy Simpson was being given a leg-up he smashed his head on the fuselage and cut it. He then had this ridiculous bandage tied under his chin and knotted on the top of his head which earned him a ribbing.

MIKE TEAGUE

I took a little bit of heart because Murray Mexted, who had given me a lesson in the series, and their coach Brian Lochore, said they liked the way I played. They said that if I stayed in New Zealand they'd make me an All Black. I knew then that I was going in the right direction although I was never tempted because I was an Englishman, and wanted to play for England. It reminds me of the Welshman who came up to me on the 1989 Lions tour and said, 'You look better in red.' I didn't like that.

JAMIE SALMON

As usual the New Zealanders took us up to Northland and down to Southland before the Tests. After we beat Southland (15-9) in Invercargill their guys came up to us after the match with their programmes, which they asked us to sign. It was because that was one of the highlights of their careers, it was their Test match.

NIGEL MELVILLE

To avoid the demonstrators before the second Test in Wellington we were taken to a convent, where we stayed for three hours before the match. It was terrible preparation, but by that time we had pretty well run out of steam. At the time the New Zealanders were almost professionals, and we were amateurs, so there was a big gap in conditioning.

PAUL DODGE

That was my last Test, and I knew at the time that it might be. Jerry Guscott and Jamie Salmon were just pushing up, and you had the feeling it was time to go. At 27 I was not old, and I carried on playing for the Tigers, but I felt I'd had my time. Overall, I enjoyed international rugby. There were great days in front of 60,000 people, whereas in club rugby in 1985, even at the Tigers, there would be crowds of only a couple of hundred people. It wasn't until Leicester's successful cup runs that it picked up.

MIKE TEAGUE

When I came back from New Zealand I joined Cardiff. The idea was that I'd fill John Scott's shoes, but I struggled. I found it difficult to play for a club side other than Gloucester, and I was out of form. Cardiff dropped me and then Jack Rowell, who was South-West coach, said that he would not pick Welsh-based players. I was disillusioned, and had gone into the rugby wilderness.

STUART BARNES

In 1986 I sat on the bench for the whole Wales match, but then I came on again at fullback in the French game at Parc des Princes. It was quite enjoyable, but I was immediately asked to do the goal-kicking. I also conceded a dubious penalty try when I intercepted a French pass, caught it, and walked into touch. It was a 29-10 beating and I remember Blanco, Sella and Charvet picking beautiful lines. If I'd been in the crowd as a neutral I'd have enjoyed that.

DEAN RICHARDS (1986-1996, 48 caps plus 6 caps for the Lions)

My main reaction on hearing about being selected to play for England was just the huge sense of honour and delight. I was interviewing someone as a policeman at the time, and I had to leave the room to take the call from Don Rutherford. This was on the Monday before the Saturday game against Ireland in 1986, and then the nerves set in. I hadn't been involved in any of the training, and wondered about the preparation. I was even more nervous when I turned up and we pottered around a bit on the Thursday before some of the guys disappeared for a pint. We did a little bit more on the Friday morning, but I was very anxious and nervous.

Dean Richards celebrates scoring against Ireland in 1986 in the 25-20 victory.

I felt totally underprepared. We had a monster pack with Colclough and Dooley in the second-row, and Rees and Winterbottom on the flanks, so we were able to dominate up front. So my two pushover tries against the Irish were really credit to the others around me.

I feel incredibly honoured to have represented my country, and never felt I had a God-given right to be there. You have to earn it. Sometimes your face fits, and sometimes it doesn't – that's life.

But it's odd. There was a huge amount of pride in selection for England, but as a group of players we felt it was the norm to have a couple of pints the night before a match – and it wasn't only us. The French would have a meal of steak, mashed potatoes and red wine before they played an international in the afternoon. In terms of conditioning, there was none. It proved costly in the next game against France. We flew over to Paris on Friday and had a few beers that night. The people I was playing against in 1986 were guys such as Jean-Luc Joinel, who I had aspired to be like a couple of years before. The next day we lost 29-10 and just didn't perform. We were comprehensively beaten, and even though I knew what the French were like, it was a bit of a shock to the system.

STUART BARNES

I came off the bench and went to fullback for the last five minutes of the 1986 game against Scotland at Murrayfield. They scored 16 points, including three tries, in that time. It was pathetic. I don't blame myself for any of the tries because by that stage they were flooding through. On the bench when you see the starting 15 have not done well you are almost dreading the call, and that's how it was. Horrible. You just watch them come at you.

NIGEL MELVILLE

By 1986 the team was starting to grow, and we beat Wales and Ireland to finish mid-table. Then, in 1987, I did my knee again. I would have been captain for the World Cup campaign, so it was deeply disappointing.

EIGHTEEN

THE FIRST RUGBY WORLD CUP
1987

THAT ENGLAND WERE *ill-prepared for the first World Cup held in 1987 in New Zealand and Australia was not surprising. The RFU had initially voted against the inception of the new global tournament – but having been outvoted agreed to participate.*

Against that background, and an increasing awareness among England internationals that, despite the big commercial gains made the RFU, they were lagging behind in terms of preparation, perks and player welfare compared to other teams, coach Martin Green did his best to raise standards. He tried to improve fitness levels in the squad by engaging the athletics conditioner, Tom McNab, only for his England side to hit the headlines for regressive rather than progressive tendencies in the 1987 Five Nations.

Having been beaten by Ireland and France in the opening two matches of the campaign, England – including a contingent of Bath players who were no strangers to winning in Wales with their club – were on a mission to settle old scores in Cardiff.

After a blood and thunder changing-room speech by England's fiery new captain, scrum-half Richard Hill, the match at the Arms Park soon degenerated. With the line-outs turning into a street-corner brawl two Welsh forwards were forced off, No.8 Phil Davies with a broken cheekbone following a punch by giant England lock Wade Dooley, and second-row Steve Sutton with a broken nose after being elbowed by his team-mate, Rob Norster.

Wales won the match 19-12, and the RFU controversially disciplined four members of the England team – Bath's Hill, Graham Dawe and Gareth Chilcott along with Dooley – dropping them from the last game of the season against Scotland. A re-shaped side under the captaincy of wing, Mike Harrison, with Brian Moore making his debut at hooker, staved off the Wooden Spoon with a 21-12 home win over the Scots at the beginning of April.

With their first pool match of the World Cup, against co-hosts Australia, barely six weeks later in Sydney, Green's squad had to make further gains quickly – and it proved beyond them. England were competitive at the Concord Oval, where they were beaten 19-6 by the Wallabies, with Jonathan Webb winning his first cap after replacing the concussed Marcus Rose two minutes into the match.

They overwhelmed Japan 60-7 then racked up a 34-6 win over the USA to book a quarter-final showdown against Wales in Brisbane. What followed was a mute England display devoid of passion, invention or initiative as they went down 16-3. There is the suggestion from some players that overblown RFU concerns about another outbreak of Anglo-Welsh warfare pulled England's teeth, while others say it was nothing more than a sub-standard performance.

Whatever the truth, it led to more change with Green sacked and Geoff Cooke appointed as manager in an attempt to arrest the slide and build, over the next four years, an England team capable of winning the 1991 World Cup.

STUART BARNES

I was called up at fullback against Ireland at Lansdowne Road in 1987. The wind blew and the rain poured, and by that stage I'd pretty well forgotten how to play fullback because I was playing fly-half every weekend for Bath. I was exquisitely awful.

JAMIE SALMON

Anglo-Welsh relations were not at their best by the time we went to Cardiff that year. There's no doubt Richard Hill had delivered a team talk at Cardiff Arms Park which was not about tactics, but more about, 'If you see anything in a red shirt just climb in.' Chilcott, Dawe, Dooley and Winters were all foaming at the mouth, but apparently Don Rutherford was stood by the door in a little passageway and heard every word – whereas Martin Green had left the room before the captain's big speech. I'm sure that Don reported back.

I can't remember what Phil Davies did, but England had not won in Cardiff for a long time, and there was a sense that if we were going to go down, we were going to go down fighting. That sort of 'climb in' language happened at that time, and you would not call that Welsh pack timid, or slow in coming forward.

BRIAN MOORE (1987-1995, 64 caps plus 5 caps for the Lions)

The season had started with an awful game in Ireland when England lost 17-0, a home defeat against France, and then that brawl down at the Arms Park after which four England players got disciplined. It was kamikaze stuff and Graham Dawe was one of those dropped. I was a travelling reserve in all games. Hill's team talk before the Welsh match was inflammatory to the point of being ludicrous, it wasn't even about rugby most of the time, while Dawesy got wound up because that's the sort of person he is. I would say, of course, that I deserved to get the call up for the final game against Scotland but the simple fact is I got my chance because Dawe was banned by the RFU for a game. Normally I had no truck with the RFU, but on this occasion I think it's fair to say they had to act following Cardiff. In fairness to

Hilly, in particular, he became a much better, more controlled, player for England afterwards. He channelled all that fury and feistiness.

JONATHAN WEBB (England 1987-1993, 33 caps)
The 1987 Five Nations game against Wales was the first international game I had watched live. My wife is Welsh, and her father got tickets, so I was at Cardiff Arms Park for that game. I heard later that Richard Hill's team talk was spectacular, but I was a bit neutral about that attitude – I thought it was over the top. Dudley Wood, the RFU secretary, commented on Anglo-Welsh relations in the aftermath of that match by saying, 'Our relationship is based on trust and understanding... they don't trust us and we don't understand them.'

BRIAN MOORE
On one hand I was lucky to get the opportunity against Scotland, but it is not lucky when you take that opportunity. It really hit home at the team hotel, the Petersham, just before we left for the ground and *Grandstand* came on, and of course that theme tune, which had a real resonance for our generation. It meant the main events of the sporting weekend were about to start, and there they were presenting from Twickenham. And a picture of me came up. Suddenly, I was very proud but very nervous. There was a real understanding now that I would really

Peter Winterbottom prepares to tackle Simon Poidevin during the Pool 1 match against Australia at the Concord Oval in Sydney.

be under the microscope that afternoon. It wasn't anymore just my thing, this was England.

The secretary and the RFU committee were the constants while players and teams came and went. It was an honour to play, but in two senses. I felt proud to have been selected, but Dudley Wood used to make it quite clear that we the players were honoured to get the invite, which isn't quite the same thing at all. I was pulling on an England shirt because I had trained and played like a dog for years.

STUART BARNES

I quit England in 1987 because I was fed up with sitting on the bench and boring third-rate training. I believed also, as an amateur, that my club was a better team than England and was far more enjoyable to play for. I thought, I'm working five days a week, England training is rubbish, and I'm nowhere near the team. So, I made myself unavailable before the first World Cup. I disappeared again from 1988 to 1993, when I was again not available for England duty.

JONATHAN WEBB

When we got to Australia, I assumed that Marcus Rose would start at fullback, and that I would be there for experience and perhaps to play against Japan in the pool stage. However, he was knocked out in the first 10 minutes of the opening game when his head hit the ground hard after a tackle by Peter Grigg. He was unconscious for two minutes, and that meant a statutory three week ban for concussion. I had a chocolate eclair in my mouth at the time, and had settled down on the bench trying to maintain a useful optimism in the face of the cynicism of Bailey, Clough and company. I had no time to think – which was the best way – and on I went. I remember very little of the match other than that I caught a kick and ran the ball back. Troy Coker caught me, and dumped me on my head. The rest of it went in a hard, fast blur. When I saw Marcus the next morning at breakfast he said, 'The king is dead, long live the king.' It was very magnanimous in the circumstances.

I felt a massive sense of pride and honour at being selected by England. I got very nervous before games, and had to calm myself down. I suppose it was just fear of failure, especially with the goal-kicking. It is one of the clearest ways in which you can exert superiority over your opponents, and if you have a bad day goal-kicking then all the hard work of the team, and the forwards in particular, comes to nothing. One of my tricks was to think that there must be 20,000 blokes who would bite your arm off to be in the same place. It put it in perspective – that idea that you are a link in a chain, in a culture, that people relate to.

DEAN RICHARDS

There were huge question-marks over whether the World Cup would happen even four weeks before the tournament was about to start. There were also unresolved issues like the format, and whether players would be able to get time off from work.

BRIAN MOORE

Because we were in Australia the media coverage was small and you would hardly know it was on. There was hardly any reporting of it. We didn't understand what you had to do to play in a tournament and if other teams are honest I suspect they might say the same. Only the Kiwis were flat-out in tournament-mode. England had tour courts, a bit of messing around old tour style, it was amateurish in every sense of the word – but then again we had all taken our annual holiday to be there.

JAMIE SALMON

The quarter-final against Wales was dire. RFU officials were adamant that there would be no repeat of Cardiff, and with Dudley Wood, the secretary of the RFU, in Australia, the message was stressed repeatedly. They had banned Hill after the Five Nations, and then given the captaincy to Mickey Harrison on the right wing, who was one of the quietest, nicest guys you could meet.

It meant that post that game, rather than the announcement of the World Cup squad the focus was about the player bans from the Wales game. You will also find that they told Wade Dooley to jump at the front of the line-out so that he wouldn't be tempted to whack Bob Norster if he lost a throw or two. Instead, poor Nigel Redman had to jump against Norster.

So, especially in the forwards, England were muted – to put it mildly – in conditions in Brisbane where we needed them to front up. It was reflected in the game. We had a terrible training session which went on for three hours, when we were just going through the motions. We didn't need it.

DEAN RICHARDS

The inaugural World Cup was a very exciting prospect, but we approached it with no professionalism at all. The attitude was that it might be the first and last World Cup. Everyone was incredibly sceptical. We had a hell of a party anyway.

JONATHAN WEBB

When I got the invite to go to the 1987 World Cup it led to an extraordinary chain of events. I was in my last year as a medical student at Bristol University, and thought I would have to say no because it clashed with my finals. I was pondering what to do when on a ward round being led by Professor Alan Read, who was an eminent professor of medicine at the Bristol Royal infirmary and was grumpy, moderately terrifying and unsmiling. He summoned me to the front, ahead of all the junior doctors, and said, 'I hear you've been selected by England.' It was totally unexpected that he knew I played rugby. I said yes, and that I'd have to say no to the trip because of the finals. He told me he would look into it. He spoke to all the department heads and it was arranged that I would do my finals, which were normally spread over three weeks, in two days. It was a daunting prospect. All I can remember is belting around Bristol on my bike from department to department doing clinical exams and vivas after discussing cases. I had none of the camaraderie of doing exams with people in my year – but it all worked out.

DEAN RICHARDS

The first thing a lot of players did when we got to Australia was to hire motorbikes so that they could roar around Sydney. Fortunately, no-one came off.

PETER WINTERBOTTOM

We were in a pretty average hotel in Sydney and it soon became obvious that the World Cup proper was going on over in New Zealand, and we felt very isolated and out of it. We hadn't clocked that we needed to go into tournament mode. It wasn't even like the Five Nations when you always had two weeks between matches and sometimes a month. Here the games came thick and fast.

DEAN RICHARDS

We should have beaten Australia in the opening game, but they were given a try that wasn't. Then, after the remaining pool games, we came up against the Welsh. It's often forgotten that between the end of the pool round and that game in Brisbane we were taken up to Hamilton Island for a four-day holiday. There were no rugby pitches up there, so there was no preparation at all – other than scuba-diving, waterskiing, golf and tennis. There are times when you need some R&R, but just before a World Cup quarter-final is not one of them.

BRIAN MOORE

The quarter-final against Wales in 1987 – along with the third-fourth play-off game in 1995 – were the two worst games I ever played in, and I pity anybody who had to watch them. Awful. That pitch in 1987 was like a bog, it drained everything out of you, it was a dreadful game and we played very badly. It was a watershed moment. I sat in the changing room afterwards and thought – in fact, I didn't just think I told everybody in earshot – if we are going to put all the effort in it is pointless playing like that.

JONATHAN WEBB

That World Cup quarter-final against Wales was my fourth game for England, and one of my least happy as an international because we were so woefully poor. Arriving at Ballymore it was a sea of red – the whole Welsh population in Australia seemed to have gone to the game. It was just crammed with Welsh supporters, and you thought, 'Where have they all come from?'

RORY UNDERWOOD

We were so used to the Five Nations, where there's usually another game, but suddenly we had to get used to knock-out rugby. It was a shocking wet day at Ballymore, and some argued that our forwards got carried away with trying to dominate the young Welsh tight-head, Dai Young. It never really happened. It was frustrating, and with so few opportunities you always got two defenders at the same time.

Richard Harding of England is clattered by Jonathan Davies and Ieuan Evans during the quarter-final at Ballymore Stadium.

DEAN RICHARDS

Before that quarter-final we didn't really talk about the game in Cardiff. There had been repercussions with people banned, but it was done and dusted – even though some players were not pleased because it felt like double standards from RFU officials. I don't feel that it pulled our teeth at all. We underperformed because we underperformed. We went out that night and the next day we were on the plane back home. We thought, 'Jesus, we are out of here.' That was the stark reality of it. Everyone said they did not want it to happen like that again.

JAMIE SALMON

It was a safety-first attitude all the way through, and a very forward dominated style. The whole thing manifested itself in the 1987 World Cup – although it's worth remembering that the players on that trip formed a huge foundation of the team that got to the 1991 World Cup final.

Looking back now the whole 1987 debacle changed the way England thought about the international game.

PETER WINTERBOTTOM

We were slow on the uptake, and everybody got caught out by New Zealand. They sent what was almost their World Cup team on a tour of Britain at the end of the 1987 season – I think they called themselves the New Zealand Barbarians – to get valuable game time together. This was the trip when it also became obvious that some players in the southern hemisphere were doing very nicely thank you out of playing amateur rugby union.

JONATHAN WEBB

We were just rubbish. We had no real conviction that we could do well, it was more like just turn up and do your best. That's what Geoff Cooke changed. Before he took over there was a sense that you played to avoid being dropped, that it was more self-centred then team-centred, and more, 'Oh well, let's just move on,' after losses. But when it's just your fourth cap, and you're a junior boy, you do as you're told and keep your nose clean.

PETER WINTERBOTTOM

I wasn't prepared to flog myself around athletics tracks and gyms after work three times a week if this was as good as it got. Things had to improve, and thank God once Geoff Cooke arrived on the scene they did.

BRIAN MOORE

I have no fond memories really. Was it a tournament? Was it a tour? Nobody knew what it was going to be like, nobody knew if it was going to be a success or a turkey. As it turned out it wasn't a particularly great tournament, but it was sufficiently interesting to warrant a second go – and by the end of the 1991 tournament it had clearly arrived.

NINETEEN

THE CARLING YEARS

1988-1996

SOMETHING HAD TO *change. England had made a poor showing in the inaugural World Cup, the nation's rugby team seemed too often to be stuck in a rut, with high hopes but little direction, consistency or confidence. There was a realisation that England had to go back to the drawing board and a new coaching/management team of Geoff Cooke, a Cumbrian not especially well known in the elite end of the game, and Roger Uttley, the grand old flanker, began to sow the seeds for long term improvement. Cooke, immediately, struck people as the organiser England so badly needed.*

In the short term it was still a struggle. As if to underline that, by the time England returned from their unsuccessful summer tour of Australia in 1988 they had appointed no less than four captains – Mike Harrison, Nigel Melville, John Orwin and Richard Harding. All had fallen by the wayside for one reason or another.

So the most pressing need was a captain, a leader who was guaranteed his place in the team and an individual who bought in totally to Cooke and Uttley's methods as they tried to introduce England to new scientific training methods, especially when it came to conditioning and match analysis. The search was on.

Just about every senior name in the squad was mentioned – Simon Halliday, Brian Moore, Peter Winterbottom, Dean Richards, Rob Andrew – but the one name never mentioned was the player who eventually received a call from Geoff Cooke. WDC Carling, aged 22 who had won just five caps at centre at the time, was a trainee officer in the Welsh Regiment studying at Durham University at the time. To the outside world it was an outrageous punt and even within in rugby circles it caused mystified shakes of the head.

Expectations were low but what transpired was the most successful and dominant period in English rugby history. Three Grand Slams in five seasons and another that went begging at Murrayfield in 1990. A World Cup final appearance at Twickenham, a semi-final in South Africa four years later, which was almost considered a failure so high had hopes and expectations become. These were the halcyon days, even if they were not necessarily recognised as such at the time. For all their excellence since 1995, at the time of going to press, England have garnered just one more Grand Slam, in 2003 – that year of all years.

What was the Carling influence and magic? Quantifying it precisely is difficult,

Opposite: Will Carling after the 1991 World Cup final.

as we will see below as colleagues discuss the phenomena, but above all else it does appear a case of synchronicity. Right person, right time. Nothing had worked since the early eighties and that alone spoke eloquently for a complete change in direction, a new face receptive to new training methods, a player not in any way identified with the underperforming England team that he had recently stepped into. Carling was a winner, that was the true joy of sport in his book, while he was also very relaxed in front of the cameras and at the top table answering questions. Rugby's profile was about to go through the roof and England's new captain was more than capable of dealing with that, or at least in all outward appearances. He was never, in fact, quite as confident as you would think and by his own admission his devotion to the job started to exact a high personal cost.

That came much later. Initially all his considerable energies were spent winning over the grizzled veteran forwards in his team, the discarded captaincy candidates – a task he soon completed after a middling 1989 Five Nations in which an 11-0 win over eventual champions France was the highlight – and England started playing a high tempo and exciting game in 1990. An apparently unstoppable momentum built and England looked certain to complete the most attractive of Grand Slams when they crashed to an unexpected 13-7 defeat against an inspired Scotland team who were themselves challenging for a Slam.

Not only did the defeat hurt per se, it was a massive momentum changer as well. England, in their bitter disappointment at the result and themselves for an over-confidence, reverted to a much tighter safety-first game and vowed to grind out that elusive Grand Slam the following season. Which is exactly what they did.

For a while it seemed such an approach might also garner a World Cup in 1991, but England fell at the final hurdle against a very accomplished Australia team. A more ambitious approach in that final failed to catch the Australians by surprise but 1992 saw Carling's England in their pomp, sweeping to a second Grand Slam and then heavily defeating the Springboks on their return to these shores after the apartheid years with a comprehensive win at Twickenham. Thereafter there was a dip in fortunes for two seasons: a classic case of a great team growing old together and perhaps being kept together en masse for half a season too long. England had to rebuild but still the enduring Carling was the man in the middle, a figure of even greater authority than before.

By 1995 England were back in good shape and their third Grand Slam under Carling was largely without drama or alarm. That was all saved for the end of the season when Carling found himself sacked as captain in the run-up to the 1995 World Cup for his off-camera remarks on a Channel Four documentary. When he had taken his mike off and was heading for the door and home, he referred to the full committee of the RFU as '57 old farts'. For one long hot Bank Holiday weekend chaos reigned as the England squad effectively threatened to go on strike before Carling was restored, although not before he was forced to apologise publicly at a hastily organised press call at Marlow Rugby Club.

The flippant remark by Carling was the catalyst, not the reason, for the stand-off. It was the tip of the iceberg. What in effect was happening was that Carling – as the representative of a senior player group – was being taken to task for a number of acrimonious fights in the previous four or five years over rugby union's seemingly inevitable move towards professionalism and the players' attempts to be rewarded in some way – or at least to not be out of pocket – for their efforts.

The smell of cordite had scarcely dispersed when England found themselves in the firing line again as they ran into a Jonah Lomu-inspired New Zealand at the World Cup. They had travelled to South Africa with hopes of going one better than they had in 1991, but they were cruelly dashed as they were ripped to pieces by New Zealand in a remarkable first half. It was little consolation that probably no other team on the planet would have lived with New Zealand that day.

The Carling years were coming to a close. The mind and body were still willing and able in 1996 and but for a sloppy defeat against France he would have claimed a fourth Grand Slam in charge, but by 1997 he was running on empty.

He had stepped down as captain for that final season and although he played in the Five Nations not even the carrot of a possible Lions tour and captaincy to South Africa could change his mind. He could no longer summon the energy or mental focus. He bowed out at Cardiff along with his long-time colleague Rob Andrew who had also contributed massively to the glory years. It had been some journey, not without its dramas on and off the field, but English rugby was in their debt along with the other mighty warriors of this era who still rank among the greatest players ever to represent England.

ROGER UTTLEY

The 1987 World Cup was perceived as a failure and manager Mike Weston was told there had to be a change of coach. Honourable man that he is, Mike said that if Martin Green goes, I go. They then alighted on Geoff Cooke, who had been a North selector when I was playing. He called me at Harrow, where I was teaching, and said he had been asked to take charge, and that he couldn't think of anyone else to help coach, but would I? I had a good think. I had seen previous coaches end up in a disillusioned state but thought I would only get asked once.

I got on well with Geoff, and with John Elliott, who was a very astute selector and became an important figure in the England revival that took place over the next four years. Geoff and John were both detailed planners who asked the right questions. Don Rutherford, the RFU's technical director, was also an excellent sounding board and source of support. Geoff was a good communicator and educator but something of an unknown quantity on the national stage. I brought the experience and credibility of a former international player and, by then, was an established representative coach having been involved with Wasps and London & South East Division. I felt it proved to be a good combination and I wouldn't have missed the experience for the world.

RORY UNDERWOOD

The 'revolution' started in 1988, and the biggest change was Geoff Cooke coming in. His man-management style was good, as was his organisation, and he saw the bigger picture. All of a sudden there was a challenge to us as players, which is how it should be at international level. Whereas in the past if the move didn't work, or if you didn't score, there was no real discussion about what you did next – you just played off-the-cuff. Some people hated it when Geoff used a flip-chart in team meetings. He would draw a line-out or scrum scenario 15 yards out from the opposition line, and pull a name out of the hat and make that player talk the rest of us through the next couple of phases. Some people thought it was boring, but I thought it was fascinating.

DEAN RICHARDS

There was a bit of an incident with the Calcutta Cup after that '88 match at Murrayfield. All I can remember about it is that I was incredibly drunk, and that John Jeffrey and I took the Calcutta Cup outside and it came back in a worse state. The SRU were having huge problems with their players at that time – and the RFU weren't – and the handling of it showed a stark contrast in attitude. My view is that I should have had a longer ban and John Jeffrey a shorter ban for what happened. However, I had no impact on what his union said and did. After my RFU hearing I expected the same ban as John got [five months], if not worse, and was quite surprised to get only one match. I felt embarrassed about the incident.

NIGEL MELVILLE

We had Ireland at home next. We were beginning to read each other, and were building a bit more belief, so you knew that at some point it was going to happen. However, bang on half-time, in what later became known as Chris Oti's game with the crowd saluting his second half hat-trick of tries by singing 'Swing Low' for the first time, I was running an outside line. I put the ball inside to Rob Andrew and, as the Irish cover hit me, my foot got stuck underneath me, and I suddenly felt my foot go through 180 degrees. I could see that it was pointing back the wrong way, and there was bone sticking out under the sock. I thought, oh no, another injury, and then it started to hurt.

I was carried off and from then on was looked after by the St John's ambulance guys. It's funny looking back. It hit me that I was captain of England, but there I was being taken in the back of an ambulance to a local hospital – the West Middlesex – where we had to wait our turn in accident and emergency. It was as busy as hell, a local casualty ward, and there I was lying on this gurney with a ward nurse saying I had to fill in a form because I wasn't from around there. It seemed a bit unfair. And then a nurse asked me if I'd donate my England shirt for a raffle they were having...

Later on an RFU doctor arrived and said, 'It was such a fantastic second half, I just couldn't tear myself away.' I'd had no pain-killers by then, but that night they straightened the dislocation and told me that I would have to have an operation to have the ankle pinned. On the NHS!

At the time I was writing a column for the newspaper, *Today*, and they said they would pay for the operation privately – and then the RFU said that they would do it. So, that morning I was driven to a private hospital in Windsor only to find that they did not have a free bed. I was told come back on Monday. I went back to my flat where my landlord, Neville Compton, an old-school Wasps forward and a lovely fellow, came along with a bottle of brandy that evening which we polished off. I'd still had no pain-killers and had a really painful night, despite the brandy. The next day I had the operation done in Windsor.

After that I didn't have the will to come back, and I was watching an England game on TV when there was a defining moment. I thought, this is it, you're done. No more holding a candle, it's over – move on.

JEREMY GUSCOTT (1989-1999, 65 caps plus 8 caps for the Lions)
Will Carling was often seen as a fairly negative, boring player, but his contribution to England rugby was huge. He was hard, tough, quick, squat and powerful, and he could distribute, and at inside-centre he worked well with Peter Winterbottom. He did not have to lead too much – and it was hard for a young three-quarter to lead an England team in which the forwards had a very significant influence – but he managed it. I would say he was a world-class rugby player.

WILL CARLING (England 1988-97, 72 caps plus 1 cap for the Lions)
We had finished the '88 summer tour to Australia and it was the new season the week before the first England squad announcement. The way it worked in those days was if Roger Uttley rang you it meant you had been picked and if Geoff phoned you were almost certainly about to be dropped. I had moved into a flat with no phone – this was pre-mobiles – and I was back around my parents' one evening for a bit of home cooking when Mum said Geoff Cooke had phoned and

could I phone back ASAP. My heart sank and I sat there for fully half an hour going through the tour in my mind. OK, I hadn't set the world alight but I didn't think I had done too badly either. Oh well, I'd better get it over and done with. I phoned and whether by accident or design Geoff seemed to milk it a bit. 'Hi Will, thanks for getting back. I've just been phoning around all the guys who went on tour in the summer who aren't going to be playing against Australia in two weeks' time . . . (long pause, very long pause) – no, not you, I want to know if you would like to captain England.'

I still wasn't sure if he was joking around or not and laughed which was possibly not the reaction Geoff had been hoping for. Meanwhile my brother Marcus had been picking up a bit of the conversation and looked at me questioningly. I reached for pen and paper, wrote 'I'm captain' on it and held it up for him. His jaw dropped, he shook his head in disbelief. By the end of the phone call it was quite clear that Geoff was serious and eventually he rang off with me in a state of shock.

I had the weekend off at Harlequins and Geoff asked me to keep the news under my hat until he announced it to the England squad on the Sunday. In the meantime I went to watch Quins play London Scottish and I was in the bar afterwards when the subject of who should be England captain came up. A lot of names were mentioned and mine wasn't one of them, the hot favourite seemed to be Simon Halliday. Just for the devilment right at the end I piped up, 'I think it's going to be me.' They all looked around killing themselves laughing. 'Do shut up Will, of course it won't be you. Get the beers in.' Not a great omen.

When Geoff did announce his decision in the team room there was utter silence for a few seconds before everybody started chattering and guffawing.

To this day I'm not really sure why Geoff opted for me, it was a pretty radical move. I've tried to have the conversation a few times but he's a Yorkshireman and doesn't give much away! I've seen him quoted in a few places saying that he had identified a winning mentality in me and perhaps that was it. I was definitely obsessed with winning. I looked at the terrific players available for England around that era and I couldn't understand at all why England weren't doing much better. Great players, heroes of mine, but very little was happening results-wise.

As a player I'm not sure I did a huge amount and any more than a number of other good centres might have done given a decent run in the team. Did I actually make any difference at all? I'm not sure I did as aplayer. That group might have gone on and achieved exactly what they did and even more without me ever getting the tap on the shoulder and being made captain because good things were happening under Geoff. There was a consistency of selection that suddenly came into the England team with Geoff, we embraced new training methods, got really fit, were much more 'professional' in the way we went about things.

Perhaps my main contribution was on the mental side. We hadn't been successful for a good while so we had done that classic English thing and pretended it wasn't really important, and a number of the guys even tried to make out that club rugby was the main thing. Most of the Bath guys used to bang on about Bath and the Leicester guys the same, as if playing for England was a step down from playing for their clubs. Well I wasn't having that. When we were all really young schoolboys our dream was playing for England, pure and simple. Let's make that dream happen was my message. In fact let's go one better, let's make sure we start winning in an England shirt as well as pulling one on.

PAUL ACKFORD (England 1988-91, 22 caps plus 3 caps for the Lions)
My memory is that it was the Friday night before Will's first game as captain against Australia (and the night before my first cap) that he gave his little speech. He was 22 and he had many fewer caps than a lot of the guys and after the coaches went out he got up to address the team. There was a pool table at the back of the room and I think people like Dean Richards were playing pool and somebody else was mucking about in another corner.

Carling got to his feet to address the troops and nobody paid him the slightest bit of attention. Because it was my first game I was in the front, legs crossed and waiting. He stood there and said nothing. There was a fifteen, twenty second silence and one or two people stopped doing what they were doing. But still, there were four or five not paying any attention. So he waited another twenty-five, thirty seconds. He stood there and stood there. It was becoming embarrassing. He waited until everyone had stopped, until people took their seats, and only then did he speak. It wasn't a tub-thumping address or strategically important but it was that he had the presence of mind, the character, the force of personality to command silence from a group of people who were more experienced than him. It was an astonishing display.

PETER WINTERBOTTOM
I was injured and out of the squad when Will was named as the new captain for the Australia game in 1988, so I missed the announcement from Geoff but in all honesty I wasn't the slightest bit surprised. It was a good appointment at the time and looking back it was actually a master-stroke. Something had to change radically. It needed a brand new approach, a fresh face, a new voice, somebody who believed in new ideas and methods. It was time for a real shake up. From the outside it might have looked like there were other more suited candidates – Mooro, Rob Andrew, Dean Richards and even myself maybe – but in all honesty what had we achieved in the previous three or four seasons? None of us had put our hands up and said, 'I'm the man. Make me captain.'

BRIAN MOORE

There were tensions at the time over the appointment. At the time of the announcement everyone was astounded. I was disappointed. I thought I might be in with a shout, others even more so, but when you look back it was the right appointment on several levels. It represented a new start, a new approach, Will was young, personable, aesthetically pleasing and I'm not belittling that – when you are entering a media era that is invaluable.

His face got rugby into sections of papers it hadn't been in before. For all those reasons he became a figurehead. The one thing that did annoy some is that Will was quite reticent in dispelling the myth of the England captain, which is that the captain is largely responsible for everything. There were many leaders in that team and I believe a number of them could have led the group to equal success – but again that's not to say Will was the wrong appointment. Somebody has to be captain, you have to make the call.

Geoff Cooke has told me subsequently that he looked around the dressing room in 1988 and didn't really see any candidates among the older group. I didn't like that and I didn't agree with it but that is how Geoff assessed the situation, it was his call, and he had seen something in Will and in hindsight you can't say he got it wrong. None of these tensions ever amounted to much because we were basically a happy winning team. There were strains but no fractures.

WILL CARLING

I don't know if my Army background helped generally but I do remember one specific phase of my training which made a big impression. I was a trainee officer, we had a big three-week exercise planned and I asked the senior officer if I could just go in the wagon with the guys because I didn't have a clue about them, their lives and what exactly they did in the Army and what they thought of us blokes who were supposedly in charge. I was in with a load of Taffs and for the first couple of days they were a bit suspicious but after a while they started to thaw and we enjoyed some really good banter.

It got to the point where I felt I could ask them outright, 'Who are the good officers, what makes a good officer?' To a man they answered that the officer didn't have to be popular and all things to all men; no, he just had to be honest and fair. The trooper doesn't want his commanding officer to be his mate, they just want to know where they stand. And when I came to be captain I really tapped into that. I didn't have to be everybody's mate, I didn't have to be at the heart and soul of everything and on the back seat of the coach singing with the guys, I didn't even have to make the right calls all the time – although that would help. Ultimately it was about creating an atmosphere and culture in which everybody was doing their best and respecting each other for that.

The main thing about that opening win against Australia is that we played some very decent rugby and got the crowd on side, although I didn't feel I had contributed much. I really felt the pressure though. I got knocked out just before the end and was led away to the changing room and remember sitting there, more or less on my own for a few minutes and crying my eyes out. It was just a huge relief. I hadn't let England down.

I started to think what the captaincy involved and to my mind it was very hands on. I made an effort to phone all the guys once a fortnight or so just for a chat to see if anything was on their minds. How they felt, were they over that bout of flu etc. Sometimes no more than just quickly touching base.

And then when the team gathered, along with Geoff and Roger we would talk to the players for hours and find out how we all wanted to play. We had a strong pack and a great set piece, we had Rory on the wing, Jerry was coming through and even I used to make a few breaks in the early days. It was really a case of, 'Guys, how do we maximise this?'

RORY UNDERWOOD

The measure of the change in England's approach was that I scored four tries between 1984 and the 1988 summer tour. Two of those came in the 1987 World Cup win over Japan. Then, with that new team from the start of the Cooke era until 1996, I scored 45.

JEREMY GUSCOTT

Rory was one of the best finishers I've ever seen – as good as Jeff Wilson, Christian Cullen or John Kirwan. If you score 49 tries for England you've done really well. I remember him scoring a try when his body was in touch, and his arms, and yet he somehow avoided hitting the ground and the corner flag – which in those days was in touch – and got the ball down. He was lightning quick and knew where to go. He was a tough cookie as well, and pound for pound the most powerful man in the squad.

JAMIE SALMON

I was available in 1988 but Geoff Cooke didn't select me. In 1989 I did get a call to sit on the bench against Romania in Bucharest, and just beforehand I'd had a call from Clive Rowlands, the 1989 Lions manager, asking if I was available for the tour. I said I was and he replied, 'It's Jerry Guscott or you.' Jerry made his England debut in the game against Romania, and scored a hat-trick. Simon Halliday had said to me beforehand that he would try to come off in the final quarter so I could get on, and towards the end he caught my eye and gave a 'What can I do?' shrug. I took my boots off, and that was it. It's funny how it all started for me in Romania [with New Zealand] and finished in Romania [for England].

DEAN RICHARDS

After the Lions in 1989 I had a shoulder reconstruction, so I was out for the whole of that 1990 season. I then had to have it re-operated on to free a trapped nerve. I didn't want to watch the Grand Slam game against Scotland, so when I had the option to go to Filbert Street on police duty I took it. Instead, I was at the front of the double-decker stand being spat on and pelted with coins. I'd had a couple of calls from the boys – Wints and Teaguey – saying they were going to win, and

I said, 'Just make sure you do.' I knew what it meant, and when I heard the result I was gutted for them.

WILL CARLING

Murrayfield 1990 was easily the most painful defeat of my life and that includes a World Cup final of 1991 and semi-final of 1995. It was entirely down to us and our own personal failings. We were arrogant and it came back to bite us.

From a captaincy point of view I totally misread things and failed to notice an unhealthy vibe in the squad. There was still a huge hangover from the Lions tour in '89, which I had missed through injury. On that tour the Scots, bar Gavin Hastings and Finlay Calder, pretty much gave second best to all the England players in Test selection issues and there was undoubtedly an unhealthy feeling of superiority among England's

Jerry Guscott, 'the prince of centres', sets off on a trademark gliding run.

Lions over the Scots. Mooro was going around saying these guys were no good and generally we went around believing the hype.

We badly underestimated them, from me the captain downwards, which is ridiculous, that's a great team they had. From very early on I didn't think like we were ever really in that game.

BRIAN MOORE

It was a big staging post for the team and the immediate consequence was it made us tighten up and go into our shells, which meant we stopped playing the extremely good brand of rugby we had been playing that season. We ground out the 1991 Grand Slam and to a certain extent did the same in 1992 although we played a bit more rugby then. The short term result was that I experienced an excruciating Sunday lunchtime in Edinburgh after the Scots had clinched the Grand Slam. I never forgot that.

PETER WINTERBOTTOM

Our attitude hardened after Murrayfield and we decided to just drill it from then on and get the results needed for Grand Slams. For me, either side could have won, it was a 50-50 game which we lost. But the consequences were big. We went on to win the 1991 Grand Slam and reach the 1991 World Cup final but we certainly didn't play as well as we did for most of 1990. It railroaded us a bit.

PAUL ACKFORD

Bill McLaren came to one of the sessions at Peebles before the game. We were so well-prepared, everything was picture-perfect. As we were coming off, Bill told me that he had rarely seen a team look so good and train as well as that. That's the way we went into the match but in the game itself everything felt difficult, everything you tried to do felt laboured.

In the changing room afterwards there was just silence at first, then some began to talk about it. I was already thinking that we had to move on and confront what had happened. So after the dinner, the wives and girlfriends were there, Wade and I went up Princes Street wearing our blazers, just to show our faces, show that we weren't cowed and we weren't going back into our box. The reception was just fantastic – completely counter to what I thought it would be.

SIMON HODGKINSON (England 1989-91, 14 caps)

I had never felt so wound-up and tense as I did before the Wales match in 1991. I was definitely in the hot seat. We were down in Cardiff to do a job, plain and simple. Our game plan was not a thing of beauty, we had learnt our lesson from

Murrayfield the previous year, when we tried to play too much rugby, too soon.

The Welsh fans were never a problem, the noisier it was the better as far as I was concerned. I took it as a challenge those days when taking my goal-kicks, it made me more determined. As most goal-kickers will tell you, it is much more difficult kicking in front of two men and a dog when you can hear every word they are saying than in front of a 60,000 crowd.

It turned out to be one of the best days of my rugby life and was the start of the best season of my life, which ended with winning the Grand Slam against the French.

WILL CARLING

Cardiff in 1991 was pretty eventful. Firstly it was just a huge monkey off our backs to win down there for the first time in 28 years. That lack of success had haunted England for a long time. Two years earlier had been a disaster. Mike Teague got knocked out in the first minute; I had food poisoning and possibly shouldn't have played. Robert Jones box kicked beautifully in the rain. The next day I stopped off at a motorway service station on the M4 on the way back and a load of Welsh fans formed a guard of dishonour as I came back out and headed for the car park. The abuse I got was unbelievable and back in the car I was shaking, not from fear or because I was upset, just from the emotion of it all.

Come 1991 and we were in business-like mode. We had let a Grand Slam go begging through arrogance and that wasn't going to happen again. We were going to seal the deal this year, grind out that elusive Grand Slam and of course that meant beating Wales away. End of story, we were going to do it and basically that meant the pack going to work and Simon Hodgkinson kicking his goals. Geoff Cooke put a load of Welsh music on when we trained down at Kingsholm and instead of staying at the St Pierre Golf club – as near as it is geographically possible to get to the English border, we then went and stayed right in the middle of Cardiff to soak up the atmosphere, to acclimatise if you like. We even walked from the hotel to the ground.

BRIAN MOORE

Everybody has their own versions of history. Not least our refusal to talk to the media after the game, and our first win for ages in Cardiff. For me this was all about our argument with the RFU over the 'communication for reward' issue. Myself and a number of others had worked hard to present the case for an approved payment by the BBC for squad access throughout the season. We did it properly and professionally and got it approved by the full RFU committee.

Progress was being made. We are talking peanuts, by the way – £500 to be shared by the entire squad! – but it was the principle. The BBC were happy to pay it, we would receive it almost as a token payment but hopefully as that relationship developed we might achieve a more realistic figure. Then the RFU vetoed them point blank. The payment would have been rugby related and therefore contravened IRB regulations. No can do.

As far as I'm concerned that is what the boycott was about, it had very little to do with press intrusion. We got on well with the press and don't you think that we would have been happy to share that, of all moments, with the media? It felt like a 'them and us' situation during this period and how much it affected our enjoyment of what we were doing.

SIMON HODGKINSON

I didn't have a clue what was going on afterwards in Cardiff. I was never part of the inner circle, the senior players' cabal who ran the show. I didn't have any inkling that there was going to be a press boycott and had certainly not been consulted or asked my opinion on it. With all the stars in our team, let's face it, I was never one of the players the press came looking for anyway even though I think I equalled a world record that day with seven penalties, so in many ways it didn't seem any different to me. It was always the others that did the talking.

Getting that win in Cardiff after 28 years was a pretty big event. I suppose that might be why the press boycott was quickly organised for then, for maximum effect. We were a very close-knit group at the time. We had our clearly identified leaders – Will, Brian, Rob – and the rest of us automatically followed them. It was an 'over the top' mentality from the trenches, if you like. I didn't stop to question the press and media boycott at all after the game. I didn't let it ruin my evening I can assure you.

PETER WINTERBOTTOM

I never really got involved in any of the off-field issues or indeed the general debate about professionalism. I was working in the City by this stage and it was pretty busy combining work and top class sport, but I simply wouldn't have bothered if it was a serious problem. It was the choice you made. I worked on a desk with seven other guys and they were fantastic in covering for me when I needed to be away playing for England or when I needed to disappear and do some serious fitness work. My part of the deal was that most of my allocation of ten match tickets went straight to them and I was delighted to do that. I appreciated that others in the squad might not have enjoyed that same luxury and that I was very fortunate.

JASON LEONARD (England 1990-2004, 114 caps plus 5 caps for the Lions)
When we won the Grand Slam in 1991 it all seemed so easy. It was only the

previous year that I had made my England debut in Argentina. I remember looking around the changing room after our win against France and thinking, 'What's all the fuss about?' I saw what it meant to some very experienced players like Wade Dooley, Paul Ackford and Peter Winterbottom but as a young man I was blasé and just assumed this level of success was the norm for England!

We beat Ireland 16-7 in Dublin to tee up the French game and I remember celebrations were muted just a tad when we heard France had stuffed Wales 36-3 and stuck six tries on them in Paris. It was going to be a huge showdown game at Twickenham.

After we beat the French there was a very grand dinner at the Hilton, but what with all the speeches having to be translated it dragged on even more than usual and I slipped off with the usual suspects for a few pints just before desert. I was lucky to be involved in four Grand Slams in my career – 1991, 1992, 1995 and 2003 – and looking back you realise every one was incredibly hard earned. It requires complete commitment to the cause – plus the bounce of the ball.

I don't care how cynical people might become when you say this, but representing your country is the be all and end all, it makes you so proud. It was an absolute buzz. I'm very good at remembering games. I remember them all. Name a game and there'll be something I can recall to trigger things off. There are still characters about now, but when I look back at some of the early games, there's a real pleasure in it – the pleasure of going into battle as an amateur, with the likes of Moore, Winterbottom, Richards, Dooley, Ackford. I still laugh out loud when I remember some of those times.

We won the first Grand Slam in 1991, and there were new boys like Jerry Guscott, Nigel Heslop and myself. It was a case of saying, 'Oh look, we've won a Grand Slam. That's nice.' We were taken aback to see what it meant even to old-stagers like

Mike Teague during the 1991 Five Nations

Dooley and Winterbottom. Even the hard men were emotional. It's only when you've been around a bit that you realise that they are very special, they don't come around very often.

JONATHAN WEBB

In the build-up to the 1991 World Cup suddenly the game became cool, and *The Sun* had a rugby reporter. We noticed this phenomenal surge in interest, and the big buzz around the tournament really helped us. There was the sense that the entire country was behind you, rather than just a select audience. Just before the start, Barry Fentlow, who was one of the senior consultants at Southmead Hospital, wished me good luck and said he hoped England were paying me well. When I told him that there was no financial compensation he was amazed that I would be taking six weeks unpaid leave to play for my country. All the consultants at the hospital had a whip round on my behalf, which was very much appreciated.

One of my abiding memories is walking through Paris the day before the quarter-final with dad and mum. They were very gentle people, and reserved. An England fan came up and said to me, 'Hey Jonathan, good luck.' My dad was very old school, and turned to me and said, 'Did he just call you by your first name?'

BRIAN MOORE

I love the French by the way, their culture and their wine and the people. In another life I might well have chosen to decamp to Chamonix and ski myself into old age. But the simple truth is they are so easy to wind up! I would never have gone on doing it if my little barbs hadn't been so effective. It was ridiculous. I was watching a French rugby documentary recently on this period and my name kept cropping up and then they had an interview with Philippe Saint Andre and I paraphrase his comments: 'When I was captain I used to tell the team, "Do not listen to a word this idiot Moore says, he is brainless." And I would look up at the forwards who clearly had not heard a word I had said. All they wanted to do was go out there and punch somebody, preferably Brian Moore. And of course that's what Moore and England wanted all the time.'

WILL CARLING

The World Cup of 1991 all still felt a bit new – well it was to me, because I had missed out on the '87 World Cup – and as good a team as we were in '91 we still had a bit of an issue with southern hemisphere teams. We weren't playing them enough and deep down didn't believe we could beat them on a consistent basis. The quarter-final in Paris was the most violent game I ever played in but also one

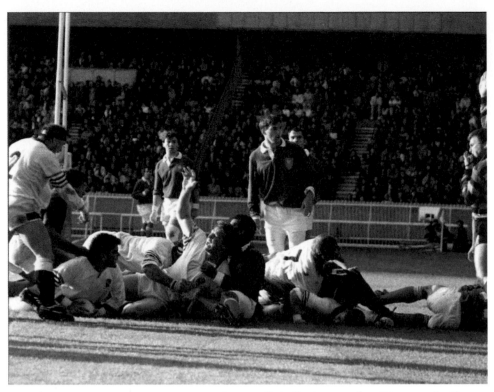

Brian Moore and Mickey Skinner celebrate Will Carling's try against France at the Parc des Princes in the 1991 World Cup quarter-final.

of my favourite matches of all time. And that was a hell of a French team; but from the moment Nigel Heslop slapped Serge Blanco in the second minute we were right into our stride and never really felt like losing.

Then came the Scotland semi which in many ways was a horrible match, with almost zero rugby played, but the stakes were so high and the rivalry so intense after 1990 that that was probably always going to be the case. Gavin Hastings' miss in front of the posts at 6-6 with ten minutes to go was a huge moment. I was under the posts talking to Jerry assuming we were about to go 9-6 down and trying to make some plans when suddenly we were off the hook and all we needed was a Rob Andrew drop-goal to win it.

RORY UNDERWOOD
I find it hard sometimes listening to talk about the 1991 final because you wonder whether you were there or not. My memory is that we as backs saw an area, instigated by Will, where we could attack the Australian backs. Look at how we played against other teams – we didn't play a 10 man game, we could play in

a variety of styles. We wanted to attack their outside-centre area. However, we still needed first phase dominance from our forwards given that we were playing against an Australian side that had beaten New Zealand, and let's not forget that we conceded a sloppy try from a line-out. I didn't have a great game, and nor did a lot of others.

JONATHAN WEBB

There wasn't a massive shift in emphasis, but there was a feeling we could spread it a bit and test Australia's defence.

WILL CARLING

Plenty has been written about our so-called change of tactics for the final so here's my version. We had toured Australia in the summer, lost 40-15, and basically our pack got hammered up front and they also produced a better kicking game on the day. We had meetings about this a couple of times in the week and discussed tactics. It was decided we had to open up a bit, try and stretch Australia, and this notion that we just woke up on Saturday morning and decided to change tactics is a complete nonsense. Two things worked against us on the day. We did try and put tempo into the game and we had the players – but we were inaccurate and didn't make the final pass tell. The tactics didn't quite come off. If we made a mistake at all it was not to realise that our pack had progressed since the summer and were now shaping up against the Australians better. We might have tweaked our tactics on the hoof but bottom line it made no difference. They were better than us.

BRIAN MOORE

In the summer we had seemingly shredded their backs in a Test in Sydney but to little effect, we didn't finish off moves and lost heavily 40-15 and I believe we let our debrief on that influence our game plan unduly. We should have looked at those tapes and said, 'Hang on, we lost that game 40-15.' In the event we played quite a bit of decent attractive rugby in the final, good attacking intent, but it didn't take us anywhere. Our pack was getting stronger with every match and I am convinced we would have won if we had kept it tighter.

PETER WINTERBOTOM

There is no great debate in my mind. The lesson from Sydney was that we had to do quite a bit more than produce our forward orientated game from the Grand Slam to live with the likes of Australia. We lost a tight game of rugby against a very good side, there isn't much more to be said really.

PAUL ACKFORD

That was it for me, I retired after the World Cup, although I did make a brief comeback for Harlequins for the 1992 cup final. This might sound a bit pompous but I was 33 and I had played a World Cup final, won a Slam and been on a Lions tour. By the next Lions tour I would have been 35 and the next World Cup was four years down the track. I could have hung on to go for another Grand Slam but it just seemed like a good time to get out. I was still in pretty decent nick in terms of performance and fitness so I thought well, step away now, say goodbye.

WILL CARLING

We really hit our stride in 1992 and I remember a good feeling from the time we gathered for our warm weather camp at Club la Santa in Lanzarote. Under Geoff we had started having four- or five-day warm weather training camps around New Year, firstly in Portugal and then down in Lanzarote. One New Year's Eve Mark Linnett appeared in the bar wearing world 200m champion Merlene Ottey's running leotard which he had borrowed from her washing line outside the apartment next door. He returned it early the following morning about nine sizes bigger. I'm not quite sure what Merlene made of that.

BRIAN MOORE

I enjoyed those training camps. I worked very hard generally on my fitness and started to get really fit. I had the skill for the hooker position, I like to think, but physically I was unremarkable and knew it was an area I could improve massively if I took it very seriously.

I started taking fitness really seriously in 1989 when I gave up alcohol for six months. I was determined to get on the Lions trip to Australia and win the Test spot. It went well down there and I just carried on when I got back.

It was a big commitment. I was working flat out as a lawyer in the City, horrible London commuting every day. I would be in the office well before 9 and work through to 1pm when I would have an hour in the gym before eating my sandwiches at my desk. Then at 6pm I would dash for a train at Waterloo down to Harlequins for training. That would end about 9.30, I'd have something to eat at the club and then head home. On other nights I would get home, drive to what was Borough Road College and climb over the fence and train in spikes on their athletics track for an hour or so.

The headlights from the traffic on the A4 lit up one of the straights but the other would be pitch black. Friday was the only day I didn't do anything. It was remorseless, a very demanding time. My poor first wife. In ten years I think we had one week's holiday apart from our honeymoon, the times she had to go to weddings and parties and family gatherings on her own because I was tied up playing rugby or training. It was very hard on her.

This was where amateurism and elite sport clashed horribly.

JONATHAN WEBB

My best season was 1992 – I hardly lost a game – England won a Grand Slam, and Bath won a double. I played well and kicked well, and scored a really satisfying try in Paris where I dummied to Rory Underwood and outpaced Sella, who had drifted onto him. I troubled the records left, right and centre, became England's most capped fullback, highest points-scorer in a Five Nations tournament season and totalling 296 in my England career, beating Dusty Hare's tally.

RORY UNDERWOOD

By 1992 we were a complete team. We could be steely and tight but also expansive and free-scoring. We had learned how to always take our chances. And we were in the groove. It might have been the old amateur days but I played 14 games for England in 1991 including 12 Tests despite pursuing a career with the RAF.

DEAN RICHARDS

I came off the bench against Scotland at Murrayfield when Tim Rodber went down injured. I was sat on the replacements bench in the stand, and you had to get in a lift to go down to the ground floor. I was in the lift with Dick Best when it got stuck, and I only got on the pitch because we forced the door open and there was a three foot gap to wriggle through and get out. We went on to win the game, which was already going our way.

It came down to France in Paris again, and we said we would just go about our business. We knew that Moscato and Tordo were livewires with a propensity to lose the plot. So, in the pack beforehand, the policy was that if they hit you, you smiled and then gave them a wink to wind them up even more. And, hey presto, they had two people sent off on the day. They were daft – they had no self-control – and once the Moscato incident happened we ran away with it. When Lascubé was sent off soon afterwards they just capitulated.

JASON LEONARD

That was some match in Paris. I remember at one stage Dewi Morris was pointing into a ruck which the French were killing and screaming at the referee, 'Monsieur, monsieur, le ballon, le ballon!' The referee was Steve Hilditch, of Ulster. He said, 'Dewi, it's all right, I can understand you. I speak English.' Ben Clarke and I cracked up. We were laughing helplessly.

WILL CARLING

We were good, very good in 1992, at the height of our powers, and we won the Grand Slam with plenty to spare, which is rare. I would in all honesty say that for an England team to win a Grand Slam is much harder than for others, it just is – because everybody will raise their game and the chances are that at least one team every season will play an absolute blinder against you and you are never quite sure where it is going to come from. That is what England discovered for a long time under Clive Woodward when they got thwarted three times before finally landing the Grand Slam in 2003.

PETER WINTERBOTTOM

We had a great win over the Boks late in 1992 but that was deceptive, the last major performance from that England team. By the 1993 Five Nations we needed freshening up, we weren't firing properly at all. There is nothing like dropping the old buggers to gee them up a bit. Still at least we got Johnno [Martin Johnson] involved when Wade Dooley got injured. I'm not saying we needed to wield the axe as such but it does no harm to remind people that their place is in danger. Isn't that what Alex Ferguson did brilliantly for decades at Manchester United?

Wade Dooley celebrates scoring England's second try against Wales in the Grand Slam clinching match at Twickenham in 1992.

MARTIN JOHNSON (England 1993-2003, 84 caps plus 8 caps for the Lions)
I was staying at the Leicester Hilton with the England A team ahead of our game against France that night at Welford Road and was about to leave for a meeting of the forwards when the manager, Graham Smith, came in and said Wade Dooley had a leg injury and they needed me down at Twickenham as cover.

When I got to the Petersham Hotel there was nobody around in the foyer but then Geoff Cooke and Kevin Murphy the physio came down and told me Wade was out and I was playing. The players were all over the place but I found Martin Bayfield and Brian Moore and we went over the calls. Then we had to drive down to a menswear shop in Richmond to get a dinner suit for the bash at the Hilton the following night, they had to alter my trousers a bit. Wade came and saw me in my room the next morning which was great of him. We went through a few things that could be useful, how they would try and upset me. We came back from 12-3 to win the match and at dinner that night the RFU president Danie Serfontein got up and said: 'This morning Martin Johnson was a young man of 22, this evening he is an old man of 22.' It only really sunk in when I started to play the recording of the game back at home the following evening and found that I was on it.

WILL CARLING
1993 was a poor year for England, the least enjoyable I can remember, although we picked up a bit in November when we beat the All Blacks, and 1994 was better. The 1993 Lions tour was a distraction, a lot of guys had lost the edge and we really needed to make changes to freshen things up. We scraped a win against France, had a scrappy win against Scotland, lost to Wales and got absolutely thumped by Ireland when we didn't even come second. I found out years later that quite a few of the guys, mostly the older boys, got on the beers Thursday night in Dublin and that really annoys me still.

BRIAN MOORE
1993 was very odd, we couldn't get it together. It was time for a big changing of the guard and we just didn't do it ruthlessly enough. 1992 was the last throw of that exceptional '88-'92 group and despite our fine achievements there needed to be a clear out. The likes of Ben Clarke, Tim Rodber, Victor Ubogu, Steve Ojomoh and others should have been given their heads a season earlier and we lost a lot of momentum as a consequence.

STUART BARNES
The high point of my England career was the Scotland game in 1993. That brought me to national attention, and essentially got me a job with the *Daily Telegraph*

and Sky. I remember going to Oddbins in Teddington later that week where the manager gave me four bottles of very good Burgundy as a memento. I wanted a crack at the Lions. I was on the long list in 1983 and 1989, so when it came to 1993 it was a case of being aware of your sporting mortality. I thought I had to give it a go, and in 1992 I phoned Geoff Cooke and said I was available. They made me captain of the England B team to prove my commitment.

Early in 1993 Rob Andrew had had a few poor games, and I had played well for the Barbarians against Australia, so Geoff decided England needed to sharpen up their game and I was selected at fly-half against Scotland. The Friday evening before the game I went and drank a bottle of wine with Jerry (Guscott) after a meal. He had a packet of fags, and I had most of the wine, it was just his way of keeping me calm. It worked. I made a lot of breaks against Scotland, but then got frustrated. We were on the verge of destroying them, but our forwards held onto the ball too long, and it became slow ball. If it had been a Bath pack, we'd have put 60 points on the Scots.

I did not feel a sense of vindication after that game because I was always very self-critical. The Rory Underwood try was picked out as one of the best of the era, but I seriously thought that it was overestimated. I always waited for the openside to come onto me, and because I had good acceleration we scored loads of tries like that at Bath.

I'd have liked to have played more international rugby with Jerry because we were on the same wavelength, so that's a great pity. However, if you make yourself unavailable you cannot take issue with it later. England could have got a bit more out of Jerry, but we saw some great stuff in any case.

PETER WINTERBOTTOM
1993 was the end of the road for me, time to step down after the Lions tour that summer. I enjoyed a great time with England but it had got to the point where I was training to keep up rather than training to get ahead.

KYRAN BRACKEN (England 1993-2003, 51 caps)
I was playing well for Bristol, but it was quite scary when I got the call for my first cap against New Zealand in '93. When Jamie Joseph stamped on my ankle, I knew when I stood up that it wasn't good. It came out and then went back in, a sub lux of the joint. I remember Joseph called me a 'whingeing Pommy', but I was so driven to stay on because Matt Dawson was on the bench, and in those days you did that. I stayed on the whole game, and the adrenaline kept me going. Afterwards I was in severe pain, and I was on crutches for a month before training again. But it was all worth it – I had made my Eng;and debut and we had beaten the All Blacks. It was incredible.

WILL CARLING

There were some fresh faces and new energy establishing themselves in the team by '95 – Mike Catt, Kyran Bracken, Victor Ubogu and a few others like Matt Dawson emerging fast, and England rugby was back on an upward curve. Johnno was beginning to become a real force, Tim Rodber and Ben Clarke as well. For the only time during my captaincy I sat down in a team meeting before the campaign and set us the very specific target of a Grand Slam. I felt all this new energy and talent needed something very definite to focus on.

Working with Jack Rowell was a bit different, a very bright and accomplished man who could suddenly seem to have massive dips in confidence but generally we got on well and there were always a few laughs and smiles around with Jack, which I liked. It was just a good accomplished Five Nations campaign with a feeling of a lot more to come.

KYRAN BRACKEN

1995 was the last amateur Five Nations and we went out with a bang. I remember the good times and the laughs, not the matches and the scores. Dublin? A fantastic all-nighter on the town with the Irish lads. Cardiff? That was when Victor Ubugo bought us champagne all night after asking a mate to put £100 on him at 18-1 to be the first try scorer. Victor duly obliged and was celebrating large when his mate turned up to admit he thought Victor had been joking and hadn't placed the bet after all.

WILL CARLING

At the end of the season I was interviewed for a Channel Four documentary by Greg Dyke who, unbelievably, went on to run the BBC. The interview was over, I had taken my microphone off, got out of my chair, walked past the camera and was on the way out of the room when I passed Dyke who still evidently had his microphone on, although I didn't know that at the time. In a friendly conversational way he said, 'So Will, what do you really think will happen if the game goes professional?' I replied something along the lines of, 'I've no idea but you certainly don't need 57 old farts running it.' We both laughed and I left.

The transcript of the programme they were to put out was leaked and when the story broke all hell broke loose. I was on the golf course with Gary Lineker and there were twenty missed calls from the office when we stopped for a drink at the halfway hut. I racked my brain. If I'm honest, it had been a pretty boring, uninspired interview, nothing of interest had really been said by either of us.

I quickly got up to speed with what the story was about and was amazed, I wouldn't really put it stronger than that. It was all just too stupid. Then the RFU phoned. It was very serious and I needed to phone Denis Easby, the RFU

President, at the East India Club to apologise. I had no problem with that, I hadn't done anything wrong. I got through and was in the process of apologising and explaining that it had been pretty sharp practice when he interrupted me and said, 'I must stop you there, Will. You are no longer the England captain.'

The week wore on and eventually Denis sat me down and asked what this was all about and actually, in fairness, he listened long and hard and we then had a very good conversation in which I detailed the long and growing antipathy and tension between the team and certain members of the RFU – it rather sounded to me like it was the first time Denis had ever been given our side of the argument. He promised to do what he could to ease the situation. Denis was alright, he had been placed in a very difficult situation by others and we appreciated that. When he travelled to the World Cup he was made welcome in the camp.

BRIAN MOORE

Will's old fart comments were neither here nor there – they were clearly off air, not for use and not particularly offensive. In fact they bordered on the generous in my opinion. What was absolutely incredible is that some of those in power – a very small minority, not the majority – chose this moment, five or six weeks before a World Cup in which we were well in the frame, to sack the England captain over something so utterly trivial.

Will Carling begins the celebrations after England clinched the 1995 Grand Slam with a 24-12 victory over Scotland at Twickenham.

By way of an olive branch I will give the RFU credit for one thing during this otherwise acrimonious period. They handled the rebuilding of Twickenham superbly, they were ambitious and professional in that area, which has a certain irony in itself, and even when it was a building site they disguised it very cleverly and we always felt we were playing at the home of English rugby.

WILL CARLING

As I say, I quite fancied our chances at the 1995 World Cup, or I did at least until we turned up and saw how New Zealand were playing! In the end South Africa, inspired by Nelson Mandela, became a different proposition but New Zealand, inspired by Jonah Lomu, started playing rugby from another planet. It's the only time I think the best team in the world at the time didn't win the World Cup.

We eased through the pool games; well, the idea is to just get through them, no point in leaving your best rugby in the pools. And then we nicked a tight quarter-final against Australia with Rob Andrew's dropped goal and the madness really started. I was pleased enough but a bit concerned with how we had been playing. I saw Winters, over to support us, in the bar that night and asked him what he thought. He always gives it to you straight. 'So-so at best, loads of work to do. Mooro has finally gone, you need fresh legs at hooker and the other older guys are struggling as well. We need fresh legs and more pace in the pack against New Zealand.'

Rob Andrew strikes the drop-goal that knocks defending champions Australia out of the 1995 World Cup during the quarter-final match in Cape Town.

Straight after the Australia game England had booked two full days off at Sun City for a spot of R&R. Our jolly attracted plenty of criticism; almost all of it warranted, looking back. We should have got straight out on the training pitch first thing Monday and hit it hard for a couple of days before tapering down in the build-up to the semi-final. Mentally I don't think we were anywhere near where we needed to be against New Zealand and then they exploded out of the traps and hit us with 20 minutes of rugby from the gods. They were incredible. I stood under the sticks after their third try and the game was over. There is nothing in the captaincy handbook which prepares you for that moment.

DEAN RICHARDS
After we had beaten Australia thanks to that Rob Andrew drop-goal, we went to Sun City for three days, two nights. We obviously hadn't learned from the Hamilton Island trip in Australia in 1987. We asked for footage of Jonah Lomu – and New Zealand's style of play – and were told he'd only played against Scotland. We didn't do the preparation well and the semi-final was an accident waiting to happen.

MIKE CATT (England 1994-2007, 75 caps plus 1 cap for the Lions)
I think because we had a lot of players from the '91 squad who had lost in the final to Australia it made the quarter-final against the Wallabies in '95 another cup final. We were not meant to beat southern hemisphere sides and when we did it was amazing. That gave us a semi-final against New Zealand. They were such an incredible team, all sorts of amazing individuals from No 8 Zinzan Brooke, who landed a drop goal from near the touchline, to Jonah Lomu out wide who ran in four tries, including, of course, one when he ran over the top of me.

JEREMY GUSCOTT
Lomu terrorised every team he played against. People can talk about George North, Julian Savea and Israel Folau these days, but they are nowhere near as quick as Lomu. He was 6ft 5ins and 18 stone, and he ran like Brian Habana. He not only had speed, but nimbleness and dexterity – a hippo doing ballet. He had amazing skill, and was an amazing rugby player – the most amazing I have seen.

BRIAN MOORE
The end of my career was strange, stressful and downbeat. For a start I was going through my first divorce which was hard in itself. Meanwhile on the rugby pitch I knew my career was coming to an end and that my time was up. I just wish it could have been in any other match than that awful third/fourth place play-off

game against France in Pretoria. I was knackered from the New Zealand game, Dawesie [Graham Dawe] should have played, I should have insisted.

There was one extraordinary incident surrounding that game though. There was quite a bit of drug testing in those days despite comments to the contrary, and the process was that 21 balls numbered from 1 to 21 – we only had six replacements then – were placed in a bag and somebody would pull out two numbers and off you trotted to give your sample. In the 1991 season I got tested six times in a row and people cleverer than me tell me that's an 85 million to one shot. I was always getting tested, constantly. Fast forward to 1995 and I was on four consecutive tests going into my final game and would you believe it out I popped again. Five tests in a row, a 4.1 million to one shot.

It was my last game and I just didn't believe this nonsense anymore. There was no way these tests were random, I was being targeted. I refused to go. Don Rutherford told me to go to the testers or I would be banned. I said, 'No, I'm retiring anyway, I don't care.' In the end I didn't go and they had to pick another number out of the bag which was probably highly illegal but what did I care? I was already de facto retired. Later we had a fantastic evening on the ale with the French after six or seven years or real enmity and warfare. We rebuilt a lot of bridges that night and although it was an utterly dreadful game, the après rugby at least felt like a proper farewell to Test rugby.

Decompressing from playing for England is hugely difficult; well, I've found it a real issue and continue to fight some of the psychological aspects to this day. That life you have been living with England is your real world and for a time it can seem normal and routine but the moment you step outside of that world you realise how extraordinary and totally abnormal it is. You have to fight that temptation to see everything else as normal and mundane – which of course it isn't because those who don't happen to play Test rugby find ultimate fulfilment and excellence in a million different ways – and you must sternly resist the urge to recreate what you had in some way because you will never match it. Take my word on that.

You can try and recreate something else entirely different and special in some totally unrelated walk of life – that might work for you – but you need to understand you can't go back to where you were and if you try you can encounter serious problems. One of the things I did soon after finally retiring was to splash out on a Chelsea season ticket, not just because I support them, but so that I had somewhere to go most weekends other than a rugby ground and a rugby club bar. Clive Woodward phoned me up when he got the England coaching job and asked if I would be a selector but I had to decline because I had just made the conscious decision to get away from rugby for a while.

I get very vivid England rugby flashbacks all the time, re-living the game in real time and in precise detail. Part of that is possibly that my commentating job and all the rugby chat and debate I get involved in prompts such thoughts, but I also got them before I was involved heavily in the media and I know other guys get them as well. I've normally got a rubbish memory, I'm always forgetting to pay bills and bailiffs are turning up on the front door, absolutely disgraceful behaviour really, but I can recall entire multi-phase passages of play from over 20 years ago and long-involved discussions at team meetings and all that stuff.

DEAN RICHARDS

Jack Rowell said to me after the 1995 World Cup that he wouldn't pick me again. I said fine. Then, in the 1996 Five Nations they had injuries going into the France game, and I got a message saying that Jack would like me in the squad. However, a couple of days before that I'd had a call from the RFU and they'd asked me to return the rowing machine and pager I'd been given. At the time the pager was in the bin, and the rowing machine was under a stack of construction material where we were building a conservatory. I had a think and then phoned the RFU and told them that I wanted Jack to call me. When he phoned back he said that he wanted me at least on the bench, and I said, 'Look, I don't want to give back my pager or rowing machine.' He said OK. When we saw each other at Twickenham

Jonah Lomu on the rampage during the semi-final.

for training I told him what had happened. He broke down laughing. It was a hot and cold relationship – but I had huge respect for him.

I came off the bench against the French in Paris, and then started the last two games. The game at Murrayfield was when the Scots kicked the ball to me all afternoon and I wouldn't let them have it back. Scotland had been saying that they'd thump us, and in the team talks I said to the England lads that all we had to do was win. Afterwards Jack and I just sat down with a beer and had a laugh. After that we beat the Irish at Twickenham, retaining the Five Nations title. I didn't call a halt in 1996, and I have always wondered why anyone would retire (specifically) from international rugby. Retire completely, yes. If your body has given up, you accept it. But not 'retire' and turn down the chance to walk out at Twickenham and miss out on special moments.

WILL CARLING

In 1996 I wanted one more Grand Slam to make up for the disappointment of the '95 World Cup and it could have happened, but we played badly against France and that was that and after that I took a good look at myself and didn't like everything I saw. As captain I wasn't doing all the things I used to do, the weekly phone calls, I wasn't as diligent as I used to be, I wasn't pushing as hard. I decided to resign as captain. It was a hard decision to make in that I had grown up being England captain, it's what I did and to a certain extent, an identity crisis followed for a while.

Jack seemed genuinely stunned and I flatter myself that he tried to talk me out of it before he accepted my decision.

At the time playing and captaining England was everything, it was my life, and if I'm honest, throughout that period it caused all sorts of issues in my personal life because always number one was my devotion to England and the 'job' of captaining England. The rest of my life came and went – not in a malicious way – but it always took second place. For a while it was everything, all consuming, and yet now I don't miss it at all. Your priorities change, family and loved ones are everything now. Mentally my England rugby career is tucked away in a little box which I occasionally open up and I smile at the good times and great memories.

TWENTY
THE MAKING OF CHAMPIONS
1997-2003

THE SIX YEARS *from 1997 to 2003 were dominated by Clive Woodward, the maverick with a mission. Woodward's tenure as England's first full-time professional coach culminated in the most successful period in the nation's rugby history, and, while he was a controversial character who divided opinion like no other, there is no doubting his effectiveness.*

Woodward was an unlikely figure to become the driving force behind England not only making the transition from amateur to professional eras successfully, but also turning them into the world's leading rugby power by the end of the 2003 World Cup.

That Woodward was adventurous and ambitious was evident in his illustrious playing career. He was a mercurial outside-centre for Leicester, before coming to international prominence as a member of the 1980 England Grand Slam side, and also for the Lions (1980 and 1983).

His adventurous spirit was mirrored in his decision to leave the East Midlands and start anew in Australia, where he joined the Manly club and became an admirer of their expansive playing style, while at the same time pursuing his career as a sales director at a computer leasing company.

However, he was not a part of the English coaching establishment, and when he returned to the UK and began coaching in earnest it was with Henley, a junior club in the Thames Valley. After four years with Henley he joined London Irish, and then spent a year with Bath.

His appointment as the England Under-21 assistant coach while at Bath indicated that he had admirers in high places in the RFU hierarchy, notably his former teammates Fran Cotton and Bill Beaumont. Even so, Woodward's appointment as England coach in 1997 as successor to Jack Rowell was a shock to the English system, mainly because his track record at the highest level was sketchy.

What was clear from the outset was that Woodward brought energy and dynamism, as well as a vision for the future. By creating a high performance environment he wanted to challenge the England players, but he also wanted to demolish the perception from the outside of England being hostage to a conservative approach. He says that his initial objective was to play a style of entertaining rugby that got, '70,000 fans at Twickenham on their feet going nuts'.

Opposite: Martin Johnson

In the autumn of 1997 his new-look England, with Lawrence Dallaglio as captain, faced a daunting itinerary with two Tests against New Zealand, and a further two against Australia and the world champions, South Africa.

After a draw against the Wallabies (15-15), with debuts for Matt Perry at fullback and Will Greenwood at inside centre, two defeats followed. After an eyeball to eyeball confrontation at Old Trafford during the haka between the hookers, Richard Cockerill and Norm Hewitt, the New Zealanders proved too fast and accurate for England, winning 25-8 in a Test that was the first outing for a back row of Richard Hill, Neil Back and Dallaglio – a trio destined to become an England institution under Woodward. A further reverse against South Africa (29-11) saw the Woodward experiment faltering, with the second Test against the All Blacks to come at Twickenham.

Woodward persuaded his players to play that game at the highest pace they could, exhorting them to leave nothing in the tank in an attempt to surprise the All Blacks by running them off their feet. It almost worked. In an epic encounter England ran everything from the outset, and a three try blitz with touchdowns by David Rees, Hill and Dallaglio saw New Zealand trailing 23-9 at half-time. With England tiring after the interval the New Zealanders fought back to secure a 26-26 draw – but Woodward had come out of the series with the greatest of gains. By pushing the All Blacks to the brink he had proved to his players that with the right mindset and levels of fitness, the sky was the limit.

In the first Five Nations campaign of the Woodward era in 1998, England won a Triple Crown, and although beaten by France to a Grand Slam, with Jason Leonard and Martin Johnson as front five stanchions, they could lay claim to having the best pack in Europe.

The coach also had the foresight to fast-track Jonny Wilkinson, who, when he came on as a last-minute replacement against Ireland at the age of 18, became the youngest red rose player since Henri Laird in 1927.

The honeymoon period for Woodward came to an abrupt halt with the ill-conceived Tour from Hell that summer. This saw a severely weakened England tour party play reciprocal fixtures against the southern hemisphere big three, starting against Australia, continuing with two Tests against New Zealand, and finishing against South Africa.

With most of England's Five Nations starting line-up rested, the tourists were on a hiding to nothing. Disaster duly struck when a callow red rose second/third-string side was dismantled 76-0 by Australia in Brisbane – far and away England's worst international defeat.

The embarrassments also came thick and fast on the other side of the Tasman. Woodward's side succumbed to the New Zealand Maori and New Zealand Academy sides, before being overwhelmed 64-22 and 40-10 in the Tests, with Danny Grewcock sent-off for a prod with his boot in the first of them.

The final leg of the tortuous journey saw England offer sterner resistance, losing 18-0 to South Africa in wind and rain in Cape Town. However, the tour ended on a controversial note when Woodward – who had returned to the UK briefly during the tour for his father's funeral – became embroiled in a row with RFU officials following his decision to move the squad from the hotel provided by the host union to one of Cape Town's most salubrious establishments.

Woodward's view – and one he adhered to throughout his tenure – was that as England's elite force, his squad should have the best facilities, coaching, and treatment available if they were expected to become the best team in the world.

There were more trials and tribulations to come for Woodward and his squad on the road to that goal. There was a good start to the 1999 Five Nations campaign, with Wilkinson becoming first choice goal-kicker after being picked at inside-centre, with Mike Catt inside him and Jeremy Guscott outside. This saw England go into the final match against Wales at Wembley (minus the injured Guscott) with a Grand Slam there for the taking. However, the chance was lost when, despite being the dominant side, they were sucker-punched by a last minute Scott Gibbs try soon after Dallaglio had spurned a penalty to kick for the corner. Their 32-31 defeat in the last game in Five Nations history gifted Scotland the title.

This was followed by another serious setback when Dallaglio was snared in a newspaper sting rigged by the News of the World, with the England captain lured into having a few drinks and then saying on tape that he had experimented with recreational drugs in his late teens. The subsequent furore resulted in Dallaglio's resignation and withdrawal from the summer tour of Australia.

In his absence, Johnson took over the captaincy when England, wearing the red, blue and white of the 1899 British touring side, played Australia in the host nation's Centenary Test in Sydney, losing 22-15.

By that time the focus had switched to preparations for the imminent World Cup. England embarked on a series of warm-up matches for the first time, but these were more notable for the reintegration of Dallaglio than as a serious playing exercise. The USA were buried 106-8, and Canada accounted for (36-11) in late August, before the tournament started in earnest in October.

With England drawn in the same pool as New Zealand, along with Italy and Tonga, the crucial early encounter was always going to be against the All Blacks – and, with England's 1995 nemesis, Jonah Lomu, and fly-half Andrew Mehrtens spearheading the New Zealand assault, England came up short again (30-16).

Matters did not improve when Jeremy Guscott, who had already suffered a groin strain in one of the warm-up games, was forced out of the tournament by a recurrence of the injury against New Zealand. It proved to be the end of the great centre's international career, as he announced his retirement the following week.

By finishing as runners-up to New Zealand, Woodward found that the deck was stacked against his team because they had to play a midweek quarter-final eliminator

– in their case against Fiji – allowing them only a three-day gap to travel and prepare for South Africa, should they win.

England beat the Fijians 45-24 to clinch their place in the last eight, but Woodward made changes, most notably by benching Wilkinson. The youngster had started at fly-half against New Zealand, but the England coach decided to go with experience against the Springboks, picking Paul Grayson ahead of him.

However, it was the opposition's replacement fly-half who stole the show, with Jannie De Beer executing a pre-planned strategy to perfection with his five drop-goals putting paid to England making any further progress (44-21).

Woodward, who had said before the tournament started, 'Judge me on my results', was now in danger after such an unsatisfactory exit – and he returned home with his position in jeopardy.

Woodward was given the reprieve he so desperately wanted, and thanks again to unwavering support from Cotton, Beaumont, and the RFU's new chief executive, Francis Baron, he was confirmed as England coach through to the 2003 World Cup.

The coaching and conditioning infrastructure that he had been putting in place during his first two seasons was now beginning to bear fruit in terms of England becoming one of the fittest, best prepared sides in the international arena. This involved specialist coaches, trainers and nutritionists providing unrivalled attention to detail.

It was a period in which Woodward also switched his main emphasis, putting the autumn series against the southern hemisphere big three at the top of his priorities. It is notable that following the defeat by New Zealand in the 1999 World Cup, England turned Twickenham into a forbidding fortress. They did not lose again at home on their own turf to anyone for more than four years.

Yet, in many respects, they were not the finished article, and there were more disappointments to shoulder, especially in the Six Nations Championship. Although England were clearly the dominant force in Europe from 1999 to 2003 they found their Grand Slam holy grail to be horribly elusive.

In 2000, despite 10 tries for wings Ben Cohen and Austin Healey, England fell at the final fence again, this time losing 19-13 in the rain at Murrayfield against a Scottish side which outplayed them as they failed to adapt to the conditions.

They made amends on their summer tour of South Africa when, having been robbed in the first Test in Pretoria (18-13), they outmuscled the Springboks to win 27-22 in Bloemfontein, squaring the series.

However, the growing support for the side was jeopardised during the autumn series five months later when the England players threatened to go on strike when negotiations with Baron over a rise in their £6,000 match fee stalled. With Woodward and his coaching staff backing the RFU's position there was the potential for a nasty rift, but it was averted at the last minute when a compromise was reached, and England proceeded to beat Australia (22-19), Argentina (19-0) and South Africa (25-17).

Back on the Six Nations front Woodward's side were thwarted again in 2001. With Jason Robinson emerging as a lethal convert from rugby league, England produced a series of scintillating displays to beat Wales (44-15), Italy (80-23), Scotland (43-3) and France (48-19), only for the final match of the season to be postponed due to an outbreak of foot-and-mouth disease.

In the summer the Lions tour intervened, and, by the time England reassembled for the rescheduled match in Dublin in the autumn, they had lost their spark. Ireland took full advantage to scupper a third England Grand Slam opportunity in succession, and deserved their 20-14 win.

The French raised their game in Paris in 2002, and, with Serge Betsen detailed to hound Wilkinson, England were derailed again by a single defeat (20-15). This put France on the road to the Slam so cherished by their opponents.

Then, at last, in 2003 all the stars aligned in England's favour. A clean sweep of the Tri-Nations in the autumn of 2002 – with wins over New Zealand (31-28), Australia (32-31), and the annihilation of South Africa (53-3) – saw England in irrepressible form. With Johnson at his glowering best, Wilkinson as a steely controller and goal-kicker without peer, and Hill, Back and Dallaglio as the complete back-row, they had world class credentials to spare.

The advent of Will Greenwood and Mike Tindall as a highly effective midfield pairing, and the arrival of Josh Lewsey as the last component in a razor-sharp back three, saw Woodward's side soar to new heights. They beat France (25-17), Wales (26 9), Italy (40 5), Scotland (40-9) and, finally, Ireland (42-6).

England's refusal to be fazed as favourites for the Six Nations, or by their new world number one status, was evident in Johnson's stubborn insistence that his team would stay put when asked to swap places before the anthems in Dublin.

Their five tries to nil haul against the Irish in a Grand Slam decider was equally uncompromising. Nor were they done. Woodward's England then embarked on a three match summer tour of New Zealand and Australia, breaking new ground by beating the All Blacks and the Wallabies on consecutive weekends, after warming up with a victory over the New Zealand Maori (23-9).

What was most remarkable was that the 15-13 victory over New Zealand in Wellington was achieved by an England side well below their best, and also handicapped by being reduced to 13 men at one stage with two players sin-binned. However, with the help of an epic goal-line stand and Wilkinson's unerring accuracy, they became the second England side to beat New Zealand on their own soil.

A week later Australia were on the receiving end of a comprehensive 25-14 beating in Melbourne, outscored three tries to one, as England produced a performance straight out of the 'Total Rugby' book beloved of their coach.

With the 2003 World Cup just around the corner England could not have made a more emphatic statement of their intent.

ROGER UTTLEY

When Jack Rowell was in charge in 1997 the cult of the coach had developed to the extent that he was the sole spokesman for the side. There was a view that it had become too complex, and that a manager was needed to take the pressure off the coach by doing some of the speaking and media duties. Bill Beaumont called me to ask if I be interested in the role. He said that they were also looking for someone to coach the side and that there were various individuals in the frame. It was at the start of professional rugby in the northern hemisphere and most of the top choices were already under club contracts. Clive Woodward's name came up, and although he was at Bath as an assistant coach he wasn't under contract and was therefore available.

MATT DAWSON (England 1995-2006, 77 caps plus 7 caps for the Lions)

Clive came with all these ingredients and a completely different style of management, which some might have thought of as controversial, but I just found it so refreshing. It may have taken a few years for the players to really get used to it all, but it was such a breath of fresh air.

CLIVE WOODWARD

Don Rutherford came to my house to ask me about doing the job. I asked him what the financial side of it was as my business was going well at the time. He couldn't answer me. He said no one had actually thought about it. So he eventually came back and said: 'This is the salary.' It was just ridiculous. I remember talking to my wife, Jayne. 'I've got good news and bad news... we have got to sell the house, all the kids have got to change schools, and we have to sell the cars... But the good news is that I'm the England head coach.' This went on for ages. I remember it took a long time to sort it all out.

ROGER UTTLEY

People thought that Clive and I knew each other well, but he had only come into the 1980 Grand Slam side following injuries to Tony Bond and Nick Preston. He was just starting whereas I was a senior pro at the fag end of my career. As the senior partner in the new set-up, I arranged to have a drink with Clive at a pub in Harrow-on-the-Hill. I said this was a great opportunity for everyone concerned with English rugby but that the one thing I knew above all from my past experience in the game was that we had to operate in a 'We' culture not an 'I' culture if we were to have any chance of being successful. He agreed.

CLIVE WOODWARD

It was about 13 years since I was last in the full England set-up as a player, and suddenly I am sitting in this massive media conference at Bisham Abbey with all these RFU grandees – Billy Beaumont, Cliff Brittle (RFU Chairman), Don Rutherford, Fran Cotton, Roger Uttley. They are announcing me as England coach. One question was, 'What's it like to be second choice?' And I said, 'I'm fifth choice.' I knew that the RFU had approached Graham Henry in New Zealand, and Ian McGeechan had already said that he had been approached. Ian didn't think he could coach England because he was Scottish. I think they went through various people and there was me, coaching the England Under-21 team. Fran, who had always been my biggest fan, must have said, 'Hang on a sec, maybe we should go with this guy.'

MATT PERRY (England 1997-2001, 36 caps plus 3 caps for the Lions)
Clive was coaching England Under-21 and I was playing in the centre, just coming through the Bath ranks in 1996, being coached by Brian Ashton, and with Mike Catt, Jerry Guscott and Phil de Glanville in the backline. Clive asked me if I fancied playing fullback, and I said yes. You learn that life is about timing and taking opportunities. When Clive went to England, I went on that journey with him. I was 20, spotty, two years out of school, but I had been tested at Bath.

I had a very clear vision. I had a place to do law at Cardiff University, and I went to South Africa for six months and played rugby in Durban. My aim was just to play one game for Bath, and playing for England wasn't in my head. However, I got in the Bath side, and stayed in, and decided to defer going to university. At that time we were in the transition to professionalism, and I was on an academy contract at Bath worth about £5,000. There were additional fees for playing in the European Cup, with a £450 match fee and a £750 win bonus. The following season, when I got in the England side, my earnings went up to about £40,000.

It was a dream when I was selected against Australia in the autumn of '97. To have all that at such a young age was unbelievable. It was everything, and I was living off pure adrenaline that year, especially during the 1997 autumn series. It was almost as if I was living in the third person. You were just reacting to every moment and doing what you could – you were being tested to your limit.

CLIVE WOODWARD

There was nothing in place (in 1997). The game had gone pro less than two years before. I'm not saying it was anyone's fault. I think England were the great amateurs in a real positive way. We were amateur. All this stuff you hear about brown envelopes – well, I never saw a brown envelope.

I was the first professional national coach so in that sense I had a blank sheet of paper. But the flip side was that experience told me that the first two or three years of any new venture are the toughest, and if you're smart you come in after three years when some other idiot has taken all the initial rubbish. However, it was a fantastic opportunity for me and I jumped in with both feet. I had various ideas but the bottom line was that I had to win Test matches otherwise I wouldn't survive.

JEREMY GUSCOTT

Clive's appointment was new, refreshing and rejuvenating. It made us think – and you did not know what would happen next. Everything happened very quickly. You knew England was a sleeping giant and that Woodward had locked all the doors and thrown a hornets nest in the middle. He revitalised England.

In the autumn of '97 I remember Clive sticking a flip-chart up of the New Zealand fitness and conditioning results. He said where they were and then told us we were 25 per cent below them – and that we needed to be 10 per cent above them. It got you thinking, 'How much better can we be?'

Clive's attention to detail was amazing and like nothing I had experienced before. There was the brown leather Filofax with the English rose. It was your property. There were also nameplates in the changing room. It was the start of an identity.

JASON LEONARD

What Clive created was a no-excuses set-up. You'd always have some excuse in the early days. The food was bad, you'd trained badly because you'd been working all day, the bed was too small, you were stiff from the journey. Now, all that was taken away. We were pampered. But to get all these perks we had to perform, and there was no comeback whatsoever if we didn't.

RICHARD HILL (England 1997-2004, 71 caps plus 5 caps for the Lions)
One of the major things that he did was to put a fantastic coaching group together. He tried to look for the very best experts in their fields – the guys who were the best at coaching scrummaging, line-outs, defence and so on – guys who could lead the best players and make them better. That, of course, had its own challenges: if you want to be a world leader in your specific coaching area, you want to have a good amount of time with the players – you don't want to get to a World Cup and say, 'My area was a let-down.' So we had all these coaches who would want maybe thirty minutes a day with us, but you can't train that much as a rugby player. Three-hour sessions just do not happen; even two-hour sessions were a stretch. Clive was very adept at managing that workload so that we got the benefit of the specialist coaching but without overworking our bodies.

JASON LEONARD

We hadn't had backs, forwards, defence, attack, scrummage and kicking coaches before, let alone throwing-in coaches, tactical analysts and all the other people who suddenly became associated with the team. I realise now that it was the right thing to do but, at the time, we were a bit alarmed at how quickly everything was changing and what all these new and varied coaches were going to do.

RICHARD HILL

He was obsessed with detail and changing things that you would never have even thought of before. I remember one of the first things he did was to bring in a TV make-over company to revamp the changing rooms at Twickenham. We were all asked what sort of things we would like, from the paint colour to whether we wanted cubicles. We were locked out of the place in the build-up to a Test match and then shown in before the game and we were all bowled over with how much it had changed. We went in and it was all bright and spacious, with huge pictures on the walls and plaques with our names on them above individual cubicles. It certainly made you feel like you were a part of an elite environment.

MATT DAWSON

And he made the away changing rooms worse! He made them as dull and cold as possible. Then you'd walk into the tunnel and line up next to the opposition before running out and there would be all these plaques to great England victories that went right back to the first internationals dotted all along the walls, and on the doors to the pitch in giant writing were the words: THIS IS FORTRESS TWICKENHAM. At the time as a player I didn't really appreciate all the little things that Clive did but you look back now and think, 'He was a clever so-and-so...'

JEREMY GUSCOTT

Woodward gave us freedom, but you never felt safe in your place. It was not so much through fear as it was about being in a highly competitive environment. He shook things up – he didn't do the obvious. For instance, Martin Johnson was the obvious choice as captain, but he went for Lawrence Dallaglio.

LAWRENCE DALLAGLIO (England 1995-2007, 85 caps plus 3 caps for the Lions)
I was a lot more talkative than Martin. That was more Clive's style. In the early years, he was full of ideas and I think he liked to feel he could discuss them with his captain. What I particularly liked was Clive's vision. He didn't want England to be the best team in just Europe, he wanted them to be the best in the world. And Clive definitely wanted to be the man to bring about that change.

JEREMY GUSCOTT

Lawrence is a good mate, and I have such respect for him as a person and a rugby player. As a player he was an unrelenting force of nature that added unbelievable belief, and was all about winning. He loves being English, and loves everything English – which is interesting given his Italian heritage! You all think that you're passionate, but Lawrence is full-blooded emotion – all the elements, fire, earth and water – and he wore that passion on his sleeve. He is a product of hard work and determination. Lawrence was not a Zinzan Brooke or Kieran Read, in that his skill set was not huge. But he was fit, hard, and quick and he made the most of what he had and became the best No.8 in the world at that time.

CLIVE WOODWARD

That first season, 1997-98, I just threw the kitchen sink at it. There are people now who probably haven't forgiven me for a few things that happened behind-the-scenes. I still saw it as a player. I still do. I see from a player's point of view. If I thought something would make a difference to the team, we did it.

JEREMY GUSCOTT

I don't believe that England coaches should be doing anything but fine-tuning. All I ever wanted from a coach was someone who challenged you.

Woodward was a game-changer, just like Geoff Cooke. Quirky as it sometimes seemed it was enjoyable, and it was becoming a no excuses environment. It's a bad place to be when people are looking for excuses, a bad vibe. You felt good playing for England, not just because you were winning, but because it was a good place to be. Nothing frees you more than a coach saying, 'Go out and give it a lash.' Woodward was clearly a visionary, just as Cooke was, and fitness was a big point. Cooke had a clear idea of what he wanted to do, and how he was going to do it.

A new captain and a new era. Lawrence Dallaglio leads his team out to face Australia at Twickenham in the autumn of 1997.

Jack Rowell did not have anywhere near as big an impact as Cooke or Woodward. A politician never answers a question, and rarely makes a difference.

Geoff Cooke changed the dynamic of English rugby, and so did Clive Woodward – and it is what Stuart Lancaster is trying to do now. They deserve credit for challenging the players and the establishment.

JASON LEONARD

I remember that after the New Zealand team put together a booklet of their training drills, coaches in England got hold of it and we all copied it slavishly for years. Clive's theory was that we should find a way that worked best for England and not copy what other rugby nations were doing. We should establish the England way of doing things, and let other countries copy that.

KYRAN BRACKEN

Woodward said that he was annoyed that everyone was always bigging-up New Zealand, and he refused to buy into the mystique. He made a point of never calling them the All Blacks. Clive said we were going to run them off the park, and that he wanted the nines and sevens to be absolutely hanging. He said he'd rather lose like that than never know how far we could push them. It had never been done before, and after 25 minutes I was knackered. By that time we were 20 points up and I kept on saying to the coaching staff, 'I'm gone – I can't keep up'. I came off after 65 minutes. It wasn't easy, but it proved to all of us that if we could do this to the best team in the world, we could do it to anyone. I didn't feel that England could play that well again for a long time.

MARTIN JOHNSON

Clive came in and wanted to change how we were playing, to move away from the stereotypical English game dominated by the forwards. He insisted, in those first games, that we play without a game plan as such – in fact, the term 'game plan' was banned from being mentioned – and that we were to play off the cuff whenever we could. At first it was all a bit chaotic but in retrospect I can appreciate what he was trying to do – he was wanting us to free our minds and to think differently.

I think we surprised ourselves with how well we competed in the first Test that autumn against the All Blacks. I think they had become an even bigger test in our minds than they actually were.

LAWRENCE DALLAGLIO

We started the match at Old Trafford with a back-row of Richard Hill at 7, Tony Diprose at 8 and me at 6. Clearly, Clive felt the back-row hadn't performed in the first half and at the interval he came into the changing room, looked at Diprose and said, 'Right, you're off.' Turning to Neil Back he said, 'You're on.' It was brutal. Rugby substitutions didn't happen like that, at least not in an England dressing room. But that was the start of the successful back-row of Hill, Dallaglio, Back.

NEIL BACK (England 1994-2003, 66 caps plus 5 caps for the Lions)
Geoff Cooke and Jack Rowell denied me of many years of international rugby and the honour of representing my country on many more occasions. I firmly believe I should have been playing for England from the early 1990s.

WILL GREENWOOD (England 1997-2004, 55 caps plus 2 caps for the Lions)
I remember thinking when we played the Springboks a week later how much bigger and more powerful than us the South Africans seemed that day. Perhaps it's a trick your mind plays on you when you are beaten, but it certainly felt a little like boys against men… If we gained anything that afternoon, it was the realisation that we had a vast amount of work to do if we were going to turn the tables on the southern hemisphere and start bullying them.

LAWRENCE DALLAGLIO
Clive spoke from the heart before the final Test of that series against New Zealand. 'Let's have a go at this New Zealand team. Let's tap everything, we've lost the last two games anyway. We don't have much to lose, so let's absolutely go for it. Let's go for the jugular with these guys… let's get some pace into the game.' He then wrote 'three tries' on the board and told us that was the target for the game. It was a brilliant approach.

CLIVE WOODWARD
So we were coming into the fourth and last game of that autumn and I was feeling frustrated with how it had all gone. Paul Grayson was at stand-off and I remember standing in a team meeting and saying to Paul, 'We have nothing to lose now, we've not had a great autumn, we've drawn one and lost two, so we have to try and do things differently now. I want you to push up flat to the gain-line on attack, I want you right up in the All Blacks' faces. And I mean right up there.' And the whole team was listening in to this. I said, 'I don't care what you think about this or how you feel, you're going to do it. And if you don't, if we're only five minutes into the game, I'll sub you for someone who will do it.' And that's what we practised all week. And Grayson was awesome. It requires an incredibly high skill-level and also a fitness level because if you start to tire that's when your skills start to drop-off and the whole thing falls apart. And, in all honesty, you need a

player like Will Greenwood. You expect your nine and ten to be able to pass well, but you need intelligent operators in midfield who can read the game and pass – and since Will retired, he's never been replaced.

Will was absolutely key to the success of the England team while I was in charge. Was he the best passer? No. Was he the best kicker? No. All round was he the best player? By a mile. His big thing was hitting the line flat and being able to offload the ball. He had everything. In terms of his communication skills and understanding of the game, his offloading ability, he was the best player I have ever seen play in the centre for England.

MATT PERRY

That New Zealand game was the quickest game I was ever involved in. We were massive underdogs, and we played at a pace which was at times out of control. The second half was like a game of sevens, with bodies and space everywhere, and we were hanging on after giving it a massive go. It took me two weeks to get over that 26-all draw. My body was just buzzing with the pace of it all. In the first Test at Old Trafford I remember standing there and bricking it when Richard Cockerill advanced on the Haka. To see one of your own team step forward and rile them even more, you thought, 'Oh. That might not help.'

LAWRENCE DALLAGLIO

But even after that magnificent effort, you only had to look at the scene in our changing room at half-time to realise why we were miles away from the best countries in the world. It was carnage. No one could speak. Players were sprawled on the floor, others were vomiting into the bins and it was simply a question of allowing players to regain some semblance of physical normality. We should have gone out and closed the game down, but instead we started falling off tackles and allowed them to get into our territory. One try came, then another and, at the end, we were happy to hang on for a 26–26 draw.

MARTIN JOHNSON

Looking back, we weren't a good enough team to beat those sides at that stage. We might have defeated the Aussies if we had had a really good day, but the New Zealanders and the South Africans were a level above us. It had been a pretty tough baptism for Clive: four games, two heavy losses and a couple of draws. If that wasn't enough, our first game in the 1998 Five Nations was France. In Paris.

PHIL VICKERY (England 1998-2009, 73 caps plus 5 caps for the Lions)

My first time on the bench was in Paris in 1998. The team seemed to be very

Leicester-orientated and in the build-up in the week no-one talked to me. I was hardly allowed to join in training because I didn't know any of the line-out calls. We're getting pummelled up front, the crowd were roaring. I was thinking, 'Please, please, please, don't send me on!'

I started against Wales in the following match. I remember being absolutely terrified, thinking, 'I cannot do this.' But then you start getting letters and cards and telegrams, notes from the old school teachers, and people from Bude, and all over the country.

Then there was Jason [Leonard]. I was a young prop just come on the scene but then, like always, he was there. He was always brilliant to me and I remember him saying before the game, 'Enjoy it, because before you know it, it will be all over.'

I had so many injuries throughout my career that by the end I suppose I lost as many caps as I won. But when I hear those people on reality TV shows dressing up in stupid things and saying they are living the dream, well, I can say hand on heart that I have lived the dream. When I started out as a young man in rugby and when I first fell in love with the game at Bude rugby club in Cornwall, I'd never ever have dreamt that I would do what I did. When I retired I suppose I had a few dark times but I came through. I looked back to playing for Bude colts at the age of 12 or 13, then to playing for Redruth colts at the age of 17… then for Gloucester with all their pride and passions. Then I remember what London Wasps did for me in prolonging my career. In the end, I didn't give a damn about being in the media, or being a celebrity. What I missed was singing my national anthem. When I retired something died inside me because I couldn't stand and sing it any more. Standing there and, especially on away grounds, letting people have it – even when they hated us for it – was just the best feeling ever.

CLIVE WOODWARD

To be fair, I am sure anyone that coached England would have picked Jonny Wilkinson. So, it wasn't as if I had plucked him out of nowhere… but they may not have stuck him in at 18. If I choose one player that you wouldn't want to replace for the whole time (you were coach), it would have been him. So, my whole coaching career had him in the pivotal position. And he was awesome. I would never hear a bad word heard against him. He was just the most amazing guy.

PHIL VICKERY

A lot of people criticise him but I have the utmost respect for Clive Woodward. You could say he found me and identified me, and stuck with me – just as he did with Jonny Wilkinson. He found people with the right attitude, and then he put the pressure back on them. All you had to do was work your backside off, and he put things in place to give us all the rest of the tools. I respected him for his ambition, and for wanting to change the mind-set. And the goal-posts. I was really up for that. Let's do this!

ROGER UTTLEY

Of my three stints with England it was the least satisfying experience. Clive and Don Rutherford didn't get on. I soon found that as a manager there is no release as there is when you are a player, and to a lesser degree as a coach. Playing politics has never been my strongest suit, and my relationship with Clive was never quite right. He was soon talking to Bill Beaumont about who should be responsible and in charge. As coach and the only full-time paid member of the England staff he argued that he should be that person and that I should be reporting to him. This seemed to make a nonsense of the original reason for having a manager. But with the backing of Bill and Fran Cotton, the RFU said that Clive was to be the man in charge. That rankled with me for a time, but I continued to do the manager's job for a further two years, including the Tour from Hell in 1998.

CLIVE WOODWARD

At the end of the first season we made the notorious Tour from Hell, when we took what was in some places a third and fourth team, with losing 76-0 to Australia the centrepiece.

I'm hugely proud of my overall results by the time I finished, but you go through those early fixtures and you say, 'No sane person would ever pick those fixtures.' Australia, South Africa and New Zealand (twice), then France in Paris and then that brutal summer tour. Can you imagine flying to Brisbane to play a Test match, then flying to Auckland and you don't just play two Test matches against the All Blacks but you also play a midweek game against the Maoris. Then my Dad died in the middle of all that and I had to fly back, and then we had to fly to South Africa – and the team I've got, because all the players are in bits, was our second choice… but more our third choice if I'm honest. It was just madness – but that was how madly things were run with England. No one had ever tried to do a tour like that before and no one ever will again.

ROGER UTTLEY

Whoever drew up the itinerary had given no thought to the enormity of the challenge. The defeat by Australia in the opening game was embarrassing. It was Jonny Wilkinson's first start, and England's biggest defeat in history. The Australians had these press-up boys, who had to do a cumulative amount of press-ups with every point Australia scored to earn money for a charity. They had given up long before the end. We then lost a game heavily in Rotorua to the New Zealand Maoris.

PHIL VICKERY

I'd only had one cap, against Wales, and I was cited for punching Colin Charvis. So, then my second is 76-0 in Australia. Then the third and fourth caps come (in the big defeats) against the All Blacks – and so when we went to Cape Town and lost only 18-0 we were almost thinking of it as a victory.

LEWIS MOODY (England 2001-2011, 71 caps plus 3 caps for the Lions)

On the Tour to Hell, only Jonny Wilkinson was younger than I was. The coaches were keen for us all to go out for a few beers on the first night as a bonding exercise. Pete Richards and I took them at their word, except for the 'few' part of the instruction…

We returned at six in the morning as drunk as you can be while still standing. We did not get to into any trouble and in my mind it became acceptable to behave like this on tour. It set the tone. On day two of my first-ever senior tour with a Test match against Australia looming, I contracted a violent gastric bug which ruled out any chance of a debut. I was bedridden for the rest of the week, lost a load of weight and watched what befell England in Brisbane from my hotel room in Melbourne in growing disbelief. That 76-0 defeat is something that none of us will ever forget.

MATT PERRY

The opening Test against Australia in Brisbane was like chasing shadows. We were understrength and simply could not match their physicality. They had these 'Press-Up Boys' doing reps based on every point scored, and at the end they were so absolutely knackered that they changed from press ups to sit-ups. I was moved to centre for that game, and had Tim Horan and Jason Little opposite me.

PHIL VICKERY

After one of the games when we had been shocking, Clive said whatever we do, we don't draw any attention to ourselves whatsoever, we don't want to embarrass ourselves. But then someone organised a trip to a bungee jump. I didn't do it because I didn't have the balls to – I couldn't even go out on that little platform – but then Garath Archer decided to do it. Stark naked. He gets ready, takes all his clothes off and jumps. All I want to do as the new man is make sure to do the right things, like Clive said, and not draw attention to ourselves.

ROGER UTTLEY

On the field we were totally outgunned in two Tests by New Zealand, who could afford to start with Jonah Lomu and then bring on Joeli Vidiri, who was just as big and fast. After the first Test I felt we were the victims of disciplinary stitch-up by the New Zealanders after Danny Grewcock had been sent off for a minor incident, while Ian Jones, who had looked as if he had stamped on someone's head, escaped completely. It was not the only bad news.

Although good things were being done on the Tour of Hell by a coaching team which included Phil Larder, Brian Ashton, John Mitchell and Dave Alred, this number of coaches meant a lot of training sessions were too long.

JONNY WILKINSON (England 1998-2011, 91 caps plus six caps for the Lions)

I thought I was getting somewhere in the game until I went on that tour. It was as if someone was saying to me: 'You think you've done well, but hold on. You've got a long way to go to even get close to this level.' I raised my standards. In one respect I spent years trying to distance myself from the experience, but I have always maintained that it taught me more than anything else I have gone through, or ever will.

MATT PERRY

For some players it was a step too far and they were never seen again. It was a really tough tour mentally, and we were getting abuse left right and centre from the media. But it was part of the contract, and some came through it to greater things. The second Test against New Zealand at Eden Park came soon after Sean Fitzpatrick announcing his retirement, and they were determined to give him a big send-off. After being over-run in both Tests against New Zealand we finished the tour by flying across the Southern Ocean to South Africa.

We were staying at the Holiday Inn in Cape Town, and that was when Clive got his credit card out of his pocket and moved the whole squad to the six star Mount Nelson. I think what prompted it was that he had put his laundry into the wash, and it didn't come back. Then when he went looking he found some of it in the team room, where his pants and socks had been stuffed down the pockets of the pool table.

CLIVE WOODWARD

I caused a stir when I checked us out of this poor hotel in Cape Town where there was noisy building-work going on – and we moved into a really good one, the Mount Nelson. It caused ructions so I had what I expected to be a last supper with the media guys that night. The RFU complained about my claim for my credit card bill, and said I had upset the South Africans and done all sorts of bad things and changed protocol. Players like Martin Johnson and Lawrence Dallaglio, who couldn't tour, rang and told me to keep going. We did know what we were doing, we had beaten Wales by a record score in the 1998 Six Nations and, remember, it was all on the back of a Lions tour. Somehow I survived it and carried on.

ROGER UTTLEY

We were staying out at Newlands. The hotel group were one of the main sponsors of the South African union, and although the hotel wasn't brilliant it was adequate. On the Thursday evening before the Test match we got back to our rooms after a management night out to find a note shoved under our doors from Clive telling us that there would be a 7.30am meeting the following morning. At the meeting Clive announced that the hotel wasn't good enough. As such he had taken the unilateral decision to book the squad into the Mount Nelson, one of Cape Town's plushest and most expensive hotels. Despite protestation from Graham Cattermole and myself that we should not be thinking of moving the team en-masse the day prior to a Test match, and the fact that SARFU were incensed at the lack of respect shown to them and their sponsors, Clive insisted on the move. Graham and I were

Jonny Wilkinson in action against Australia on the 1998 Tour of Hell.

left to pick up the pieces, and the political fall-out. I felt very sorry for the hotel manageress at Newlands who was understandably distraught. If we had won the Test the move would have been judged a master stroke, as it was it just seemed completely unreasonable and unnecessary.

MATT PERRY
Against South Africa the weather was horrendous, but we made it a real dog-fight. We had come on as a team. Like the English do when their backs are against the wall we came through in adversity. Some guys, like Matt Dawson and Jonny Wilkinson, had started to talk more and by the end of the tour we were more together.

CLIVE WOODWARD
When we landed back in London I'm thinking: 'Thank God for that. I'm going to take two weeks off.' Jayne is there with me. We are walking through the airport and Don Rutherford is there to meet us. Or to meet me. I had done all that stuff checking us out of the hotels using a credit card. I had a last supper with the press guys – I thought it was probably the last time I'd ever speak to them so I said, 'We are going to have a big party.' Now we've arrived back and I didn't know that Don was going to be there. None of the (RFU) officials were on the trip, and it had been such a disastrous tour – which everyone knew it was going to be. Don't forget, I have had the Tour from Hell, my dad has died, I've just flown back from South Africa, and I'm absolutely shattered. I just wanted to go home, shut the door, have a cup of tea. Don has looked at me and said, 'I need to speak with you.' I say fine, and he says, 'No, I need you to come to Twickenham now.' I tell him I'm not going to Twickenham and ask what it's about. He starts going on about the changing of the hotels. 'You have upset the South Africans.' And I am going, 'Don, that's great. Can I just remind you we have also lost four Test matches? We have been stuffed in all four. If you had said to me that you wanted to come and talk to me about rugby, why you have lost all this stuff, I may have even gone. I may even be civil to you.' Jayne has grabbed me. I'm going to kill this guy. I lost it completely.

ROGER UTTLEY
My third association with the RFU ended when Clive rang me on the day of the England squad review announced by the then new CEO Francis Baron. He came up to Harrow and told me that Don Rutherford had to go – and that I had to go too, as part of a cost-cutting exercise. I thought it was good of Clive to come and break the news personally as we seemed to have achieved a working relationship by this stage. I was fortunate that I still had my full time employment at Harrow to

fall back on, and, in all honesty, it was with a sense of release I stepped away from the various pressures involved in running a team in that particular environment.

CLIVE WOODWARD

We never looked back. Less than two years later we went back and beat South Africa in Bloemfontein. The Tour of Hell was really the making of me. And it was the making of many of the players.

RICHARD HILL

Phil Larder joined the backroom team in 1998 and developed a new defensive system for the entire team. Backy [Neil Back] was central to this, effectively becoming Phil's general on the pitch. Our training changed to reflect the fact that 50 per cent of the game is about defence. That was completely new. So were the handouts that Phil gave us, detailing each player's tackle count. The target was a 95 per cent success rate. Backy and I compared results and took our rivalry very seriously. The whole thing didn't come easily to the team, though, and took several years to perfect. We certainly hadn't cracked it by the 1999 Five Nations, as Scott Gibbs illustrated at Wembley. I've never forgotten what he did to us that day. The game was being staged there because the Millennium Stadium was being completed for the World Cup. It felt odd, being the away team in the middle of London, but the Welsh supporters really made the place their own. It was an amazing atmosphere, with Max Boyce and Tom Jones whipping up the crowd.

LAWRENCE DALLAGLIO

Deep in the second half we got a penalty that was kickable but I chose to go for the corner, aiming for a try that would have clinched the Grand Slam. At the time, we were six points clear but I was a disciple of Clive's have-a-go philosophy. Both of us were naturally opposed to the lack of adventure traditionally associated with England. Another factor in my decision was that Jonny Wilkinson was not the kicker then that he subsequently became and taking a shot at goal was no guarantee of three points. I remember the moment vividly. It was quite a long way out, on the left-hand side of the pitch, which was the wrong side for Jonny. I turned to the players close to me before speaking to the referee. 'Come on,' I said, 'let's go for the corner.' Johnno and I looked at each other for a second. 'Are you sure?' he asked. 'Yeah, why not?' 'Ok, fair enough.' The key mistake was my belief at that point in the game, Wales weren't going to go down to the other end of the field and score a try. I should have known better. In hindsight, it was a big mistake.

RICHARD HILL

Almost immediately Rodber was penalised for a high tackle, they booted it back into our territory and suddenly we were facing an attacking Welsh line-out in injury time.

The ball came off the top to Scott Quinnell, he passed to Gibbs who went on a jinking, bullocking run. With a guy like Scott Gibbs, you have to bring him down as early as you can but we did not lay a finger on him. I think he went between me and Rodber, danced to his right past about three other would-be tacklers and scampered in. Jenkins added the conversion, we lost 32-31 and the Grand Slam had gone.

LAWRENCE DALLAGLIO

The changing room was like a morgue – complete silence. Guys sat in stunned bewilderment. How did we lose that? We had blown it and we knew it. If you looked around, some guys were quietly shedding tears. What hurt most was that we had contrived to lose a match when we were the better team. I blamed myself for the decision not to kick for goal.

MATT DAWSON

I cannot imagine a worse memory than that. The combination of it being my first Grand Slam game and being played at Wembley Stadium, a mecca for every Englishman. Later that evening the England squad went back to the Petersham Hotel in Richmond for dinner and a few drinks. Clive stood up and said, 'I believe good things come out of bad days. In time, this will do us the world of good.'

LAWRENCE DALLAGLIO

Following the Six Nations the *News of the World* story broke. When it was revealed that it was a sting [a series of nights out with three individuals who Dallaglio believed were interested in a sponsorship deal] and that every conversation had been taped, I felt sick. And it all made a different kind of sense. Having got me into a situation where I felt obliged to consume a lot of alcohol they steered the conversation into the gossipy and titillating areas. They wanted me to dish the dirt on all sorts of things relating to rugby. What did I know about Will Carling and Princess Diana? Had I ever taken recreational drugs? Like most teenagers I had experimented in my late teens but that wasn't going to impress them, so I embellished the stories. They set the trap and I didn't so much get caught as throw myself headlong into it. That's part of the reason I never felt too bitter about the hassle that followed because I certainly wasn't blameless.

But do you know what? In comparison with what I'd experienced after [my sister] Francesca's death, the pain I felt then and the sense of crisis for the following 18 months, the *News of the World* story didn't even scratch the surface.

MARTIN JOHNSON

The build-up to the '99 World Cup was like nothing I have experienced before or since. We spent the whole of the summer and early autumn together, working hard on our fitness and skills. We were probably stronger and fitter than we had ever been, but we felt a massive weight of expectation on all of our shoulders. Clive had always insisted he be judged on the World Cup, which put a lot of pressure on him and us.

PHIL VICKERY

This was the start of the new-style training regimes and proper professionalism. I can remember Jerry Guscott being broken at one session. I remember going on fat-burning sessions in Richmond Park, and Victor Ubogu had to do a fat-burning walk.

MATT PERRY

We went on a summer tour to Australia before the World Cup and we played a Centenary Test against the Wallabies in Sydney. We were beaten 22-15, but I scored two tries and got the man of the match award. My body felt good, I was free of injury, and training well. We had New Zealand in our World Cup pool, and although we played well we just weren't good enough to beat them.

CLIVE WOODWARD

I realise now that I made a fundamental mistake in selection against the All Blacks. I played Wilkinson at fly-half with De Glanville and Guscott in the centre. I should have played Grayson at fly-half with Wilkinson and Guscott in

Jonah Lomu was once again devastating against England in a World Cup.

the centre. Selection is the most important part of the job. Selection wins or loses you more matches than anything else. Jonny had played most of the season at centre, with Paul Grayson at fly-half. Playing Grayson at fly-half would have given us real leadership and experience, which Wilko was still acquiring.

NEIL BACK

We were doing OK against New Zealand and then Lomu made his entrance... Christian Cullen sent a long pass out to the left wing and Jonah was away. It was like a re-run of 1995, a horrible sequel, and I could scarcely believe my eyes. He brushed off Jeremy Guscott, swatted aside Austin Healey and powered on to the line from 40 yards out despite Dan Luger and Matt Dawson also doing their best to halt him. No other wing in the world would have come close to scoring that try.

JEREMY GUSCOTT

I remember, as a child, I was being chased and I ran into the road and into the side of a car. A split-second earlier and I would have been squashed, but I hit the side of the car and I bounced off it. I was shocked and didn't really know what had happened. It was exactly the same when I tried to tackle Jonah at Twickenham. I didn't quite have the right angle on him and he just brushed me off as if to say 'Go away'.

I had pulled my groin in a warm-up game but had a strong anti-inflammatory injection and afterwards felt good and thought, 'I can play.' But when it went again against New Zealand I knew my World Cup was over, and then I thought maybe my career was over too.

I spoke to Clive Woodward, and because I was injured he said to stay on for a week and come to Paris for the quarter-final against South Africa. We announced my international retirement early in the week, and it was a disappointment. I tend to set disappointments to one side, but, although I didn't want to retire, I knew it was time to pass the shirt on. I don't remember much about the quarter-final, just that there was a load of drop-goals, making it a pretty boring game.

CLIVE WOODWARD

The World Cup in 1999 was fundamentally not fair. What happened was that if you won the group you went straight to the quarter-finals. In our group we had New Zealand. So, New Zealand win the group, and if you come second, you play a midweek game against the runner-up from one of the other groups – in our case, Fiji – to get through to the quarter-finals. Imagine it. We have got to beat Fiji on the Wednesday, which is a tough game. Now, we won easily. But it was the Wednesday before the Sunday quarter-final! So we finished that game and on the Thursday we are travelling to Paris, on the train. When we get to Paris we are knackered from the match. Then we have one training session before we are playing on the Sunday against a South African team that has been there all week waiting for us. Then you get Jannie de Beer who drops five goals against us! You lose. And deep down you are thinking, 'That's rubbish. That is not how it should be.'

PHIL VICKERY

I remember in the quarter-final just craning my neck time after time as Jannie de Beer kicked all those drop-goals – it was almost like watching it in slow motion as they flew over your head. Then I remember Os du Randt, who had always been a bit of an idol of mine. I was up against him in the scrum and we did all right – we didn't have much trouble at all up front. But he really hit me. I remember going back to pick up the ball and, as I stood up, he hit me. I thought my body had snapped in half.

CLIVE WOODWARD

I did write once that I got the fly-half selection wrong, that I should not have switched Wilkinson and brought in Paul Grayson for the quarter-final at fly-half. But I am not sure I actually believe that myself. It wouldn't have made any difference.

LAWRENCE DALLAGLIO

It was a sad end to our 1999 tournament. You can try and find all the positives you want but you can't get rid of the feeling that you're leaving and the big boys are getting on with it. We wanted to be among them but we weren't good enough, and that hurt.

NEIL BACK

When a guy has a freak day – and that's what it was – there is not a lot you can do about it. De Beer would not even have been playing had Henry Honiball's hamstring cleared up and all most people knew about him was that he'd had an average season with London Scottish. We had looked at him, of course, and knew he was a fine kicker. But five drop-goals in half an hour. No-one saw that coming.

LAWRENCE DALLAGLIO

Clive never let us forget how we felt on the journey home from Paris. Any booklet he produced for us carried photos of us at the end of that game and there was one shot of Backy crouching down on all fours, utterly distraught. Another shot showed Johnno and I looking hopelessly over our shoulders at a De Beer drop-goal as it flew between the posts. Clive touched a raw nerve and when he saw us wince with pain, he touched it again and again.

MIKE CATT

I was a bench player but it was still the start of the Clive Woodward era. I was fighting for the No. 12 shirt with Will Greenwood. Although we lost in the quarter-final to South Africa, the seeds were beginning to be sown. People forget that the team who won the World Cup were together for six years. After that 1999 quarter-final defeat to the Springboks there were the three Grand Slam losses, and I honestly believe if we had not lost those games when we did – and learned what we did – then we would never have won the World Cup in 2003.

CLIVE WOODWARD

Franny [Cotton] supported me again after that World Cup when many thought I would be sacked. I got a battering in the press, which I understood. You take it. Deep down, I was thinking, 'I want to stay, absolutely we have got the players, I have learned huge lessons about who has got to go and who has got to stay.' So I went to a meeting with Fran Cotton and Francis Baron. We sat and spoke for about two hours about the whole thing. They were deciding about whether I was staying or not. Then they went to the management board and said, 'The guy should stay.' Which was a big call. Because it would have been very easy to fire me. But I stayed and I completely changed. I absolutely changed after that. I thought, 'Right. I have somehow survived this. There's no more compromise. No more putting up with one or two players being negative. No more energy-sappers.' And then we rebuilt the team. We totally rebuilt the team. We started again, on my terms. I told myself that I was not going to allow anyone at Twickenham to get in my way. If I didn't win, I was going to get fired anyway.

RICHARD HILL

We played brilliantly in the 2000 Six Nations – until we went to Edinburgh for the final game. The Scots wisely played the percentages. They played the conditions perfectly. Scott Murray was at his niggling best for Scotland in the line-outs, getting under the skin of a few players and making them lose concentration. To complete the humiliation, I went down with cramp, and had to be stretchered off, which felt idiotic. I don't think I have ever known a more despondent dressing-room in all my time playing rugby. Later we heard we'd also managed to snub the Princess Royal. We had slunk off after the game and forgotten to pick up the Championship trophy. Inevitably the result led to renewed accusations that we lacked bottle. We were fine beating out-gunned opponents, the media said, but caved in at the slightest hint of pressure, just as we had done in the [1999] World Cup. It was more a lack of brains than bottle that day, though. We just got it all wrong.

JONNY WILKINSON

We tried to open up a bit in Edinburgh despite the weather, but in such horrendous conditions every tackle had the potential to knock the ball out of our hands. Scotland were smart and didn't really move the ball at all. They just sat tight in the driving seat, and as the weather deteriorated, that was a great place for them to be.

NEIL BACK

What went wrong at Murrayfield? Failure to adapt. Bad weather. Poor line-out. Martin Johnson and Danny Grewcock were available but Clive, not surprisingly, decided not to change a winning side. Would they have made a difference? We will never know. You can't take it away from the Scots. They played better and, roared on by a desperate crowd, they out-fought us too.

KYRAN BRACKEN

I had a very good pass, so it suited me when England expanded their game, and for the last couple of years before the World Cup we were ahead of everyone in every respect. Whether it was nutrition, sports science, conditioning, skin-tight shirts, specialist coaches we were leading the way. I didn't care for some of the psychobabble, but overall the Woodward way was very good.

MATT PERRY

We started to out-think sides, as well as using our physicality to establish dominance up front. The big turning point for the team was the tour to South Africa in the summer of 2000. After losing the first Test in Pretoria, we showed real steel to win the second Test in Bloemfontein. After 2000 we matched the southern hemisphere sides for physicality, and that tour was a turning point.

LAWRENCE DALLAGLIO

I went to the South African changing room after the first Test and was shocked by what I saw. There were bodies everywhere, bandages being taken off, ice-packs on knees and heads, players having wounds checked and everyone too shattered to talk… They were completely gone whereas I felt we still had 20 to 30 per cent of our energy left. At that moment I knew we would take these guys the following week. I also knew that in their bruised and smashed state, they now respected us. With that thought came the certainty that we were no longer the old England.

KYRAN BRACKEN

We were always improving, and we were lucky to have Jonny Wilkinson, who could always build a score. I was back for the summer tour of South Africa in

2000, when we were cheated out of a try in Pretoria after Tim Stimpson was impeded. The win in Bloemfontein was memorable, and it was during a period when Joost Van der Westhuizen was at his best for the Springboks. Many say that the turning point for the team came on that tour, but for me it was the summer tour in 2003 after the Grand Slam. Before that we would take two steps forward and one back, but, in Dublin, Martin Johnson made a really important decision not to move the England line up ahead of the game. Those two games on the 2003 summer tour when we beat New Zealand and Australia said, psychologically, that we don't care who we meet, because we know we can come here and win. I was in form on that tour, but one year you do well and then you get an injury and someone else does really well. I had a very good relationship with Matt Dawson. We both respected each other, and what Matt did is he produced the goods when it really mattered, whether it was in New Zealand on the Tour from Hell when he scored two tries, or for the 1997 Lions in the first Test, or in the final in helping to set up Jonny Wilkinson's drop-goal. It was a fierce rivalry but we got on fine. It was not always the same with Austin Healey, who was very confident, assured, brash and sharp. With him it was dog-eat-dog, and I had the last laugh.

CLIVE WOODWARD

The 2000 tour to South Africa was a big moment for the squad. Arguably we should have won that first game in South Africa but Bloemfontein in the second Test was massive. For me, the big heroes were Baron and Fran, who supported me, who allowed me to keep developing the team for another crack at the World Cup.

The players celebrate after their win in the second Test during the 2000 summer tour.

LAWRENCE DALLAGLIO

Without doubt, it was a turning point in the development of the team. We had come to South Africa and drawn the Test series 1–1 but we all knew we should have won it 2–0. That tour convinced us all that Clive was the right man.

MATT DAWSON

The first time I realised that we really did have the makings of a great team happened when we beat Australia at home in the autumn of 2000 when Dan Luger scored the match-winning try in injury time. We got into the habit of winning tight games that previously we would have lost – so that game sticks in my mind as a turning point.

CLIVE WOODWARD

There was a bit of negativity around Jason Robinson when we brought him across from rugby league, but after a couple of games I remember sitting in the stand at Twickenham and as soon as half-time started, you had about four hundred people sitting around you shouting, 'Bring on Robinson! Get Robinson on!' And then when he came on everyone would just go nuts. He brought a real superstar factor to the game whenever he touched the ball.

I remember a great quote from Andy Nicol in 2001 when we played Scotland at Twickenham: 'There were twenty minutes to go,' he said, 'and we're getting stuffed, we're out on our feet, and there is a stop in play – and they bring on Jason Robinson. And you're just thinking, give us a break!'

KYRAN BRACKEN

In most respects Clive Woodward got things right, and if it wasn't for him there would have been no signing an 'X Factor' rugby league player like Jason Robinson. He was the only player to come across from rugby league for us at the time, but what a player to make the change. He was just unbelievable.

JASON ROBINSON (England 2001-2007, 51 caps plus 5 caps for the Lions)

I had done almost 10 years for Wigan and had done almost everything possible in rugby league. And because I had not signed a renewal the news got out, and that's when I spoke to Clive. One of the things I never did in league was to win something at international level. I played for Great Britain and England but the set-up was not right and I could not see either team achieving what I wanted to do at international level. It was either now or never. I was 26 and in the prime of my career so I thought the time was right. At the end of the day I thought I could always go back.

I played my first game for Sale on 5 November and to go from that to being on the bench for England in the 2001 Six Nations was quite something. And it continued because that summer I was playing for the Lions. The first year was unbelievable.

Once I got involved I realised the set-up was fantastic. It was the best I had ever been involved in and you had the feeling that this was special. Clive made sure every stone was turned. He wanted us to be the best prepared, the fittest team going into the World Cup. I could see that and things just got better and better. When you looked at the staff we had – all the different coaches – it was great for me having come from a rugby league background to have a guy like Dave Alred there who looked after my kicking. I had a lot of good people around me. When you have Martin Johnson, Jonny Wilkinson, Lawrence Dallaglio, Jason Leonard etc it makes life a lot easier. They helped to bring the best out of me and, I hope, I did the same for them.

I always wanted to play for England and that was one of my main aims for making the switch. I had also met Clive before moving over and I had bought into his vision for the 2003 World Cup. He believed I could play a part in that, but it was up to me to prove that I was worthy of a place. I'll never forget the feeling I had when I was stood on the touchline waiting to come on against Italy, because I never knew how the Twickenham crowd would take to me having come from league. But I can remember spectators shouting 'get him on', and that was a nice feeling because I was full of nerves. Whilst I did not get much of the ball in that first game there was still a lot of excitement from the crowd, and in the games that followed the fans wanted me to get my hands on the ball. It was the start of a fantastic time in an England shirt.

KYRAN BRACKEN

I was very disappointed not to be on the 2001 Lions tour. A lot of it is just timing. Instead, I went on the England tour to North America, which gave me the chance, and the honour, of captaining my country.

LEWIS MOODY

The England players not wanted for the 2001 Lions tour played the Barbarians at Twickenham and then moved on for a tour of Canada and America, with full caps awarded for the internationals. The way I saw it, after my antics on the 1998 Tour from Hell, this could be my only opportunity to play for England again. Clive did select me to make my first start for England in the Test against Canada in Toronto, and winning my first cap was very special, of course, but the scenario was not quite how I dreamt it would be. I'd imagined I would run out in front of a massive crowd in one of the great rugby stadiums of the world, all singing, and dancing and fireworks. In reality, we were in the middle of Canada in front of 3,000 people either sitting in temporary stands or playing with their kids on grassy banks, while we got changed in a shed.

MATT PERRY

From 20 to 24 I basically exhausted my body. I spent four years playing a lot of rugby, and I was burned out. Basically, faster guys like Jason Robinson and Iain Balshaw were coming in, and really I was a fly-half or centre playing at fullback. After the 2001 Lions tour I started getting groin problems – sciatic problems in the nerves down my left leg which then affected my back. When my back started giving me grief I couldn't get to the levels of fitness required, and at 25 and 26 I was working very hard just to stay in the game. It was not an easy time. It was frustrating for me that my body couldn't keep me at the level required to compete. I came back for Bath, but from the ages of 25 to 30 I spent a lot of time battling injury, and lost a lot of confidence. Also, I probably wasn't proactive enough in going and chasing Clive and asking what I had to do to get back in the running.

RICHARD HILL

We ended the truncated [2001] Six Nations with four wins and no defeats, 215 points for and 60 against and a record 28 tries.

Well, a fat lot of good that did us when we eventually went over to Ireland, after the Lions tour to Australia, for the final game. You can look for excuses but the fact is that they beat us 20-14. It was a bit like Scotland the year before. We were handed the Six Nations trophy after the game and struggled to smile for the cameras.

To be honest, Ireland were up for it and we didn't play well. The Irish guys had also learnt a lot about some of our players and our line-out work during the Lions tour. I suspect they even managed to read some of our calls, because they certainly disrupted us there.

It was a major disappointment – missing out on all those Grand Slams were major disappointments. They all felt pretty much the same – wretched.

MATT DAWSON

We were playing sensational rugby in 2001. Iain Balshaw was carving everything up and Mike Catt in midfield was world class. Then we had Ben Cohen in there and Jonny Wilkinson was in great form – we had a lot of world class players in great form – and the forward pack were on the front foot. Then there was the break and in Ireland we got beaten fair and square – but it did not mirror the Six Nations campaign as a whole, which was a great campaign.

MATT PERRY

All those Grand Slam chances…

It was an immense disappointment to lose to Wales at Wembley in 1999, and it was the first year of three in which we had a Grand Slam in our grasp and lost it. We lost to Wales, Scotland and Ireland in the last game of each season. Overall, the team had started to take shape, and we were dominant up front and were consistently dangerous in the back-line.

That Wales game shows how hard it is to win a Grand Slam. We made mistakes at the wrong time at Wembley. The Scott Gibbs try came from nowhere. He was like a baby bull on the run, and when he got through the middle a good step inside took him over. Then Neil Jenkins kicked the conversion. No-one spoke in the changing room for two to three hours afterwards. People weren't getting changed, and there was no chat whatsoever. I can still picture the blokes around the ground who had hoped to sell England Grand Slam T-shirts piling them all into the back of their vans. I do look back on that and think it was a missed opportunity. However it was small margins, and those disappointments pushed England towards their 2003 World Cup journey.

The weather came in when we went up to Edinburgh in 2000, rain and mist, but whereas England had learned by 2002-03 to close games out, we thought we had it won in Edinburgh when we got to half-time. We weren't tight enough at the right time, and we didn't deserve it because we were slack when it mattered. Martin Johnson was an unbelievable man, with great integrity, and it was a massive loss when he was unavailable. He would have pushed us in the right direction because he could lead and influence while he was playing – he had this calm ability to read the game on the hoof. However, the players who went out on the pitch that day had accountability for the result.

There are sometimes a lot of moving parts you cannot control, and that was the case in Dublin in 2001 with the game against Ireland that had been postponed from the previous season after the foot-and-mouth epidemic. That 2001 campaign was the third year on the bounce for me where I had been averaging 35 to 40 games a season. A lot of us had done that. For instance, two weeks after the 2001 Lions tour, in which I played in the three Tests, I was back in training with Bath. And then we had to regroup and try to finish off a Grand Slam. It was just a step too far. A lot of England players did not have good Lions tours, and on the day we just didn't adapt. We were dominated. Like a balloon, we were deflating. We were light-years from the team that had beaten France 48-18 six months earlier.

MATT DAWSON

The mistake we made was to think we could play the way we did in the spring in a one-off game, when Ireland had two games already under their belts and had ironed out the creases in their game, and we'd not had even one.

BEN KAY (England 2001-2009, 62 caps plus 2 caps for the Lions)
Coming from the outside I could tell the group was really strong. When you think of the likes of Martin Johnson, Lawrence Dallaglio, Neil Back and Jonny Wilkinson, who you could tell was going to be world class. Add in Will Greenwood – and I was aware of what Jason Robinson had done with the Lions – and there was a group you could really dominate with. I was desperate to be part of that group.

PHIL VICKERY
The big turning point for me was the win over Australia in 2001. That's when we realised that the team could really get somewhere. The whole thing had changed. We just thought, 'This is what we do. It's not a great sensation any more to beat these southern hemisphere teams.' We were expecting to win those games. It wasn't England arrogance, it was just what England expected as a squad. It felt like you were living in a bubble, where you felt you were almost bullet-proof. It came from Clive and the management team, and the coaches – but also from the players.

Jason Robinson explodes past Scott Murray during the 2001 Calcutta Cup.

RICHARD HILL

After the disappointment of Dublin we turned things around really quickly. We saw off Australia without the injured Johnno, Lawrence and Daws, which made a statement. It was also back-to-back wins over the world champions. Johnno was back for the Springboks and made an even bigger statement after that match, saying that it was no longer such a big deal for us to beat southern hemisphere sides.

CLIVE WOODWARD

That was our third straight win over South Africa and our fifth successive win against a Tri Nations side – the first European nation ever to do so.

RICHARD HILL

Our third game of the [2002 Six Nations] Championship was the most important – a 20-15 defeat in France. Crucially, their flanker Serge Betsen gave Jonny a wretched time. As for us, we were just too lax. For years the England team had prided itself on playing pragmatic rugby, but we failed to live up to that.

Johnno made exactly that point afterwards: we needed to go back to those roots in crunch games, playing it tight where necessary.

CLIVE WOODWARD

Jonny won't mind me saying it was probably one of his poorest games. Wilkinson's mistake was that he decided to take on Betsen. He let it become a personal battle and started flying into rucks to clear out Betsen, to show him he was not intimidated, but you do not want your No.10 flying into rucks, you want him playing quarterback. Betsen won that battle only because he got Wilkinson playing in a way England didn't want him to play. Both myself and Wilkinson learnt a lot that afternoon. The next time we played France, I put Charlie Hodgson outside Wilkinson to offer him a get-out route and we won the game comfortably.

JASON LEONARD

There were lots of reasons for our loss of form but the main one was sheer exhaustion. It was the end of an awfully long season – the Lions tour had taken up the previous summer and we'd rolled straight into a tough autumn international season, the delayed Ireland match and then straight into the Six Nations. We didn't have the zip and snap of the year before. There was an irony in the fact that while we were all tired and needed a break, we also needed more sessions together as a team.

PHIL VICKERY
I captained England for the first time in Argentina in the summer of 2002. We had bricks thrown at us on the coach, and when we walked into the ground through a long metal cage people were shouting at us and insulting the Queen. I absolutely loved all that.

TREVOR WOODMAN (England 1999-2004, 22 caps)
I never really considered myself a capped player until 2002 when I started against New Zealand at Twickenham. That was my first cap because everything else was off the bench.

MATT DAWSON
The management were announcing to the team (in the autumn of 2002) that if we wanted to have a realistic chance of being contenders we had to win every single game at home, and those three games were the opportunity. New Zealand did not send a full squad – they had a good team but not everyone came. Danny Grewcock nicked a line-out at the death to win it. Against Australia we were trailing before winning it. Martin Johnson picked up individuals and told them what he wanted them to do and what roles they had in decision-making, scrummaging, strategy. He turned to his leaders. He was just very pragmatic and told us what we were going to do for the next five minutes. He was at the top of his captaincy then and was very impressive.

LEWIS MOODY
It was bizarre that I eventually got picked ahead of Backy (Neil Back) for the first time, in November 2002, against New Zealand. I got picked for England before I got picked ahead of him at Leicester. That was a massive day because Neil had been one of my heroes and was one of the first to congratulate me.

TREVOR WOODMAN
Things got incredibly frustrating with injuries in my career. When you're really striving to be the best player you possibly can be, you do push yourself, push your body slightly harder. You might end up training and playing with certain injuries, and once you start doing that, that's when the bigger injuries suddenly kick in. On the England tour of South Africa in 2000 I lasted three days – stuck my head between two tackle bags and spent six months out with a bulging disc. After the New Zealand game in 2002 I had the worst one. We were doing a scrummaging session on a wooden scrummage machine – if health and safety actually looked in they would have stopped it. I popped a disc in my neck. Then I had back trouble at Sale.

In my head I would love to have won 50-caps plus. A lot of people would think that 22 is not bad, but the ones I missed did hurt.

LAWRENCE DALLAGLIO
Our general improvement was obvious from the 2002 autumn campaign. We won all three matches and yet didn't feel like we had done anything fantastic.

CLIVE WOODWARD
This is one of my favourite records: between losing to New Zealand in the 1999 World Cup pool game to winning the 2003 World Cup we never lost at Twickenham. That was massive. Then you start to plan to beat these teams away too. One of the keys was that we started to go totally full strength to those countries.

KYRAN BRACKEN
With Woodward, he wouldn't have won a World Cup if he didn't have our team, but we wouldn't have won a World Cup without what he put in place. It was a marriage made in heaven.

SIMON SHAW (England 1996-2011, 71 caps plus 2 caps for the Lions)
Clive brought in so much. He really took England from being an amateur team to

Ben Cohen makes a break against New Zealand at Twickenham in November 2002 and flies in to score as England go on to record a famous 31–28 victory.

being a highly professional team – probably, the most professional. We also had an exceptional bunch of players who were all very driven. The training pre-2003 was extraordinary. The effort the boys put in was the best I've ever been involved in, because there was such a high level of competition.

JOSH LEWSEY (England 1998-2007, 55 caps plus 3 caps for the Lions)
The 2003 season was huge for us even before the World Cup after three consecutive unsuccessful shots at the Grand Slam between 1999-2001. England were ranked number one team in the world, but we had effectively won nothing, and next stop was the 2003 World Cup in Australia. We needed a concrete achievement as a launch pad.

One of our ploys was to set ourselves the highest possible performance levels throughout the season. For example we wanted a minimum of a 95 per cent tackle completion rate in every game because if you achieve that you are unlikely to lose any game, it's almost impossible. And once you are extremely unlikely to lose you can concentrate fully on winning it by as comfortable a margin as possible.

MATT DAWSON
We got to Dublin late and only stayed a couple of nights in the hotel. It was all very relaxed. It was the coming together of the last three years, as well as the expectancy that Clive Woodward put on us. We quite enjoyed that pressure. Maybe before we had been a little bit worried about upsetting the opposition by saying we were good and expected to win. We were scared of being called arrogant – but that time the England players quite enjoyed being favourites.

CLIVE WOODWARD
I think in previous years when we dropped the odd game that cost us Grand Slams it was because we weren't so much focused on winning as we were on really playing. But by the time 2003 came around I changed things and I wanted to put the pressure of winning on the guys. I said that if we were to have any chance of lifting the World Cup, we had to win the Grand Slam – it wasn't about entertainment any more, it was about results. I wanted to put that pressure on them to see how they handled it.

The night before we played Ireland, Tony Biscombe put together a montage of clips to the Eminem track 'Lose Yourself', with the lines, 'If you had one shot, or one opportunity, to seize everything you ever wanted, would you capture it or just let it slip?' And I really rammed home that unless we won the game and won it well, we had no chance in the World Cup. I really turned up the pressure – which is the exact opposite of what you're meant to do as a coach, but I felt it was really important to do it. And the players responded magnificently.

BEN KAY

With what had happened in previous years when we were playing Grand Slam deciders, the Six Nations is a really good preparation ground for a World Cup. If you look at the Rugby Championship, or the Tri-Nations as it was then, you are going into games against some teams knowing that if you lose you will still play that team again in the tournament. And then if you beat them everyone believes you are great. The Six Nations is different. If you don't beat all the teams and get to a Grand Slam, and just win the Championship, it does not feel quite the same. It feels a bit flat. In that way it is bit like knock-out rugby – like the World Cup – and there is the same pressure in the Six Nations if you are aiming for a Slam. Sometimes you are playing a game against a team who have got nothing to lose. There is no pressure on them, and all the pressure is on you. Clive said if you have more pressure coming from outside than you put on yourselves then it gets on top of you. So, we put more pressure on ourselves than we were getting from the outside.

JOSH LEWSEY

Straight after we beat Ireland in Dublin I looked at the match stats sheet and our tackle completion was nearly 99 per cent. That is remarkable at Test level – especially against such a good Ireland side who were going for the Grand Slam themselves. That's why we won. We soaked up an incredible amount of pressure for the first hour. I remember looking at the tape soon after and during one 22 second period Jonny Wilkinson made three massive tackles – Geordan Murphy, Denis Hickie, and then to complete the hat-trick, Justin Bishop. Unbelievable stuff from Jonny.

WILL GREENWOOD

Jonny Wilkinson was magnificent. He was awe-inspiring that day. We had our tactical differences, but after that match I vowed to always back him up. If he was willing to put that much effort in for a team then the rest didn't matter.

JOSH LEWSEY

Eventually Ireland were like a heavyweight boxer punching themselves out. In the final quarter they had nothing left and we ran in the tries. The score-line was really tough on Ireland but in fairness it was one of England's most complete performances.

TREVOR WOODMAN

Coming into 2003 I found that the neck surgery had helped – you'd gone to the point where you think there isn't much chance of playing on, I couldn't even lift my hand off the table at one stage. But Dean Ryan coming to coach Gloucester helped me fitness-wise and playing-wise and I got back in time for the 2003 summer tour to New Zealand and Australia. That squad was growing all the time and the end goal was to win things, to put England on the map.

LAWRENCE DALLAGLIO

When we went on that summer tour Clive was basically asking us if we wanted to do what no England team had done in New Zealand for 30 years. Of course we did. Then there was Australia, where no England side had ever won a Test match. I listened to that statement in disbelief... But it was true, and Clive was there asking us to create history by changing that statistic. As we listened, the World Cup did seemed irrelevant, which was the object of the exercise.

PHIL VICKERY

We started the tour by going to New Plymouth to play the Maoris and it's horrible driving rain, and wind – like Crediton in the winter. They were a really good side, so it said in the papers. We mullered them. We really battered them, and I was getting into my game and played better. That set the scene, and then we were coming into the All Blacks game at the Cake-Tin. Wind and rain again. I sat on the bench, which was frustrating, but you have to earn your right.

After five heart-wrenchingly close attempts, England finally win the Grand Slam on Clive Woodward's watch in 2003.

KYRAN BRACKEN

With Wellington being on the coast there was a swirling wind in the Cake-Tin, and the atmosphere in the build-up to the game was amazing because England were seen as a real challenge. However, I really don't think that most of New Zealand thought we could win. There were moments when they could have sneaked it when we were down to 13 men but we kept them out, and looking back I don't know how I got the ball away from some of those scrums. That was when one New Zealand writer described us as 'white orcs on steroids' – we made a bit of a signature theme of it by having a photo mocked-up of us as orcs, and used it in the build-up to the World Cup.

BEN KAY

We never underestimated Australia, but we believed we would beat them. We thought we were better than New Zealand but we had to prove to ourselves that we could go to one of the most hostile places to tour – where the chambermaids in the hotels were telling us how much the All Blacks were going to thrash us –

Martin Johnson powers into space against the All Blacks in Wellington in the summer of 2003 as England record a famous win against the odds.

and win. That we did it with 13 men was the biggest thing, because we really outmuscled them.

PHIL VICKERY

The plan was to drive the ball up to try to get penalties, or Jonny to kick. Then we lose two players to the bin and I am on. The ball came out to me and I look up and Johnson was outside me. Only him. No-one else. For some reason I shape to kick the ball and Johnson shouts: 'Don't kick it!' But the ball travelled on and went into touch just outside their 22. Johnson comes up and says through those big rubber lips: 'Good kick.'

MATT DAWSON

In New Zealand I was watching in the stands and I was itching to get into the team. By now every single time you were not in the team it was an opportunity for somebody else to stake a claim for a World Cup shirt – that was the pressure we were under for 18 months leading up to the World Cup. Every player was playing as if it was their last game. To beat New Zealand with 13 men on the pitch was an unbelievable performance. You don't beat New Zealand on their home patch, and you don't beat them with 13 men. It will never be done again.

PHIL VICKERY

When we were two men down we had these amazing scrums. It was one of those emotional moments for me. I needed emotion when I played rugby. I used to have running arguments with sports psychologists, who talked about judgement and calm and all that. Ice in the head and fire in the belly, and all that rubbish. But I needed fire in the head, legs, feet, toes and ears – that is when I played best. When I was in those six-man scrums I was playing for everyone who ever helped me, everything I'd ever worked for. I'm thinking about my mum who drove me thousands of miles in an old Fiesta to every trial and session and match; all the good people at school and Bude, and Gloucester and Wasps. All the fans and all the physios. We held up in those scrums. We should not have. It should never have happened, but it did. We beat the All Blacks in New Zealand. Just wonderful moments.

TREVOR WOODMAN

I played in the game against a really powerful Maori team while the top team were getting ready for the All Blacks, but on that trip Clive was very up front. He said, 'You're playing against Australia no matter what happens against New Zealand,' and he changed the front-row for the Australia game, which was a brave call.

KYRAN BRACKEN

The roof in Melbourne was closed, and it was like playing in a sports hall when you were a kid – hot, humid, and with a slippery ball. However, the pace that we put on the game meant that the ball moved so quickly that it was unbelievable, and the pressure on Australia phenomenal. They didn't know what hit them, with runners like Ben Cohen, Josh Lewsey and Jason Robinson coming at them from everywhere.

TREVOR WOODMAN

We really hammered Australia in Melbourne. One of the things that really stands out is a driving maul that made about 40 or 50 metres before I got pulled down about a yard from the line. From that point, their legs had gone. We always said that we wanted to be the fittest team in world rugby – so you knew that if you were hanging, then the other team were going to be even worse. I think that's when we really set a marker down. I just remember the physicality that we had in our back three – Josh Lewsey, Ben Cohen and Jason Robinson. Ben came crashing through the line in that game to score a great try, Josh broke Mat Rogers in half with a tackle. There were all sorts of reasons for Australia to remember us, for all the wrong reasons for them.

PHIL VICKERY

I was never the greatest trainer but we all used to do extras. I liked a smoke and a drink, but when I left Pennyhill Park and got home after sessions I used to do extras because I knew Jonno was doing extras, Backy was doing extras, so was Will Greenwood, Trevor Woodman, Danny Grewcock. Everyone.

JASON ROBINSON

When we beat New Zealand we were down to 13 men, and we then knew we could beat any team anywhere.

KYRAN BRACKEN

Once we had finished the playing side of the tour Clive decided to fly us to Perth for familiarisation with our pool base in the World Cup – but the only familiarisation most of us did was getting on the sauce for three days.

BEN KAY

That was clever of Clive Woodward. With a training camp and a World Cup coming up it [Perth] was a chance to have a blow-out at an ideal time so we would have some good stories to get us through what was going to be a tough, hard camp at Pennyhill Park.

JASON LEONARD

Our preparation immediately before the 2003 World Cup was quite different from the preparation we did in 1999. There were no army assault courses or complicated team-building sessions. I think Woodward had learnt the lessons from 1999 and our training was quite specific to the task in hand and less harsh than it had been. We didn't feel we had the natural enthusiasm trained out of us – we went into the tournament feeling fresher and fitter than we had done four years earlier.

MATT DAWSON

As candidates for World Cup selection we wanted for nothing. The pitch outside [at our Pennyhill Park base] was a beautiful surface, the gym inside as comprehensive as I'd ever seen. There were three lanes of equipment and never any wait to get on the machine of your choice. With no contact work scheduled, it was a great chance to get in really good shape.

JOSH LEWSEY

The training was intense and tough but incredibly well structured, planned and orchestrated. Weekends were a welcome break in which everyone busted away from captivity back to their wives and girlfriends. The Friday feeling was heightened when we had team Olympics – a series of team-based fitness competitions designed to knacker everyone just before a couple of days' rest and before it started all over again the following Monday morning.

PHIL VICKERY

It was like training with a club side because we all knew each other so well. You knew other people's scrum machine settings and what they liked and didn't like about training, just like you would in a club environment. I knew the system, the techniques and the personalities. It was Club England, which is exactly what Clive had been keen on achieving. There's no question that he did that. We were all part of a club that felt very familiar and were all very confident.

WILL GREENWOOD

There was a fantastic atmosphere in the camp in those weeks building up to the tournament as the squad was honed into shape. Everyone pushed themselves to the limit of their endurance. The aim was to put the hard work in the bank at the beginning of our preparations and concentrate on the skills and tactics later.

CLIVE WOODWARD

I defy any coach in international rugby to say, 'We are trying to peak at this moment, we are trying to peak for that moment.' We weren't. What I was trying to do was win the next game. People say the team was at its greatest on the 2003 summer tour or maybe the Grand Slam of 2003. I don't know when we peaked. I didn't understand peaking. We were trying to win the next game. Having gone on the Tour of Hell, having been battered by not having your best team, all I said was 'Right, I'm going to pick my best team – because it might be my last game.' That was my mindset. The players loved it. The players knew that I was picking the strongest team. Against Ireland, in the Grand Slam game before the World Cup, we just had a great game of rugby. We played really well. Did we peak on that day? I don't think so. I just think we played really well.

Then we beat New Zealand in New Zealand. Did we peak then? I haven't a clue. When we beat Australia in Melbourne? I haven't a clue. You get to the World Cup, and then maybe you don't play quite as well – but maybe because the other teams are full strength. They are better. And we have to play a different way. As long as you win, you move on. If people are saying that we peaked before the World Cup, I'd say to them, 'I wasn't paid as to when we peaked. All I wanted to do was win the next game. And, with the pressure on at the World Cup, it doesn't matter how good or experienced you are, maybe you can't play that way because they are better than they were. Or maybe you are under more pressure and you are playing a different way just to win the flipping game.'

So, I can't say we peaked at any time. I still think that England international rugby is all about the 'next game'. Your mindset as a coach should be, 'If I don't win, I am going to get fired.' Then you will say, 'I'm going to pick the best team.' I think that is such a powerful statement to make. That is the New Zealand way. They don't rest players unless they have got a really Mickey Mouse game. They wouldn't dream about resting a player against England because there's a chance that they could lose. They wouldn't even think about it. And that's the way you have got to be.

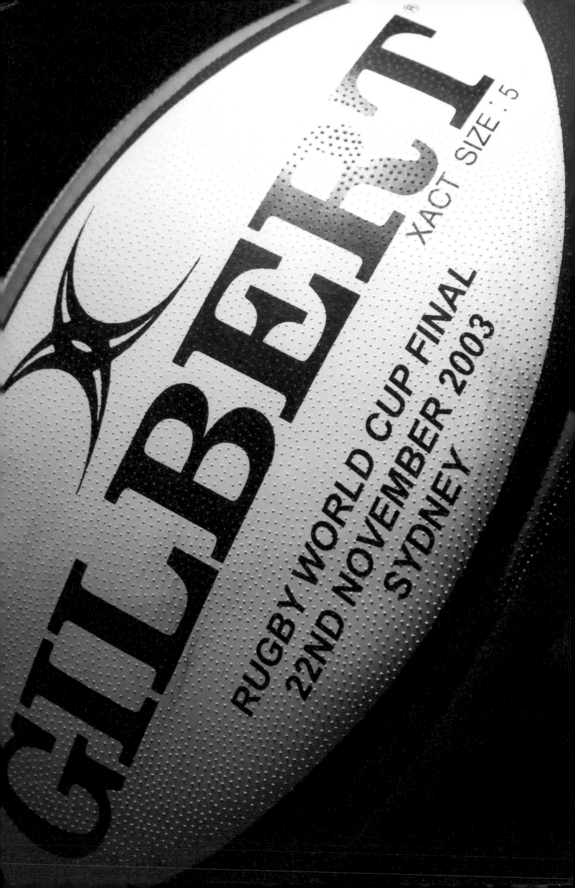

TWENTY-ONE

SWEETEST CHARIOT

2003

WHEN THE ENGLAND *squad under Clive Woodward and Martin Johnson, head coach and captain respectively, left London for the 2003 Rugby World Cup, they were already at a high point in the history of England international rugby.*

It seemed that England had almost always approached internationals throughout their history in hope rather than expectation, but Woodward's men travelled with a unique, undeniable and yet well-founded confidence. They also travelled as officially the number one ranked team in the world, superbly fit and well prepared.

Woodward, drawing on the lessons of the failed campaign of 1999 and also on his own strengths – his rich ability to refine all aspects of his preparation culture and to employ the best men in their fields in the sport – had developed a team which had many talents and were light years ahead of any other England side.

They were the Grand Slam champions and this after a glorious performance in the deciding match in Dublin when a fine Irish team were also going for the Six Nations clean sweep.

After that incredible afternoon at Lansdowne Road, England had gone on their tour Down Under and beaten New Zealand, even though they had two forwards in the sin-bin at one stage. They then went on to Melbourne and secured a thunderous victory over Australia, a highly-rated team who were to be the hosts of the World Cup itself.

The three warm-up matches in Europe's summer had also gone well. They beat Wales 43-9 and France 45-14 and although they lost 17-16 to France in Marseille, they rested almost all their normal starting team, indicating that the reserve strength was far from negligible. They also played outstanding, stylish rugby.

It was a heady time and the fact that the World Cup was to be concentrated in one nation, a concept which had taken too long to dawn on tournament organisers, insured before a ball was kicked that it would be the finest of the World Cups to date. Would it also prove to be England's finest hour, the best time in a history set in motion by the pioneers back in 1871?

And the marker which above all had turned all rugby history on its head was that when they touched down in the southern hemisphere they were protecting an unbroken and record run of ten winning games against Tri-Nations opposition dating back to 2000.

Opposite: One of the match balls from the World Cup final, now on display at the Twickenham Museum.

Statistics have been produced which indicate that it takes a team of vast experience to become world champions. Johnson was approaching the end of his magnificent career as one of his country's finest sporting warriors but he was to prove graphically that his powers had not declined. He had with him the hard-nosed trio of Lawrence Dallaglio, Richard Hill and Neil Back, who had played together as a back-row in more Tests than any other trio in history.

The anchorman of the backs was the clever Will Greenwood in midfield and at fly-half there was a young man already seen as a phenomenon, and something of a national darling. Jonny Wilkinson, as kicker, defender and tactical controller, was seen as one of the best fly-halves in the business, with an indefinable star quality that was to be wonderfully burnished.

Covering the back-three positions were Josh Lewsey, one of the last parts of the jigsaw at fullback, rugby league convert Jason Robinson, and Ben Cohen. Greenwood formed an effective midfield partnership with Mike Tindall, in the form of his life, while Mike Catt was also vying for selection. Up front, Steve Thompson, Phil Vickery and Trevor Woodman, backed up by the titanic Jason Leonard, who had already passed the 100-cap mark, were the cornerstone of a pack that was bested by no other team.

Of the three scrum-halves in the party, it was Matt Dawson who emerged as the starter above Andy Gomarsall and Kyran Bracken.

Woodward's meticulous organisation created a back-up team probably second to none in rugby history. It was led by Andy Robinson, with whom Woodward had initially worked in Bath; Phil Larder, the experienced and driven defensive coach who had once unsuccessfully coached the Great Britain rugby league team in Australia; Dave Alred, kicking coach and mentor of Wilkinson; and various other specialists, led by scrum professor Phil Keith-Roach and the throwing coach Simon Hardy.

Woodward had assembled a large cast in supporting roles – he took a refereeing consultant (Steve Lander), chef (Dave Campbell), visual awareness coach (Sherylle Calder) and QC (Richard Smith) – who had all been initially judged surplus to requirements by the RFU.

The conditioning and medical staff were also of the highest order. Staggeringly, every member of the 30-strong England squad was available for selection for the World Cup final. After a long season and a harsh tournament, that remains arguably the most incredible statistic about the whole campaign.

It would not be true to say that England sailed through the tournament. Indeed, looking back it is remarkable how self-critical they were as they went along and how much they were criticised by outsiders – notably by Australian commentators. The most frequent jibe expressed was that England's experienced team were 'Dad's Army', suggesting they would tire late on in games.

England opened their campaign against Georgia in Perth. Although they won 84-6, scoring 12 tries, the players described it as a real challenge and a decently physical game, because the Georgian forward power, which was to become a feature of succeeding World Cups, was first exhibited.

Among the most impressive England players were the massive hooker Thompson, and the huge wing Cohen, whose size and power and athleticism made him one of the most dangerous attacking players at the tournament.

The build-up to the key pool game against South Africa was conducted in a baleful atmosphere. England had savaged the Springboks in the autumn of 2002 at Twickenham, running up 50 points, and the Springboks had reacted with a performance of considerable violence.

Prior to the World Cup game, Corné Krige, the South African captain who seemed to be at the heart of a good number of the unsavoury incidents in 2002, declared that Johnson was 'the dirtiest captain in world rugby'. Some could think of another contender.

Yet for all the talk, South Africa did not have a great side, not even a unified side. England never had to play near their best to win easily, 25-6, although it was obvious that Wilkinson and Dallaglio were among those still searching for their best form.

The match was sealed when Louis Koen, the fallible South African fly-half, had a kick charged down and Greenwood ran on to score. It had been a match of high tensions and England had safely negotiated it, but The Sydney Morning Herald was not impressed. It published a picture of a rather downcast Wilkinson under the heading: 'Is that all you've got?' England rugby followers might have reflected that if a 25-6 win over South Africa was to attract criticism then standards must be encouragingly high.

England then moved to Melbourne to play Samoa, and found themselves in a mighty and thrilling confrontation against supercharged opposition. Samoa led 10-0 early on after a magnificent team try touched down by Semo Sititi, their inspirational captain. They led at half-time, too, and led again in the final quarter by 22-20. England then pulled clear with two excellent tries to win 35-22, but they were given a real scare by the Samoan team, which had rich talent but eventually ran out of steam.

During the match, Tindall was injured. Due to anxiety and the lack of communication between Woodward and Dave Reddin, his lieutenant on the touchline, they sent on Dan Luger as replacement. By this time Tindall had recovered and for just under half a minute England had 16 men on the field. It was an offence for which the Australians called for savage penalties, but the powers that be levied a fine and suspended Reddin from the touchline for one game.

Woodward's meticulous preparations paid off again. Smith, the team's QC, apparently gave a strong performance in the hearing to head off any suggestion that England might be docked points.

England crushed Uruguay in Melbourne by 111-13, with Lewsey showing glorious running skills in scoring five of England's seventeen tries, Paul Grayson kicking eleven conversions and Iain Balshaw, almost as effective as Lewsey, scoring two tries.

Joe Worsley, the powerful back-rower, incurred the wrath of Woodward by gesticulating towards the crowd as he left the field for the sin-bin and there were items to concern England in other areas, including the hamstring strain that Richard Hill had picked up against Georgia that should have cleared up in a few days but was still nagging away. But England had reached the knockout stages and the rest of the world was worried.

The quarter-final at the superb Suncorp Stadium, Brisbane, was an epic. Wales had been improving rapidly as the tournament progressed and they scored a dazzling counter-attack try by Stephen Jones early on. Another by Colin Charvis made it 10-3 to Wales at half-time.

Woodward acted. He took off Dan Luger, moving Greenwood and Tindall out one position to accommodate Catt at inside-centre to take the pressure from a faltering Wilkinson. England began to motor, powerfully. Robinson made a brilliant run to create a try for Greenwood and the pressure exerted on Wales meant that England forced a hatful of penalties, six of which Wilkinson put over. England recovered to win 28-17 with their self-belief restored and one of their oldest enemies dispatched.

The tournament now moved to Sydney, a city that provided a magnificent showcase for the closing stages. England were to meet France in the semi-finals, one day after Australia thrilled their followers and electrified the tournament by disposing of New Zealand in the first last-four tie.

Again, there was a tetchy build-up period with the two European camps stressing the old sporting enmity between the nations. France had come to life with periods of excellent play during the tournament, though occasionally they had shown a lack of concentration and frustration.

And against England, they fell flat on their faces. At the time, England had France in a vice-like psychological grip and the wet weather appeared to convince France that everything was running in favour of England. Wilkinson took advantage of a growing superiority by kicking five penalties and dropping three goals, gradually and expertly kicking the heart out of the French effort.

The French had scored the only try of the match through Serge Betsen at the back of a lineout, but England were worth every point of the 24-7 victory and the massed ranks of England followers amongst the thousands in the stadium looked at each other in some incredulity. England were once again in a World Cup final.

Suddenly, both the Australian and the English nations were enraptured by rugby. The build-up to the final in Sydney was colossal in both countries, it was all that Woodward and his colleagues could do to keep the team on track mentally. But here again, the wise old heads in the England team – Dallaglio, Back, Greenwood, Vickery and Johnson – were able to shape the week.

Again, the day dawned cheerless and wet. The Olympic Stadium was not only a sea of Australian gold, but also a sea of English white. The support England had for the final was incredible. So was the drama, the spectacle and the standards. World Cup finals in many sports often tend not to be classics because of the stakes involved, but the 2003 Rugby World Cup final was a classic in every respect; it sat easily on the shoulders of the rest of the tournament.

Australia struck the first blow when Lote Tuqiri leapt high above Robinson to catch a cross-field kick from Stephen Larkham and scored in the corner. But England – the superior team for much of the match, defending with passion but also attacking with class – struck back.

Wilkinson, in his element, kicked three penalties to put England in the lead. England missed further chances, notably when Ben Kay, horrendously, dropped the ball when the easiest try of his career was waiting under his nose. But England did score a try before half-time, a splendid one involving Dawson, Dallaglio and Wilkinson, with Wilkinson sending Robinson slithering over in the corner, and it was 14-5 at the break.

Some of England's massive scrummage authority was taken away by the performance of André Watson, the South African official, which has gone down in notoriety. He continually penalised the superior England scrum. Elton Flatley kicked two penalties for Australia to make it 14-11 and agonisingly for England, he kicked the goal to level it in the last seconds of normal time. The drama was heart-stopping.

Woodward and Johnson gathered their men before extra time began, and safety-first was the call. Wilkinson, majestically striding the biggest of stages, kicked a magnificent penalty from near halfway. It was one of the greatest kicks of his outstanding career.

Still England's defence was brutal; still the agony continued. By this time, Leonard was on the field to try to bring some sanity to the scrummaging, but Flatley came again with a penalty to make it 17-17 towards the end of extra time. At this stage, what would be a horrendous conclusion beckoned – a drop-goal shootout.

But England kicked off, chased hard and forced Mat Rogers, the Australian fullback, to make the hurried kick to touch. The next move made history. Thompson threw the ball immaculately, Lewis Moody caught it at the back and England cut loose with a well-sustained and beautifully-executed drive, heavily involving Catt, Johnson – who was playing the match of his career – and then Dawson, who made a superb break to take England into range.

Johnson drove one more time, Dawson fed Wilkinson and, using his weaker right foot, Wilkinson dropped the goal of English rugby history. As the ball approached the posts, vast banks of England fans went berserk.

Prop Woodman, of all people, caught the kick-off, and recycled it. Catt kicked the ball out of play. The whistle went. That set off delirious scenes round the stadium and, so we discovered later, in rugby clubs and bars and homes and streets back in England.

The victory let loose a torrent of celebrations. The squad were mobbed on laps of honour, on the flight home, by massive crowds at Heathrow, and then again on an open-top bus ride through London, stopping at Trafalgar Square, which was packed full of followers. Then to Buckingham Palace, for an audience with Her Majesty.

It seemed that celebratory dinners carried on for months, the numbers playing the game rose dramatically. Rugby had its finest weeks. Wilkinson ascended into the pantheon of all-time great British sportsmen, joined there by Johnson and Dallaglio. Woodward was knighted and all of the squad featured in the New Year Honours list.

We were not to know then that the team would suddenly spiral into rapid decline. In those heady days at the end of 2003, England, finally, had reached the top of the rugby world. They were the greatest team in English rugby history. One British tabloid, recalling The Sydney Morning Herald's *'Is this all you've got?' line, trumped them. 'This is all we've got!' ran their headline.*

The heading was above a picture of Wilkinson with the World Cup.

CLIVE WOODWARD

It was probably the time of my life. It was certainly the time of my sporting and coaching life. We had absolutely fantastic players, of course, and no weak links. Johnson, Back, Dallaglio, Greenwood, Dawson, the rest – and Wilkinson. I'll never accept a bad word said about Jonny Wilkinson. I have to say if they walked in now, we would still all be very close. We are just mates – every one of them. We had the time of our lives together.

The back-up to that team was world class too. There is a saying in business that you employ people who are better than you. I have absolutely no doubt that Andy Robinson was a better coach than me or that Phil Larder was a better coach than me. So was Brian Ashton, for the time that we brought him in, and Dave Reddin on the sports science side of things. Find people who have skills that you haven't got, that's the secret.

So much went on within that coaching group. They were not and are not easy people; they had strong opinions, and they got emotional and stroppy. I handpicked them because they were the best in the world. I wanted people who would challenge me. But I'd like to think that they loved that time as well.

Sometimes it kicked off. Over selection, especially. There was a game against France when I picked Jonny Wilkinson at fly-half and Charlie Hodgson, who was a great player, at inside-centre. Larder said, 'Charlie Hodgson can't tackle well enough, you can't pick him at inside-centre.'

I said, 'Well, you may be right but we are paying you to make him tackle. It's not my problem, it's your problem. You've got to make sure that he tackles properly.'

'You can't pick Charlie Hodgson at inside-centre.'

'Phil, that is why you are here – so if they can't tackle, it's your fault. By the way, if they could all tackle, then you ain't got a job. So, come on.'

I wanted us to attack. I am not going to pick someone who is a great defender and make him attack. We had to make good attacking players into defenders.

Of course, Phil is banging the table. He wanted to pick some big brute in the centre. What I would usually do is tell them I would sleep on it. That meant I'd had enough and I was leaving the room. I'd come in next morning and announce the team. I'd see Larder slapping his hand on his forehead.

Andy Robinson had a different approach. He'd say, 'Gutsy call, Clive, but we are with you, you're the boss, and you're picking the team.' Robbo has a quiet menace about him and I know he's thinking, 'That's nonsense.' But instead he's saying, 'You're the boss. We are all happy.' We had fantastic meetings. Just great meetings.

JOSH LEWSEY
Historically, all the most successful teams have encouraged accountability and leadership from top to bottom, so that it almost becomes part of the culture. Looking at the success of that England side, leadership was not generated solely by the captain. Martin Johnson was a fantastic leader, but under him was a raft of lieutenants.

Ben Kay ran the lineouts, Neil Back the defence, Matt Dawson, Jonny Wilkinson and Will Greenwood ran the attack, Phil Vickery the scrums. On top of that you put in trusted veterans like Lawrence, Mike Catt and Jason Leonard. It was a culture of excellence created by Clive.

CLIVE WOODWARD
On the surface at the time I dismissed that stuff about going in as number one, but deep down I didn't. To arrive there as favourites was confirmation that we were all doing our jobs properly and that for me is what being a coach is all about.

LAWRENCE DALLAGLIO
I was the only player who played in every minute of that World Cup campaign. I wasn't overly impressed with Clive at the time, but on reflection I am very proud and cherish that achievement more with every passing year. The Australian press called us 'Dad's Army', so it was great for us to live that label down in some style.

JASON ROBINSON
By the time we arrived in Perth we knew we were ready, we had worked so hard. Physically it was the hardest thing that I ever trained for in sport. I had never before put so much into any campaign. The tag of favourites was also unusual for an English side in union or league. It was just a great chance to achieve the ultimate

goal and when we got there, it was all rugby; a high-pressure elite environment under Clive.

BEN KAY

We knew that we were going to get it from the Australian press, although to be fair they are slightly more tongue in cheek than the press in New Zealand. When we beat New Zealand on the summer tour, the New Zealand press called us 'the ugliest pack in rugby'. They also called us 'white orcs on steroids'.

Clive had produced a video, which was a spoof of *Lord of the Rings* with the England pack in there looking like orcs. It was a way of putting the pressure on us from inside and taking it away from the outside. It showed us that we were going to take a bit of flak, but that the siege mentality could be quite enjoyable.

ANDY ROBINSON (England 1988-1995, 8 caps. England coach 2004-2006)

The scrum was a key part of our game and we set our store by it. In our first game, the Georgians started strongly up front but they tired because of the pace of the game. We, on the other hand, didn't let up for a second. In terms of statements and declarations of intent, it was very important for us.

WILL GREENWOOD

We won the Georgia match as comfortably as everyone had expected, the final score was 84-6 but we knew that we had been in the game of rugby. We knew they were going to be tough but I would go so far as to say that they were as physical a side as any I ever played against and they tackled as if their lives depended on it.

JONNY WILKINSON

It was really good to get that first game under the belt, good to do it with a big crowd supporting us and to get a win. But there was a lot to work on.

For me, one of the other challenges was to enjoy myself. The World Cup, the rugby, it all meant so much that my natural inclination was to regard it all as work and not as enjoyment. I'd see it all as just a series of pitches: get to the pitch, do my work, get off, get back to the hotel. And back in the hotel, the danger was I'd stay too much on my own, think too much about the training or a game and get too inward. I needed to think actively about breaking out of that. I wanted to take it all in at that World Cup. I didn't want to let the intensity board me up in my room.

LAWRENCE DALLAGLIO

We got the job done against Georgia but without pulling up any trees. And suddenly we were into the game against South Africa. In the previous autumn, after beating them by 50, there had been a few of the 'it will be different in Perth' comments from the Boks, which made me laugh. But this was a big Test match and the Boks are always good enough to win any one-off game.

Looking back at 2003 now, they were England in disguise. Just as coming up short in the 1999 World Cup was part of our 2003 success story, the Springboks of 2003 were on the upward curve which led to their World Cup win over us in 2007.

CLIVE WOODWARD

We had to forget that match the previous November when it had all kicked off. It was a day we didn't want to go back to. I was expecting a very tough and physical game in Perth and no more. We were going into that game with a lot of injury niggles. Kyran Bracken had back spasms, Matt Dawson had strained his hamstring and Andy Gomarsall had a bruised shin so all three scrum-halves were affected. Richard Hill strained his hamstring against Georgia and, as it turned out, that took a long, long time to clear up.

LAWRENCE DALLAGLIO

The South African game was the Kyran Bracken show. Kyran was a really good scrum-half, a bit unlucky with injury and, of course, a contemporary of Matt Dawson's, so they fought out the starting spot for years, much to England's benefit. That night in Perth was Kyran's finest moment. We were scruffy, they missed a few kicks, it was all getting tense, but he was winning his personal duel with Joost van der Westhuizen, who was a key man for the Boks. Kyran didn't get to play in the final like a few others in the squad, but he played a massive part in bringing the trophy home.

KYRAN BRACKEN

The most important game I played for England was probably that pool game against South Africa. My back was not great and considering that I couldn't touch my toes before the game, I played really well. There was a crucial moment in the first half when Will Greenwood forgot the rules and failed to touch the ball down in the in-goal area after a missed kick. That gave South Africa a scrum near our line and when van der Westhuizen got the ball, I managed to stop him and turn the ball over. It meant that we were level 6-6 at half-time and we'd stopped South Africa getting any momentum. In the second half, we took our chances.

MARTIN JOHNSON

We turned over too much ball against South Africa and didn't give our kickers a chance to get on the front foot.

WILL GREENWOOD

Lewis Moody set off like a demented cheetah and I cantered behind him waiting to feed off any scraps. Sure enough, Mongo [Moody] lunged at Louis Koen, smashed down the kick and the ball squirted backwards towards the South African line. By now I had a 15-yard start on everyone else and I knew that if I stayed cool I was going to score.

It was quite late at night and there was dew so figuring the ball would go skidding along the surface quite smoothly, I aimed to summon up every last iota of my modest football talent and side-foot it over the line. I reached it first with a gang of 15 Springboks at my back.

CLIVE WOODWARD

We were so relieved at the end but we knew that we hadn't achieved anything like the level of performance that we could.

PHIL VICKERY

I had given everything I had against South Africa. I could not have wrung one more ounce out of myself and even though we had won, it hadn't gone that well for me. God, it can be demoralising because you've got to go back and face your team-mates. There was no hiding place in the squad. So you front up, and I suppose that is why not everyone plays for England.

Will Greenwood scores in the crucial pool victory over South Africa.

LAWRENCE DALLAGLIO

The Samoa match was a classic example of England's opponents raising their game because we were England and the world's number one ranked team. We were also 10 per cent below par and when that happens, it is suddenly game on. But the encouraging thing was that we fought our way out of a tight spot, we were trailing three times and we stole the win and that set us in good stead. But there were quite a few of us who had not brought our A game onto the field yet.

TREVOR WOODMAN

There were some twitchy backsides during that Samoa game, I can tell you.

STEVE THOMPSON (England 2002-2011, 73 caps plus 3 caps for the Lions)

Samoa were unbelievable; they scored a great team try through (Semo) Sititi. But I never thought we would lose. I had no time for all that talk on tour about us being in a dark place. I didn't read newspapers over there and didn't watch any of the rugby talkshows, I wasn't aware if we were getting any stick. From the information I was getting from friends and family back home, there was a real buzz in England. And that was certainly true in the squad as well.

MARTIN JOHNSON

We had to dig ourselves out of a hole. We had faced a team that played as well in the first 20 minutes as any team for as long as I can remember.

ANDY GOMARSALL (England 1996-2008, 35 caps)

We were not playing amazingly well in the early stages, it was just sheer bloody-mindedness and strength of character that got us through, that and the fact that everyone was the fittest and strongest they had ever been.

CLIVE WOODWARD

We had an extremely fair hearing after briefly having 16 players on the field against Samoa and I felt it proved the wisdom of bringing a QC. Richard Smith was outstanding in the hearing and Samoa's attitude was also outstanding.

Some Aussies were calling for us to have points taken away, which was ridiculous, and the Samoans were being put under pressure to say something in the press, but they wouldn't have anything to do with it. They didn't want to tarnish what was a great game of rugby. We made an error, we learnt from it and we moved on.

LAWRENCE DALLAGLIO

We had a big debrief the morning after the Samoan game. Clive went through all the penalties one by one on the big screen and after about the eighth or ninth penalty it was established, beyond reasonable doubt, that Martin Johnson had been responsible for six of them. 'At what point do you think you lost the referee, Martin?' Clive asked in the meeting and we all collapsed with laughter. It was a good tension reliever.

ANDY GOMARSALL

I had been feeling frustrated so it was great to get my chance against Uruguay, whom we beat 111-13. We all played exceptionally well and I scored two tries and felt that I pushed my case, but ultimately Clive had made his decision as to his top two.

There was a sense of deep frustration, though in the end it was the most amazing experience of a professional sports career, to be part of the World Cup-winning squad. During the tournament my wife was an absolute rock to me as I was so frustrated. It was one of Clive's great ideas to have wives and girlfriends out there for a while.

MATT DAWSON

Having beaten Wales in the Six Nations and in the warm-up game and beaten South Africa in the pool you are thinking, 'It is semi-final time'. If we had not had all those horrific experiences of Grand Slam defeats and the defeat to South Africa in the 1999 World Cup we would have lost against Wales in that quarter-final. It was not just about the players, it was about the management. We had all been through that bad stuff together.

TREVOR WOODMAN

We geared everything to winning our group so that we wouldn't have to play the All Blacks in a quarter-final and subconsciously maybe we thought we had succeeded as we were playing Wales and we could beat them.

Probably it was no surprise that the first 40 minutes happened, they scored two tries and got in front, but obviously we got back into it again and I think our fitness really came through.

MATT DAWSON

If Wales had possessed a little more experience they could have put us away in that first half. They wanted to play, we wanted to play and it made for a great half. The pace of the game was tremendous and there was not a lot said in the dressing room because we needed to catch our breath.

LAWRENCE DALLAGLIO

In all honesty at no time in the Wales game was I as worried as when we were behind against Samoa. Wales had nothing to lose, they played well and we performed like complete idiots in the first half. But I knew we would come good.

JONNY WILKINSON

The first 40 minutes of the game against Wales were horrible. Absolutely horrible. The biggest crisis of our World Cup.

CLIVE WOODWARD

I think we played the World Cup well enough, but the one game we really did stuff up was against Wales – we really stuffed it up – and I think that was partly because we looked at the fixture and were already focussed on playing France in the semi-final. We were up in Brisbane and all week things felt wrong, you could just tell people's heads weren't right. And that is the worst part of being a coach because you try all sorts of things to turn it around to make it a good week, to make training better, to change the atmosphere in the camp, but it just wasn't happening. Training was flat – I put my hands up and say we probably overworked the players – but we were just trying to do things to lift them and it didn't work. I woke up on the day of the game and I didn't feel like I normally did, I didn't think, 'Oh wow, great, we're ready to go', I thought, 'We're just not right'. And it is a horrendous feeling. You always look in the mirror and blame yourself at those moments.

At half-time we were in real trouble. Wilkinson was having a poor game, he kept hitting rucks and getting too involved in the heavy traffic. So we needed to do something to shake things up. But what do you do? I didn't want to take Jonny off because he was too important to us and although he wasn't playing that well, he wasn't playing that badly either. But we needed someone to help him out – so we put Greenwood to outside centre, brought on Catt and moved Tindall to the wing instead of Luger. It was a big call, but those are the ones that you're proudest of when you look back because it worked. I think most coaches would have left it ten or fifteen minutes into the second half to make that call. And if someone went down injured we would have been stuffed – but I just felt it was a change that we had to make at half-time to give us a change in momentum as soon as we left the changing room. Half-time had to be a scary place in that changing-room; normally it's calm and professional, but that was a T-CUP [thinking clearly under pressure] moment, we had to make the big changes, make the big statements. And within five or six minutes the game started to change our way.

WILL GREENWOOD

Shortly after the break, Jason Robinson made a fabulous burst from the back, his cheeks puffing. Jason was bombing in the general direction of the corner flag so I started jogging along the touchline on the off-chance he might somehow manage to work his way through half of Wales and end up somewhere in my vicinity.

Suddenly, he was in the clear, Welshmen languishing in his slipstream and there I was lumbering up on his outside, to take the pass and fall over the line for the try that supposedly swung the match in our favour. It was just a simple coincidence that I happened to be passing through in the period when Robbo came flying from nowhere.

MATT DAWSON

Will's ability to read the game was second to none. It's like watching a snooker player and wondering how he knew where he needed to be four shots earlier. Will could read the game so well and he had obviously thought, 'Jason could make a break here and if he does, he's probably going to be running to the outside, so I need to be there.' For me that was the defining moment of our World Cup.

I never said Jonny was playing badly against Wales but he was not right and it needed changing. I remember wondering how the hell we were going to do it. Bringing on Mike Catt was one of the best substitutions Clive ever made because it changed the intensity and the direction of the game. It had been the first time a team had thrown the kitchen sink and more at us, and we didn't expect Shane Williams to be running it at us from everywhere. Mike Catt was key.

MIKE CATT

I never understood where that myth came from that I'd come on to help Jonny and turned the match. Just study the first half and tell me that Jonny was not England's best player. His tackling was one of the factors that kept us in the game. What happened is that the England pack, unusually, didn't go well in the first 40 and the half-backs were on the back foot. We had no real second kicking option – that's why Jonny had come under a bit of pressure with his line kicking and with ball in hand.

But it was the team's failing, not his. Clive needed to provide the second kicking option, which was a simple tactical switch. We then stood either side of the scrums, Jonny left and me right, and we hoofed it downfield to get us on the front foot, and the nature of the game soon changed. For some reason I got most of the credit, but the truth is that everyone in the England team was part of the solution. Jonny kicked all his penalties and added a drop-goal as well.

JONNY WILKINSON

Mike Catt is a great talker and a great thinker. He had experience, was very strong-minded in what he wanted and he made things happened by the way he communicated and bossed people around. He played brilliantly.

STEVE THOMPSON

As individuals and as a team we were highly critical of ourselves. Amazingly, the changing room was very flat after the win against Wales. I did find that a bit strange because we were in a semi-final of the World Cup, but there wasn't much noise or self-adulation.

To add insult to injury I was chosen for drug testing and didn't leave the ground until midnight because I was too dehydrated to provide a sample. Then when I went to bed I couldn't get to sleep. I was exhausted, but my head was full of things that I hadn't done as well as I would have liked.

CLIVE WOODWARD

I went into the press conference after the Wales game knowing exactly what I was going to do. I knew the press were going to have a go at Jonny because he'd had a poor game by his standards and I also knew that we had not played that well while France had won their quarter-final comfortably.

I decided to go on the front foot. I told myself I was going to cause a ruck. As soon as someone said anything, I was going to bite their head off. The first question was from one of the French journalists, Benoit [Pensivy] from *L'Equipe*. He said something quite innocently, like, 'Well done on winning but France must be favourites for next week?' And I just launched into him and told him that we would beat France.

I was trying to take the pressure off Wilkinson. Benoit was looking bewildered and wondering if something had been lost in the translation.

LAWRENCE DALLAGLIO

After the Wales game we had a great old codgers' rugby chat while we were rehydrating in the corner of some bar in Sydney and the consensus was that we were doing too much training and that there was no reason to have sessions in the heat of the afternoon when our matches were all in the evening. We were all as brave as lions after a few beers so we decided to bring this important matter to Clive's attention at our next team meeting.

When Clive asked for any other comments at the end, I was the only one who seemed to put his hand up. Anyway, the point seemed to go down well and we did ease back. The coaches were totally dedicated to the team, and players do know what the exact balance between training and resting should be.

We were in a good place then, happy and relaxed in our hotel on the seafront in Manly and preparing to do a big number on the French. Without being big-headed, it was where we were meant to be.

RICHARD HILL

I was so happy to be fit at last for the semi. It was an immensely frustrating time. When I first did the injury, no one thought I would be out for so long. It was just a slight hamstring problem and once I missed a few games, I must admit I was beginning to get a bit concerned. But the physio team and management stayed positive.

NEIL BACK

There are certain players who do not need games to be ready to play and Richard Hill, who had been out for a few games, was one of them. Before the tournament we did an awful lot of conditioning work and he was one of the guys leading the way. That back-row of myself, Hilly and Lawrence had played together so many times, we were tried and tested and knew we would play off each other's strengths.

CLIVE WOODWARD

But just as we got it wrong against Wales and got out of jail against them, we got it so right against France. There was no way that French team would beat us. We had almost slipped up against Wales because we had been looking forward to playing France and once we got over that hurdle, all minds were just set on doing a job on them in the semi-final. All week was perfect. I woke up the day of the game and I just remember feeling, *I don't care what happens today, I don't care what the weather's like, we're going to smash them today, they have no chance.*

MATT DAWSON

That semi-final was an awesome night to be an England rugby player and supporter. A World Cup semi-final is something you always dream about and we delivered. It was tough, but our forwards were magnificent from the first minute. And so were the fans. I couldn't believe the sight when we ran on and the noise they made was extraordinary.

RICHARD HILL

I was happy with my performance in general against France but I had to take responsibility for Serge Betsen's try. It was a missed tackle. But it didn't get me down and it was important to get myself back into the game early and that is what I did.

JASON ROBINSON

Against France, we knew we had a forward pack that could squeeze the life out of anyone in any conditions. We played those conditions well and held our nerve.

TREVOR WOODMAN

We knew they were going to be huge up front and that was an area they would want to target us. Then due to the wet conditions, it was always going to be a forward battle. That showed with every point that came from Jonny's boot.

It was a matter of frustrating the French, if you can get them frustrated by taking away the strong part of their game then you've got half the battle won. My opposite number was Sylvain Marconnet and what was telling was that in one of the first few scrums I remember him sending in right hooks. You could quite easily react in the heat of the moment and get yourself sent off, but we didn't have to react. We knew that if they were doing that that we'd got them. They're throwing punches? Great, we'll stand there and take them but we'll just keep trying to drive them back in the scrum. I think we all had a wry smile. 'We've got you now.'

PHIL VICKERY

France had a great team on paper and we knew it was going to be big up front, but I felt we had a big edge on them – and then it's over to Jonny. Penalty, three points, penalty, three more points, drop-goal, three more. I could see France just shrinking and shrinking and shrinking. That was the memory that sticks in my mind more than anything.

They really wanted it. Fabien Galthié was playing his last game at scrum-half and it was his World Cup supposedly. They were a great team on paper but, suddenly, it's us in the final.

LAWRENCE DALLAGLIO

Like all world-class players, Jonny bounced back after that Welsh game with a magnificent performance against France. Now, knowing as I do that Jonny is a perfectionist, I realise he was making amends in his own way for what he considered a below-par performance against Wales.

WILL GREENWOOD

The momentum was all ours, the hex was on them. Comparisons were made between Wilkinson and his opposite number, Frédéric Michalak, but on the day there was no contest. It was a case of the master and the apprentice.

LAWRENCE DALLAGLIO

As well as Jonny being immense, the semi-final was all about our front-row of Vicks, Steve Thompson and Trevor Woodman having the collective game of their lives and smashing their opposite numbers into the next parish.

Contrary to popular belief, France's defeat had nothing to do with the rain and Freddie Michalak not liking the conditions. We would still have beaten France by the same score or more if we had them played in 90 degrees of sunshine on Manly beach.

ANDY ROBINSON

It was a magnificent effort by the forwards. There were various comments made about them and about whether they were too old but, as always, they went out and performed.

CLIVE WOODWARD

The biggest round of applause in the changing room afterwards was for Jason Leonard. For him to overtake Philippe Sella to be the most-capped player of all time was incredible. There was a huge amount of history made that evening.

TREVOR WOODMAN

You try to tell yourself that the final is just another game. Throughout the tour I always tried to keep as low key as possible, to hang out with my mates. Phil Vickery, Jason Robinson and I would always go out and try to relax; we were all fairly relaxed individuals. But then we'd think, 'Christ, we're actually in a World Cup final.' You don't know how to respond to it because you've never been there before.

Luckily I had some good friends in Manly and they had this incredible penthouse near where you come off the ferry from Sydney. I went over there for dinner. It was just good to be away from the hotel and up there I could look down on everyone. It was just nice to see everyone in the bars, people getting off the ferry, all the England supporters from the outside rather than being in the middle of it.

Aussies were trying to disrupt us but it was one of those surreal moments where you do the same things that you've done for every game, and it is the same but different.

STEVE THOMPSON

When we went training there were always 200 or so supporters cheering us on to the bus. You couldn't walk out of the hotel for a coffee without someone coming up and wishing you well. The English fans were terrific all trip.

JONNY WILKINSON

The team had been together for five years, through thick and thin. We had stuck together through strikes, through horrendous defeats and glorious victories, whether we'd been slagged off or praised.

LAWRENCE DALLAGLIO

We had to stay chilled and let the gravitas of the match itself kick in on the day and that's pretty much what happened.

PHIL VICKERY

In the build-up to the final, there was just a sense of nerves and the surreal. I remember being at the hotel, which was a massive focal point for all the fans by then. How do you go anywhere with the fans outside? I remember that team meeting, the one before the final, and it was probably one of the most emotionally charged but quiet meetings I'd ever experienced. I can't even remember what Martin said, which is not unusual.

MARTIN JOHNSON

We had a team meeting on Friday night. We had a motivational video – big hits, tries, good moments set to music. We watched that and I said my usual few words to the squad. I kept it short. My main message was, 'Let's play our normal way. Let's not force things. By the same token, let's do the things we want. Don't let the occasion get to you.' If you start thinking, 'It's the rugby World Cup final' as you receive the ball, the likelihood is you will end up paralysed by the moment.

JASON ROBINSON

I had never felt pressure like that for the final of any competition. The media coverage and the frenzy around the team meant that we could hardly get out of the hotel. It was all very tense but we genuinely did believe that we could win.

PHIL VICKERY

I remember the trophy being there as we ran on, and I remember thinking this is not real; it's like you're in a movie and it's not really happening.

LAWRENCE DALLAGLIO

Australia got a great start in the final courtesy of a wonderful cross-field kick from Steve Larkham, who was as good a Test ten as I ever played against. He found Lote Tuqiri, who jumped above Jason Robinson and scored. It was a shock, but caused no panic.

JASON ROBINSON

It was a great kick and it worked perfectly. I'm just surprised that they didn't do more of it. The night was wet and horrible and those kinds of kicks are always 50–50 – in fact more than that for the attacker as they are going forward and have the momentum to take them over the line if they have the ball – and he had a big height advantage on me. But from our point of view there was no panic, we just thought, 'Right, let's get back into doing what we do. Let's focus and play to our patterns'. And that's how we went about it.

WILL GREENWOOD

There are only 10 minutes to go before half-time when Ben Kay only has to fall over the line to score, but he drops the ball for about the first time in a year. Ben just didn't drop the ball; he's got hands like buckets.

BEN KAY

At the time I was gutted for missing the opportunity of scoring a try in the World Cup final. I did everything I teach schoolboys not to do. I saw Phil Waugh coming across to tackle me and I gave him a glance to see how he was going to approach the tackle, but I had not caught the ball then. Matt Dawson tried to dummy him so he would worry that Daws would go himself but I bought the dummy and missed the pass. I wanted the ground to swallow me up but I thought we were so on top that we would go right back and score.

A lot of people get the timeline wrong and think that was after Jason Robinson's try but it wasn't so when he went over I thought that was me off the hook – but the game got tighter. These things happen and I've got to live with it.

MARTIN JOHNSON

Credit to Ben, he didn't let it get to him. We went in 14-5 up at half-time but 19-5 would have felt even better and would probably have ended the game as a contest.

WILL GREENWOOD

From a lineout I took the ball into the midfield and got walloped by about four of them, but I managed to keep the ball in the ruck. Dallaglio took over and stormed it round the corner before offloading to Jonny with Robinson flying out on his shoulder. No one is stopping Billy Whizz from there. Jonny places his pass right in the breadbasket and Robbo bombs off. We were leading 14-5 at half-time.

LAWRENCE DALLAGLIO

We threatened to break their line almost every time we moved it and when Matt

Dawson went, I knew we had a chance. I made a bit of ground and I could hear Jonny screaming on my right. So when the time came, I let him have it. He had the choice of Ben Cohen on his right and Jason Robinson on his left – he opted for Jason, who was always going to score. It wasn't a bad choice, was it?

MARTIN JOHNSON

At half-time I felt calm, strong and full of running. The rest of the boys looked in a similar way. The Wallabies had been breathing hard as they came off.

LAWRENCE DALLAGLIO

After the break we played as poor a 40 minutes as I can ever remember from that group, losing the second half 9-0. We lost concentration and André Watson started to find fault with our dominant scrum. It could easily have gone pear-shaped but we still had that inner core of belief and crucially we never slipped behind the Aussies. It might have appeared otherwise in the stands and back home on the TV, but we still felt we were dictating terms.

PHIL VICKERY

The aggravating thing for me was we'd played the whole tournament without giving a single scrum penalty away! I remember speaking to referee André Watson before the game. I told him we didn't want to mess about at scrum time, we wanted to be solid and we wanted to play. He said that would be excellent, blah, blah, blah. Then on the field he starts penalising us when we are on top. Then the touch-judge or the referee starts penalising Trevor for not binding. Al Baxter, his opposite number, is over somewhere near my left knee, right across the scrum and nothing was done about it.

TREVOR WOODMAN

We knew that there were going to be a lot of collapsed scrums. Bill Young was up against Vicks and we knew that if they don't get a comfortable hit for channel-one ball, they go down, reset and try again. It was so frustrating and the opposite of the semi-final.

In the final we were on top and obviously we wanted the scrums to be challenging so that we could push them around and wear them down. Not to get that opportunity, to have so many free-kicks and penalties against us, took a weapon out of our game and played into their hands.

When Jason [Leonard] came on for Vicks in extra time we decided we may as well not push, we will just hold on our own ball and they will win theirs and we will win ours. We just couldn't afford to give away a penalty. That was sad but that was what we were forced to do.

PHIL VICKERY

People asked me if I was gutted to be taken off in a World Cup final. I can honestly say that Jason would be the only bloke I'd actually be happy to come off the rugby field for. Jason had always been a fantastic help and a great influence on me and on the squad.

I wasn't upset with Clive. I had total respect for all those coaches. They even taught me about kicking – what did I know about kicking?! I knew what they stood for, I knew what they were about. I would have sacrificed anything because I hundred per cent trusted those guys and their decisions and what it was that they wanted to do.

JONNY WILKINSON

Australia were awarded another random penalty at a scrum, so Elton Flatley had a chance to level the scores before full-time. The pressure on that kick was remarkable and Flatley showed stupendous mental strength to come through it.

MATT DAWSON

Before extra time we were huddled up and Martin Johnson had control – he just told us to keep doing what we had been doing. I looked over at the Australian team and they were scattered over the field, cramped up and taking on fluids, and there were coaches everywhere. We were very cool and calm and I remember thinking everyone knew exactly what they needed to do. There was no screaming and shouting, just a bit of frustration that we had not finished the job.

MARTIN JOHNSON

I would have backed our fitness against anybody's and the proof was in which side that made the biggest number of substitutions. They'd used most of theirs while we made just a couple of changes at the end of the second half.

STEVE THOMPSON

It was a weird experience. There was no panic. We just thought that we had to carry on and we could win. Johnno told us that we had plenty of rugby left in us. The plan was to keep running at the Australians and keep hold of the ball, which we hadn't done all that well in the match.

JONNY WILKINSON

We soon got a penalty, 49 metres out, and there and then, all those late nights at Middlesbrough with Dave Alred [kicking coach] became worth it. We were 17-14 up and we took our lead into the second half of extra time.

LAWRENCE DALLAGLIO

That pain we went through when Wales scored at the end and Neil Jenkins kicked a goal to deny us a Grand Slam at Wembley in 1999 – that stood us in good stead in extra time. When Jenks knocked over that conversion there was a lot of cursing and a feeling of panic from us England boys. We couldn't believe we had allowed a game we had dominated to slip away from us at the death but we simply weren't a mature enough side to appreciate we still had time to put things right. Losing that match was a massive disappointment but a good lesson.

I always contrast that moment under the Wembley posts with the similar scenario facing us at Olympic Park when Elton Flatley made it 17-17 with two minutes of extra time to go. There was a complete calm. The rest of the rugby world might have been having a nervous breakdown but as Elton went through his long routine we were already mentally rehearsing our World Cup-winning reply. He was never going to miss but we had two minutes left to finish the job.

JASON ROBINSON

In those big games, it can be easy for players to lose focus and for individuals to do their own thing. But, in fairness, it was all about the team and achieving the ultimate goal. That was summed up by the winning drop-goal. We had practised that until we had almost got sick of practising it. That's how we would always finish a training session. 'We need a drop goal to win – how are we going to do it?' Just watching that back it was what we had been trained to do. By keeping our nerve we got three points and secured England's greatest ever win.

MARTIN JOHNSON

And suddenly the whole World Cup is down to 90 seconds. But again you can either throw your hands in the air at the ref and complain, or you refocus. Flatley is taking a kick at our goal and I'm talking to Benny Kay who is calling our lineouts, Jonny who is going to kick off for us, and Steve Thompson, who is going to throw-in the lineout. And your choices really are at that point, you either kick the ball long, put the ball in their court and make them kick it back to you, or you kick the ball short and try to regain possession. We had enough time so I said to Jonny, 'We'll go long. They'll kick it, we'll get the lineout and we'll play off that.' And we said to Lewis Moody, who had come on, 'Make sure you're there to put pressure on the kick.'

LAWRENCE DALLAGLIO

We didn't think Australia would run from their own line and we were right. They looked for Mat Rogers, who – under pressure from Lewis Moody – found a short touch. From the moment the lineout formed 40 metres out it was like a training drill at Pennyhill Park; we were oblivious to all the noise and tension.

Though we had spent so much energy in the first 80 minutes we just knew that all our hard work would pay off. I can remember looking round at the boys and there was an expression in their eyes – it meant that this was ours.

CLIVE WOODWARD

What people don't realise, I mean Jonny and I have a laugh about this, Jonny has dropped a goal. And my kind of strapline is, 'That's great but he has already missed three.' If he had done his job properly, we wouldn't have gone through all that nonsense. But I say that with tongue in cheek.

We kick-off and we kick long. It goes to Rogers on his left foot. Moody almost charges it down because he has gone haring after them. The amount of work we did with Phil Larder on charge-downs. Lewis absolutely knew that this guy was left-footed, what to do, how to do it. We had practised charge-downs relentlessly.

LEWIS MOODY

I replaced Richard Hill three minutes into extra time. I played a small part in the drama, for which I am for ever grateful. The ball went to Mat Rogers in his own half and I was able to put enough pressure for the former rugby league star to slice his clearance.

CLIVE WOODWARD

That gave us field position. The lineout call is massive because you've got Steve Thompson, who has played the whole flipping game and extra time. The obvious call was Martin Johnson, because it's the simple call, the less risky option, but the Aussies are there. At the back Lewis Moody is unmarked. So Ben Kay calls the back. You see Thommo going: 'Are you sure, Ben?'

Thommo wants it at the front. He's thinking if he doesn't throw it straight, we lose the World Cup. A few years earlier Thommo is a flanker at Northampton. You hire Simon Hardy to work as a specialist and all the stuff you have done comes down to one throw. If we don't win that lineout, we don't win the World Cup. So he throws it. It wasn't the greatest throw but they weren't marking Lewis and he catches it.

MARTIN JOHNSON

The key was the lineout. We had to win it. Benny Kay was calling it and Thommo was throwing it – and he'd missed a few, he was probably going to be a little uncomfortable throwing it long, but that's where the space would be. The Aussies were going to be marking the front, so it had to go long. They were daring us to throw it long, where Thommo had missed a few times.

And the key to that moment, the pressure of the situation, was the communication – me talking to Benny and Thommo and saying, 'Mate, we're going to go long at the lineout,' and we could see that Thommo wasn't very comfortable, but Benny said to him, 'Look, if it goes wrong, it's our fault.' Thommo had overthrown it a few times, so Benny just said, 'Underthrow it, you've gone too big before now. Throw it short. If they steal it, don't worry, that's our problem.'

If you watch the video you just see Benny nodding his head at Thommo, just trying to catch his eye to say, 'Yeah, it's on.'

BEN KAY

I think the last play signified everything we had worked towards. Some senior players sometimes play down the work of Clive in what he did, but he had built a framework which allowed players to flourish. A lot of his thinking was to make sure we could handle the pressure and could remain calm.

CLIVE WOODWARD

When you watch it back that is where you are most proud. All the detail. We used Sherylle Calder, who did all this stuff about peripheral vision. We are teaching Dawson that if they think it's going to be a drop-goal, there are going to be gaps. Dawson sees this and he goes ten yards. That puts the drop-goal on. All these things we had worked on, which all came together. Of course, everyone remembers Jonny, and rightly so, for his amazing kick. But what has gone into that drop-goal I could do a two-hour talk on – about every player and what they were doing. It just needs one player to bottle it under pressure, one player to ruck wrong and Watson penalises us.

WILL GREENWOOD

You've probably been through those situations on the training field or in certain games, you back your lineout, you know that you're just going to hit the midfield with this drop-goal routine, we're just going to try to get Jonny in the right position, but I think the break that Dawson made almost shocked everyone because we thought, 'Christ, this is actually going to work.' Jonny's bit was the icing on the cake.

MATT DAWSON

We had practised that move so many times in training. Sometimes we had called it in games for the hell of it to make sure everyone knew exactly where they were supposed to be. Part of the routine was that Jonny Wilkinson would never be in the ruck so I did not have to worry about where he would be. That is why Martin

Johnson takes the ball up that extra time because he knows I am at the bottom of the ruck. If I was, a forward had to recycle so the scrum-half, whoever it was, could get back to their feet. It was done with military precision.

TREVOR WOODMAN

Daws was able to run through their defence and how it set up everything pretty much came off 100 per cent. It was just great to suddenly see it all going to plan. All you do as a front-row forward is make sure you don't get in the way of the bugger who's got the ball.

LEWIS MOODY

I was on the other side of the pitch, virtually unmarked, waving frantically at Jonny. If you chucked the ball over towards me I was convinced I would score. Happily for the sake of English rugby, Jonny ignored me.

The drop to glory. Jonny Wilkinson seals his place in rugby's Pantheon.

JONNY WILKINSON

I'd had a couple of goes before which were very much pot shots, having a dig almost. But for this one I was thinking that because of where the guys had put me, I can't miss… this must go over. I almost remember feeling like 'the others drifted wide but this one will go over'.

I knew I'd hit it in such a way that it wasn't going to be the most powerful kick, but it was going to be accurate. I knew from fairly early on it was going over. What surprised me was I actually got lost in that moment, I didn't know where I was. I remember half celebrating, but not really celebrating. It felt like a surreal, dream-like situation. I had to ask 'is this really happening?' and that was my facial expression.

Then there was the realisation that there was still time left and I really wasn't up for a third game-tying penalty from them before the end. There was the panic to get back and the urgency to get the ball off the field and finish the damn thing.

We spent years and years with that team working on a framework to manufacture three points when needed. We demanded that people knew their roles and also everyone else's roles so that it was as professional and ruthless a manoeuvre as it could possibly be. There was no great communication, but under the greatest pressure everybody carried out their roles impeccably.

It always seemed strange to me that the World Cup played itself out like it did. Not only did we play the final against the host team, but also that it went down to the very last seconds of extra-time and a drop-goal. All that hard work we did over the years we were obliged to put into practice in one passage of play. The time when we got it exactly right was the time when we needed it most. That made it feel like a really special moment when many destinies came together at one point. It was our time.

I've tried to preserve the quality of the memories I have which are wrapped up in the feel, the senses, the smell, noises and atmosphere. I'd rather keep it there and then in that first-person experience than watch it back, which can taint the memory. I want to keep it exactly as I remember it, which was one hell of an experience.

PHIL VICKERY

You became a supporter at the side of the field, when that drop-goal went, we knew what was going on and when that ball left his foot it was like… man… it was like slow motion… wait, wait, what's going on, is it over? The only sign that you knew it was over was the people at the end standing up going crazy.

CLIVE WOODWARD

I have come down to the touchline now, where I'm not normally. They are all celebrating and everyone is high-fiving. I am screaming at people: 'GET BACK IN POSITION!'

When they take the kick-off, Trevor Woodman is stood in the middle of the pitch. He should have been over with Johnno. We are all out of position. The Aussies being the Aussies they see Woodman, they kick to him, thinking, 'That's our best chance.'

Even now I get emotional about this. They kick and if they win that restart, you have probably lost the World Cup. All I am thinking is, 'If we don't get this restart, I am going to kill them!' They kick and I can still see it now. Trevor Woodman just soars like a salmon, like an Australian Rules footballer, and takes the ball with two hands.

MATT DAWSON

At the whistle it was pure enjoyment. To have that moment when Jonny kicked the ball between the posts just gave me a huge rush of adrenaline. We had been playing 100 minutes or whatever and I did not feel knackered at all. After the kick it would be my job and Martin Johnson's to run back and tell everyone to keep concentrating – but everybody was shouting, 'Next job, next job', 'We've got to concentrate'. Everybody was so switched on and it epitomised where we were as a team – there was no panic. It ended up with Trevor Woodman catching the kick-off and probably the only time a prop has caught a kick-off was in the 2003 World Cup final.

TREVOR WOODMAN

Within the last 12 months or so of that final, Dave Alred had the tight five catching high balls. He's a big Aussie Rules advocate and he had everyone going through the technique of catching a high ball and that's exactly what went through my mind. At the time you just think, 'Oh, okay, we'll practise it but I don't know why we're practising it.' But it obviously paid off in the end.

PHIL VICKERY

Who kicks the ball out to end the game? Mike Catt. The man they used to boo at Twickenham. I hated that. I can't even talk about it without getting tears in my eyes. Horrible, horrible, horrible. That's a guy who was so passionate about playing for England. He helped me massively as a prop. He could have easily chucked it all in and let people get to him, so for him to kick that ball off the field for England in a Rugby World Cup final, I'll tell you what, brilliant.

MIKE CATT

I loved every single minute of my international career. I had my critics. All that sort of stuff when the Twickenham crowd did not take to me. I think all those sorts of things helped make me very resilient. If anything my career shows if you stick at it and work towards your goal you can achieve your dream.

CLIVE WOODWARD

After the game I am furious with Watson and talking to some players about not being in position and they just turned to me and said, 'Calm down a bit, Clive – we have just won a World Cup.'

PHIL VICKERY

I just couldn't begin to take it all in. England are world champions, we have just won the World Cup and I got to lift the Webb Ellis Trophy.

LEWIS MOODY

John Howard, the Australian Prime Minister, virtually threw our World Cup winners' medals at us.

TREVOR WOODMAN

You begin with huge relief at the final whistle and then it was just about finding your closest team-mate and giving them one of those celebration hugs. Enjoy that moment for as long as you can – get your medal, do a lap of honour, don't rush it, enjoy it because once you walk back through the tunnel that part of the whole experience has gone.

WILL GREENWOOD

I was sad that my little boy Freddie [who died after being born prematurely in 2002] wasn't there. I was tackling my heart out for him in that final. When I got my medal, I looked to the sky and hoped he was up there somewhere.

LAWRENCE DALLAGLIO

There was the extra-time drama and the epic conclusion, but my over-riding memory of the night was the sheer pleasure of sitting in the changing room for an hour or so afterwards when we shut the door and just enjoyed the moment en masse, a group of guys who possibly may never all be in the same room together again at any stage for the rest of our lives. Some were crying with the emotion, some were laughing. I was in the laughing camp.

CLIVE WOODWARD

One of the most satisfying moments for me was just sitting in the coaches' room after the final. We'd had the match, the extra time, the drop-goal, the presentation and the laps of honour. After all that we just sat on the floor together. There was Robinson, Larder, Dave Alred, all the rest. And we started giggling, we were saying: 'We did it!' Amazing moments.

KYRAN BRACKEN

I found it quite hard to cope with being on the bench for the quarter-final and the semi, even though I came on late in both. Then in the final, three of the seven subs didn't get on: myself, Martin Corry and Dorian West. It was disappointing, but I think now, 'Does it really matter if you'd got on for a minute or two at the end of the match?' I would have liked 100 caps, but there are some people who don't get one. You were there, unlike Austin Healey who was back in the UK. I felt I had played a part.

ANDY GOMARSALL

I remember at the very end of the tournament speaking to Andy Robinson. I told Andy that I was going to be the scrum-half in the next World Cup, and there and then I set the goal to play in the next World Cup final. There were

The squad celebrate their historic achievement.

some low times, but I did achieve the ambition to be there at scrum-half in the final in 2007.

JASON ROBINSON

There was no real normality after that. We had a week off and I went back into club rugby for Sale. It was a great period and we had won the World Cup. The big thing is that when the country has a big win at sport it affects so many people. And we affected millions and millions of people by winning. Even now, having retired from the sport some time ago, there are not many days go by when I am not stopped by someone to tell me where they were when England won the Rugby World Cup in 2003. It does not get better than winning a World Cup.

TREVOR WOODMAN

I was never one who ever chased the spotlight afterwards. I turned down a lot of things because it was like, 'Right I am back at the club now.' It was a matter of focusing on my rugby because that's what I enjoy doing most. When someone says, we'll pick you up, we'll do this, we'll pay you that, you can stay in a hotel – I've stayed in probably the best hotels in the world in the last six to seven months, you know, I don't want to see another hotel room.

For me, it was about going back to Gloucester, who'd got me into this position. We came back and the whole Shed was singing 'Swing Low Sweet Chariot' when Vicks and I ran on the field. You get back to people you know, friends and family and sort of enjoy the whole experience that they've been through because they make a lot of sacrifices when you're on tour.

LAWRENCE DALLAGLIO

We gave it a good belt but I still felt very energised and motivated as soon as we got home. We had five Wasps in the squad, we were all in the shape of our lives and we buckled down more or less straight away. The result was a great season and an epic Heineken Cup title. There was no sense of anti-climax and no World Cup hangover, nor has there ever been. It's all about what happens next.

JONNY WILKINSON

A problem with reaching the peak of your tallest mountain is that there is only one way to go and that is down the other side.

TREVOR WOODMAN

I enjoyed the ten-year reunion because you never really get to meet up with everyone or chat to everyone. It was really good to see how everyone was years down the road, you know, how people had changed – even Jason Robinson was drinking alcohol.

PHIL VICKERY

Winning the World Cup wasn't something that changed me as a person, I don't think. But it does change your life because you've suddenly won the ultimate rugby trophy; it changes the way people think about you. If you've had that success it is so important that you use it to inspire. That is the best thing about the entire World Cup and everything I might have achieved.

One day some time ago I went to school to pick my daughter, Megan, up and the teacher came out looking really sheepish. She said they'd been worried about what Megan had brought in that morning. She had taken my MBE insignia and my World Cup winners' medal and taken them into school for show and tell. The teacher said that they didn't know whether to put it in the safe. But you don't want to lock things away, you want to share those things. What is the use of keeping it all hidden? That's a lovely thing with rugby, that it inspires other people.

Whatever people say about me – and I can be a miserable so-and-so – I hope that we inspired people. My family had very little; the only thing we had was the love of my mum, who grafted for us. So it's also important that people understand what rugby is and the nonsense about rugby being a game for the privileged; 90 per cent of people talk about 10 per cent of the game. Go into rugby clubs wherever they are and you find what rugby really is. Yes, the elite game is brilliant, but the game is a wonderful thing apart from that – the people, the relationships, the emotions the winning, the losing, the friendships. So what if the third XV is the best you can manage? That's why you want to share things and not leave the medals hidden away.

TWENTY-TWO

DECLINE

2004-2007

ONE OF THE *most glaring flaws in the English – and British – sporting psyche in international team sports is that having sculed the summit it is rare that anyone has worked out successfully how to stay there.*

The most obvious example is the failure of England to build on winning the 1966 Football World Cup, but the rapidity of England's fall from grace after winning the 2003 Rugby World Cup comes a close second.

England were unsettled in their new status as world champions from the outset. Clive Woodward – who soon became Sir Clive Woodward after receiving a knighthood in the 2004 New Year's Honours – became disenchanted by the RFU's failure to negotiate greater access for the England coaches to the players in the squad, or to approve the new facilities he wanted.

At the same time, Woodward's single-minded pursuit of World Cup success had made him enemies as well as friends, alienating an influential caucus within the RFU committee.

There was also a sense of staleness within the squad with the senior players concerned that they were listening to the same coaching voices delivering the same messages they had heard for the previous five years.

The irony was that at the same time as England were struggling for inspiration, the Wasps team captained (like the national side) by the reinstated Lawrence Dallaglio, were kicking up a storm. Where England finished third in the 2004 Six Nations, losing their 22 match unbeaten home record to Ireland (19-13) after their line-out was picked apart, and also lost away to France – who clinched a Grand Slam with a 24-21 victory in Paris – Wasps bucked the trend.

Their young, overwhelmingly English side, coached by Warren Gatland and Shaun Edwards, won the European Cup for the first time in 2004, beating Toulouse 27-20 in an epic final at Twickenham.

Matters did not improve for England when they were ambushed on their summer tour of New Zealand. Woodward's side lost the first Test convincingly (36-3), and then, after a promising start in the second Test, were forced to play 70 minutes with 14 men after lock Simon Shaw was sent off for the use of the knee on opposite number, Keith Robinson, which was more yellow card than red.

Opposite: Martin Corry's body language epitomises the slump that hit the England team following the triumphs of 2003.

The dismissal killed the game as a contest, England eventually losing 36-12, and the deflated outfit were then overrun 51-15 by an Australian side desperate to avenge their World Cup defeat six months earlier.

With a disillusioned Woodward unable to get the off-field changes he wanted, he resigned amid an acrimonious exchange with the RFU top brass at the start of the following season, and was succeeded by his assistant, Andy Robinson.

After a bright start to the 2004 autumn series with wins over Canada (70-0) and South Africa (32-16), Robinson was criticised for his selection of a former Kiwi rugby league star, Henry Paul, against Australia – and then panned when, after multiple errors by the centre, he replaced Paul after just 26 minutes. England lost 21-19.

The perception that Robinson's selection skills were not his strong suit was reinforced in the 2005 Six Nations when he picked the novice Mathew Tait in the 11-9 defeat in Wales on the opening weekend. When the 18-year-old came second in the midfield collisions against Gavin Henson he was replaced and dropped for the remainder of the season.

The campaign was the worst for a generation, and finished badly agsin in 2006 when they lost their last three games to Scotland and France (away), and to Ireland at home. The 2006 summer tour thrashings in Australia (34-3 and 43-18) saw Robinson's stock plummet further, with the 2006 autumn series billed as make or break for the coach.

The loss to New Zealand in the opener was no shock – however, the next reverse, when Argentina claimed their first win at Twickenham (25-18) – settled Robinson's fate.

A narrow win over South Africa (23-21) in the first of the two Tests merely delayed the moment. After the Springboks won the second Test 25-14, Robinson, who had lost eight of his last nine games, left by mutual agreement.

It was a sad episode because Robinson had played an important role in England's World Cup success 25 months earlier, and, despite his intense demeanour, was well-liked. Yet, his win-loss ratio of 13 losses in 22 games, justified the decision.

With less than 10 months to the start of the next World Cup in France, the focus now turned swiftly to Robinson's successor. England world champion captain Martin Johnson, former South Africa coach Nick Mallett, Harlequins coach Dean Richards and former Wasps and Ireland coach Warren Gatland were all linked with the post. So were Andrew and England attack coach Brian Ashton.

Soon afterwards Ashton, who had a reputation as an exceptional backs coach, accepted the RFU's offer of the England head coach role. One of his first moves was to ask Jonny Wilkinson – who had not played for England for three years due to multiple injuries – if he was fit enough to make a comeback in the 2007 Six Nations.

Wilkinson, who wanted to help England to retain their title as world champions, was more than willing and responded with a virtuoso display against Scotland on the opening weekend. Wilkinson's 27 individual points haul included a 'full house' of a try, conversions (2), penalties (5) and a drop-goal, in a 42-20 victory.

However, despite following that with a home win over Italy (20-7), the malaise of skin-deep confidence resurfaced when England were destroyed in Dublin on their first visit to Croke Park, losing to Ireland by a record 43-13. A home win over France (26-18) stopped the rot, only for the season to peter out with a 27-18 defeat to Wales in Cardiff.

The robust health of the English club game contrasted starkly with the Test arena, with Wasps winning their second European Cup title by beating Leicester in an all-English final in May 2007, before going on to do the 'double' by also winning the Premiership final against Bath a week later.

A combination of internationals at those clubs being ruled out of the summer tour of South Africa by the end-of-season finals, and a rash of injuries, saw Ashton travel with a squad minus 30 leading players.

They were on a hiding to nothing, and Ashton's reputation took a pounding as understrength and outclassed England line-ups were smashed 58-10 (Bloemfontein) and 55-22 (Pretoria) by the Springboks.

It was not the best portent ahead of the 2007 World Cup, but England got back on the rails with an nine-try 62-5 rout of Wales at Twickenham as part of their warm-up. However, the two-steps-forward, two-steps-back routine under Ashton continued with two defeats by France, 21-15 at home and 22-9 in Marseille two months prior to the event.

CLIVE WOODWARD

Looking back, post-World Cup I would do so many things differently. But that is hindsight. What we didn't do well, what I didn't do well, was to actually plan 'What happens if we do win it?' You almost didn't even want to think about that – and it's probably right not to. The thought in November 2003 that in nine months I wouldn't be coaching that team, well I would have just laughed. I would have gone: 'What do you mean? I have just won the World Cup. We have won 44 out of 50 games – how could I not be coaching the team next September?'

I felt that we had won in spite of the system and the next time I wanted to win because of the system. So I wanted us to have a complete overhaul with how we dealt with the clubs and how we had access to the players. I wanted us to keep evolving – because if we stood still, others would catch us and overtake us.

MATT DAWSON

I don't think I saw the big drop in form that hit the team coming at all. Maybe we got a bit ahead of where we were. In 2004-05 we were really disappointing. There were some players who should not have played for the extra couple of years after 2003 and maybe I was in that category. But I was enjoying the euphoric wave England were on and thought it would go on forever.

JASON ROBINSON
Any team who wins the World Cup is under more pressure because every team you play against wants to beat you from then on. There were many adjustments to management and players and it was always going to be a tough time. Sometimes you have to take it on the chin. We had had the good times and it was now a time for rebuilding.

ANDY GOMARSALL
The frustration was that we had such an amazing ride, an amazing journey, but then the mood dipped, and there were loads of retirements. However, there were still a lot of experienced guys who were still young enough and still hungry, like Simon Shaw, Lewis Moody and myself, who hadn't started the final and wanted to be in the next one. There was also maybe a bit of a distraction with all the huge euphoria of the aftermath and all the celebrating, and ultimately there was a loss of form, a loss of those players which had a big impact.

BEN KAY
When you have just become world champions everyone is gunning for you and we didn't have that belief in the squad that we had built up in the six or seven years before 2003. The pressure started to build outside rather than inside and we did not deal with it particularly well up to 2007. We became reactive rather than proactive. Everyone felt really bad – the major thing was the succession planning, and we didn't really have that and we paid very heavily for it. It was a very public fall and very difficult.

LAWRENCE DALLAGLIO
The first defeat came against Ireland in the Six Nations at Twickenham, where we had not lost for four and a half years and where we had won 22 matches. Confirmation that we had allowed things to slip came at the Stade de France where we suffered defeat against France in our final game. It was Clive's seventh championship and the first campaign in which the team had lost more than one game.

BEN KAY
I am not sure if Clive had a succession plan or not, but we had never been in the position of being world champions before. We did not know how to be world

champions and there was the wrangle between Clive and Francis Baron, and it ended up with Clive leaving.

JASON ROBINSON

At the end of the day that World Cup team of 2003 was something very special. It's going to take something very special again to match where that team got to. You look through that 2003 team and everything was right. After the World Cup it was never going to be the same. You want to do your best, but... it was a difficult time because England had got used to success. We had regularly beaten New Zealand, Australia and South Africa whereas prior to that we hadn't beaten any of them home or away on a regular basis. There was a lot of weight on the shoulders of the guys. But that's just how sport goes.

CLIVE WOODWARD

I got very frustrated. I am sure people you talk to would say, 'Clive changed'. I don't think I changed. I just think that the people I was dealing with suddenly felt really threatened by me. I don't think getting a knighthood helped me one little bit. You don't apply for these things. You just get them. I think that caused a lot of problems. I could just feel it. I was going to meetings and things were different.

RICHARD HILL

We began 2004 well enough by winning 50-9 in Italy and 35-13 away to the Scots. The next game, though, was the start of the team's downfall. We hadn't lost at Twickenham for 22 matches going back to 1999, but Ireland turned us over 19-13. Our line-out went wrong that day and the Irish knocked us out of our rhythm early on. We missed certain players as calming influences and panicked a bit. We lost to France 24-21. It didn't look too bad but we were always struggling.

I suppose it is interesting to see how little most of the World Cup-winning squad played for England after Sydney – Johnno, Backy, Kyran and Jason Leonard never started an international again while Jonny had to wait four years. And as for Clive, well, he had resigned within nine months.

CLIVE WOODWARD

I am sure people on the board felt that after that I needed my wings clipped a little; they already felt I was a bit of a maverick and I honestly feel that they thought the knighthood was just going to my head and my new ideas were based on me getting ahead of myself, thinking above my station – and of course that was all bollocks. I don't think it's made any difference to me at all, I'm just the same as I've always been. It wasn't something I wanted to turn down and I took it on behalf of the team. And suddenly they were saying no to things, and that hadn't happened before. They just said, 'Go away, Clive, and do it again. You've got a four year contract, go and do it again.'

I was coming in with ideas that made complete sense and I wasn't asking for things that they couldn't afford. All I was asking was for them to take a little bit of money from one area and put it into the elite end – because that's the area that drives all of the rest of the game in England.

RICHARD HILL

The 2004 England tour to New Zealand and Australia which followed was even harder to bear. Probably for the first time, I wasn't sure about the wisdom of going.

LAWRENCE DALLAGLIO

We lost the first Test in New Zealand 36-3, the second 36-12 a week later and got smashed 51-15 by Australia. The tour disillusioned me and probably many others. Playing for England is not about getting beaten by 36 points.

RICHARD HILL

We went into the games with a new defensive system, blitz rather than up-and-out. Blitz relies on everybody moving up absolutely together. If someone is out of line it becomes very obvious. We didn't get it right that day. In Auckland we lost 36-12 and if that felt bad, worse was to come against Australia. We started that game with five players who had started in the World Cup final against the Australians. By the final whistle they had buried us 51-15. It was their first win over us for five years.

We had barely got back home and started preparing for the new season when the next shock hit us. First Lawrence called time on his England career then, in the same week, Clive called it a day. Lawrence complained about the structure of the game in England and the number of games we were playing, while Clive argued that he was not being allowed enough time with the players.

LAWRENCE DALLAGLIO

With the benefit of hindsight, the 2004 summer tour to New Zealand and Australia was a seriously bad idea. That summer we all needed a rest, players and coaches. After winning the World Cup, the team should have celebrated its status as champions by producing a string of top-class performances. Mentally and physically, we didn't have it. Trevor Woodman, Phil Vickery, Steve Thompson and Richard Hill all picked up injuries, Neil Back retired, and the pack that won the World Cup was no more.

ANDY ROBINSON

Instead of getting more time with the players, Clive was getting less and he thought, 'What's the point?' I believed I could manage this situation and get the necessary structures in place. But I couldn't.

CLIVE WOODWARD

What was really the final straw with me was I wanted to build what I called 'the pressure dome' (a high-performance centre). It's exactly what they are building at Pennyhill Park at the moment. We are now in 2014. I put forward plans in 2003. Ultimately I quit out of anger.

Do I regret it? No. But I regret bitterly the way I left. I should have left with far more grace and aplomb and explained to people, especially the players. Did the England team deserve an explanation? Absolutely. Did the English public deserve one too? Yes. Everyone did. I had had this amazing time and what I should have been doing is saying 'thank you'. Not coming across as this person who had just fallen out with everyone. I should have stepped back gracefully and said, 'Thanks everyone, especially the team, the fans.' I had a press conference which all turned a bit nasty... So I regret hugely the way that I left. Not so much leaving because I knew it was the right thing to do. Because I would have been fired if I hadn't – and I didn't want to give anybody the opportunity to fire me. That wasn't going to happen.

ANDY ROBINSON

Clive set a standard for all of us to follow. His successful record at the helm was unique and very special. It was my privilege as his assistant coach to be part of that achievement. My challenge when I took over was the next era, and to ensure the World Cup remained at Twickenham in 2007. But it was a huge task.

PHIL VICKERY

We had never won a World Cup before so no one really knew what to do. Those years were very tough. Andy Robinson is a great coach, he typifies what rugby is all about and then Brian Ashton too, a man who I have the highest respect for. But then people started talking about what it used to be like without setting out the new stall. I felt like saying, 'It's not like that any more, this is where we're at now.' You need to have a bit of a longer vision. We're in the results business and when you're used to winning, you know 80-90 per cent of all your games, and then suddenly it doesn't happen it's difficult. I'm not trying to blame anybody, but everyone was to blame really – players, coaches, and management.

MIKE CATT

There was no legacy. We didn't pass anything on. A bunch of players came in and failed to live up to their predecessors' achievements. There's been a very poor return from England in the ten years or so since we won the World Cup.

JASON ROBINSON

I was made captain for the 2005 Six Nations and it was such a fantastic experience. I look back now and think, 'How has little me from a council estate in Leeds gone on to play not only rugby league for England but to play rugby union and to be captain as well?' It was a huge responsibility but also a fantastic experience. It should have been Jonny Wilkinson, but he got injured. I could not say no to the captaincy. It was a huge responsibility, especially when there are significant changes taking place in the way the team looked.

LEWIS MOODY

The autumn Test against Samoa in 2005 made me re-address my psychology when playing. I had gone through a number of injuries and I realised, having just come back from the Lions tour, that my frustration in having not played was manifesting itself in anger on the pitch. After that game I went away and sat down with a sports psychologist. The match itself was full of cheap shots and late tackles and off the ball incidents. It culminated in Jonny Wilkinson putting across a great kick into Mark Cueto who competed for the ball with Alex [Alesana Tuilagi]. The clash finished in Cuets landing on his head and I went over to separate the two. I knew Cuets was a fiery character and Alex also. I tried to separate them and got tangled up in the middle... Alex then caught Cuets with a punch to the head and I reacted in a way I should not have done. I was sent off and became the first Englishman to be sent off at Twickenham. My first instinct was to separate the two but the red mist then came over. We quickly made up afterwards, shook hands and embraced. That's rugby.

LAWRENCE DALLAGLIO

The 2006 Six Nations wasn't a good time for England and neither was it much fun for Martin [Corry] or me. In that campaign I spent far more time warming up on the stationary bikes that England's replacements use than actually performing on the pitch. It led to some funny texts. 'Don't think you'll be winning the Grand Slam this year but I'd back you to win the Tour de France,' wrote one. I felt for Martin because I had captained England on days when we were stuffed and it's no fun. The next day you feel you can't walk down to the local shop and buy a pint of milk without the sense of shame being written across your face. I had a long conversation with Andy Robinson, who was a coach I admired. We had a very honest talk during which he asked what I thought he could do to improve as a coach. 'Perhaps if you would pick up the phone and talk to players on a more regular basis it might help,' I said. 'Tell guys how good they are and generally treat them like human beings, and you'll get a phenomenal response.'

MARTIN CORRY (England 1997-2007, 64 caps plus 7 caps for the Lions)
Every single game we played I thought we were going to win it. I never thought, 'We are rubbish and this is terrible.' But if I knew what went wrong it would not have happened. We had beaten Australia in 2005 and South Africa in 2004 at Twickenham and people were saying we should have beaten New Zealand in 2005 when we lost 23-19. So it was not all doom and gloom, but 2005 to 2006 was a really difficult time and as a team we were just not good enough. I know Andy Robinson took a lot of flak but you can't make a silk purse out of a sow's ear. We'd taken a lot of criticism and in my eyes the vast majority of it was justified. People used to say, 'It's England and everyone else' but we had fallen behind Ireland in the rankings and northern hemisphere rugby was the most competitive it had ever been. So many games were won or lost by one score.

The nights were the worst. I couldn't help replaying the games in my head, again and again. If I got a couple of hours' sleep after a loss I'd take that as a good night. The instinct was that nothing would help until you pulled the boots on again. That's what made a Saturday or Sunday night pretty hopeless. You couldn't even talk to your teammates and say, 'Right, this is what we do to get things back on track.' It's only on Monday when you started training again that you began to lose the pain.

ANDY ROBINSON
There's no hiding from it – especially when we lost 31-6 to France in Paris – we were awful.

JOSH LEWSEY
The France game was a shambles. It was an embarrassment in terms of the players involved in it, for everyone involved in the RFU and for every England supporter, and it is them you feel sorry for. It was a sad state of affairs. England is the wealthiest union in the world with the biggest player base and a competitive league and as far as we saw it, there was no reason why we shouldn't be the best in the world.

LAWRENCE DALLAGLIO
On and off the field, we were letting standards fall... After the victory against Italy in 2006, it was decided that because Matt Dawson and I had come on so late in the game, we could return to London that night and play for Wasps the next day.

That was fine but we needed to get from the ground to the airport and, standing outside the Stadio Flaminio, we realised no-one had pre-booked a taxi. We waited for ages, eventually got a cab, ran like lunatics through the airport check-in, arrived sweating like mad and missed the flight. Useless!

ANDY GOODE (England 2005-2009, 17 caps)
We played some decent rugby against Ireland at Twickenham in 2006 and they scored three tries that, on another day, they might not have been given. We got pretty close to winning it, but a bounce of the ball and a couple of decisions denied us. The first try was shown on the big screen. Afterwards the touch judge was smiling under the posts when he realised he'd made a mistake. When your luck's down, things like that tend to go against you.

LAWRENCE DALLAGLIO
After that Ireland match I went into the toilet area alongside our changing room and spoke with Andy. 'I'm sorry you didn't get on,' he said. 'Just explain one thing here,' I responded, 'because there's something I don't understand. Of the 44 players involved in today's match, I was the only one who didn't enter the field of play. And of the 44, I'm the most experienced, the guy with 76 caps... Surely you realised when we went in front with Steve Borthwick's try that was the time to get me on. If we lost then, you could have blamed me.' I left Twickenham a very disillusioned man that evening. I just thought, 'Lawrence, you're fooling yourself here... You haven't come back for this.'

ANDY ROBINSON
We looked back at the stats after we were hammered 43-18 in Melbourne in the summer of 2006 and saw that we had had 63 per cent of the possession. But it's about what you do with that possession. We turned over 27 balls and our game management was so poor. I'd said for a long time that the Premiership was good at developing good international rugby players, but it was not developing world-class players. We had to reflect on how we gave players the opportunity to become world-class.

MARTIN CORRY
Look at the two games we played against South Africa back-to-back in 2006. Jake White was under huge pressure, and so was Robbo, and the second game was one where everyone was saying that the coach who lost would get the sack. We were 14-3 up going into the last ten minutes of the first half and had just scored. I was telling everyone, 'Just give 100 per cent concentration and don't give them a sniff.' They

kicked off long and we went back under our posts and gave them a scrum and they scored. We kicked off, they came back and we gave them a penalty and they were in front at half-time. That was where we were as a side. We could play well but it was built on flaky foundations and when the pressure came on we did not have belief.

We should have won that match but there is a fine line between winning and losing, and confidence is a big part of getting you over the line. After 35 minutes of that game Jake White was gone – he was writing his resignation letter – and we let them back into the game. How can coaches be responsible for things like that? That is really down to the players.

ANDY ROBINSON

A key mistake was my inability to manage upwards. I didn't manage Francis Baron and the management board well enough to get the necessary changes. I asked to be allowed to work with somebody to achieve that. Eventually Rob Andrew came in as a director of rugby and the changes that I wanted in 2005 were in place after the 2007 World Cup. Why did we waste two years?

I became a bit like the Monty Python character, Black Knight, who gets his arm chopped off, says it's only a flesh wound, and keeps fighting. He gets his other arm chopped off, but he's still fighting. His legs get taken off; he still keeps battling. That's how it became. Ultimately you're just going down and down, lessening your own performance. I just accepted things I shouldn't have accepted. I allowed the New Zealand game to be added to the autumn fixture list in 2006 when I knew it was wrong and would have knock-on effects, but I didn't say, 'No, we can't have this, because it gives us four extremely tough Tests on four consecutive weekends'. I should have been true to myself. It's a question of restraining the warrior spirit, then standing back and seeing the bigger picture.

Another thing – for me to allow Phil Larder and Dave Alred to be made redundant, two quality coaches, that was wrong. There were mistakes and I've got to accept responsibility for not managing things better. I had six great years with England, even if the last six months were deeply disappointing. Our strength as a family helped us to get through the tough times, and there were some very tough moments for the kids, whether at school or on the rugby pitch, where people have had a go at them. 'Your dad's a rubbish coach.' Dealing with that has been hard for them. But they came through it and I just don't know why people should be that nasty. To level that at a vulnerable child… boy against boy I could understand, but I've heard a couple of coaches from opposition teams levelling it at my son. But it teaches you a lot about your family and the strength they give you.

I was confident that I would coach the England team through to a successful

World Cup in 2007, notwithstanding the setbacks that we had through the autumn of 2006. It was my understanding that I had the support of the England players and the England management team, but the RFU management board would not continue to support me as England head coach.

ROB ANDREW (1985-1997, 71 caps plus 5 caps for the Lions)
The decision to terminate Andy's contract was made with a great deal of regret. He'd played a significant part in England's Grand Slam, unbeaten tour to Australia and New Zealand, and World Cup success in 2003. He also recorded excellent wins against Australia, South Africa and Wales during his tenure as head coach and was always totally committed to the role. Unfortunately, with the exception of the win against South Africa, England's run of results just weren't good enough for him to continue.

ANDY ROBINSON
You deal with it. I loved my whole time coaching England. I don't really want to dwell on what's been and gone but rugby is about winning, that's what counts. That's the big lesson I learned, this game is about winning. The way that we play, the style, the performance, doesn't matter. You've got to win the game.

LAWRENCE DALLAGLIO
Walking into the England camp under Brian Ashton, my first impression was of a man determined not to follow the Clive Woodward blueprint. Clive used to have meetings about having meetings, but then you always knew what the plan was, on and off the field. Brian's England was different. But as you looked closer, it was obvious all wasn't well. Our three principal coaches were Brian, John Wells and Mike Ford. Brian wanted England playing with width and imagination, while John Wells had a very different view. He is the epitome of Leicester; great set pieces, a bit of a dog and a lot of efficiency. They didn't appear to gel, something that players will pick up on in a millisecond. It seemed to me that the difficulty lay in Brian's personality and the issue of whether he was particularly comfortable in the role of overall boss.

BRIAN ASHTON (England backs coach 1998-2002, England head coach 2006-08)
It has been well-chronicled and I've never denied that I passed over a lot of responsibility to the players. I felt that was the right thing to do with where we were at the time. I happen to believe I managed the situation. I have never seen a coach or manager cross the line and take part in a game.

JONNY WILKINSON

I was quite surprised, a couple of days into the new year [2007], when I got the call from Brian Ashton. I hadn't played any rugby for over two months but Brian asked if I was ready to come back to play for England. I'd been out for over three years so I was never going to say no, and he picked me to play against Scotland. It was unbelievable how well that comeback game went. Looking back, I am glad that I got injured, to a degree... because it enriched my career afterwards in terms of experience, in terms of coaching, in terms of progressing as a player and a person too.

Yeah, there are games that have worked out, winning the European Cup late in the career was something that you search for but you don't bargain for. Obviously there is the World Cup and things like that, they're fabulous, but doing what is written in the sports books is never the whole story. It's never been that satisfying. Looking back on the World Cup in 2003, it doesn't satisfy me, it happened when I was 24 years old. What does satisfy me is knowing that day in and day out I went for it and I loved doing what I was doing.

BRIAN ASHTON

Jonny had a voracious appetite for the rough and tumble aspect of the sport, to the extent that it was devilishly difficult to stop him involving himself in the tackle area, whether or not he was the actual tackler. I can think of very few other backs, and no outside-halves, who had to be held back from hitting too many rucks. It was a reflection of his nature, of his enthusiasm for rugby. This remarkable physicality took its toll: between 2003 and 2007, Jonny experienced more injury trauma than any professional sportsman should have to suffer. Yet he battled through regardless, and it seemed to have a positive effect on his outlook, rather than a negative one: indeed, it appeared to bolster his already exceptional determination. When he returned to the England side after a prolonged absence, against Scotland in 2007, my first game as head coach, he was brilliant.

JONNY WILKINSON

I struggled with the frustration and disappointment of not playing for the three or four years in between the 2003 World Cup final, when I was injured the whole time, and coming back and playing for England in 2007. I lost a lot of my identity and my value, I really struggled without rugby. But then when I came back, the expectation was so mismatched because when I played my first game for England for three years I hadn't actually played a minute of rugby in the previous three months because I had punctured my kidney. I'd suffered fourteen injuries on the trot and there was only one that was a repeat – I did one knee twice in a row, but the rest of them were somewhere else on my body every time. And with each injury

I felt like I was getting further and further away from where I'd been in 2003 – not so much physically because I was training harder than ever, but mentally. Watching people doing what you want to do is so difficult and I felt myself just getting lower and lower. I think it was in 2006, around a year before I came back, that it just got to its worst. I suddenly turned inwards on myself and my obsessive side went from being a massive help on the field to being a massive problem off it. Then, when I made the comeback, I probably went about it the wrong way. I was holding on to the way things had been before all the injuries. I wish I had just looked at it and realised that times had changed and it was time to start a new path for myself and my career. It took me a while to come to that conclusion.

NICK EASTER (England 2007-2011, 47 caps)
Initially, I thought I would be just going to Bath, where England were training, to be a bit of cannon fodder. I got down to the hotel and was told Brian Ashton wanted to see me. He said, 'Congratulations, you are starting next weekend.' It took me completely off guard. I had been unaware that Joe Worsley had injured his neck against Scotland.

In the end I was happy with my game although the match itself [against Italy at Twickenham] wasn't as free flowing as we would have liked. I must admit after that first cap it was quite a messy night. Back then, you had to have a drink with every member of the squad and to sing a song on the bus.

JONNY WILKINSON
England-Scotland was a ludicrous game because it went so well. We didn't play so well against Italy, but we won 20-7. Then we had to travel to Dublin to play at Croke Park where we faced the most passionate Ireland performance that I had ever had the misfortune to come up against. We were blown off the field. We were 23-3 down at half-time.

BRIAN ASHTON
The Wales game wasn't much better. We needed to beat them by 57 points to overtake France to win the title, while Wales were trying to avoid the wooden spoon. I thought we maybe had a chance to do it. But Wales led 15-0 after 15 just minutes and 18-15 at half-time, and although we managed to draw level in the second half, they went on to beat us 27-18.

It was obviously hugely disappointing to finish the tournament like that, but we had to shift our focus pretty quickly and turn our attention to preparing over the summer for the World Cup in France later that year.

TWENTY-THREE

LONG RUN FROM THE BACK

2007

T HIS WAS AN *extraordinary odyssey for England rugby. It was a tournament in which they plumbed the depths, played occasionally as badly as any England team has played in any World Cup, and yet they made such an incredible late run in the tournament after they had been written off and even humiliated, that it could be said that they came within millimetres of retaining the title.*

It is possibly true that had they indeed repeated the win of 2003 then it would not have said too much about global rugby standards in 2007, but on the other hand, never in their history had England failed to react to adversity, and the team from nowhere was to come so close.

The world champions crown always sat heavily on English heads. There were hopes after 2003 that the triumph would be the start of hegemony but, in fact, it was a high point followed by a rapid and worrying decline which had seen Sir Clive Woodward and Andy Robinson both leave the position of head coach.

Whereas the 2003 team had gone storming into the World Cup as the number one ranked team in the world, England in 2007 almost tip-toed over the Channel for the event. The coaching tenure of Brian Ashton had begun only nine months before the World Cup and he had problems in reversing the decline. Ashton had always been seen as one of England's cutting-edge coaches, especially with his visionary ideas in attack, and the tournament would indicate whether he was a natural fit for the number one position as well.

Under the captaincy of Phil Vickery, the warrior prop, England were still able to call on some veterans of 2003, such as Lawrence Dallaglio, Jason Robinson and Mike Catt, though for various reasons, none reached the form of their greatest years – and Dallaglio had to be content with a place on the bench for major matches.

The team was in a state of flux even as it gathered for the tournament, a situation never alleviated as things progressed. Jonny Wilkinson, who had endured horrendous periods of injured absence since 2003, was back in the fold but his performance levels were never quite as high, even though his aura was undiminished.

England did appear to have power up front, with a Vickery and the mighty Andrew Sheridan seen throughout the world as formidable scrummagers, with the combative Mark Regan at hooker and Simon Shaw and Ben Kay still around in the second-row

– and both played to their normal elevated standards – with the experienced Martin Corry influential in the back-row and Nick Easter installed as a ball-carrying No 8.

One of Ashton's priorities was clear – he had to develop an all-round attacking game to take advantage of this forward power. He had available Andy Farrell, a great former rugby league player – but whose transition to his new code had been savaged by injury. Olly Barkley's footballing ability gave England presence in midfield but the backs were never to fire, even though scrum-half Andy Gomarsall came through to have his best time in the England jersey.

It was a bizarre campaign from the start. England opened against the United States in Lens and struggled horribly against a rather limited opponent, winning 28-10, although even that margin flattered them. Robinson, Barkley (who was to shine during the tournament) and Tom Rees scored tries but there was a notable lack of dynamism and energy about proceedings. Rees, incidentally, was to suffer injury in the pool stages and was overtaken by Lewis Moody for the position on the openside. This was just one in a succession of injuries which eventually forced Rees retire, a great loss to the English game.

The USA game was also poor preparation for the first of the mighty challenges. Just as in the 2003 World Cup, it was clear from an early stage that the game most likely to decide the pool would be that between South Africa and England.

And it did. England were massacred, and the Springboks won 36-0 without ever really extending themselves, and with Wilkinson missing these early games through injury there was a total lack of presence about the team. They also lost Robinson to a hamstring injury, and there was a warmer moment when the whole stadium applauded him as he limped from the field, an ovation which included the South African contingent on the bench.

At this stage, the remaining pool matches loomed as a fierce assignment for England, with both Samoa and Tonga standing in the way of qualification, and both of those Pacific island teams were much improved. As it was, with Wilkinson back in the fold and with Gomarsall teaming up with him at half-back, England were significantly improved against Samoa in Nantes, winning 44-22 with two tries each from Corry and the dangerous Paul Sackey on the wing. Wilkinson, without ever being dominant in the run of play, scored 24 points with the boot.

There was much talk in and around the England camp at this stage of what amounted to crisis meetings, with hard talk from the players and suggestions that coach Ashton had been forced to change the shape of the team and the way they played, which before the clash with Samoa had been horrendously stilted.

England still needed to beat Tonga in the final pool game in the Parc des Princes in Paris and the Tongans took an early lead. However, England again showed improvement, Sackey scored two more tries in a period of the tournament when he was one of the most dangerous runners. Mathew Tait added another from midfield and Farrell scored a try at a crucial stage.

The final score was 36-20, England had qualified, if rather fitfully, for the quarter-finals stages and while the team showed signs of coming together going into that quarter-final, against Australia in Marseille, they were still the rankest of outsiders. Cohesion and true star quality had eluded them.

Then, the miracle. That day in Marseille will never fade in the memory. First, England overpowered Australia when Sheridan and Vickery and company demolished the Wallaby scrum. Australia had motored impressively through their pool but ran into an England team revived and playing with iron will. Looking back, it seems bizarre that England won only 12-10 – with four Wilkinson penalties – and that Stirling Mortlock of Australia had a long shot at goal which may have won it for Australia.

But England, almost from nowhere, had found a shape and a spirit, Ashton had focused them and the big forwards had done the rest. Later that same day over in Cardiff, France ejected favourites New Zealand from the tournament, and in the old port area of Marseille that evening there were vast thousands of celebrating English and French, celebrations tempered only by the knowledge that the two teams would meet in the World Cup semi-final in Paris, a match clean out of the blue.

By the time of the semi-final, the English nation had woken up to their unlikely heroes and Paris was suddenly awash with white jerseys. Although France had lost, sensationally, in the opening game of the tournament, beaten by an inspired Argentina, Les Bleus had their monumental win over New Zealand to inspire them. As they prepared for battle in a semi-final for which they were warm favourites, however, there were signs that the pressure on them was growing, and that they were having difficulty living down in their hearts and minds the threat of Wilkinson and England. There were memories of the semi of 2003, and England's win.

As it turned out, the English revival continued. They won 14-9 to reach their second World Cup final in succession and to win the first match against France on French soil for seven years. They began beautifully when a chip ahead by the increasingly influential Gomarsall brought a try in the left-hand corner from Josh Lewsey – sadly, he was injured in the match and missed the final. Wilkinson kicked England home with two penalties and a drop goal and France, dumped from their own tournament, were devastated by their own paucity.

Matters then went into overdrive as the final approached – against South Africa. Vast armies of English fans arrived, hotels were booked solid for miles outside Paris, and many fans arrived simply to watch the game on giant screens. There was fervent hope that Vickery's men could pull it off against what was believed to be a fine, powerful yet not a vintage South African team.

As it turned out, South Africa were just too good in what was, for the neutral, a disappointing final, winning by five penalties to two by Wilkinson. England could never really establish themselves in the game, and the only dazzling attack they launched began when fullback Mathew Tait carved through the middle and sent Mark Cueto diving over the line in the left-hand corner. A try then could easily have altered the whole shape of the game but after protracted examination, the television match official ruled that, by millimetres, Cueto had put a foot out of play before he touched down. It was a decision which Cueto himself was always to dispute, and England after that could never shake themselves free of the grip of the South African forwards, and ultimately the long run of the English finished just short of a remarkable success.

The post-tournament analysis was also difficult as people contemplated the grim build-up, the mediocrity of the opening stages and the joyous and hopeful nature of the knock-out stages. There was nothing predictable about England, although, in the final analysis, for them to reach the final of the World Cup without any initial momentum, was a stunning achievement.

BRIAN ASHTON

When you looked at the players who possibly would be available for the 2007 World Cup, many had been there, done it before and were playing well in the Premiership. My hope was that over the period of time of a tournament, they would galvanise into a team that was very difficult to beat. By and large, that is what happened. We weren't the prettiest side in the world but not many liked playing us.

TOM REES (England 2007-2008, 15 caps)

I had been capped in the Six Nations and I had had a good build-up to it, things had been going well. We were staying in sensational hotels – the nicest ones I had ever been in – and I turned 23 when we were at the World Cup. I was just enjoying it. There did not seem more pressure because we had won it in 2003. I had not been involved then and we had not been hugely successful in the run-up.

LEWIS MOODY

In 2003 we wanted to be the best and fittest team in the world. We set high standards and it helped us to grow the spirit within the squad. In 2007 it was the exact opposite. The team kept changing and we had no consistency. The captaincy kept changing as well. It was just all up in the air. Just before the start of the 2007 World Cup when I was battling injury, was the worst time of my career.

BRIAN ASHTON

You want players to express themselves in all regards, to help create the right environment. At the World Cup, the environment ended up creating itself, and there's nothing wrong with that. We all had to be adaptable, and although adaptability is one of the traits I want, I hope we don't have to be as adaptable as that in the future. The beginning of the World Cup was bizarre. We didn't get there until the Monday of the opening week, and as we ran out against the USA for the first game, I was thinking, 'Blimey, where's the preparation time gone?' On reflection, we could have handled that better.

SIMON SHAW

That campaign gave me tremendous satisfaction because I had missed out on 2003, when I travelled but didn't play. I loved the 2007 World Cup. It's probably the reason why I went to Toulon for the last couple of years of my career. People talk about South Africa and New Zealand, but the passion for rugby in France is amazing. I just loved the whole thing. For many of us, such as Andy Gomarsall, Mark Regan, Martin Corry, and Lewis Moody – those of us who spent 2003 on the bench – it was a realisation of our ambitions. And we did it when no one gave us a chance of reaching the final.

Brian Ashton had taken on the team and had not an awful lot of time to work on things. It was the most close-knit England team I had ever been involved with. We all got on and that was shown in our style of play. We did not play champagne-style rugby but we had so much guts and just battled it out for each other, especially in the later stages.

MARK CUETO (England 2004-2011, 55 caps plus 1 cap for the Lions)

I struggled with injury in the build-up and it affected me in the tournament. I missed all the pre-World Cup games but still made it out to France. I learned an unbelievable amount from that campaign through all the different emotions. It was an incredible experience.

NICK EASTER

The 2007 World Cup is a bitter-sweet memory. It was the best time I had with England – it was an incredible journey to the final. The group ended up becoming very tight, which wasn't the case when we came together because there was a real mix of new and old and a lot of players in the squad who had not played in the Six Nations or been on the South African tour that summer. We had a 10-week build-up which took us from being with the Royal Marines in Poole, to Portugal and then to our base in Bath in order to get the best preparation.

JONNY WILKINSON

Because I had been out of the game for so long I found that the simple connection between the players wasn't there and then everything you do feels like you're trying to force it. I was playing with guys who had never even seen me play rugby because I'd been injured so long. Guys didn't know how to talk to each other: 'Apparently this guy played in 2003 and I'm supposed to respect him but I've never met him.' I was supposed to tell these guys what to do, but I didn't know if they believed in me yet, and on the pitch I didn't know where the ball was going to go.

JASON ROBINSON

It was a total contrast to 2003, when we all knew each other inside out and had been together for a long time. We knew what was expected. But in 2007 that was not the case. There was chopping and changing, and injuries. We hadn't had a great run going into the tournament and had been unable to play consistently well. It was quite a different challenge but we did have some talented players. We struggled through the pool stages and we weren't very convincing.

BRIAN ASHTON

It was the biggest tournament in world rugby and we all felt privileged to be involved in it, but we had a crisis because Jonny Wilkinson had injured his ankle. Going into the USA game I wanted a win, a performance and no injuries. I got two out of the three.

PHIL VICKERY

Before the match against America we got fed up talking about things. I must have gone to 400 press conferences and I couldn't remember looking forward to a game as much as that. The build-up dragged on and on and we were fed up with training. It made the hairs on the back of my head stand-up thinking about getting started.

LAWRENCE DALLAGLIO

I had first shot at it [the number eight position] and blew the assignment against the USA. I looked no further than myself in terms of blame.

JOSH LEWSEY

The players knew that the USA game was a disaster but we had to stick together.

LEE MEARS (England 2005-2012, 42 caps plus 1 cap for the Lions)
Our opening match was a hard-fought 28-10 victory against the USA. The

scoreline suggests a relatively comfortable win, but the reality was a poor English performance. Next up were the South Africans, the match we try to forget. We were outplayed in a 36-0 mauling which left me finding it hard to come to terms with the fact that our preparation had been so magnificent and yet within a couple of weeks everything was turning sour.

ANDREW SHERIDAN (England 2004-2011, 40 caps plus 2 caps for the Lions)
I thought we were all physically in good condition and the warm-up games had gone quite well – and then it all came crashing down when we lost 36-0 to South Africa.

SIMON SHAW

I have always been disappointed in how we have been described after the pool game against South Africa. We were incredibly depressed about being described as the worst defending champions ever. During the game I thought we had got them because, as a forward pack, we were very confident against them. I wondered what we could have done differently. The bounce of the ball did not go our way and Fourie du Preez had a blinder at scrum-half. We could not say we were awful in any department. The Springboks just exploited every mistake we made.

ANDY GOMARSALL

I found myself on the bench against South Africa and when we went into the changing room at the interval and sat there in silence and Brian just looked at me and he said, 'You're on.' That was it. I got the guys up, we all got into a huddle and we just took over from that moment. I felt the style we were playing wasn't the way Brian wanted to play so I took over with Jonny, Olly Barkley people like that, the decision makers, and we actually played better in the second half but we were so far away.

JASON ROBINSON

The first hamstring injury I got, I thought, 'Oh no,' because I was on 48 caps and I really wanted to get to 50 because I knew I was retiring from international rugby at the end of the tournament. I should not have played again in the tournament because the medics said it would normally take five weeks to recover. I got back within two and a half weeks, but during each game I tore some of the hamstring fibres again in each match. I managed to get through, and looking back now a lot of credit has to go to the physios and doctors because so many of us were on the treatment table. They were patching us up right, left and centre.

LEWIS MOODY

There were a lot of frustrations. We lost our captain [Phil Vickery] to suspension after the first game. Martin Corry took over a role he had relinquished six months earlier. I never felt we were prepared for that World Cup and it was only after the drubbing by South Africa that we sat down and said it was not good enough and attempted to address the issues alongside the coaches.

MARTIN CORRY

The lowest point I have been was after that 36-0 defeat by South Africa. We were playing as individuals. Brian was a very different coach to Clive Woodward and Andy Robinson, who were very prescriptive. Brian is a facilitator and we needed

Nick Easter offloads the ball against Samoa.

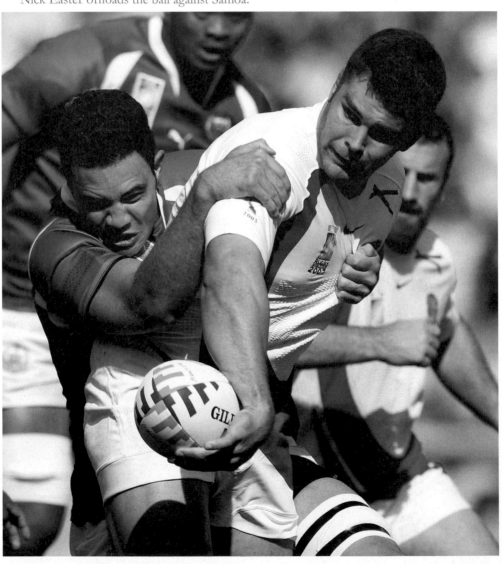

someone more prescriptive because confidence was so low. The great thing about being in that situation [before the Australia game] is that nobody gives you a chance and everybody writes you off. The over-riding feeling for me was that if we had lost that quarter-final then all that people were going to remember was the 36-0 game and I couldn't have that as the stand-out memory of the World Cup. We needed to show everybody how important playing for England was for the players.

NICK EASTER

The South Africa match was played on a Friday night. Everyone was devastated but we had Saturday off and did not meet up until the Sunday when we had a crisis meeting. The coaches wanted feedback and it was a desperate situation. It was much to do with ball in hand. There were a few issues to sort out over defence – we had conceded 36 points – but we failed to put pressure on when we had possession, and didn't know what we were trying to achieve from our game plan with the ball.

After about two hours things were sorted out as well as they could be given we had the hard-hitting Samoa and Tonga in our next games. Those wins made us more battle hardened and more confident by the time of the quarter final.

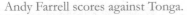

Andy Farrell scores against Tonga.

ANDY GOMARSALL

We all had this meeting afterwards and a couple of guys put their hands up after analysis and said it was their fault. I sat there and thought, 'We haven't actually sorted anything out here,' and a few of us that stayed back – about six of us. Eventually Brian came back into the room and we questioned him and he said, 'Well this is what I tried telling you, this is what I want.' We said it wasn't the message we were getting. Obviously there was a difference of opinion among the coaching staff and there was no internal organisation.

JONNY WILKINSON

Word was that we had been 'humiliated'. I disagreed with that, but frustration in the camp was tangible. Something had to be done. At the next squad meeting, a few home truths were finally laid on the line. We didn't really know what we're doing out there. That was the message from the players to Brian. Olly Barkley delivered it in the strongest language. He told Brian that we didn't have a clue. Brian could have dug in his heels and refused to listen. But he is not like that. So he did the opposite. He heard our grievances and invited us to come up with the solution and wanted us to deliver it our way. This smart bit of player empowerment took the sting out of the situation. Soon, another meeting was under way. The main playmakers were encouraged to discuss how we wanted to play. Immediately, there was a connection. I'd not played a lot with Olly but he and I seemed to share the same vision for the structure, Catty was on board, too. We had a game plan. The next question was whether we could play it.

ANDY GOMARSALL

We weren't idiots, we knew what we were doing and we were being forced to play a structured game, but structure sometimes doesn't work. South Africa killed us. We had one of the best players in the world, Jonny Wilkinson, at No 10 and I was asking why we weren't giving the ball to the best people on the pitch, why were we trying to get this go-forward game and getting absolutely smashed.

MARK CUETO

There was a conflict of ideas and interests in how we wanted to go forward. But the differences are always so minimal. It's not like a completely different concept. It is pretty well documented that the players got together with the coaches and thrashed it out.

PHIL VICKERY

There were lots of big personalities among the players and coaches, we got quite emotional and had a little bit of a rant and stuff but after about half an hour we all realised we all wanted the same thing. You start off at loggerheads but then when we actually sat down and talked about it, it got clearer.

MARTIN CORRY

After that South Africa pool match we changed a few things to make it a bit more prescriptive – it was rugby by numbers but it did not really show in the Samoa game because we were still learning.

ANDREW SHERIDAN

We managed somehow to get through to a quarter-final against Australia, where the world and his dog thought we'd succumb to a pretty severe drubbing. I remember Graham Rowntree speaking to the forwards before we left for the game that day, and although I'm not normally a fan of great Churchillian-like speeches before a game of rugby, the emotion, the content and the intensity with which he spoke truly struck a chord with all of us.

MIKE CATT

That tournament proved how resilient and competitive the England rugby team is. When they have time together and time to gel it is a hell of a wagon to stop.

JASON ROBINSON

When you have characters like we had there's always going to be a few challenging times. Ultimately, you have to pull together and do your best to try to win the games. When we turned up for that quarter-final against Australia many people thought we weren't going to win. And no wonder. But we put in a performance and everyone wanted to be an England fan again and you couldn't get a ticket for the games.

TOM REES

There was no sense in the camp that the quarter-final was a lost cause. There was an overriding sense that we had things to put right but that it just hadn't clicked yet. We knew we just had to go out there and be a bit smarter, and there was just an overwhelming sense of frustration that we hadn't been playing as well as we could have. I was rested for the Samoa game and in between that and the Tonga game I got a hamstring tweak and Lewis Moody went out there and had a stormer. That was my World Cup.

ANDY GOMARSALL

I remember getting out of bed, showering and drawing back the curtains to see bright blue sky. We'd been told the forecast was for rain and at that stage, with our confidence at best fragile, we believed that our best opportunity of beating Australia was in the wet. We required something to level things up a bit. This was not going to be my day, or England's, I told myself.

LEWIS MOODY

It was credit to all the coaches for the analysis they did and credit to the players for taking it in hand. We took one focus into each game. John Wells had realised that the Australians had had an easy run at the breakdown and they were not putting numbers in. They were able to win the ball quickly and to dominate their games. This helped them score a truckload of tries. Our focus was that every time we got into contact we would flood the breakdown because they were so used to putting one or two players into the breakdown. They were not ready for us – and Vickery, Regan and Sheridan were so dominant in the scrum. Sheridan was an absolute machine that day, he destroyed them.

ANDREW SHERIDAN

Weight training was something I have always enjoyed. Something I got a high from doing. There is definitely something addictive about it. That's partly down to the improvement you can see, but it's also to do with how you feel afterwards.

England's scrum, spearheaded by Andrew Sheridan, was decisive in the quarter-final victory over Australia.

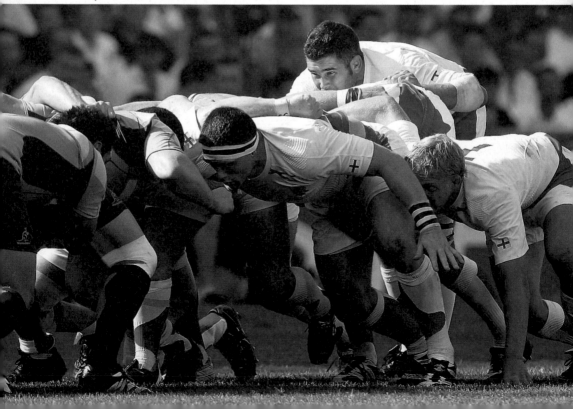

They talk about endorphins or something being released – not that you can go and pick up your car after a hard session, but you do feel good. I liked the feeling of being able to shift a weight that to the average person seems very heavy. It's whatever works for you. Some people get that feeling from having a cigarette; others will have a large scotch.

I remember the first game I played at prop for Bristol, it was against Newport and a prop called Rod Snow. After the first half I sat in the dressing room and I couldn't get my chin off my neck. My neck muscles weren't used to it, and that's where the pressure goes. After that I went back to playing No 6 and No 8 and it was the following season that I made the permanent move to prop.

Phil Keith-Roach, the England scrummaging coach, helped me to make the change and you learn as you go along, especially from those opponents who make you struggle. And there were guys like Jason Leonard, who was always open to helping. I have spoken to him a few times since I moved to prop and you couldn't meet a nicer bloke.

There is no secret to the way I try to scrummage, I don't try to be underhand about it. I try to get into my strongest possible position to use my strength. Sometimes I am able to, sometimes the other scrum and the other prop are able to put me into a position that I can't use my strength to the maximum.

Martin Corry celebrates at fulltime in Marseille.

PHIL VICKERY

George Gregan was having a go at me on the early stages after I gave a few penalties away and it wasn't about me being fat for a change. He was saying, 'Thanks for the leg up mate, didn't realise you were going to make it this easy for us.' Then things started to change. We were hammering them in the scrum. We did everything that we practised on the training field and we absolutely battered them. I don't like seeing other people suffer but I love seeing an Australian disappointed and I remember seeing George Gregan on that field on his haunches, tears running down his face. I've got a lot of respect for him but I knew they were on the next flight home. That made my day.

ANDY GOMARSALL

I got to George Gregan during the game, which gave me amazing confidence. We ruffled them in the rucks, we got in their faces. They were shocked and they didn't have an answer to it, which was amazing for such an experienced team. We battered them, it was just the best feeling in the world. George is one the greatest scrum-halves ever to play and he's a good friend, but that was an amazing experience for me. The forwards were phenomenal – Sheridan, Vickery, Regan, Shaw, Kay, all of them. After the game I collapsed, I was so emotional. Suddenly you realise we're in the semi-final. Later that night as New Zealand lost to France, we realised we were playing the host nation.

PHIL VICKERY

Shez and Ronnie [Sheridan and Regan] were awesome that day. They proved that rugby hasn't changed a huge amount in that sense, if you can get some dominance up front you are still going to choke the other team.

We had to strip everything back going into it – no good thinking ahead, it's right now, this moment, this lineout, this tackle, this breakdown, that pass, that break, that clear-out. I hated getting beaten but I remember lots of things I talked about before that game – don't come off the field with any regrets, so we can look each other in the eye afterwards, no matter what.

NICK EASTER

It was a scorching hot day in Marseille but we still managed to play well and surprised the Wallabies. They missed a penalty in the last minute and we managed to hang on.

JONNY WILKINSON

Despite everything, something amazing happened out there on that Marseille pitch. We won it. We were still alive. The atmosphere afterwards was incredible. There were moments when I thought we'd be going home, and in the changing room, everyone was saying the same, laughing, amazed. Cozza [Martin Corry] had so much tape holding him together, he looked like Mumm-Ra the Ever-Living from the cartoons. Lewis [Moody] is bruised and battered and looked like he's been to war. And Simon Shaw was a bit older than us but consistently world-class. I loved playing with that guy.

MIKE CATT

Beating Australia in the quarter-final was an amazing feeling because, before the match in Marseille, I had a call from my tearful young daughter asking when I was coming home. I replied, 'Don't worry I will home on Monday.' Pretty much everyone had written us off in Marseille so it was a great win. I remember telling Jonny it could be my last game of international rugby and I did not want to go home without trying our best to win. We played some good rugby and surprised everybody. But, like the 2003 group, we had some amazing people – players and coaches.

TOM REES

It was bitter sweet – I wanted to be out there. I felt I had played okay in the first two games and I was putting myself about well but given how the team went changing things and given how well Lewis Moody played I can't complain. For those 80 minutes in that stadium in the sunshine it was fantastic. The Samoa and Tonga games had been different types of opposition and although they are hard to beat, to go into a game against Australia and perform like that showed us how far we could go and showed how far that group had come. We had a pack that just drove into Australia and the guys behind were committed – everybody puffed out their chest and showed a lot of resilience.

That night I caught the last 10 minutes of the All Blacks game then I wandered around a couple of bars and had a few beers. You couldn't help but get caught up in the euphoria – everyone was so ecstatic. People always say we got better in the World Cup after I stopped playing! Bearing in mind it was an old team and what happened with Brian Ashton after taking a team to a World Cup final it was probably not the best outcome in terms of planning for the future. But the World Cup is not about that. It was not getting to the final that caused the slump, but what happened after.

PHIL VICKERY

Suddenly you're in another semi-final, you're playing France in France. Imagine what's going through their minds – and my opposite number as captain is Raphael Ibanez, of Wasps at the time, one of the best hookers I've ever played with. I remember one thing more than anything – I remember walking down the tunnel for the toss thinking, 'If we go down we're going down in blaze of glory.' I hated the French that day, but that captain, I hated him in a nice way. He didn't make eye contact with me. The referee did his chat and I gave Rafa a handshake and he still didn't look at me. I went back in and told the boys, trying to get them fired up.

JOSH LEWSEY

On a personal level, the World Cup ended for me in the French game, after scoring the early try. My hamstring went and at the time you kid yourself that it might be a muscle spasm but you know deep down that it is your hamstring. The next day I went for a scan and was devastated to have it officially confirmed. I kept going in the hope that it would all come right because we had been through some bad times for three years. When I remember the bad times it wasn't the rugby itself because I still loved playing the game. I was thinking of the times when I had sat in meetings where things were being said that I didn't agree with, and I just had to grin and bear it, nodding politely.

PHIL VICKERY

Andrew Sheridan was everything I wanted him to be – big, strong, powerful. But if

Josh Lewsey powers over Damien Traille to score an early try in the semi-final against France.

you don't get him fired up, then he's not nearly as good. I said some things to Shez in that changing room before the French game that I wouldn't ever say to anybody again. So he head butted me, actually split my head open. I can remember the atmosphere even before that, the boys were fired up, some were crying, I tried to cover over the cut, the blood was running down my shirt. Then there was a knock on the door, the official calling us out for the match. I've got blood stains on my shirt, ball under my arm and I'm walking down the tunnel leading England out against France for the World Cup semi-final.

That feeling of coming off having beaten France in France in their home stadium, in the semi-finals again, I don't think that game gets enough credit, not for the standard of rugby that was played but what we achieved.

LEWIS MOODY

There was such a big difference in mind-set. Even though the two teams were not that different in personnel, the difference was that in 2003 we expected to reach the final whereas in 2007, the win over France in the semi-final, was our final because it had taken so much to get there. I felt a little embarrassed because I knew how much had gone into that 2003 tournament and that we had 'winged' it this time.

Jason Robinson breaks through the French midfield.

LEE MEARS

We had stumbled on through the group stages and then secured a decent victory over Australia in the quarter-final. Although the victory gave the team a degree of confidence, things were still not right. The organisation and structure was not as it should have been. This is best illustrated by a comment from one of the former England captains in the squad, Martin Corry. Cozza is a stand-up guy, with a good sense of humour and is a passionate Englishman.

I was heading back to my room one afternoon when I saw him walking along the corridor towards me. 'Okay, Cozza?' 'Fine, Mearsy,' he replied, 'although I do feel as though I'm a member of a pub side that's just found itself in the-final of the World Cup.'

ANDY GOMARSALL

I vowed after 2003, when I didn't make the bench for the final, that I would be there in 2007. I made it, even though I had some career lows in between. But 2007 was the best time of my career. I felt that it was my time and people said some very, very nice things. I remember Martin Johnson saying I was one of the players who really turned it round for England. That was an amazing compliment for me.

NICK EASTER

By the time it came to the final, what had gone before in the pool game against South Africa did not count for anything. This was another one-off game and we were a much better side. We had guys that had been in the final four years previously and won – Wilkinson, Robinson, Vickery and Kay – it was a very tense game and it boiled down to discipline. We gave away a couple of silly penalties but if that try had been allowed when Mark Cueto scored it might have been different. South Africa also made a mess of our lineout and were also blessed in having scrum-half Fourie du Preez. He was outstanding that day especially with his kicking.

I felt we needed to open up and were a little too cagey compared to how we played in the previous games as South Africa were probably the best side in the world at winning arm wrestle-type games. Ultimately, it was a bridge too far but one hell of a journey.

LEE MEARS

By hook or by crook we reached the final, where once again we came unstuck against South Africa, although our performance was much better than it had been just over a month earlier. Had the Mark Cueto 'try' been given early in the second half who knows, things might have been different. You can never be satisfied with defeat, but if someone had offered me a place in the final after our group matches I would have gladly taken it.

BRIAN ASHTON

Mentally, we should have had the edge going into that match. It was a bizarre situation because South Africa must have thought they had buried us with that 36-0 group stage win. Then suddenly, we were lining up against them in the final. I don't know how much general, real deep-seated belief there was among the players that we could win that final. I had the belief but I don't know whether they did. Unfortunately, around the time we had that try disallowed, I felt we tried to play catch-up rugby and lost mental clarity.

MARK CUETO

I remember at the time, when I flew home, my left foot was pretty much on the front of every newspaper. It was incredible. I remember thinking was it a good thing or a bad thing that it was not given? I was disappointed it was not given but on the other hand it got my name out there and it could lead to other opportunities. I remember thinking that it would be a 'flash in the pan' and people would talk about it for a month or two. But all these years later, I must get asked at least once or twice a week.

I still believe it was a try. Even now there are decisions going to the TMO which are far more ambiguous than mine. Look at the try which settled the 2014 Premiership final between Northampton and Saracens. If you are telling me that was definitely a try and mine wasn't I think you are looking at a different video. I still stand by the gut instinct of a try scorer or a goal scorer. There are times when you know you haven't. Generally, you get it right even watching the video. There is no conclusive shot because you either get the shot when my foot was in touch and the ball has been grounded or you get the shot where my foot is a millimetre from touch and the ball is a millimetre from being grounded. It's a tough one.

JASON ROBINSON

We played down the injury, but I should have been out for five to six weeks. I could feel it constantly during the quarter and semi-finals, and it meant I did no training in the week of the final, save for 15 minutes.

Then, in the warm-up, I hit a tackle bag and felt the hamstring go. I'd never injured my hamstring throughout my whole career, but here I was in a World Cup final carrying an injury that hadn't had enough time to recover.

I thought about pulling out. If I'd thought I'd be a liability, I would have done, but I'd got through the previous two games and, although this was worse, I reckoned I could hold out. It was the one game out of the three where I was most conscious of my hamstring. What frustrated me more than anything was that it prevented me from being my true self. I had a constant mental battle between the confident me and the negative me who kept saying I wasn't fit.

It was a shame because the final needed something out of the ordinary to happen to win it. The defences were on top and, apart from Matt Tait's break, nothing worked. Maybe if I had been fully fit, I could have made something happen.

MARTIN CORRY

Comparing 2003 to 2007, in 2003 Lote Tuqiri scored early and it did nothing to shake the self-belief of that team. In 2007 our big opportunity came through Mark Cueto but think about how that came about. There was a Barnes Wallis pass from Andy Gomarsall that was picked up by Mat Tait who made the break – it was not constructed play. In 2007 we needed luck to win and we did not have it and South Africa were the better team. It was about us stopping them and we didn't get the breaks. For me the biggest call [of the Cueto incident] was that when Mat Tait made the break Schalk Burger dived in on the wrong side. If the break had not happened we would have got the penalty [they did eventually] and Burger would have been binned but he wasn't because it was a long way back – but it is all ifs and buts.

A game of inches: Mark Cueto's try is disallowed after the TMO decides that his toe skimmed the touchline before scoring.

ANDREW SHERIDAN

After the disappointing pool game against South Africa a big group of players spoke with the management and thought: 'We all want to give this a decent crack.' We then got a couple of good results and managed to win the quarter-final.

Once you reach the semi-finals you know you are not very far off from being in a World Cup final and being in with a chance of winning it. At that stage it will be so close, so you have to make sure you get all the little things exactly right. If you are going to win games at that stage it is tiny margins you are dealing with. Losing the final was a massive disappointment, but I didn't feel as though we let

Phil Vickery, the England captain, reacts as the fulltime whistle is blown in the final.

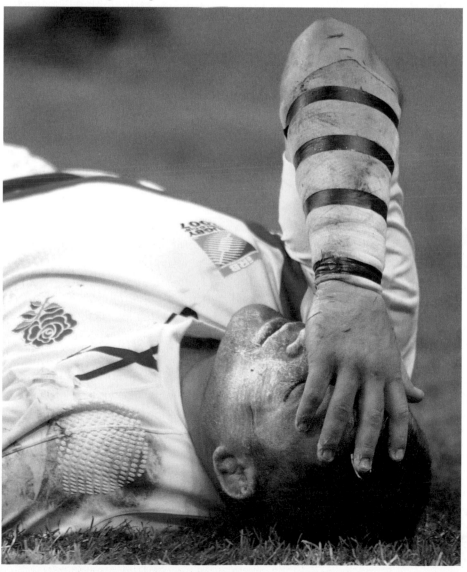

ourselves down, as individuals or as a team. We did our very best, but it was not quite good enough and South Africa deservedly won.

The players worked really hard to reach that final, and Matt Stevens started the banter with the song 'The Gambler', and played it in the changing rooms. He plays the guitar and sings well and everyone joined in.

As a group we developed a real dogged spirit which took us all the way to the final. Despite the loss I don't think we can have any regrets. The trend in modern parlance is to describe any semi-momentous occasion as 'a great journey', but on this occasion the cliché is the right one.

PHIL VICKERY

I didn't feel any pride in losing the final, my sense of pride came from how hard we had fought to try and keep that trophy.

Over the years I'd built up a relationship with John Smit, the South African captain. He was just a great guy. I thought if I had to lose to someone, as much as I was gutted and disappointed, then the cup went to a captain who probably typifies everything I believe in in sport.

NICK EASTER

It was an incredible experience. I had never been through anything like it.

TOBY FLOOD (England 2006-2013, 60 caps)

The feeling at the World Cup, especially in the final two weeks, is pretty hard to replicate. It's so exciting... you're not sleeping until 3am but you feed off the fear, the anxiety and the excitement. It's a massive adrenaline dump when you lose but it's something very, very special. I consider myself extremely lucky to have played in a World Cup final. It's a short list of those who have.

PHIL VICKERY

You know, when I look back on 2007 it is probably with more fondness than 2003. Playing for England has meant everything to me – and that's not saying Gloucester or Wasps or the Lions weren't important – but to represent your country and to be able to sing your national anthem before playing the greatest team sport in the World Cup is unbeatable. They [the players] always used to take the piss out of me. They used to call me Churchill. Not because of the nodding dog but because of the way I spoke before a game. For me, it was like representing the entire nation, there is a huge level of emotion.

Things did get bad on the field but then you have a choice. You can either go home, or you can do something about it. We didn't let ourselves down, we fought to the very end, and the sense of disappointment was outweighed by a sense of pride that we had done everything that we possibly could.

It was totally different to 2003. My God, I felt so proud of everybody, the players, the coaches, the physios, everyone in the group.

MARTIN CORRY

I got on well with Brian Ashton but he may have been the wrong type of coach for the players he had. England played their best rugby when Brian Ashton and Andy Robinson were coaching and Clive Woodward was in overall charge.

SIMON SHAW

One of the things that Brian [Ashton] did, and Jack [Rowell] as well, is that when you have the confidence of the coach you feel there is a release of pressure, so that you can do the things you are picked for. Sometimes players get stifled by thinking what they have to do.

If you have a coach who allows you to 'do what you do' a player is more relaxed. I remember in the 2007 World Cup I put in a couple of kicks and a couple of chips which I would happily do for Wasps but would never have ever considered doing under, say, Clive. But under Brian I knew that he had confidence in my footballing ability. He would say, 'If it's on, do it.' That's why I think 2007 was my best period. I was at my peak. My England career had been littered with bouts of a lack of confidence because it does not matter how many times you are picked or dropped, it always affects confidence. I always felt I had to play way above the standard to get picked again. That was my feeling. A lot of the games I never played with total confidence in what I was doing.

PHIL VICKERY

Some very strange things happen in sport. You write people off at your peril. There's a little spark inside me which died the day I knew I would never be able to do that again, you can't replace it, I wouldn't want to try to replace it but my God I look back with so many wonderful, wonderful memories of coaches, of fans, of highs and lows that I will always remember. And all I can say is, thank you.

TWENTY-FOUR

THE FALL

2008-2011

THE FEEL-GOOD FACTOR *from the 2007 World Cup was soon replaced by intense scrutiny of coach Brian Ashton, especially after the 2008 Six Nations began badly when a late Wales surge at Twickenham saw them overhaul England 26-19 in what was to become a Grand Slam season for the visitors. Equilibrium appeared to have been restored with away wins over Italy (23-19) and France (24-13). However, Ashton's plans to bring the mercurial Danny Cipriani into the side against Scotland at fly-half for Jonny Wilkinson were undermined when the player was seen coming out of a London nightclub a couple of days before the match, breaking a squad curfew.*

Ashton dropped Cipriani from the line-up and Wilkinson went on to pass Neil Jenkins' world record points total by kicking three penalties at Murrayfield. It was the only high point in an otherwise dismal performance, with England unexpectedly losing 15-9 to the Scots.

Having served a one-match ban, Cipriani got the chance to make amends in the last game of the tournament against Ireland, and was inspirational in a 33-10 victory. Nevertheless, it did not save Ashton from becoming embroiled in a messy transition as the England coaching structure was overhauled ahead of the 2008 summer tour to New Zealand.

Ashton, and Andy Robinson before him, were happiest coaching players and were not as adept at the public role and media duties that Woodward relished. Both felt the need for a manager to deflect some of the media glare.

At the same time there was a desire in the RFU corridors of power to bring in a 'big figure' to lift England's flagging fortunes going towards the 2011 World Cup – and they didn't come any bigger than England's 2003 World Cup winning 'Captain Colossus', Martin Johnson.

Ashton may have coached England to the World Cup final in 2007, and to second place in the 2008 Six Nations – their best finish since 2003 – but he did not fit into the RFU's grand plan.

Johnson's appointment as England manager was announced on 16 April, 2008, with Ashton offered the post of head coach of the RFU's National Academy, a role he had performed previously. Ashton had won 12 of his 22 tests in a sixteen month reign as head coach.

Opposite: Chris Ashton performs the 'Ash Splash' as he crosses for one of the four tries he picked up against Italy at Twickenham in the 2011 Six Nations.

Johnson's brief was that he reported to Rob Andrew, but had 'full managerial control' of the England team, including the appointment of a new backs coach. The hitch was that Johnson was unable to take up the reins for the 2008 summer tour of New Zealand because his wife was expecting their second child. This meant that Andrew became interim England manager for the duration of the tour, although Johnson was a tour party selector.

It proved to be an unhappy tour with England not only second best in the two Test series (losing 37-20 and 44-12), but also with some of the younger players embroiled in a sex scandal following a night on the town after the first Test in Auckland. This involved an 18-year-old girl claiming to Auckland police that she was 'sexually violated' by up to four players after going back to the team hotel and having consensual sex with one player.

However, because the girl decided not to make a formal complaint, no arrests were made. A report by the RFU disciplinary officer, Jeff Blackett (a circuit court judge), stated that there was no evidence of illegal activity by the players, who vehemently denied any criminal wrongdoing. He fined fullback Mike Brown £1,000 for all-night drinking, and wing Topsy Ojo £500 for staying out all night, whilst clearing scrum-half Danny Care and wing David Strettle of any wrongdoing.

The disciplinary report suggested also that the England management needed to keep 'a tighter rein' on players.

When Johnson, untried and untested as a top tier manager/coach, took over for the autumn internationals he had a promising baptism, with England beating the Pacific Islanders comfortably (39-13). It did not take long for him to become acquainted with the harsh demands of elite coaching, with England crashing to defeat to the southern hemisphere big three following Johnson's selection of Steve Borthwick as his first captain.

Borthwick was a controversial choice because the Bath lock, whilst a model professional, was not considered in pure playing terms to merit being one of the first names on the team sheet. England lost 28-14 to Australia before being trounced 42-6 by the world champions, South Africa.

A hat-trick of defeats ended with New Zealand winning 32-6 against an England side whose indiscipline proved terminal as they were reduced to 13 men twice with four players yellow-carded for infringements (Lee Mears, James Haskell, Toby Flood and Tom Rees).

The lack of tactical savvy left Johnson irate, and although England made headway during the 2009 Six Nations with home victories over Italy (36-11), France (34-10) and Scotland (26-12), away defeats to Wales (23-15) and Ireland consigned them to second place as the Irish claimed a rare Grand Slam.

The 14-13 defeat in Dublin, when England conceded 18 penalties and had Danny Care and Phil Vickery sin-binned, saw the England head coach's frustration boil over as he was caught on camera smashing his fist down on a desk.

That summer England played a home and away two-Test series against Argentina (during the 2009 Lions tour), winning the first at Old Trafford 37-15, and losing the second in Salta 24-22. However, when the serious southern hemisphere business started again in the autumn, Johnson's England were unable to break their SANZAR duck.

Argentina were dispatched again (16-9), but either side of that England were beaten by Australia (18-9) and New Zealand (19-6), with growing questioning of Borthwick's Test credentials and England's faltering attack.

This intensified when Johnson's second Six Nations saw them finish third, displaying a marked lack of attacking enterprise after the opening 30-17 home win over Wales. When a narrow win over Italy (17-12) was followed by a loss to Ireland at Twickenham (20-16) and a turgid away draw with Scotland (15-15) there was widespread disenchantment with England's safety-first strategy. Their tournament ended with a 12-10 reverse in Paris where Johnson had intended to stubbornly stick by Borthwick. But the captain was injured and advised to rest and recover fully, so Johnson appointed his former Leicester and England teammate, Lewis Moody, as interim skipper.

During the Five Nations Johnson had belatedly blooded three young players, Ben Youngs, Chris Ashton and Dan Cole, who all showed promise. The summer visit to Australia was an opportunity to give them and three other up-and-coming caps of limited experience, Tom Croft, Ben Foden and Courtney Lawes, greater exposure on the international stage. Borthwick's continued absence through injury, moreover, presented the manager with the opportunity to experiment further and Moody wore the captain's armband throughout the tour. After losing the first Test in Perth 27-17, despite forcing the outclassed Australian scrum to concede two penalty tries, England caught Australia on the hop in Sydney. Their attacking zest resulted in tries for Youngs and Ashton and helped them to a landmark 21-20 victory.

With a drawn away series against the Wallabies in his locker, Johnson made the biggest sea-change of his tenure soon afterwards, dropping Borthwick from the England squad for the new season and confirming Moody as captain.

The 2010 autumn series saw England notch their first home victory over one of the southern hemisphere big three under Johnson the manager. After being beaten 26-16 by New Zealand, they cut loose against Australia sending the Twickenham crowd's hopes soaring with a 35-18 victory crowned by a spectacular end-to-end try by Ashton. The wing celebrated his touchdown with a swan dive – immediately dubbed the 'Ash-Splash' – which sparked debate over whether it was gloating gamesmanship or legitimate flamboyance. Johnson's response was not to prohibit Ashton's dive, but to warn him that he had better not drop the ball. England followed that with a win over Samoa (26-13), before losing to South Africa (21-11).

There were high expectations of England going into the 2011 Six Nations, and, with Mike Tindall replacing the injured Moody as captain, they started the campaign strongly.

The win over Wales in Cardiff (26-19) saw Ashton score twice, and the wing was even more prolific in the home win over Italy, scoring four of England's eight tries (59-13).

Further home victories over France (17-9) and Scotland (22-16) saw England on the brink of their first Grand Slam since 2003. All that was required was to beat Ireland in Dublin.

They suffered an early disruption when Tindall was ruled out by an ankle injury, and the captain's armband was handed to Nick Easter. The loss of the two experienced World Cup winners (Tindall and Moody) left England exposed in the face of the Irish gale, and their Slam hopes were scattered to the four winds as they were bowled over 24-8.

England finished the tournament as champions by name, but the comprehensive nature of Ireland's victory indicated that Johnson's team still had a long way to go.

The manager's introduction of a young Samoan-born centre powerhouse, Manu Tuilagi, for the World Cup warm-up games – including his spearheading of a 20-9 win in a rematch in Dublin – offered a diversion. However, the seeds of doubt had been sown already over England's credentials as 2011 World Cup contenders in New Zealand.

England were based in Dunedin for most of the pool section, opening their World Cup account with a hard-fought 13-9 victory over Argentina thanks to a late Ben Youngs try. They went on to record comfortable victories over Georgia and Romania, before meeting Scotland in the group decider in Auckland for 100% record.

In the interim, news broke about the England players binge drinking in Queenstown in celebration of their win over Argentina, including attending a hostelry which listed 'dwarf throwing' and 'Leprechaun Bar Wars' among their attractions.

When temporary captain, Mike Tindall, who had recently taken up residence in royal circles by marrying Zara Phillips (the Queen's grand-daughter), was revealed to be among the most inebriated of the revellers the story was seized on by the media, and Johnson was left with a major fire-fight on his hands.

Rather than imposing a couple of one-match bans on the Queenstown revellers, Johnson's staunch defence of his players meant that England lost the PR battle, and by the time they played Scotland they had become the pariahs of the tournament.

Sympathy was in short supply for professional players participating in the biggest tournament of their lives allegedly behaving like a bunch of amateurs on an Easter tour, and the disjointed brand of rugby that they had served up also did little to win them friends. Nor did a ball-swapping row during the Argentina match help – prompted by Jonny Wilkinson's concern about their aerodynamics – with Johnson forced to ban conditioning coach Paul Stridgeon and skills coach Dave Alred for a match.

An error-prone England squeezed past a Scotland side coached by Andy Robinson by the slenderest of margins (16-12) thanks to another late try, this time by Ashton, securing a face-off with France in the quarter-finals.

England were dumped out of the competition the following weekend after an abject first half showing gave the French a 16-0 head start. Despite hitting back through second half tries by Ben Foden and Mark Cueto it was too little too late and, outplayed by France (19-12), the squad left New Zealand shores with its reputation in tatters.

It was a sad end to the England careers of the last of the 2003 world champion squad, with Wilkinson, Tindall, Simon Shaw, Steve Thompson and Lewis Moody all playing their last games for England.

When a review was held into the tournament by the RFU, the Rugby Players' Association (RPA), and Premier Rugby, Johnson's England regime was in the dock.

Johnson said he took responsibility for the World Cup failings and in mid-November he made a dignified exit after tendering his resignation. When the review was leaked soon afterwards it was clear that Johnson's position was untenable because of the picture painted of poor discipline, internal divisions, greed, and mismanagement, following anonymous interviews with 90 per cent of the squad.

The 2011 World Cup and its fall-out left England in a state of disrepair – and Johnson's successor facing a major rebuild of squad morale.

BEN KAY

Looking back, I think that coming second at the 2007 World Cup was probably the worst thing that could have happened to English rugby and it set us back at least 18 months to two years in terms of trying to get back on track. We had come second in the World Cup even though we had been thrashed by South Africa in the pool stages. Getting to the final was a blip, we were still very much in a transitional period and that showed the following season.

PHIL VICKERY

We lost to both Scotland and Wales in the Six Nations and finished second in the table [as Wales secured a Grand Slam]. Scotland deserved their victory against us up in Edinburgh. It wasn't pretty. I don't think there was ever going to be a great deal of rugby played. We weren't under any illusions how difficult it was going to be. We were bitterly disappointed with our performance – certainly in that first half-hour: we pretty much did everything we said we would not do.

BRIAN ASHTON

When we lost to Wales at Twickenham in the 2008 Six Nations, there was a touch of the surreal about it. In fairness to Wales, to fight your way back from a 19-6 deficit at half-time takes a bit of doing. But we did give them a helping hand.

When it came to it, it seemed we didn't have the players that could put teams away consistently. Against France and Ireland we did but we couldn't do it on a consistent basis. If you look at the 2003 World Cup side, about eight England players would have been contenders for a world XV side. Now, if you are in a world XV team, you must have massive leadership qualities. With all due respect to some of the players that played in the Six Nations that year, you wouldn't say that. But we were also aware that we had some exciting players emerging in the squad and Danny Cipriani's first start, which came against Ireland at Twickenham, was pretty sensational.

DANNY CIPRIANI (England 2008-2014, 9 caps)

I'd played that game in my head a million times before we kicked off. I'd been told I probably wouldn't sleep that well but that it wouldn't affect the way I played.

After what had happened the previous week with my one-match ban [imposed for appearing in a nightclub], I thought when I woke up it was too close to kick-off for me to be deselected!

It must have been gone five by the time I dozed off again but by then I was happy with all the positive thoughts about what I was going do. I was just so excited I couldn't wait to get on to the field.

I'd been given the job of playing fly-half for England and I could not go into the game quietly. I know people think I'm confident and arrogant but if I'd gone about it half-heartedly it would never have worked. I had to make sure we were going the right way. I was talking all the time, trying to make sure it was the right talk. It's crucial you tell the forwards what you want, that you need them to be running hard and smashing people back. I had to make sure that was in their heads before the match.

BRIAN ASHTON

It was a pretty tricky time in 2008. I was never clear about what was likely to happen next with my job and the whole decision-making process seemed to drag on for a long period of time. It didn't spill into my private life, although I'd have to be honest and say I have slept better. But the worst thing was it affected the people around me. They became very anxious and stressed about what was going to happen.

You go through all the emotions on a daily basis, and sometimes all of them every hour. It would be unusual, against the make-up of human nature if you didn't.

I wasn't sure what was going to happen, to be honest. The week before the decision was made, the RFU announced a new management structure was to be put in place. It was said they hoped all the present coaching staff would buy into it. I assumed that included me. But it didn't.

I never got out of the England team what I and other coaches got out of those England sides from 2000 to 2002. Those sides of that era went on to the field and really showed the rest of the world what they were all about. In international terms, that era was my greatest achievement and brought me real pleasure.

My approach then was exactly the same as later. But we had different personalities, people not afraid to have an informed opinion and players and coaches not afraid 'to have a go'. And maybe the environment we were operating in by 2007 made that quite tricky.

It was a fabulous honour to be asked to be England coach. It was the excitement of fire-fighting my way through 15 months and we came out with a pretty good record. But, ultimately, I left frustrated that, having got to the point where a lot of new-generation players whom I knew well from my time running the Academy were beginning to appear, I did not have the opportunity to continue working with them.

SIMON SHAW

It was tough on Brian. We lost two games and finished second equal. I thought Brian was a bit harshly dealt with. Johnno came in and there was a lot made about it because of his lack of experience. But all the ideas he had and what he said were never doubted. We all bought into it.

MARTIN JOHNSON

I went into it all with my eyes open. It was a fact I had no coaching or management experience but I had a lot of experience in rugby. This game is always about players. It is not about the ego of coaches: that sometimes gets overplayed. It is about trying to create an environment where these guys can thrive and play. It is about team culture. It's not about having a way of playing, but finding the way to win.

TOBY FLOOD

Brian Ashton was very different to Martin Johnson, more laissez-faire: he'd let things happen. He was very much about player power. So he let you go out there and work things out for yourself. Martin knew what he wanted and brought a cool approach to the way he spoke to the team. He brought a real depth of belief with what he said because he'd been there and done it. There was a huge amount of respect within the side for him.

NICK EASTER

It was a transitional period in 2008. In the Six Nations we had some good performances. We beat France away heavily and we smashed Ireland at home, but there were some under-performing games – such as away to Scotland – and that was Brian Ashton's undoing. It was very unfair. After all, he had taken the team to the final of the World Cup and had finished second in the Six Nations. Johnno came in for the autumn series. Ultimately, what he wanted, like all successful teams, was for a core group of senior players to lead. You need direction from coaches but out on the field, certainly towards the end of the training week and in matches, the players have to make the decisions.

He realised the need to blood youth as the previous year at the World Cup we had taken a very old team and lots of those guys had retired or were overlooked. In his first game in charge against the Pacific Islands he started Danny Cipriani and Danny Care at half-back, who had around four caps between them. I also remember Delon Armitage and Ugo Monye making their debuts.

TOM REES

After that World Cup a lot of the senior guys had moved on and there was a sense I had to stand up myself having been one of the young guys. I had now been involved a bit more than some of the other players and this was the start of the next stage.

I remember sitting in the dressing room after the first Test on the 2008 summer to tour to New Zealand and catching the eye of James Haskell and Luke Narraway and we just looked at each other and I was thinking we'd had a good day at the office. How can that happen when you have just been smashed by the opposition? But we had put it all out there. There was a sense that after the tour we could kick on, but Luke got his back injury, James went abroad, and my injuries are well documented.

I had played against Schalk Burger in the 2007 World Cup, and while we got hammered in the pool game I felt I had at least contributed. Richie McCaw was the best player in the world, he was the yardstick, and it was a chance to see where I was. Everyone was very complimentary about me and it made me think I could mix it with these guys.

MARK CUETO

I was injured after the World Cup with a niggle with my back. The following season I hardly played any rugby. I fell out of the team and came back when Martin Johnson was appointed. I remember getting a call from him that I was not going on tour to New Zealand. You always worry when a new coach comes in that you are not going to be part of a team. You think, 'Is that going to be it?' Johnno rang me and he knew that I had not been playing a lot but he said, 'Have a good break and get yourself right.' The next autumn I was back in.

We started the series off well with a 39-13 win over the Pacific Islanders, but it got a lot tougher after that. We lost to Australia [28-14] and then got hammered by South Africa [42-6].

STEVE BORTHWICK (England 2001-2010, 57 caps)

The Springboks handed out a pretty brutal lesson. It was much the same the following week against New Zealand. It showed us how far we had to go to get back to the top of world rugby.

MARTIN JOHNSON

Mistakes kill you, especially against the big teams from the southern hemisphere. When we made them, they made us pay. When they made them, we let them off the hook. When we were playing back in 2008 we were not as good as Australia, South Africa or New Zealand in terms of composure. If you are not listening to the referee you are going to upset him. We paid the price.

Steve Borthwick came in for a lot of criticism in the media but I thought he was fantastic and there was never a question in my mind that he would be captain for the 2009 Six Nations. A lot of captaincy is done off the field. Everything he did was of the highest quality, and for him to get the criticism he got was totally unfair.

MATT STEVENS (England 2004-2012, 44 caps)

Steve can be quite a miserable bastard, but we all loved him for it. He also happens to be the best captain I've ever played under. Categorically. Yes, he's good at

Steve Borthwick issues commands during England's 32-6 loss to New Zealand at Twickenham in November 2008.

tempering overenthusiasm and keeping things in balance, yet he can be charismatic when he wants to be. He gives a great team talk.

I was annoyed by the way Steve was treated. It was really bad. England weren't playing well and he took the blame, which was ridiculous. At that stage of the team's development, why wouldn't they want his kind of experience? There are so many perceptions about individuals in this game, and they're so often wrong. There was a time when people assumed that because I did a lot in the loose I couldn't scrummage. In Steve's case, people reached the conclusion that because he was so good in the line-out he didn't do anything else. That's not how it works. The reality is that he did a lot of things incredibly well.

STEVE BORTHWICK

When you are a winning captain, everyone wants to know you. When it's not going so well, nobody wants to know you. I experienced both sides of the coin at Bath, Saracens and England.

I made a point of not reading or listening to what people had said about me, but I had constant calls from family and friends irate about the accusations levelled at me. They seemed more upset about it than I was.

I had a great many setbacks in my career, notably failing to make the 2003 World Cup squad, serious injury, and my failure to make a meaningful impact at the 2007 World Cup, so I was well used to the knocks and learnt to deal with them much better than I did before. My family got pretty upset at times, though. The only accusation I heard that got to me was being described as 'brainless'.

The English rugby public, the media and former players had every right to be disappointed, to be upset and to be angry after what happened in the 2008 autumn internationals, but I can promise you with total conviction that nobody in the country got anywhere close to feeling as bad as the 22 players sitting in the home changing room in silence and in shock. I wish the millions of dejected people could have seen the scene that I did.

We lost three games by unacceptable margins because we simply were not good enough. The biggest lesson from that autumn was that you don't get many chances against that calibre of opposition, so when you do, you must take them. Our conversion rate in terms of points gained from scoring chances just had to improve.

MARTIN JOHNSON

It was the same when we went to Dublin and lost [14-13]. Indiscipline cost us that Test match. All that work you try to put in to win a game is gone, wasted. It wasn't one individual doing it all, it was a number of individuals at key moments. We worked on discipline all the time. One of the fundamentals of the game is not to be penalised. Once you get behind on the penalty count the referee and touch-judges are on your back, and things like the Danny Care sin-binning happen.

MARK CUETO

In defeat in Paris [in 2010] we found something as a team. I thought our performance as a whole was a significant improvement on what had gone before. Ben Foden and Chris Ashton [on his international debut] brought a lot of confidence from the season they had been enjoying at Northampton and played really well.

MARTIN JOHNSON

Before we went on tour to Australia in 2010 there was a lot made about Danny Cipriani's celebrity status. There was a perception that I had got a problem with celebrity. It suits some guys – some guys enjoy it – and some guys don't. I played with guys who are on television. There is a balance to have to your life, and different people look for different things. That is not the issue for me. It is what you do when you play, how you prepare, what you are as a rugby player – that is what is important.

LEWIS MOODY

It was hugely frustrating to lose the first Test against Australia in Perth. We really felt like the game was in our hands but we just weren't at the races. But the following week, in Sydney, was something really special.

Ben Youngs' first start for England was brilliant... what a legend. I'd played with him since he broke into the Leicester team as a 17-year-old and we could all see then that his potential was huge. He was absolutely tremendous in that win.

BEN YOUNGS (England 2010-2014, 38 caps plus 2 caps for the Lions)

It was an instinctive moment really, Thommo [Steve Thompson] threw a nice ball in and my housemate Crofty [Tom Croft] threw it down to me – I think he got every line-out that day – and there was a gap so I managed to go through and sneak round Drew Mitchell.

STEVE THOMPSON

Some people had totally written us off before the second Test, but we went out there and showed we weren't just one-paced. It meant everything to pull the England shirt on, bounce back and prove people wrong. I love doing that.

CHRIS ASHTON (England 2010-2014, 39 caps)

My dad had an operation on his knee in 2010. It should have taken him three to four weeks to recover, but it was taking twice that time and, dad being dad, he refused to go back to the doctors. He never wanted the operation in the first place and only did it because the family insisted.

Then things seemed to get worse. On the afternoon of my debut for England in Paris, he used my hotel room to have an afternoon sleep. We all thought it was some kind of reaction to his knee. In the end we forced him to go back to hospital. Something was clearly wrong. For two weeks dad deteriorated. Then he came home and announced that he had lymphoma. He was obviously upset but said that chemotherapy would make him better. He seemed keen to get on with it. The family all sat around his hospital bed and watched him just fall asleep. The life-support machine was turned off. The fact that he didn't suffer for too long gives me a great deal of comfort.

He'd always been there to help and advise. It wasn't always nice. Sometimes after a game he'd tear into me, although it would be for the right reasons. When I was about to return to rugby league at the start of 2009, it was him who persuaded me to stick at union. After he had died, one of my sisters found a diary that he had kept that none of us knew about. From my very first game in league to my England debut in union against France, dad wrote down his real thoughts on

The squad celebrate their victory over Australia in Sydney.

a Monday in his diary. To my face he'd tell me what I should have done and where I went wrong. Behind my back he'd write about his pride in seeing his boy playing rugby for a living. His diary is full of the things he wanted to say to me but couldn't. He just couldn't bring himself to open up. But I can't tell you what it means to me to know he kept that diary.

It was hard to get back into playing rugby again at first, but since then I've had extra motivation, a drive to do something for my dad. That was one of my first thoughts when I was told I'd be touring Australia with England.

I scored my first Test try out in Sydney on our way to winning that match. It was a big moment for me. And then, of course, there was my dad. It meant a lot to me at the time and I thought about him while i was out there on the field.

BEN FODEN (England 2009-2013, 34 caps)
That win took a bit of pressure off us and we were all happy for the coaches and management who had taken a lot of flak over the previous few months. We owed them a big performance and result. That win in Sydney was one of my greatest days as a rugby player. It was an unbelievable feeling to beat Australia out there and in the manner that we played.

Chris Ashton flies over after his length-of-the-field break against Australia at Twickenham in the autumn of 2010.

MARTIN JOHNSON

If I'd listened to everyone, we'd have dropped all the players from the first Test. You have to have trust and loyalty to get success. It was a great win in Sydney but I knew that if we lost the next one, people would be on our case again.

NICK EASTER

Johnno had to develop the team and it was going to take time, and casualties, but in the summer of 2010 we beat Australia away and beat them again heavily in the autumn. We were playing a good brand of fast but winning rugby, as our record going into the 2011 World Cup, in which we won 13 out of 18 Tests, showed. The likes of Ben Foden, Dan Cole, Courtney Lawes, Tom Wood, Ben Youngs and Chris Ashton are further examples of the youth that was blooded and proved more than up to it.

MARTIN JOHNSON

You get rewards for all the work you put in. We played well in patches against New Zealand in the autumn and when we had the ball we did some really good stuff. Then you put another layer on the next week with the detail. Turn a half-break into a break. A break into a score. Keep building layers on layers. That was how we had to progress as a team and it paid off with that 35-18 win over Australia. But we knew that, as with the second Test win in Sydney in the summer, if we didn't back it up in the next game that the media would be on our backs again – which is exactly what happened when we lost to South Africa. Sometimes you do make a conservative call. People had me in that box. But I'm a practical guy. People say, 'You've got to be creative, you need the maverick'. Well, it's a brutal world out there. If you chuck guys in there who aren't ready they are going to be spat out and spat out very, very quickly.

CHRIS ASHTON

Scoring twice against the Wallabies in the autumn of 2010 was amazing. The first try was the perfect score for me. It was my first at Twickenham for starters. It's one thing receiving the ball on an overlap, running 10 metres and touching down, and another when you've cut inside, received an inside pass and have still got work to do. If there had been a lorry parked in the way, it wouldn't have stopped me going over.

And the second try was special. Really special. Not even dad could have criticised me over that second try against the Wallabies. Moments after catching the ball, I looked up at the big screen and realised it was on. The plan was to head straight for the corner, but Drew Mitchell made a move back as if expecting me to follow, so I just carried on running. I thought I might have to sprint all the way to the opposite corner, but once I had evaded his tap-tackle I had 20 metres to enjoy the moment. Scoring that try was everything I'd dreamt about. It was what my dad dreamt about as well, even if he never showed it. God only knows what he'd have written in his diary about that try!

The open way that Australia play encourages you to do the same. That is what happened on that day. It was only my second game at Twickenham and we'd just been beaten by the All Blacks, so we needed to get some confidence back. That was the first sign of us playing together and being a decent team. It was just one of those days, wasn't it? They only happen every once in a while and thankfully we took it with both hands that day. People do still talk about it. We had some new faces then so there was a 'no fear' mentality.

Even though I had the job of putting the ball down over the whitewash it was a team effort with the whole team playing its part in defending and forcing the turnover before Ben Youngs and Courtney Lawes gave me the ball. They all deserve the credit too – it wouldn't have happened without all of us working together.

BEN YOUNGS
I had a small part to play in that try. Okay, I went for it and that was the thing that got us going. Sometimes in rugby your instinct takes over.

MARK CUETO
As Ashers stepped inside Drew Mitchell, that initial step always takes a yard out of your pace, so I tried to get come in and get closer to him. I was waving my hands and screaming but then he got back into his stride and managed to dust Mitchell off. There was a split-second before that when I thought he might give it but then he finished it off brilliantly.

It was one of those days where every time I got the ball in my hands I felt like I was going to beat people and make yards. Those are special games.

NICK EASTER
We had a great Six Nations and we beat France to set up a Grand Slam game against Ireland in Dublin. We were guilty of being a little over-zealous in trying to play too much – but, more importantly, we hadn't matched the intensity of our previous performances when we needed it most. It was a little wet from memory in Dublin and we got caught out in a territory game, where the Irish completely outplayed us. I believe the group over-reacted to that defeat, and our style leading into the World Cup began to change. After that Ireland game we got together and reviewed it. The general consensus was that we had over-played, and that

opponents had worked out how we wanted to play – and that our style of a fast game was not going to win the World Cup. The training [afterwards] was geared more towards being big and strong but not mobile and fast. There was a big emphasis on weights, gym and wrestling.

TOM WOOD (England 2011-2014, 30 caps)
It felt pretty much like we'd had our hearts ripped out in that game against Ireland. We didn't go to Dublin for scars or lessons. We went for a Grand Slam and we got it wrong. It was unacceptable and a bitter pill to swallow and brought us back down to earth, even though we ultimately won the Championship.

STEVE THOMPSON
There was a lot of banter going round the squad and there was confidence there. We got hammered by the Irish but it is good to have that edge, that fear factor, that that could still happen. What happened in that game knocked the stuffing out of the boys a little bit, and also it made us think, 'Hang on a minute, we are not the finished article'. So we knew we had to work a little bit harder, which was a good thing for the World Cup. It was an opportunity for a Grand Slam and they don't come very often. It was a bit of a let-down, but we had to try to take the positives out of it and make sure it didn't happen when we got to the World Cup.

NICK EASTER
I always felt playing for England you could do all the video analysis you wanted but you always had to factor in that opponents would be 20 to 30 per cent better because you were England. Which made it an even bigger but better challenge.

There was an onus after that Ireland game, and what had happened at the 2007 World Cup, that a big forward pack and a good kicker wins World Cups. We went in with a very much territory focused, dominate up front, and kick the points game plan. That's fine if everyone buys into it. Some players in the squad could adapt their game to play that way, but some of the younger guys struggled as it took away their strengths, and everything they had shone doing for the previous year and a half. It was a game-plan that took less risks than we had before, and was more about percentages.

STEVE THOMPSON
I was a spectator at the 2007 World Cup, was drunk most of the time and eating what I wanted and I was on the rollercoaster like all the supporters. I was in the stadium when we got hammered by South Africa and I was in the stands when we beat Australia and when we beat France, and we were unlucky to lose in the final.

I had all the ups and downs with the supporters, but none of the raw nerves as a player, so it was quite nice to be on that side at that time. It was massive for me to be selected for the 2011 World Cup. I thought that I couldn't come back and play rugby and not get to the top again...The World Cup was my target... I was training to get back into club rugby, to get back into the England team, and get my 50th cap. And the end-goal was to play in the World Cup.

MARK CUETO

The World Cup build up was well organised, we had some great coaches and we had some great players. At times it did not go too well but that third year of Johnno being involved, leading up the World Cup in 2011, was a good year. We had just lost out on a Grand Slam, we had a good autumn campaign and we were going into the World Cup in a decent place.

JONNY WILKINSON

I admired some of the young guys coming through then – I loved that blatant living in the moment that they had. They didn't question things. I have been there, but with the injuries my life has been a lot about calculating things: how many months is it going to take? How long have I got? When do I need to be ready for? When do I need to prove my fitness for? It had been a long time since I had that opportunity to go out there and go, 'This is my life', just playing rugby. But by 2011 it was getting back there.

TOM CROFT (England 2008-2013, 38 caps plus 5 caps for the Lions)

We knew that with it being the World Cup that we would be in the spotlight, especially after our last trip down there in 2008. The boys had been talking about that in the camp. The 2008 tour was a little reminder at the back of our minds that if you have a beer in a pub or whatever you will be in the spotlight. We're England players and people are interested in seeing what you are doing.

LEWIS MOODY

I remember vividly watching the 1995 World Cup quarter-final against Australia when I was at school. During a break between lessons we all sprinted to the TV in the common room. We'd lost to Australia in the 1991 final so it was time for revenge and we got it. I was euphoric, jumping around with my mates. Unfortunately we then got steamrollered by New Zealand. Back then, I never thought I'd end up captaining England in a World Cup.

I struggled a little bit with the captaincy when I was first appointed. I was trying too hard to do everything like sorting out meetings and meals but the one thing

Johnno said to me was: 'Just be yourself'. So I went back to just leading through the way I played and how I behaved. I was a senior player anyway so I was very used to giving my opinion and setting an example and I soon became a lot more comfortable with it all.

TOBY FLOOD

Lewis was always a bit crazy. That is crazy in the sense that he'd do absolutely anything for the team. In training, he'd tear into things. Throughout his career he was probably injured more times in training than he was in a match. He couldn't distinguish between training and a game – it was all 100 miles an hour. And the guys responded to that really well. You looked at it and raised your eyebrows a little bit and just thought, 'Well, that's Lewis'.

MARTIN JOHNSON

World Cups are about pressure, dealing with it off the field, dealing with it on the field when you get into close games. Finding a way to win is what World Cups are about. If you talk about style, it is the team that can battle back and find a way to win a close game.

JONNY WILKINSON

There was a real issue with the balls [against Argentina in England's RWC pool opener in Dunedin]. The problem I found was that you were given eight balls to practise with the day before the game, and those are the eight balls that will be used in the match, they're all numbered. And within that eight there were a couple, maybe three, that on every single kick would veer off in one direction. The problem then was going into the game knowing that if you had to kick with one of those balls then you had to adjust for it, which is so unnatural for you as a kicker. Also you couldn't gauge how much it was going, only that it was. So I'd be kicking with one ball – straight, straight, straight – then use another ball – no, that's veered off. Then it would be straight, straight, straight again with another ball. And it was so frustrating kicking with those odd balls, because the strike felt perfect but the end point was nowhere where you thought it should be.

In all, I hit eight kicks. One of them I was definitely not happy with, one of them I didn't hit the exact line I was after, the other six I was really happy with. Only three went over.

MARK CUETO

To be honest I never really got that 100 per cent fitness you need for a World Cup.

That was partly due to having not played in the lead up to the competition. From then on you are battling against time. I had an injury for a number of seasons and I did not have the luxury of time. Though I scored a hat-trick against Romania it was not against real tough opponents. I was honest with Johnno in saying that I did not feel 100 per cent so it was a big call for him because he had put a lot of trust and faith in me over the previous 12 to 18 months. But his hand was forced when Delon Armitage got cited in the lead up to the quarter-final and Johnno had to put me back in. But at that point I was happier with my fitness.

SIMON SHAW

For whatever reason things went awry off the field, especially during the 2011 World Cup. There were a lot little incidents which all mounted up to what seemed like a team in disarray. But I was more about what happens on the pitch.

NICK EASTER

It was very frustrating. It's a pity because for the previous 12 months we had been going in the right direction. We just needed to tinker with a few things. We didn't need such wholesale changes to our tactics. From my point of view the off-field incidents did not affect me. There was a lot of hullabaloo and there were a lot of backroom staff running around. People forget a lot of the teams went to Queenstown to have a good time and a break. We had been well briefed by Johnno as to what could happen. At the end of the day we had been under a lot of pressure and sometimes you have to have a bit of a release. It was just a chance to relax. I'm a big believer in touring the country even in this age. You take your rugby 100 per cent seriously but you still need to be part of the country you are touring.

MARTIN JOHNSON

We knew they were going out to have a few beers. I had no problem with them doing that. We all know when you have a rugby team that part of it is the bonding off the field. If there was a complaint and someone said one of our players had acted inappropriately, then we would act on it.

JONNY WILKINSON

You look back on that World Cup and it was obviously disappointing and there were things that we would all do differently. The drinking thing was difficult and it was hard to hear about the punishments dished out to James Haskell and Mike Tindall; Tinds especially as I know him so well. It's disappointing. There were moments on that tour that we all look back on, especially in the tournament, and say there are things we could have done differently – and I'm involved with that as well with some of the on-the-field stuff. The thing is with me, I'd been involved with World Cups before, and guys had gone out to clear their heads. When I was younger I needed to go out after games because I couldn't deal with going: bang, game, game, game, game. It would have been too much for me. The thing is, around you, things change – and also you need to know where the line is. Because society changes round you, rugby's different, it's bigger, and you can't complain and say, 'Oh, well, guys did these things back in the old days,' because times change. It's a case of understanding where you are and what the role is that you play as England international.

MARK CUETO

We got on the wrong side of the media while we were in New Zealand and it was poorly handled. Defences were put up and it was not a good relationship. That's probably one of the best things Stuart Lancaster has done because from the start he has been so clear and so open with the media. I think credit to him. Whether you like it or not the media is a huge part of top-class sport and you might as well get them on your side rather than trying to battle against them. That was probably one of the biggest downfalls at the 2011 World Cup.

Jonny Wilkinson kicks for goal against Scotland in Auckland.

MARTIN JOHNSON

If they ever had any doubt about the goldfish bowl they were in in New Zealand in a World Cup then they were under no illusions after that whole night in Queenstown. We knew other teams had been there and had a night out and had a drink, and probably had a mess around like our boys did. We just closed ranks after that and tried to use it to bring us closer together. You get reported for bungee jumping and having a beer, well that was about five per cent of our time in Queenstown – the rest we were training and getting ready for the next game. And getting out and letting off some steam is part of it. It's part of the fun of the trip. They worked hard together, they backed each other up on the field, they went through good times with some tough times on the field, they had to deflect the criticism that was on them and the expectation that was on them. And a little bit of dealing with that is, at the right time, getting out and having a few beers together. Any team I've ever played in had nights out like they did that Sunday.

I wasn't let down by players, we were a team together. Things happen and get reported. Of course it didn't help. We didn't want that reputation. It doesn't accurately reflect what we had as a group… but how much it affected us on the field, no one can answer that.

Tom Palmer rises to win a lineout in the crucial Pool B decider.

LEWIS MOODY

I had not been captain long, having taken over from Steve Borthwick. I tried for a year and half to be the best captain I could be. I consulted a lot of people about leadership, the way I spoke to the players and how we tried to make sure the voice of the players was being listened to by the coaches. Certainly, a number of the younger players felt their voice was not being heard.

MIKE TINDALL (England 2000-2011, 75 caps)

I've stayed away from talking about what happened because people have their fixed opinions and you can't compete when people have already made their minds up. Obviously, it wasn't ideal for me to end up as hammered as I was. That's a given. People have done that in their lives before and I'm sure I won't be the last person to get drunk and then realise it wasn't a great idea to drink so much.

It's just that the reaction to my mistake turned into a rollercoaster that I couldn't control. But the people close to me, those I love, know what actually happened and it just wasn't some enormous crisis.

Given the same situation, you wouldn't repeat it, but neither did England get knocked out of the World Cup because we went for a night out. One of the great parts of rugby is the social side of it. Anyone involved in a team will tell you that.

Of course, we did not have as strong a tournament as we'd hoped we'd have and that we should have had. But we didn't fail at the World Cup because we had a night out. We won the Six Nations in 2011 and we went into the World Cup wanting to win and hoping to do so.

You don't just turn up and expect an easy ride, and we didn't get one, but we still won our first four games. Then we played poorly, very poorly, for 20 minutes against France in the quarter-final and that's why we got knocked out of the World Cup.

MARK CUETO

The build-up to 2011 was in sharp contrast to 2007. From a personal point of view, the 2007 and 2011 World Cups were injury-ridden for me. It was really disappointing because prior to both I had been in good form. From a team point of view that 2011 World Cup we had a very smooth build up. We had won the Six Nations and had won all four pool games. Yet going into the week before the quarter-final against France the press were on our backs. In terms of preparation and the form we were in, the stick we were getting was just incredible. In comparison to 2007, 2011 was a dream. In 2007 we got to a World Cup final, while in 2011 we got knocked out in the quarter-final. But that's sport. It's mad and crazy, isn't it?

TOBY FLOOD
Having played in the 2007 World Cup final and having loved the experience so much, I knew how badly we blew it in 2011. We had a path to the final via France in the quarter-finals and Wales in the semis – teams we had beaten in the Six Nations and summer World Cup warm-up games. But we didn't attack the opportunity with anywhere near enough vigour. And, of course, off the field it didn't exactly go to plan either. On a number of occasions there were situations that were poor from the individuals concerned. I'm fully aware of what we did.

NICK EASTER
For the first half hour our defence was poor against France and ultimately cost us. It would have been extremely disappointing to defend like that in any game, but in a World Cup quarter-final it was crucial. Though we fought back in the second half we were still out of the World Cup and had blown a very good chance of reaching the final, because we would have played Wales next.

There was a lot of off-field stuff and there was a lot made of it after the tournament, but that was only because we'd lost. There are plenty of examples of teams doing the same but winning, and it comes to nothing. The problems started in how we prepared because of how we reacted after that Ireland defeat.

BEN FODEN
Sitting in the changing room after losing to France was the darkest place I've ever been in. The bottom of the world had just fallen out. You couldn't get any lower.

STEVE THOMPSON
It felt like from the day we turned up in New Zealand certain people were intent on tearing us to shreds. Obviously some things had happened off the field but it was interesting to hear Wales coach Warren Gatland say during the tournament that his side were not whiter than white.

We didn't perform as well as we should have and some players got things wrong and they got reprimanded for that. They apologised and we moved on but sometimes these issues get dragged out in public rather than people focusing on the rugby. But you can't look for excuses, we came up short. Some of the combinations may not have worked as planned but I still think we played some good rugby even in the defeat to France.

SIMON SHAW
Against France a couple of missed tackles cost us. It was always going to be a

tough game. In previous World Cups we had managed to grind out a win, but this time we came up a bit short. But to put that down to what happened off the pitch is a bit far-fetched to be honest. I don't think Johnno did a bad job at all. The way he exited was a bit unkind to him because of what he had managed to put together.

BEN YOUNGS

It was hugely disappointing when Johnno stepped down as head coach. All of the players respected Johnno a huge amount and it was tough to see the kind of things that people wrote. Only the players truly knew what happened out in New Zealand. Every player backed Johnno and wanted him to stay, but at the end of the day, it was Johnno's decision.

Despite despairing tackles, the England players can do nothing to stop France winger, Maxime Médard, crossing the line to score their second try of the quarter-final.

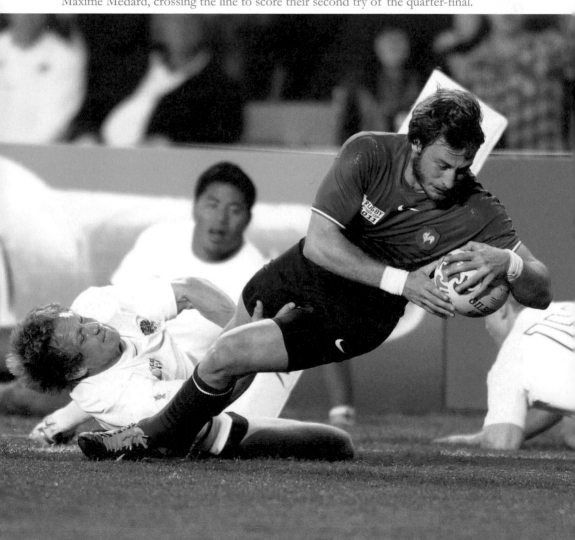

Lewis Moody and Jonny Wilkinson try to comes to terms with England's exit at the hands of France in the quarter-final.

LEWIS MOODY

My memory prior to the tournament was that things were building really well and we had plenty of confidence within the squad. A number of younger players – Dan Cole, Ben Foden, Chris Ashton, Ben Youngs, Tom Wood, Courtney Lawes – had brought a new exuberance and things looked promising. It's only when you look back, perhaps, that you realise we were papering over the cracks. There were a number of issues we could have dealt with off the field in terms of setting standards. If you look back, perhaps, we would have made different decisions. I'm not here to criticise anyone. It was a frustrating period of time and as captain you have to hold your hands up and say 'Look, we could have done better.'

MARK CUETO

I was massively disappointed in the way Johnno got handled. The regime under him was really good. I don't want to be bitter but it does grate a little bit.

Stuart Lancaster has done a brilliant job but they all seem to reflect on Johnno's era as taking the shirt for granted and not respecting the shirt and being a bit loose and everything.

But you are talking about players who played for England for 10 years and had won the World Cup in 2003, and Six Nations titles, and to reflect on that 2011 squad like that is massively disrespectful. It wasn't like that at all.

LEWIS MOODY

One of my frustrations was that I had not become captain earlier. Because by the end of the World Cup, I felt I had learned a lot. But for me it was time to retire. I could no longer do my position justice and it was pointless to cling on when there were other players coming through. The frustration was, 'God, I learned so much from that,' and [you think about] what I would have done differently in terms of training. Ultimately, we knew we were good enough to win that quarter-final. The biggest disappointment on the field was that we did not deliver and we allowed all the off-field stuff to distract us from what we needed to do. There were a lot of disappointments.

TWENTY-FIVE
THE HOUSE OF LANCASTER
2012-2014

IT WAS CLEAR *by the end of 2011 that having plumbed the depths in terms of perception during the World Cup, the only way was up. After Martin Johnson's resignation and the leaked review there was a sense that there was very little left that could go wrong – and with a putsch in the upper ranks of the RFU administration, with acting CEO Martyn Thomas leaving all his posts in December 2011 and being succeeded by a new chief executive, Ian Ritchie, a line was drawn in the sand.*

Initially, despite candidates of the calibre of Nick Mallett (former South Africa coach) and Wayne Smith (2011 World Cup champions New Zealand assistant coach), the England reins were handed to Stuart Lancaster, who was given the title of interim head coach for the 2012 Six Nations.

Lancaster's route to the top job raised eyebrows because his experience as a Premiership coach was limited to two seasons with Leeds Carnegie, in which they were relegated (2006). However, having been appointed as the RFU's head of elite player development in 2007, and also had success as Saxons coach, winning three Churchill Cups, he was a Twickenham insider with a good knowledge of the country's young playing talent.

Lancaster started his tenure by stressing core values to the players, emphasising the privilege of playing for England, the need for discipline and responsibility, and putting the team first. When Danny Care, who he had mentored at Leeds, became the first transgressor, the interim coach demonstrated that he meant business, dropping the scrum-half for the entire Six Nations.

Lancaster also overhauled the squad, replacing 15 players out of 32 in the Elite Player Squad, and naming eight uncapped players in the 23 for the first Six Nations game at Murrayfield. In a side averaging just 15 caps per player, his new captain, Harlequins flanker Chris Robshaw, had only one cap, as did the Anglo-South African lock Mouritz Botha, while the debutants in the starting XV were the Saracens centre pairing of Brad Barritt and Owen Farrell, and the seasoned Northampton back-rower Phil Dowson.

Lancaster's first game in charge was against Scotland at Murrayfield. With Brad Barritt proving outstanding in defence, it was the veteran Charlie Hodgson who stole

Opposite: Manu Tuilagi makes an audacious break against the All Blacks during the 2014 summer tour to New Zealand.

the show with a late charge down of Dan Parks' clearance which secured England a 13-6 victory over the impressively enterprising Scots.

The team then travelled to Rome – where it snowed for the first time in decades. Despite being outscored two tries to one in front of 71,000 at the Stadio Olimpico, England prevailed 19-15 thanks again to a Hodgson charge down, and a conversion and four nerveless penalties from Farrell.

Lancaster's first game at Twickenham ended in a narrow defeat to Wales (19-12), settled when Scott Williams scored a brilliant solo try late on after ripping the ball off Courtney Lawes. England responded with an uplifting against-the-odds 24-22 win over France in Paris, with Manu Tuilagi, Ben Foden and Tom Croft scoring spectacular tries. The team rounded off their campaign in style, nailing Ireland 30-9 at Twickenham when the Irish scrum crumbled after losing tight-head Mike Ross to injury.

England's second place finish after starting the Six Nations with widespread pessimism about their chances, saw Ritchie confirm Lancaster as head coach in March 2012, with the term to last until the 2015 World Cup.

Lancaster's next challenge, a three Test summer tour of South Africa, was daunting, and the coach and his players were given a sharp reminder of the strength of southern hemisphere rugby when they were beaten 22-17 in Durban, 36-27 in Johannesburg (albeit with a strong second-half comeback which reduced arears significantly), and drew the final Test in Port Elizabeth 14-14.

The new head coach's first autumn series began when England overpowered a disappointing Fiji 54-12, but a 20-14 reverse at the hands of Australia ensured that a sense of perspective was maintained. This was reinforced when South Africa remained undefeated in four Tests against Lancaster's side, edging home 16-15.

At this stage the euphoria which had surrounded Lancaster's resurrection of England's fortunes had been dampened down – only to mushroom again when his side achieved one of those once-a-decade victories over New Zealand (38-21).

The world champions were outplayed at the breakdown by an almost error-free collective England effort, and were finished off ruthlessly thanks to a seven minute burst of second half brilliance by Tuilagi which resulted in three tries. The first was rounded off by Barritt after an interchange of passes with his co-centre, then Tuilagi beat Aaron Smith and fended off Dan Carter to put Ashton over, and finally he intercepted a pass to jog over himself from half-way.

This not only put paid to All Black hopes of an unbeaten season, it also saw England ensconced as favourites for the upcoming 2013 Six Nations. At first they lived up to the billing scoring four tries against Scotland (38-18) and they followed it up by beating the Irish in a mud-wrestle in Dublin (12-6), but, although Lancaster's side secured a 23-13 home win over France, they struggled for fluidity.

In retrospect, the closer England got to a Grand Slam the tighter they became. This was highlighted in a tight 18-11 win over Italy at Twickenham, in which England relied on six Toby Flood penalties to see them home.

Then, with a first Slam for 10 years for the taking in Cardiff, England froze. Their 30-3 defeat saw a rampant Welsh side inflict the heaviest reverse of Lancaster's tenure, bringing the red rose squad and Lancaster's coaching team of Andy Farrell (backs), Graham Rowntree (forwards), and Mike Catt (skills) back to earth with a thud.

To add insult to injury England did not even win the Championship title, losing out on points difference – and in selection for the 2013 the Lions tour to Australia – to the triumphant Welsh.

The 2013 summer tour of Argentina was a welcome respite, with England winning a two-Test series against the Pumas 32-3 in Salta and 51-26 in Buenos Aires.

The autumn internationals began with an England line-up deprived through injury of their established centre pairing of Barritt and Tuilagi securing a 20-13 win over Australia. The feel-good factor built further with a 31-12 win over Argentina, before another showdown against an All Black side eager to avenge its loss of a year earlier.

The New Zealanders succeeded in their mission, outscoring England three tries to one, and weathering a determined second half fightback to prevail 30-22.

Any hopes of a 2014 Six Nations Grand Slam disappeared in the opening round when England were pipped at the post in Paris, the French winning 26-24 thanks to a last-ditch Gael Fickou try.

England followed that with the new centre pairing of Billy Twelvetrees and Luther Burrell making gains against Scotland at Murrayfield (20-0), and then squeezed past Ireland in a classic nip-and-tuck encounter at Twickenham thanks to a Danny Care try from a Mike Brown break (13-10).

There was some restitution for the previous year's lost Slam when tries by Care and Burrell secured a convincing 29-18 win over Wales. However, for England to win the title it still left them needing to bury Italy under a points avalanche in Rome in the final round in the event that Ireland beat France in Paris.

England responded by overrunning Italy (52-11), but with Ireland winning the evening match in Paris 22-20, it transpired that England had needed only 11 more points to claim the title. Instead, they finished as Six Nations runners up under Lancaster for the third season in succession.

The compensations were that England's attack had gone up a couple of gears, with Mike Brown in such inspired form at fullback that he was named as player of the tournament, and finished as joint top try scorer on four (with Ireland's Jonathan Sexton). England finished their account with 14 tries (their most in a Championship since 2003), just behind Ireland (16), with Burrell marking his first international season by scoring three of them.

With only a week between the Northampton v Saracens Premiership final and the first Test in Auckland, Lancaster's crew were forced to travel to New Zealand for their summer tour against the world champions in two parties. With the eight starting internationals from the final ruled out of playing in the Test due to jet-lag protocols and a lack of training time, the England head coach presented it as an opportunity for his squad to demonstrate its strength in depth. This they emphatically did at Eden Park, with a Danny Cipriani penalty levelling the score at 15-15 with eight minutes to go, and with England reduced to 14 men with Marland Yarde in the sin-bin. However, with three minutes remaining New Zealand found a way to win, with Conrad Smith scoring the winning try in the corner (20-15).

The make or break second Test in Dunedin was even closer on the scoreboard – New Zealand eventually winning 28-27. Lancaster's side were unable to sustain a great start which saw them go ahead through an early Yarde try, and come close to stretching a 10-6 half-time lead when Tuilagi's 70 metre breakout was stopped by a brilliant try-saving Ben Smith cover tackle.

After the interval England's attempts to match the high tempo All Black tactics faltered and the hosts scored three tries – the last after Farrell was sin-binned – to lead 28-13 with sixteen minutes remaining. England still had enough running in them to hit back with late tries from Brown and Ashton, but New Zealand had enough of a buffer zone to take an unassailable 2-0 lead in the series.

The last Test in Hamilton saw a tired England side on the end of a 36-13 drubbing precipitated by their defensive system unravelling in the face of the rapidity and accuracy of New Zealand's attacking strategy from line-outs. Having conceded four first half tries the tourists trailed 29-6 at half-time, and were not able to close the gap despite Yarde scoring his second try of the series.

With a whitewash in the bag – albeit hard-fought – New Zealand used it to claim the psychological high ground before the 2015 World Cup, while England returned home knowing they had to redress a win-loss ratio against the southern hemisphere big three under Lancaster which stood at won 2, drawn 1, lost 8.

STUART LANCASTER (England head coach 2012-2014)

I had to work hard. I never played professional rugby, never coached at the highest level and came from being a PT teacher at a school in Wakefield. But you gain points along the way. You develop your credibility and eventually people respect and listen to what you've got to say.

Look, there are football managers now who never played high-level professional football: José Mourinho, Arsène Wenger, Brendan Rodgers. You do get managers like that who graduate to senior positions. A lot of coaches said to me that it was quite refreshing that someone of my background could do that.

I understood what had gone on at the 2011 World Cup and that gave me a tremendous insight into trying to put it right. That World Cup was a strange affair. People forget that England won four out of four matches in the pool stages. I'd bite your hand off to get that in 2015. But the off-field stuff began to affect the on-field stuff. We made a transition in one fell swoop. And I picked players I knew, players I trusted. I let them know what the attitudes and expectations were and they've repaid that ever since. Some of them had been waiting patiently for their chance. Chris Robshaw's a good example. I respected that and I've found that when you give respect, you tend to get it back.

You can't change your life story. You get what you deserve if you work hard for long enough, and this is the message I give to players: you get what you deserve and I have invested in myself so I have got an inner confidence. I don't sit in front of the players, or sit in the team environment and think, 'I shouldn't be here'. I have coached for 20 years. I have toured, I have run academies, I have built teams and I have been at a Premiership club and coached them. I coached the Saxons for three years… So I didn't have any fear.

CHRIS ROBSHAW (England 2009-2014, 28 caps)
When we had our first squad session under Stuart Lancaster he outlined where we stood with the public in our first week together, but I already knew. I saw the papers and spoke to people in the pub who'd happily tell me what they thought of England. Stuart told us that we had to reconnect with the fans and, with the community work we did, the public training and, most importantly, our attitude, humility and results, I hope we have now done that. It was vital that we did.

ALEX CORBISIERO (England 2011-2013, 19 caps plus 2 caps for the Lions)
The World Cup was a big learning experience and a real motivating force as well because I vowed that I didn't want the next World Cup, especially one staged in England, to be like the last.

TOBY FLOOD
The World Cup made me question whether it was all worth it. It made me ask myself if it was something I really wanted to do. I was very disillusioned. I wasn't enjoying my rugby, my form dipped and, looking back, it was pretty scary. All I knew was that I couldn't go through what I experienced during and after the World Cup again. I could easily have walked away from the game.

But what proved to be the catalyst was watching others play in the 2012 Six Nations in place of me.

I wasn't jealous of any individuals. But I realised I missed that moment of elation five minutes after the game is won, when you sit in the dressing room, look across at a teammate and smile.

TOM WOOD

It is a culture change. Stuart Lancaster made some big calls when he took over to heave out some big-name established players and to pick young guys to take England into the next era. We don't get too bogged down in analysis and we work with simple team-first principles. It's about working hard for your mates – which is what rugby's always been about.

CHRIS ROBSHAW

I loved all sports growing up, played a bit of football and cricket, played hockey for Somerset and, of course, was besotted with rugby. I had a poster of Lawrence Dallaglio on my wall. He had his back raked and the message said: 'I love rugby'. But I wasn't destined to get to this point in my life, captaining England. I was in and out of the England U18s and on the bench for the U21s. Then, in my first three seasons at Quins, I broke my foot twice, then had serious ankle and ACL injuries. I didn't really break through until 2007, when we spent a season in the old National One.

I was gutted to get Johnno's tap on my shoulder to say I hadn't made the cut for the 2011 World Cup. I watched the World Cup like any other fan but I was an outsider looking in.

I couldn't stop smiling when Stuart asked me if I would captain England against Scotland in 2012. I told him I'd love to give it a go then phoned my parents and my girlfriend swearing them to secrecy until the players knew.

It was only the next day, when it hit the media and I had hundreds of text messages, that the enormity of the job occurred to me. But the players had been very supportive and when we managed to win at Murrayfield and follow it up in Italy, I relaxed. Let's be honest, if we'd lost those two I wouldn't have lasted long in the job.

STUART LANCASTER

We often talk about the passion of the Celtic nations but my message to our players, and the ones they are repeating back to me, is that from an England point of view we want the same commitment to the shirt, to the team and to the country.

BEN MORGAN (England 2012-2014, 23 caps)

While I was getting a lot of interest from Wales, Martin Johnson phoned me in the summer of 2011 to see if I would play for the Saxons. Johnno was one of my heroes. I remember sitting in the Dursley RFC clubhouse near Gloucester watching him lift the World Cup in 2003. Then he's on the phone to me. I was lost for words but I still managed to say that I had a niggle and didn't want to let myself down by playing badly. So it was a few more months [January 2012] before I was selected again for an England squad and officially tied my colours to the mast.

I owe Welsh rugby a lot. First with the Cardiff Blues U20s and with Merthyr, and then with the Scarlets. I was a big, unfit lump when they took me on and they showed tremendous faith in me; but I'm born-and-bred English, so there was only ever really one country I'd be playing for.

The highlight of 2012 was making my debut in Scotland – the bagpipes as we arrived, the hostile reception from the home crowd, and the singing of the national anthem for the first time will stay with me forever.

OWEN FARRELL (England 2012-2014, 25 caps plus 1 cap for the Lions)
From the age of about four I used to go to training with my dad [rugby league legend and later England coach, Andy Farrell] whenever I wasn't at school. All the legends [at Wigan] used to ruffle my hair as they ran past me on the pitch. The players couldn't get away from me because I used to pass the ball to them all the time and expect to have it returned. I guess watching a very successful team go about their business was a good education.

Watching Dad practise his kicks, work on his fitness and train hard was the norm for me. You saw the hard work he put in, and what he got out of it in return. Most of all I remember Dad lifting trophies. Lots of them.

I went over to France in 2007 to watch Dad play in the World Cup for England. I remember going to watch Jonny Wilkinson in a kicking session and had a few goes myself. Jonny gave me a few kicking tips. But what I got most out of it was seeing just how precise Jonny was in his practice. It was only one session, but I've never forgotten it.

I remember playing for the England U18 side in Newcastle and Jonny was asked to speak to us before the game. We got talking and he told me that, right from an early age, he always enjoyed hitting people hard in defence.

Representing my country was what I dreamt about as a kid, I was happy with the way my debut went against Scotland at Murrayfield. The whole family were in the crowd – my mum, my nans and granddads, my sisters, my girlfriend, even my baby brother – and it was a proud day for all of us. I learnt a lot from the day. I learnt that mistakes are punished at Test level in a way they are not at club level and that there is so much less time to get your decisions right.

It doesn't bother me whether I'm compared to my dad. I do not feel any pressure at all from being his son. And there's never been an issue with having my dad as a coach. I've never really known it any different. I came into school and dad was the coach. At Saracens, when I first came in full time, he was coaching, and then I made my debut for England and he was coaching, and it was the same when we were on the Lions tour. I don't think it's difficult for either of us. He treats me exactly the same as any other player and I treat him exactly the same as I would any other coach. The other players have never ribbed me for being the coach's son. They ribbed me more for living at home with my mum and dad.

CHARLIE HODGSON (England 2001-2012, 38 caps)
I started to get called 'Chargedown Charlie' during the 2012 Six Nations after I scored a try in Edinburgh after charging down Dan Parks and doing it again in Rome when I charged down Andrea Masi. It was simple stuff really, I just tried my best to get to the kicker and put pressure on him. It is not so much about practising, you just have to go for it and hope for the best. You have to keep chasing lost causes. We were in a bit of a tight spot in Rome but to come back from 15-6 down showed good resolve in a young team.

BEN MORGAN
I got my first start against Wales at Twickenham. There was a bit of banter from

'Chargedown Charlie' scores in Edinburgh.

my Scarlets teammates during the week but what really stands out in the memory is running out at Twickenham in front of 82,000 and hearing the anthem sung. I'll never forget my debut in Edinburgh, and I'll never forget my first Test start. We lost, which was obviously disappointing, but it just underlined how international rugby can be decided by the narrowest of margins.

CHRIS ROBSHAW

People had written us off and claimed we wouldn't be fit enough to live with Wales in the final 10 minutes, but we went toe to toe with them and if Dave Strettle's score had been given it might well have been a different story.

DAVID STRETTLE (England 2007-2013, 14 caps)

I thought when they flipped me over on my back I got downward pressure on the ball… I felt the ball touch the floor. It is frustrating when things don't go your way.

CHRIS ASHTON

We might even have won the whole lot had we beaten Wales at Twickenham, which we should have done. To lose by a centre ripping the ball out and then

Brad Barritt attempts to break through the Wales defence during his debut Twickenham Test.

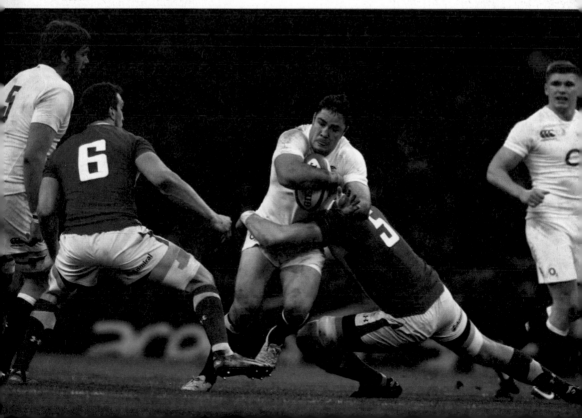

kicking on to score, and then by a TV official's decision that ruled out our try by a millimetre, underlines again the fine margins in sport.

BRAD BARRITT (England 2012-2014, 18 caps)
Defensively we did pretty well that season and it's one that we became very proud of. Tackling is about the experience you have as a rugby player going right back to a young age when you learn the correct technique. But it's also an inner competitive streak you have in you – it's that one-on-one combat and the relish of the physical challenge.

BEN FODEN
The England camp was a strange place to be at the start of that year. There was no certainty over whether Stuart would keep his job and he was someone I'd never worked with before. Also, seemingly overnight, I'd become one of the more senior players in both caps and even age, at 26! The squad he picked showed a lot of enterprise because previous coaches would have stuck with five or six experienced players to ease through the transition. But there's no point tip-toeing around. Better to jump straight in and see how it goes. As it turned out it went surprisingly well. I was worried we'd lost 'Twickenham Man' after the World Cup but, even in defeat against Wales, the support was back and the wide rugby we played that day set us up for our wins in Paris and over the Irish.

ANDY FARRELL (England 2007, 8 caps; England backs coach 2012-2014)
It was there for all to see what Stuart had done. The biggest achievement is that he put some pride back in the England jersey. That is not just the squad but throughout the country, we had some doubters along the way. We had two good wins and against a Welsh team on fire we acquitted ourselves well. Then we were told we would see what the team was about in France and to go to Paris and play like they did and fight like they did, you cannot understate how big an achievement that was.

TOM CROFT
It was a great moment to score in Paris. I saw Rougerie go, I maybe should have passed the ball to Ben Foden but I thought I'd have a go myself and luckily it came off. But it's not about my try – it was a team performance. We said after the game against Wales, we have got to take that extra step when it comes to seeing a team off and I thought we did that against France. It was a great win.

STUART LANCASTER

When you think that the team only came together eight weeks previously in Leeds, while the overall performance against Ireland wasn't perfect, our second half effort was outstanding. The weather didn't allow for it to be a free flowing running spectacle but I'm sure the England fans enjoyed the scrummaging fest and the control we put on the game. It was a great way to finish. If you had said to me two years earlier that I'd be walking around Twickenham applauding 82,000 people with a group of lads I respected and a management group I respected I would have grabbed it.

GRAHAM ROWNTREE (England 1995-2006, 54 caps and 3 caps for the Lions; England forwards coach 2007-2014)

There has been enough said about the 2011 World Cup. We were born-again as a new team in 2012 under Stuart. We came such a long way in just a few weeks and it was an emotional ride. What was created lay with the players; they drove everything with their energy and passion, and for me what they did in the 2012 Six Nations made the World Cup a distant memory. They made everyone proud of us again – even though we knew we were a long way from being the finished article.

GEOFF PARLING (England 2012-2014, 21 caps plus 3 caps for the Lions)

I loved every minute of the 2012 Six Nations. That first victory on the road in Murrayfield got us up and running. It wasn't pretty but I'd take a 3-0 win over a 50-49 loss any time.

JAMES HASKELL (England 2007-2014, 51 caps)

I made a decision after the World Cup that I wanted to try and expand my horizons as much as I could through rugby. It was always my dream to play Super 15 rugby in New Zealand and I managed to get a contract with the Highlanders. It was the best rugby experience I'd ever had. I knew I had to play for a Premiership side in the long run, but this could be my last chance to try something new. People misunderstood my motives but I knew I would return a significantly better player, and that's all I cared about.

BEN MORGAN

I had never really been on tour as a rugby player, other than to go to France and Italy in the Pro 12, and in the Heineken Cup. I had never been outside Europe before, so to be selected for the summer tour to South Africa was a very exciting prospect.

DAN COLE (England 2010-2014, 45 caps plus 3 caps for the Lions)
We saw how the Lions got on in 2009, and that showed how hard it is to play in South Africa. South Africa pride themselves on the physical nature of their game, and so do we, so we knew it would be a tour full of heavy confrontation.

MOURITZ BOTHA (England 2011-2012, 10 caps)
There was added incentive for me in the South Africa tour – I felt like I was almost representing two countries. If I went to South Africa and if I did well I wanted to think I would make England proud and make South Africa proud as well.

CHRIS ROBSHAW
Unfortunately South Africa cranked it up and squeezed us in the first Test in Durban, which we lost 22-17. They then came out with all guns blazing in the second Test in Johannesburg and really got stuck into us. Our fight back was great but you can't give sides like South Africa a lead like we did.

STUART LANCASTER
There were times in the first half [in Johannesburg] when we were hanging on by our fingernails. The guys who came off the bench in the second half, Thomas Waldrom, Tom Palmer and Alex Corbisiero, really made a difference – but we gave ourselves too much to do.

DANNY CARE (England 2008-2014, 48 caps)
We wanted to finish the series on a high and although we didn't win, getting the 14-14 draw felt like a massive step forward.

DYLAN HARTLEY (England 2008-2014, 57 caps)
We strung together a full 80 minutes at Port Elizabeth, which was great. Defence was good, ball retention was good – we just didn't come away with the result. We took pride in two-man tackles, getting off the line, stopping their momentum. But a draw's a draw.

TOM JOHNSON (England 2012-2014, 8 caps)
What we learned was that against sides of the quality of South Africa you've got to take the game to them, rather than soak up pressure. We were giving away too much easy, quick ball and they're a big side to stop.

TOM YOUNGS (England 2012-2014, 17 caps plus 3 caps for the Lions)
When Heyneke Meyer [head coach at Leicester Tigers] first mentioned the idea of

me moving from centre to hooker, I was actually quite excited. It was just a matter of looking at how we were going to go about the challenge and how I was going to get back to Premiership standard as a hooker. Heyneke and Cockers [Richard Cockerill] took it on. I will always be indebted to them for that.

I didn't play for about three months, I went into the gym and bulked up a bit and worked on my fitness as you need a different kind of engine. Then I was meant to go on loan to North Walsham, my local rugby club, but Nottingham were short of hookers, so I got called in there.

The throwing-in was horrendous, I was terrible and it was a lottery at times. It took a lot of hard work and a long time. Not only to get the technique, but to get my own personal technique. I had to find my own way and I always tell the story of the time I threw the ball and it landed in the opposition scrum half's hands. But I stuck at it and it slowly got better. After two seasons, I came back to Tigers and was sitting on the bench for the first team. Then everything seemed to just kick on. I only played nine times as a hooker for Leicester before I was picked to start in the 2012 Autumn Internationals [winning his first cap against Fiji]. I don't think you ever make anything your own, but if you get the shirt, you owe the shirt the respect to play well in it, as well as the guys that have gone before you.

It's been fantastic to do all this with my brother. You grow up together and suddenly you're working together and playing alongside each other for Leicester Tigers, then for England and then for the Lions. It doesn't get any better than that.

James Haskell takes on the Springbok defence during the 2012 summer tour.

GEOFF PARLING

It frustrates me when people said we did well in South Africa, because we lost the series two-nil, and we didn't want to just be plucky losers. We needed to be a winning side. Which made losing so narrowly to the Wallabies and then to the Springboks in the autumn so frustrating.

TOBY FLOOD

Having thumped Fiji in the opening game of the autumn series [54-12], losing to the Wallabies [20-14] was infuriating. It was the most frustrated I have been after a game. Our inability to keep turning the screw, and make our pressure count. Afterwards there were plenty of looks across the room which said: 'How did we manage that?'

CHRIS ROBSHAW

The decision to kick a late penalty instead of going for the corner against South Africa was mine and I thought potentially we had time to get the points and get back down there, and put ourselves in winning drop-goal or penalty range. But it didn't come off. We discussed it but I make the calls and, at the end of the day, it was all on me.

The mix up was the first time I'd ever experienced such negativity towards me and made me realise just how much my head is on a stake as captain. Fortunately, we beat New Zealand the following week, so we were all able to move on.

JAMES HASKELL

The atmosphere in the changing room before the All Blacks game was just electric. There was an incredible feeling in there and then it got even better when the All Blacks started the haka and the crowd began singing a deafening rendition of 'Swing Low Sweet Chariot'.

CHRIS ASHTON

It was a special moment. I could tell something special was going to happen.

MANU TUILAGI (England 2011-2014, 25 caps plus 1 cap for the Lions)

I looked into the eyes of my opposite number during the haka. I said, 'I accept your challenge, let's play some rugby'.

TOM WOOD

The biggest thing was the intensity at the breakdown. We didn't waste any bodies there. The first two guys did the job, there was no need to over-commit, which freed up other guys to carry on the front foot and be dynamic. We made a very few errors, pressurised their 9 and 10, and that's the key to winning any game.

CHRIS ROBSHAW

Everyone who stepped on the pitch against New Zealand was outstanding. We went out there wanting to prove a few people wrong. International rugby is about results – it is about wins and losses, it is as simple as that. You have to go out there and deliver. We were a bit disappointed not to get a result against South Africa or Australia. The crowd came to Twickenham expecting something and everyone stood up and delivered. It was a very, very special day.

TOM WOOD

The South Africa and New Zealand games almost felt like a second debut because I'd been out injured so long. When we lost to the Springboks I was desperately disappointed as we did just about everything right except take our chances, and that included matching and beating them up front. The injustice of the result, and the flak we received, really fuelled us for New Zealand. We knew that if we could create sustained pressure and not give them an inch we could win. Apart from a ten-minute spell in the second half that's exactly what we did.

I've heard people say we beat the All Blacks twice in that game – and they did come back at us with a real flurry. It was a challenge when we stood under the posts having been 15-0 up only for them to score two quick converted tries because we knew the whole world was thinking: 'They're going to fall apart here.' Chris said a few words, and Geoff Parling said a few, but that was all. We looked into each others' eyes in the huddle and we knew it was now or never. We had to get back on track. Everyone was immense on the day. It was a collective performance – and that's why we made it.

MANU TUILAGI

We got in a huddle and Chris Robshaw said, 'Just keep the faith. We're still leading.' We needed to get back in the game straight away. And we did – we scored three tries and the adrenaline kept us going.

BEN FODEN

Chris Ashton had gone eleven Tests without scoring a try before we played New Zealand. It was funny, he wouldn't shut up when Mark Cueto had that massive try drought. But suddenly when it was him he didn't like me talking about tries and stuff before games. I would always say, 'How many are you going to get today?', and he'd tell me to shut up because he was worried it'd jinx him.

CHRIS ASHTON

It affects me badly when I don't score a try in a game. I shouldn't let it, but it does. I get quite obsessive about it. But I guess it comes with being a wing because, just like a goalscorer in football, you're there to score tries.

The try against the All Blacks was a bit of a relief – I'd been waiting for that for a long time. You've just got to follow Manu, and every so often he will get clean through. So I tracked him, he made the break and I was there to finish it. I had no intention of doing the 'Ash-splash', and I really had no idea of where it came from.

STUART LANCASTER

To put that scoreline on an All Blacks side that good was way beyond what we could have asked for, but we had the belief all through the week building up to the Test. There was a lot of composure at halftime, real clarity of thought, and that's something that had developed a lot over the previous few weeks. We'd always had the energy and the attitude but during that Test we put the top six inches on top of that. That match became the barometer by which all our other performances were judged.

MANU TUILAGI

Playing for England, it's an honour. It's very emotional for me. You're just thinking about your mum and dad, all the people you love. You take that into the game and it motivates you. You try to go out every game and play your heart out.

Manu Tuilagi was at his devastating best against New Zealand.

Everyone counted us out, everyone wrote us off, everyone thought we had no chance, but we never stopped believing in ourselves. Put the caps of Carter and Richie McCaw together and they had more than our whole squad combined. It's not about experience, though, it's about the performance on the day. And the boys pulled out a good one.

BEN YOUNGS

By the 2013 Six Nations we were fitter than we had ever been since I'd been part of the squad. The South Africa tour was a wake-up call in terms of being able to generate intensity.

We had a great start that year, beating Scotland convincingly at Twickenham [38-18], before heading to Dublin for the second game. What happened in 2011 stayed with me, coming out for a Grand Slam game and being swept away by Ireland… I didn't play well, got sin-binned, and we never recovered from a terrible start and took a big hiding. So playing them in Dublin took on a huge significance for us all and for me in particular.

TOM WOOD

I was moved from No.6 to No.8 for the game against Ireland. The surface was

Chris Ashton flies in to score England's second try.

rough in Dublin, with mountains of turf to dig the ball out of when the scrums were crabbing, but I felt I dealt with it okay.

BEN YOUNGS

There was the great feeling of 'team', of digging in on a filthy day in Dublin in front of a passionate Irish crowd, and coming up winners. We worked very hard for one another out there against a damned good side. England hadn't won a Six Nations game there for 10 years, when I was 13. You should have seen the changing room!

ANDY FARRELL

The third match that Championship, against France, was brutal. They were wounded after losing to Italy. Everyone was saying they were coming to Twickenham with a point to prove. It started like that.

MANU TUILAGI

I took a bit of a battering against France at Twickenham but it felt good at the same time. I smacked into Louis Picamoles in the third minute and split my ear pretty bad – I had 19 stitches put in it later. I had no idea how bad the injury was at the time. The doc wanted me to go off but the ref was setting up the scrum, so I said I wasn't going anywhere, grabbed the bandage and strapped it to my head myself. The problem was I missed the ear completely, so it continued to bleed, and throughout the half the strapping kept slipping down over my eyes. My jaw hurt as well after the clash with Picamoles and for a while immediately after the injury I had a loud, high-pitched ringing in my left ear. Something like that gets you in the game nice and early. There's nothing worse than taking a while to get into it. I was almost knocked out, so I reasoned the biggest and worst collision had already happened, so now I could get on with the game. I'll have a scar there for the rest of my life but it's a small price to pay to help England win. It was a special day and it set us up for the Grand Slam showdown in Cardiff.

CHRIS ROBSHAW

Manu came back into the starting line-up against France and you could really see his power and physicality. Also his ability to hit a great line, as well as use his hands.

STUART LANCASTER

Robshaw and Wood in the back-row in the last 10, 15 minutes were everywhere against France. They were like rocks in the side.

TOM CROFT

I was recalled for the Wales game in Cardiff in 2013 and it was funny, I kept getting called the 'old man' of the back-row in the press – but I was only 26. I suppose it shows how green that team was.

CHRIS ROBSHAW

I don't know if we were quite ready for a Grand Slam game, and for them a Championship game, in the heart of Wales. The animosity we felt towards us was definitely an experience that will stay with us a long time. We've asked ourselves some hard questions since then. Did we deal with that in the right way? Did we panic a bit? Yes, we did – and I'd include myself in that.

MANU TUILAGI

The dressing room was a hard place to be after the Wales game. Credit to Wales because they played really well, but that was my worst experience on a rugby pitch. Their crowd was amazing. The noise and atmosphere was incredible and their players were clearly lifted and inspired by it. We made mistakes and paid a heavy price.

For much of the time I was powerless, standing in the backs watching Wales gain momentum and us being sent back each time we got penalised. Then, when I had a chance to do something, I dropped the ball. I knew a try could be on and that was the problem, I was thinking too far ahead and not focussing on catching the ball.

When I got home to Leicester on the Sunday the first thing I did was watch the whole match again. It was pretty painful, especially the bit when I drop the ball. I've watched that over and over and over again, hoping that I'm going to catch it at some point, but it never happens.

STUART LANCASTER

We had no complaints, the best side won on the day. To win those four games in the Six Nations was a fantastic experience for us, but to come up short in Cardiff was hugely disappointing. We just didn't turn up, it's as simple as that.

ALEX GOODE (England 2012-2014, 16 caps)

I don't want to talk about the 2003 World Cup too much, but they had their painful times to get there – and if we have to have a few painful moments to get to the final journey in 2015, then I'm sure we will handle them.

CHRIS ROBSHAW

We let ourselves down in Cardiff. We let the country down. And we let English rugby down. Looking back I think we let the occasion get to us, not just on the night but in the week, too. I felt heavy-legged in that game and I know we were emotionally tired and, of course, the atmosphere was frenzied. It was an experience as a team we had not come across before.

The end of the 2013 season was pretty hard to take. We got hammered by Wales and lost the Grand Slam and the Six Nations title; Quins then lost the Heineken Cup quarter-final at home to Munster and the Premiership play-off semi-final away at Leicester. I found out I hadn't made the Lions squad to tour Australia and, after all that, was told I wouldn't be touring with England in Argentina, but having the summer off. I'd be lying if I didn't admit that I thought the world had turned against me. No player ever wants to turn down the chance to play for England, let alone captain your country. Sport has a history of seeing people lose their places in teams through injury or by someone else taking their chance. I was concerned that it could happen to me. After all, Tom Wood did a superb job leading the team in Argentina while the competition for places in the back-row is very strong. Now? Well, it was obviously the right decision. I went on holiday, switched off and relaxed. By the time I returned for pre-season training – my first proper pre-season in three years – I was ready again.

ANDY FARRELL
You talk to all the boys and it hurt them. There was a Grand Slam on the line – it was not just winning the title. You don't get many opportunities to do that. We've used that day for motivation a lot since then. We were overpowered that day, but we are not underpowered as a team. You do find out a lot about people in those situations – and it is definitely lodged in the memory bank.

KYLE EASTMOND (England 2013-2014, 4 caps)
To be honest, I was pretty clueless about how to play rugby union when I arrived at Bath. I had no idea what to do, positionally or whatever. Luckily I played on the wing for the first 10 to 15 games, which helped me out a lot. To go on tour with England to Argentina was just brilliant and it was great to be able to make my debut and show what I could do. I had seen a couple of big Argentine forwards in front of us and thought I would have a go, and luckily I managed to score.

STUART LANCASTER
Kyle has great feet, balance, and is very strong and powerful. But what he also has is a great ability with the timing and execution of his passing game. That try he scored against Argentina was pretty special, his balance and explosive speed off the mark were on show for all to see.

BILLY VUNIPOLA (England 2013-2014, 10 caps)

It was a great experience in Argentina. It was pretty hostile but we played some good, expansive rugby. Traditionally England have their strengths – the scrum and the maul – but we played rugby out there that was heading in another direction.

CHRIS ROBSHAW

We took the momentum from the summer tour into the autumn series. Mike Brown was fantastic all season and he started the autumn Tests with a real bang. He has the ability to take high balls, make breaks, and make last-ditch tackles.

BILLY VUNIPOLA

It was very emotional having my first start at Twickenham against Australia and playing my first Test with my brother. I don't think you can top having your older brother stand next to you for the national anthem at an England game. I could feel the emotion on the bus coming to the ground – it was then that I realised I was about to achieve my lifelong dream. It was so special to celebrate that day with a win over the Wallabies.

We backed that up with a solid win [31-12] over Argentina and then got ourselves ready for the All Blacks.

I was very worked up after the haka and very happy they kicked the first ball to me – and kept kicking to me. Nothing was really said when we went 17-3 down. It was a similar sort of vibe to the Australia game when we went behind. There was no panic. We didn't rush into anything. We just dug-in – that's what we had to do.

We left nothing out there. We were all walking around the changing room with ice and bandaging around the ribs. Before the game I was getting a little bit annoyed with the way in which everybody was making us underdogs. All the talk was about the All Blacks, and that England were not good enough – yet I knew England could push them all the way, if not better.

TOM WOOD

On the one hand in the dressing room we were told to keep our chins up – we battled hard, showed a lot of character and came very close to beating a world champion side. On the other... we didn't turn up to be brave losers or close runners-up. We came to win and we blew it. We gave them a 14 point head start; I don't remember that being in the game plan.

MIKE BROWN (England 2007-2014, 29 caps)

I never look at the good aspects of my game, always the bad. I look at opportunities I missed, like an overlap or an inside pass or a better place to have landed my kick. You need to be tough on yourself if you want to be the very best. On the basis that you'll never reach perfection, you're always falling short. And that's what keeps you pushing. I was never the biggest or the best. I failed to play county or representative rugby and didn't go to a rugby-playing school. Nothing's ever come easily for me in rugby.

There's one commentator who said a few years back that I was a good club player, but I'd never make it as an international. He began to talk me up later but I've always remembered his initial comments. I guess there's been a lot of proving both to myself and to others.

STUART LANCASTER
We had to move on quickly from the disappointment of the All Blacks game to preparing for France in the 2014 Six Nations. Our preparation wasn't helped by the loss of several key players. The quality of those players was a big blow. Alex Corbisiero, Geoff Parling, Tom Croft, Manu Tuilagi – that's four key men.

LUTHER BURRELL (England 2014, 7 caps)
When Stuart pulled me aside on the Monday before the French game to tell me I'd been selected to start it was the realisation of a long-held dream of mine. As he reminded me, it had been a long journey from Leeds reserves at Roundhay [where Lancaster had been my coach] to this.

I began to study Wesley Fofana, the man who'd be opposite me at the Stade de France. He's not a bad player to start with, is he? I spoke to Alex King too, my backs coach at the Saints who had been at Clermont with Fofana. I won't lie, I was very nervous. I barely slept on the Monday or Tuesday. Then, when we travelled over to Paris on the Thursday, I didn't sleep then, either. I just had a million thoughts running around my head. It got to the point when I was genuinely worried whether I'd be able to stay awake during the game. Even in training when there was a slight break I'd suddenly think, 'Flippin' eck, I'm playing for England on Saturday!' Luckily the team run at the stadium on Friday settled me down, I slept well and ran on to the pitch loving the boos and jeers and intimidation. A lot of people asked me why I had such a big grin on my face during the anthems. It's because I remembered where I'd come from to make it to this point.

JACK NOWELL (England 2014, 5 caps)
I didn't have the best first ten seconds to my Test career. France kicked off and I dropped the ball and a few phases later they ended up scoring. I saw it late. Joe Launchbury went up and I couldn't really see the ball... but what allowed me to

keep my place in the team for the next game was the fact that I didn't really let the mistake affect my game. Afterwards I spoke with Catty [attacking skills coach Mike Catt] on the bus back from the stadium and he said, 'Yeah, you dropped your first ball but after that you got straight into your normal game'.

The whole experience was just incredible. I remember running out of the tunnel just before the anthems in Paris and thinking, 'This is what I want to be doing'.

CHRIS ROBSHAW
Looking back, it was probably a 15-minute spell against France that ultimately cost us a Grand Slam. We could have shown a bit more composure during that time.

LUTHER BURRELL
A week later we headed up to Murrayfield and again I loved every minute of the build-up. It was only after that when I sat down and tried to figure out what had happened. I called my agent and told him how I was struggling to come to terms with scoring two tries in my first two Tests for England when, not that long ago, I was playing for Otley. He said what a lot of people have subsequently said: 'enjoy the moment, keep on doing what your doing, and never forget where you've come from.'

STUART LANCASTER
The work that Faz [Andy Farrell] and Catty [Mike Catt] have done with Billy Twelvetrees and Luther Burrell really began to pay off in that Six Nations. The timing and number of options going to the line was excellent. Luther's try against Scotland was a good case in point, he hit the line flat and there was no way they were going to stop him scoring.

TOM WOOD
I came off the field in Edinburgh really disappointed because I felt there was another 10, 15, or more points out there. We knew that those fine margins might be the real difference against a really good Ireland side. We gave close consideration to the choke tackle [Ireland's defensive speciality] before the game. The solution is to go forward, be dynamic, have support with you, and don't allow people to get isolated.

DANNY CARE
The try I scored against Ireland was straight from the Quins training ground with Robo [Chris Robshaw] and Browny [Mike Brown]. We had been working all week

on supporting line-breaks and I thought I'd try to get in there. When Browny gets the ball there's always a chance. It was great to score a try like that at Twickenham. It's such an unbelievable stadium and unbelievable atmosphere when the crowd are behind us.

OWEN FARRELL

I played in the Six Nations for the first time with Danny [Care] and loved it. He's a world class player and someone who can take any opportunity that comes. He can make something out of nothing.

ANDY FARRELL

I thought we showed massive guts to go out there and play like that against Ireland.

STUART LANCASTER

The 29-18 win over Wales at Twickenham is right up there among our best wins. The game against Ireland probably had a little bit more flow to it. But because of the significance of the game in Cardiff in 2013, and obviously the pressure on the boys to deliver in the light of the World Cup on the horizon and playing at Twickenham, the boys wanted to win that game.

CHRIS ROBSHAW

To put 50 points on Italy in Rome was a great effort from the boys and we showed again that we had really developed our attacking game throughout the season.

Chris Robshaw picks and goes from a ruck against France during the 2014 Six Nations.

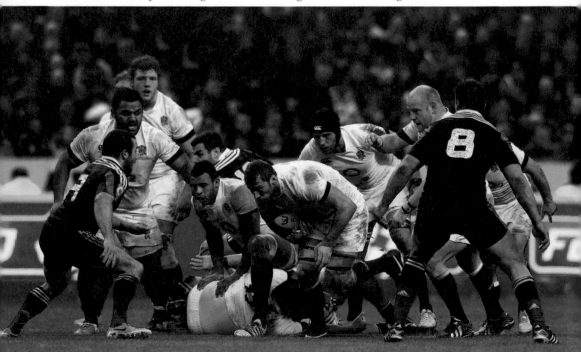

MANU TUILANGI

I was out injured for six months after the Lions tour. It was a strange feeling to watch England go so well without me during the autumn and the start of the 2014 Six Nations. Of course I wanted them to do well. You want to be a part of a winning squad. Luther Burrell was outstanding. Still, I'm not going to lie to you, I couldn't wait to get off the bench in Rome. We had won the game but had a job to do to get as many points as we could [to challenge Ireland's points-difference lead at the top of the Six Nations table]. That was one of my best tries for England simply because I'd waited a year to score.

CHRIS ROBSHAW

It was surreal to watch those final moments [of the France-Ireland match at the Stade de France that decided England's Championship fate] on a screen at our official post-match dinner in Rome, dressed in black tie, cheering on the French. It was the first time I have probably ever supported a French team.

STUART LANCASTER

Credit to Ireland, they were deserved winners, and it was a fitting finale for Brian O'Driscoll, but we were hugely disappointed.

JOE LAUNCHBURY (England 2012-2014, 22 caps)

The beauty of the England set-up is you feel welcome and part of it from day one – but you also understand that you are not too many bad performances away from being out. That's key for the whole squad. So while we have been going pretty well and people have been largely kind to us in the press, we understand that if these performances aren't driven on, you can lose your spot in the team and that the good will won't last forever if you underperform.

TOM WOOD

It was a great experience for me to go back to New Zealand for the summer tour. When I was 18 I decided to take some time out of the Worcester Academy and go to New Zealand to play out there.

I wanted to do something that would make me a bit different from the others back home.

Through a Kiwi family connection, I heard North Otago were looking for a young loose forward and so headed to Oamaru. I got a bit of stick for being 'Tom the Pom' and a posh English kid but, in general, I loved the experience.

I worked on the farm and at a local school, and trained on a Tuesday and Thursday, quickly finding my own routine and circle of friends. I'd front up to big islanders and Maoris on the field and just learned so much. By the time I had to come home I didn't want to leave. Nine months after leaving England as a boy, I felt as if I returned as a man.

In England I'd become a very hardworking, rucking, tackling back-row forward but a little one-dimensional. I felt as a schoolboy I was a good runner and ball carrier – but that went out of my game. Playing as a youngster with the senior guys, it became more important not to make mistakes. The New Zealand experience gave me the opportunity and the freedom to have a go at things you wouldn't always try. In England, we were structuring every single phase which I don't think is practical. When I told the guys in New Zealand that's how I'd been coached, they didn't understand it. They'd play a strike move but then play whatever was on.

Being in New Zealand went deep into what I wanted to be as a rugby player and I like to think people in North Otago have a vested interest in me and take some pride in seeing me achieve; so, yeah, it was very special to go back there with England in 2014.

MIKE BROWN

I would use the word 'ultimate' when describing New Zealand as a tour destination. Three Tests and a midweek game against the Crusaders, which is like a fourth Test. It's why we play this game, isn't it?

JOE MARLER (England 2012-2014, 22 caps)

They snuck the win in the first Test and that was hugely disappointing. If we want to win Test matches like that we need to go that extra step.

GRAHAM ROWNTREE

Losing a game in the final minutes like we did at Eden Park is agonising. It comes down to a few moments, fine margins like knock-ons and switching off for Aaron Cruden's quick tap which led to Conrad Smith scoring in the corner.

BEN MORGAN

Many of the general public in New Zealand had written us off before the first Test. We may have lost, but it was incredibly tight and it was satisfying to know that we were making people have a bit of a rethink about us.

TOM WOOD

The second Test was there for us. At half-time it felt like we had them. They're a dangerous team, you can't give them anything and unfortunately we gave them too much. We left the door ajar for them and they kicked it open. A lot of the credit goes to them for being so dynamic with the ball – but a lot of the blame lies with us. We can talk about the character and the positives to come out for us for weathering that storm and coming back at them, but it was all too late in the day.

COURTNEY LAWES (England 2009-2014, 32 caps)
New Zealand play very quickly and they try to tire teams out. It's just the width they play with, and the speed and intensity with which they do it. You have got to match them there, and make sure that you are as fit as they are, so you are ready on the day. That's what I'm all about. I'm a lighter second-row and I like to get around the park, hitting lots of rucks, carrying the ball and making lots of tackles.

ANDY FARRELL
The speed of thought and the speed of their game was outstanding.

TOM WOOD
Manu's breakaway was crucial. If he'd been able to get over the line that would have been a massive nail in the coffin for them and a big up for us. It's little things like that which make the difference, the white-hot pressure.

CHRIS ROBSHAW
I was proud of the way we came back in the second Test but that's not enough. We wanted more – we wanted to do something special and it didn't happen. Losing the series 3-0 was very tough to take, especially the way they dismantled us in the third Test.

ANDY FARRELL
The defence started poorly in the third Test and got worse. We weren't even near 80 per cent. You need to be pro-active against the All Blacks and we were only reactive. Once you are behind the eight-ball, there is a snowball effect. That first half simply wasn't good enough. We now know what intensity looks like and what intensity does not look like.

DYLAN HARTLEY
The third Test was supposed to be a watershed moment for us and instead that was a bit of a statement from the All Blacks so hats off to them for that. The psychological battle is key and you saw the manner in which they finished. They scored with the last play. That was not good enough from us. We were just chasing shadows.

STUART LANCASTER

I know there'll be pressure coming into the World Cup year. The Six Nations has always been an enormous challenge. I'm respectful of the tournament. But just imagine the pressure of being the host nation in a home World Cup. The expectation of being England, being English. The sheer scrutiny, it's going to be pretty full on.

COURTNEY LAWES

There's so much to say about how Stuart Lancaster has changed the feeling in the squad since the last World Cup that you wouldn't be able to put it all down in an hour. The difference basically comes down to Stuart and what he has brought to the team. The chemistry he has brought in, and the camaraderie. He really has changed us in terms of a culture we can all buy into and really get behind.

MIKE BROWN

The difference is massive – poles apart. The foundations, the culture, everyone pulling in the right direction. We've got great coaches around, and all the players are here on merit, and all working for each other. You can see the improvements in organisation and in the standards in training, both from players and coaches. We are in a much better place than we were.

There are things now that I never thought of for a second when I first pulled on the jersey back in 2007-08. You see the names on the wall now, and you think about the heritage. It's great to have that connection and bigger meaning. We know how strongly linked we are by this jersey to all the players who have worn it before. We want to do that red rose proud and to perform for the country and those we love – and for all those who have gone before us. None of us will ever underestimate how special it is to play for England.

England
Rugby

BIBLIOGRAPHY AND SOURCES

Bells' Life, 8 December 1870
Football: The Rugby Union Game, George Bell, 1889
The Award by Arbitrators, April 1890
Football: The Rugby Union Game, Cassell, 1892
Liverpool Echo, 14 September 1893
Manchester Evening News, 15 September 1893
The Daily Post, 21 September 1893
Manchester Courier & Lancashire General Advertiser, 21 September, 1893
Western Mail, 11 January, 1897
Football, Lawrence and Bullen, 1897
Western Mail, 9 January, 1899
'Chats with Celebrated Yorkshire Footballers', unidentified newspaper cutting
'Yorkshire Trade Figure of the Week', unidentified newspaper cutting
Daily Mail, 4 December, 1905
Triumphant Tour of the New Zealand Footballers, Geddis & Blomfield, 1906
The Rugby Football Annual, Williams & Walker, 1913
Modern Rugby Football, Grafton & Co, 1918
The Life of Ronald Poulton, Sidgwick & Jackson Ltd, 1919
Western Mail, 17 January, 1921
The Rugby Game & How to Play It, Athletic Publications, 1922
Rugby Football, Webster's Publications Ltd, 1923
Rugby Football, Methuen, 1925
Rugby Football, George G Harrap & Co Ltd, 1925
Sammy Woods: My Reminiscences, Chapman & Hall, 1925
Rugger, Longmans, Green & Co Ltd, 1927
Rugby Football, Eyre & Spottiswoode, 1932
How to Play Rugby Football, Constable & Company Ltd, 1933
The Sunday Times, 31 March, 1935
The Game Goes On, Arthur Barker, 1936
Evening Post (Wellington, NZ), 6 January 1936
The Sunday Times, 19 January 1947
The Sunday Times, 21 March, 1948
Let's Talk Rugger, Eyre & Spottiswoode, 1950
The Sunday Times, London: 25 February, 1951
Fifty Years of the All Blacks, Phoenix House, 1954
The Game Goes On, Sportsman's Book Club, 1954
England v Wales 1956 Official Programme. RFU/Programme Publications, 21 January 1956
Scotland v England 1956 Official Programme. SRU/Programme Publications, 17 March 1956
Western Mail, 21 January 1957
World Sports, London: January, 1958
Address at Adrian Stoop's Memorial Service, 1958
Rugby Football: An Anthology, George Allen & Unwin Ltd, 1958
England v France 1959 Official Programme. RFU/Programme Publications, 28 February, 1959
England v Scotland 1959 Official Programme. RFU/Programme Publications, 21 March 1959
Great Days in New Zealand Rugby, AH & AW Reed, 1959
England v Wales 1960 Official Programme. RFU/Programme Publications, 16 January 1960
Sunday Express, 17 January 1960
Rugby World, November 1960
The Book of Rugby Football, Stanley Paul, 1962
Rugby World, November 1962
Rugby World, Charles Buchan's Publications Ltd, May 1963
Wallace Reyburn's World of Rugby, Elek Books Ltd, 1967
Birkenhead Park: The First Hundred Years, Birkenhead Park RFC, 1971
Wallace Reyburn's World of Rugby, Elek Books Ltd, 1967
Rugby World, March, 1973
A Cap for Boots, Hutchinson Benham, 1977
Fran Cotton: The Autobiography. Queen Anne Press, 1981

Address at Lord Wakefield of Kendal Memorial Service, 15 November, 1983
The Guardian, 1 February 1984
Life at One Hundred Miles an Hour: A Biography of P G D Robbins. G&A Publishing, 1987
The Daily Telegraph, 14 January, 1991
English Rugby: A Celebration. Mainstream, 1991
Rugby from the Front, Peter Wheeler. Stanley Paul
The Sunday Times, 29 September 1991
England v France 1987 Official Programme. RFU/Programme Publications, 21 February 1987
History of English Rugby Union 1871-1995, BBC Video, 1995
'Tiz All Accordin': The Life of Peter Cranmer, Brewin Books Ltd, 1999
Size Doesn't Matter, Neil Back. Milo 2000
David Irvine interviews Bill Beaumont, Fran Cotton and Des Seabrook in *The Guardian,* November 2000
The Times, 7 May, 2004
Richard Hill: The Autobiography. Orion Books 2006
The Big Interview: Martin Corry, by Donald McRae, *The Guardian,* 31 October 2006
It's in the Blood, Lawrence Dallaglio. Headline 2007
Andy Robinson interview, *The Sunday Times,* 5 August 2007
Interview with Danny Cipriani, *The Daily Telegraph,* London: 26 November 2008
Brian Ashton interview, *The Independent,* 4 December 2008
Chris Ashton interview, *Rugby World,* December 2010
Jonny Wilkinson on TalkSport, 11 November, 2011
Jonny: My Autobiography, Jonny Wilkinson. Headline 2011
World Cup Rugby Tales, Simon & Schuster 2011
Mike Tindall interview, *The Daily Mail,* 14 April 2012
James Haskell interview, *The Rugby Paper,* April 2012
Owen Farrell interview, *Rugby World,* April 2012
Geoff Parling interview, *Rugby World,* May 2012
Ben Morgan interview, *Rugby World,* May 2012
Chris Robshaw interview, *Rugby World,* August 2012
Ben Foden interview, *Rugby World,* September 2012
Ben Youngs interview, *The Rugby Paper,* 27 January 2013
Tom Wood interview, *The Rugby Paper,* 27 January 2013
Tom Wood interview, *Rugby World,* February 2013
Time of Our Lives: World Champions 2003 England Rugby. Sky Sports, 2013
Sporting Heroes: Martin Johnson, with Gary Newbon. Sky Sports, 2013
Steve Borthwick: Happily going about his business, *The Independent,* 27 April 2013
White Gold: England's Journey to Rugby World Cup Glory, Peter Burns. Arena Sport 2013
Interview: Jonny Wilkinson, *The Scotsman,* 13 October 2013
Stuart Lancaster interview, *Mail on Sunday,* 19 January 2014
Chris Robshaw interview, *Rugby World,* February 2014
Luther Burrell interview, *Rugby World,* April 2014
Mike Brown interview, *Rugby World,* May 2014
Manu Tuilagi interview, *Rugby World,* June 2014
'England vow in Rome that 2015 will be "our year"' by Chris Robshaw, *The Daily Telegraph,* 16 March 2014
Steve Thompson: Certain people were out to get England, *The Independent,* 15 July 2014

PHOTOGRAPHIC CREDITS

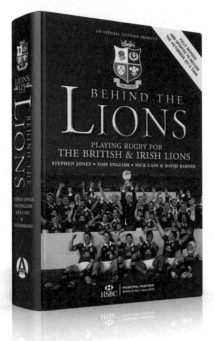

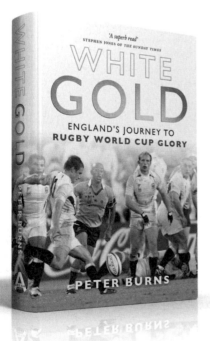